ANALYTICAL ANTHOLOGY OF MUSIC

Consulting Editor in Music

Allan W. Schindler,
Eastman School of Music

ANALYTICAL ANTHOLOGY OF MUSIC

SECOND EDITION

Ralph Turek

The University of Akron

McGRAW-HILL, INC.

New York St. Louis San Francisco Auckland Bogotá Caracas Lisbon
London Madrid Mexico Milan Montreal New Delhi Paris
San Juan Singapore Sydney Tokyo Toronto

ANALYTICAL ANTHOLOGY OF MUSIC

7 8 9 QPD QPD 9 0

ISBN 0-07-065456-5

This book was set in Palatino by Music-Book Associates, Inc.
The editors were Cynthia Ward and John M. Morriss;
the production supervisor was Janelle S. Travers.
The cover was designed by John Hite.
Project supervision was done by The Total Book.

Quebecor Printing/Dubuque was printer and binder.

Library of Congress Cataloging-in-Publication Data

Analytical anthology of music / [compiled by] Ralph Turek.
— 2nd ed.
p. cm.
Includes indexes.
ISBN 0-07-065456-5
1. Musical analysis—Music collections. I. Turek, Ralph.

MT6.5.A5 1992 91-24305

ABOUT THE AUTHOR

Ralph Turek received his Doctor of Musical Arts degree in composition from the University of Cincinnati in 1975, where he was a student of Paul Cooper. He has received grants from the National Endowment for the Arts and the University of Maryland, and he has received awards from ASCAP and the Union Civic League and Arts Foundation of Chicago. Several of his works have been published and many have been performed widely throughout the country. He is the author of *The Elements of Music: Concepts and Applications, Vols. I and II*, published by McGraw-Hill. Currently a professor of music at The University of Akron, he teaches composition, theory, graduate and undergraduate analysis, and music history courses. He developed the electronic music studio at The University of Akron and served as its director for six years.

CONTENTS

PREFACE

This second edition of *Analytical Anthology of Music* contains complete works or movements representing forty-seven known and several anonymous composers from the Middle Ages to the present time. The music is ordered chronologically and divided into five major units: The Middle Ages and the Renaissance, The Baroque Era, The Classical Period, The Romantic Period, and The Twentieth Century. I have attempted to balance musical quality, historical significance, form, medium, and complexity in order to provide an anthology of maximum practical value to students and instructors of musicianship and analysis courses at all levels. The overriding objective behind the organization of this anthology has been to provide a large and diverse body of musical material for analysis and to facilitate its use by the instructor in the classroom or by students on their own. Among the noteworthy features of this anthology are:

1. A complete Gregorian chant Mass Ordinary.
2. Twenty-one chorale harmonizations by J. S. Bach and others.
3. Five chorale melodies with figured bass.
4. Twelve Classical piano sonata movements plus other works from the period illustrating a variety of applications of the sonata principle.
5. Four Classical string quartet movements and three full-score Classical orchestral movements.
6. Full orchestral scores from the Baroque Era through the Twentieth Century.
7. Operatic excerpts from the Baroque, Classical, and Romantic periods.
8. A Twentieth Century unit consisting of thirty-two works by twenty composers.

Additional features of this edition include:

1. More material useful for first- and second-year theory study;
2. Augmented and improved indexes and pedagogical aids;
3. Enhanced legibility;
4. An expanded *Instructors' Reference Manual.*

Several brief editorial features have been designed to support the anthology. Each unit is preceded by general commentary concerning the musical period, its important features, the types of composition produced, and other pertinent information. For each piece or group of pieces, questions are provided that are designed to direct students toward the important features of the music. The questions are in two formats: (1) general questions in paragraph form, and (2) detailed *Questions for Discussion,* numbered and grouped by parameter for convenience in making assignments. This last feature grows out of my conviction that most students can profit by specific guidance, at least in the early stages of their analytical studies, and I have taken great care to be as clear as possible, to direct students to the really important points of the music without giving too much away, and to avoid redundancy.

The chronological arrangement of the music allows for any order of study. Suggestions to instructors are contained in the *Instructors' Reference Manual.* A word of caution: Because the questions about the music must necessarily assume certain prior knowledge and background, you may find it necessary on occasion to disregard selected questions. I trust this inconvenience will be minor.

A Glossary of Terms is included in the back of the anthology. Two indexes—a general Index of Devices and Techniques, and a Harmonic Index—are alphabetical and amply cross-referenced. A third index—Ready Reference: Selected Harmonic Topics in Music Theory—lists clear examples of harmonies and harmonic techniques most frequently discussed in music theory classes. (An Index of Forms and Genres is included in the *Instructors' Reference Manual,* described below).

Instructors' Reference Manual

This important and unique feature of the anthology contains a variety of material that instructors may find useful. At the beginning of each unit, suggestions are made as to how the works might be grouped for study purposes, along with an assessment of their difficulty. Each work contained in the anthology proper receives some degree of attention in this manual. Throughout, suggestions for comparison with other works in the anthology are given. For selected works, *Items of Interest* are listed, under the categories of Melodic/Rhythmic, Harmonic/Tonal, and Other, along with the location of those items. For those works in the anthology that are preceded by numbered *Questions for Discussion,* the manual provides a reprinting of the questions followed by answers and further discussion. While these discussions necessarily reflect my own background, attitudes, and opinions, I hope they will be found to be generally valid. Nevertheless, they are by no means complete, and instructors will almost certainly bring their own insights to bear. Where instructors hold different opinions, the analyses may serve as points of departure for classroom discussion and debate. A Form/Genre Index is included at the end of the manual. More specific information concerning the *Instructors' Reference Manual* can be found in its Preface.

Acknowledgments

I would like to acknowledge the encouragement and support for this second edition that I have received from DuWayne Hansen, Director of the School of Music of The University of Akron. I would also like to thank several associates who provided assistance in a variety of ways: Nancy Stokes, Director of the Music Resource Center, who served as a valuable bibliographic resource; Clifford Billions and Mary Schiller of the Voice Section for their sensitive and accurate text translations; Bob Ceasar, of the Print Media Center, who put aside many pressing projects to provide photostats of the music in a timely manner; Deborah Greene, of Cleveland State University, who was kind enough to allow me to borrow several editions that were unavailable elsewhere in the area; and Eleanor Barber, who provided me with the resources of the Bach Institute of Baldwin-Wallace College.

I would also like to thank the staff of Music-Book Associates, for their unsurpassed professionalism and meticulous care in composing the book; Cynthia Ward, of McGraw-Hill, for soliciting and interpreting several rounds of helpful reviews of the manuscript and for guiding the project through to its completion; and Allan Schindler, of the Eastman School of Music, for his valuable counsel as consulting editor.

In addition, my thanks go to the following reviewers of the manuscript, who were generous with their time and helpful with their comments: Shirley Bean, University of Missouri—Kansas City; Claire Boge, Miami University; David Brandes, Franklin Pierce College; Steven Bruns, University of Colorado—Boulder; James Caldwell, Western Illinois University; Gene Cho, University of North Texas; Donald Crockett, University of Southern California; Lora Gingerich, Ohio State University; Stephen Gryc, Hartt School of Music; William Harbinson, Appalachian State University; Joel Hoffman, University of Cincinnati; John Hofmann, State University of New York—Fredonia; Alice Lanning, University of Oklahoma; Peter Spencer, Florida State University; William Tuttle, Portland State University; and Terry Zipay, Crane School of Music.

Finally, I would like to dedicate this book to the memory of Wallace T. Williams, who ably served as Dean of the College of Fine and Applied Arts of The University of Akron from 1987 until his death on April 18, 1991.

Ralph Turek

A NOTE ON THE TEXT TRANSLATIONS

Except where otherwise indicated, the translations for this anthology have been done by the following:

French:	Dr. Russell Weingartner Department of Modern Languages The University of Akron
German:	Dr. Hans Otto Zbinden Department of Modern Languages The University of Akron
Latin:	Dr. Robert Gaebel Classics Department The University of Akron

ANALYTICAL ANTHOLOGY OF MUSIC

Unit

I

THE MIDDLE AGES AND THE RENAISSANCE

An important distinguishing feature of Western music is its level of polyphonic sophistication. For this reason, the eleventh century has long been regarded as a landmark in the history of our musical culture. It marks the beginning of a more-or-less continuous stylistic evolution that culminated in the vocal polyphony of the late sixteenth century. During this six-hundred-year time span, a large body of diverse and vital music was produced. The following developments are reflected in the music of this period: the gradual emergence of linear independence, first of contour, then of rhythm; the gradual expansion of texture from one to six or more voices; the gradual emergence of a harmonic system based upon the consonances of the third and fifth; the gradual modification of the modal system in the direction of major-minor tonality; the development of melodic techniques such as repetition, sequence and motivic variation; the development of contrapuntal techniques such as canon, invertible counterpoint and imitation; the emergence of such formal concepts as strophic, ternary, through-composed and variation; the development of a keyboard style and the beginnings of specifically instrumental forms; the development of a proportional notation system with its hierarchy of rhythmic values; and the development of a tuning system (meantone) which could accommodate the needs of instruments of fixed pitch.

Lines of development in four important categories—sacred song, secular song, Mass composition, and instrumental composition—may be studied by comparing the following works:

SACRED SONG
- Motets
  - Josquin: "Ave Maria . . . virgo serena"
  - Palestrina: "Lauda Sion"
  - Lassus: "Beatus homo"
    "Justi tulerunt"

SECULAR SONG
- Motet
  - Anonymous: "On parole de batre"
  - Machaut: "Bone pastor Guillerme/Bone pastor, qui pastores/Bone pastor"
- Chanson
  - Dufay: "Franc cueur gentil"
- Madrigal
  - Lassus: "Deh, lascia, anima"
  - Gesualdo: "Occhi del mio cor vita"
  - Monteverdi: "Dice la mia bellissima Licori" (in Unit Two)

MASS COMPOSITION
- Ordinary from *Missa de Angelis* (Gregorian chant)
- Dufay: "Kyrie" (I) from *Missa Se la Face ay Pale* (cantus firmus technique)
- Josquin: "Agnus Dei" from *Missa Mater Patris* (canonic technique)
- Palestrina: "Kyrie" from *Missa Lauda Sion* (parody technique)

INSTRUMENTAL COMPOSITION
- *Der Prinzentanz* and *Proporz* (Anonymous lute dances)

Dowland: "Faction that ever dwells" (from *Second Book of Songs and Ayres)*
Byrd: "The Carmans Whistle" (from *My Ladye Nevells Booke)*

The Gesualdo madrigal also provides an example of the middle- and late-sixteenth-century interest in chromaticism. The theme and variation form, which had its beginnings in the Renaissance, is represented by the anonymous lute dances and William Byrd's "The Carmans Whistle." Canon and two-voice counterpoint can be studied through the Agnus Dei from Josquin's *Missa Mater Patris* and the *Cantiones duarum vocum* of Lassus.

Gregorian Chant

Gregorian chant is a body of music, consisting of nearly three thousand unaccompanied melodies with Latin text, which was used in the liturgy of the Roman Catholic Church. The great majority of texts are from the Book of Psalms. Consisting of a limited number of melodic formulas, these chants were cast in different formal schemes for various liturgical purposes.

Chant melodies rarely exceed the range of a ninth. They are primarily conjunct and diatonic with few intervals larger than a fifth. An upward leap followed by an extended fall is a common contour, with cadences usually descending by a second or third. The rhythm is free and unmetered, with a slight lengthening of notes at points of punctuation in the text.

Gregorian chant is unharmonized. Although the melodies are categorized as belonging to one or another of the eight Church modes, movement from one mode to another is common.

The text setting is syllabic, neumatic or melismatic, depending upon the function and position of the chant in the liturgy. The melodic outline usually reflects the normal accentuation of the words, but dynamics and dynamic accents are *not* a feature of the style.

A complete Mass Ordinary is included in this unit. Around this core, other chants have been added to represent a variety of forms, modes, degrees of musical sophistication and liturgical functions.

Psalmody

The chanting of psalms formed an important part of the Catholic liturgy. Since the psalms used from day to day varied, a few basic recitation formulas, called "Tones," to which any psalm could be adapted, comprised the basic melodic material for chanting. These Tones, in simple and embellished versions, existed for each of the eight modes. The common practice was to frame a psalm with a freely composed melody called an "antiphon." Among the oldest melodies of the Gregorian literature, antiphons are less sophisticated than later chants, exhibiting a narrower range, less sense of tonal organization and few or no repetitive features. When a psalm was coupled with an antiphon, the mode of the antiphon determined the Tone to which the psalm was sung.

"ASPERGES ME" Liber Usualis p. 11*

This chant, consisting of antiphon, psalm verse and doxology (Gloria Patri), was sung just prior to the Introit for the principal Mass on all Sundays during the year outside of the Paschal (Easter) season. The ceremony, in which the priest asperged (symbolically cleansed) the congregation and the altar with holy water while intoning the chant, immediately preceded all Solemn (sung) Masses.

ANTIPHON

Asperges me, Domine, hyssopo et mundabor:
lavabis me, et super nivem dealbabor.

PSALM 51 (King James version)

Miserere mei, Deus, secundum magnam misericordiam tuam.

DOXOLOGY

Gloria Patri, et Filio, et Spiritui Sancto. Sicut erat in principio, et nunc, et semper, et in saecula saeculorum. Amen.

ANTIPHON

Thou shalt sprinkle me with hyssop, O Lord, and I shall be cleansed; Thou shalt wash me, and I shall be made whiter than snow.

PSALM 51 (King James version)

Have mercy on me, O God according to Thy great mercy.

DOXOLOGY

Glory be to the Father, and to the Son and to the Holy Ghost. As it was in the beginning, is now, and ever shall be, world without end. Amen.

*The *Liber Usualis* is a compilation of liturgical music for the Roman Catholic Mass and Office.

"ALMA REDEMPTORIS MATER" Liber Usualis p. 273

This is one of four antiphons addressed to the Blessed Virgin Mary, each of which was used during a particular season of the Church year. This oldest of the so-called "Marian antiphons" became the basis of many a polyphonic composition in the later Middle Ages and thereafter.

Alma Redemptoris Mater, quae pervia caeli porta manes, Et stella maris, succurre cadenti surgere qui curat populo: Tu quae genuisti, natura mirante, tuum sanctum Genitorem: Virgo prius ac posterius, Gabrielis ab ore sumens illud Ave, peccatorum miserere.

Dear Mother of the Savior, You who remain the accessible gate of heaven, And star of the sea, help the one falling to raise up one to care for the people. You who have borne, to the wonderment of nature, your holy Sire. Virgin before and after, hearing that greeting from the mouth of Gabriel, Pity the sinners.

"ALLELUIA" Liber Usualis p. 1076

The Alleluia appeared as the third item in the Proper of the Mass, immediately following the Gradual, during all seasons except Lent. This particular chant is from the Mass for the twenty-third Sunday after Pentacost. The psalm verse is from Psalm 130 (King James Version): "Out of the depths I have cried unto you, O Lord; Lord, hear my voice." Examples of responsorial psalmody, alleluias were performed as in the figure below.

The Alleluia is one of the later, and thus more highly developed, chants of the Mass. Examine its structure and note particularly the various elements of repetition present.

"LAUDA SION" *Sequence (first four verses)* Liber Usualis p. 945

The "Lauda Sion" is sung before the Alleluia during the feast of Corpus Christi (Blessed Sacrament). Structurally, this sequence consists largely of three-phrase pairs. The first four of its twenty-four verses appear below. Diagram (using letters a, b, c and so on for each phrase of each verse) the musical structure. What observations can you make regarding musical repetition? The rising cadence (as opposed to the falling variety that prevails in Gregorian chant) is typical of sequences.

Lauda sion Salvatorem,
Lauda ducemet pastorem,
In hymnis et canticis.

Quantum putes, tantum aude:
Quia major omni laude,
Nec laudare sufficis.

Laudis thema specialis,
Panis vivus et vitalis
Hodie proponitur.

Quem in sacrae mensa coenae,
Turbae fratrum duodenae
Datum non ambigitur.

Sion, praise the Savior,
Praise the leader and shepherd,
In hymns and singing.

As much as you [can],
The greatest of all praise
Is not sufficient.

Special theme of praise,
The living and life-giving bread
Today is placed [before us].

The same that on the table of the holy meal
Was broken for the [apostles] in twelve pieces,
Given without hesitation.

MISSA DE ANGELIS

The *Missa De Angelis* was a commonly used Mass, appropriate for any major feast and also as a Requiem for an infant. The following example presents the Ordinary of this Mass.

Kyrie

K Y-ri- e * e- lé- i-son. iij. Chríste
e- lé- i-son. iij. Ký-ri- e e-
lé- i-son. ij. Ký-ri- e * ** e- lé- i-son.

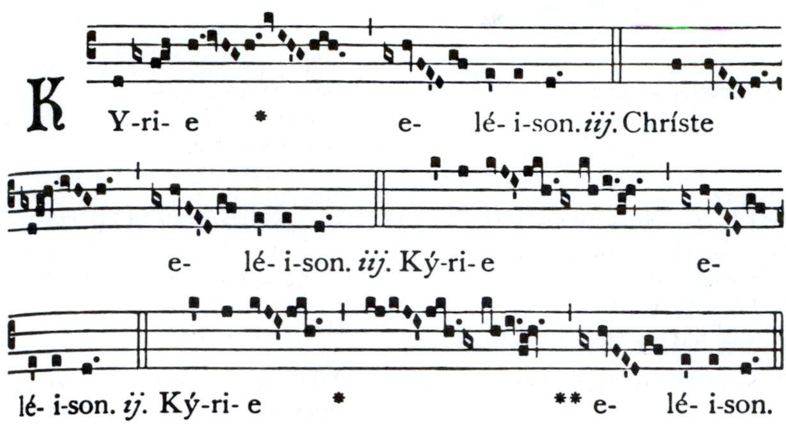

Liber Usualis p. 37

Kyrie eleison.	Lord, have mercy on us.
Christe eleison.	Christ, have mercy on us.
Kyrie eleison.	Lord, have mercy on us.

Gloria

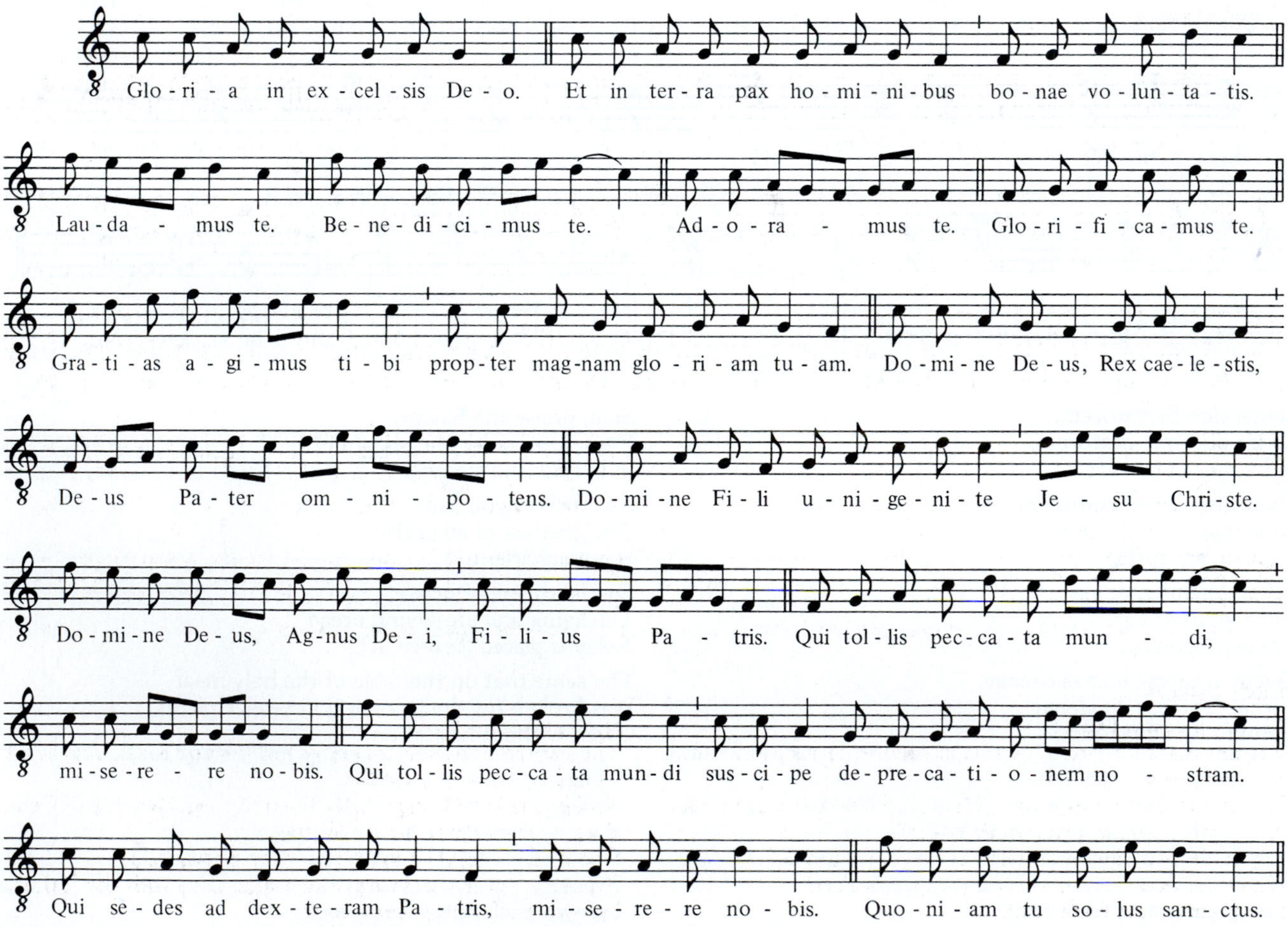

Glo - ri - a in ex - cel - sis De - o. Et in ter - ra pax ho - mi - ni - bus bo - nae vo - lun - ta - tis.
Lau - da - mus te. Be - ne - di - ci - mus te. Ad - o - ra - mus te. Glo - ri - fi - ca - mus te.
Gra - ti - as a - gi - mus ti - bi prop - ter mag - nam glo - ri - am tu - am. Do - mi - ne De - us, Rex cae - le - stis,
De - us Pa - ter om - ni - po - tens. Do - mi - ne Fi - li u - ni - ge - ni - te Je - su Chri - ste.
Do - mi - ne De - us, Ag - nus De - i, Fi - li - us Pa - tris. Qui tol - lis pec - ca - ta mun - di,
mi - se - re - re no - bis. Qui tol - lis pec - ca - ta mun - di sus - ci - pe de - pre - ca - ti - o - nem no - stram.
Qui se - des ad dex - te - ram Pa - tris, mi - se - re - re no - bis. Quo - ni - am tu so - lus san - ctus.

Liber Usualis p. 37

Gloria in excelsis Deo.	Glory to God in the highest.
Et in terra pax hominibus bonae voluntatis.	And on earth peace to men of good will.
Laudamus te.	We praise Thee.
Benedicimus te.	We bless Thee.
Adoramus te.	We adore Thee.
Glorificamus te.	We glorify Thee.
Gratias agimus tibi propter magnam gloriam tuam.	We give thanks to Thee for Thy great glory.
Domine Deus, Rex caelestis, Deus Pater omnipotens.	O Lord God, heavenly King, God the Father almighty.
Domine Fili unigenite Jesu Christe.	O Lord, the only-begotten Son, Jesus Christ.
Domine Deus, Agnus Dei, Filius Patris.	O Lord God, Lamb of God, Son of the Father.
Qui tollis peccata mundi, miserere nobis.	Thou who takest away the sins of the world, have mercy upon us.
Qui tollis peccata mundi suscipe deprecationem nostram.	Thou who takest away the sins of the world, receive our prayer.
Qui sedes ad dexteram Patris, miserere nobis.	Thou who sittest at the right hand of the Father, have mercy upon us.
Quoniam tu solus sanctus.	For Thou only art holy.
Tu solus Dominus.	Thou only art the Lord.
Tu solus Altissimus, Jesu Christe.	Thou only, O Jesus Christ, art most high.
Cum Sancto Spiritu, in gloria Dei Patris.	With the Holy Ghost, in the glory of God the Father.
Amen.	Amen.

Credo (excerpt)

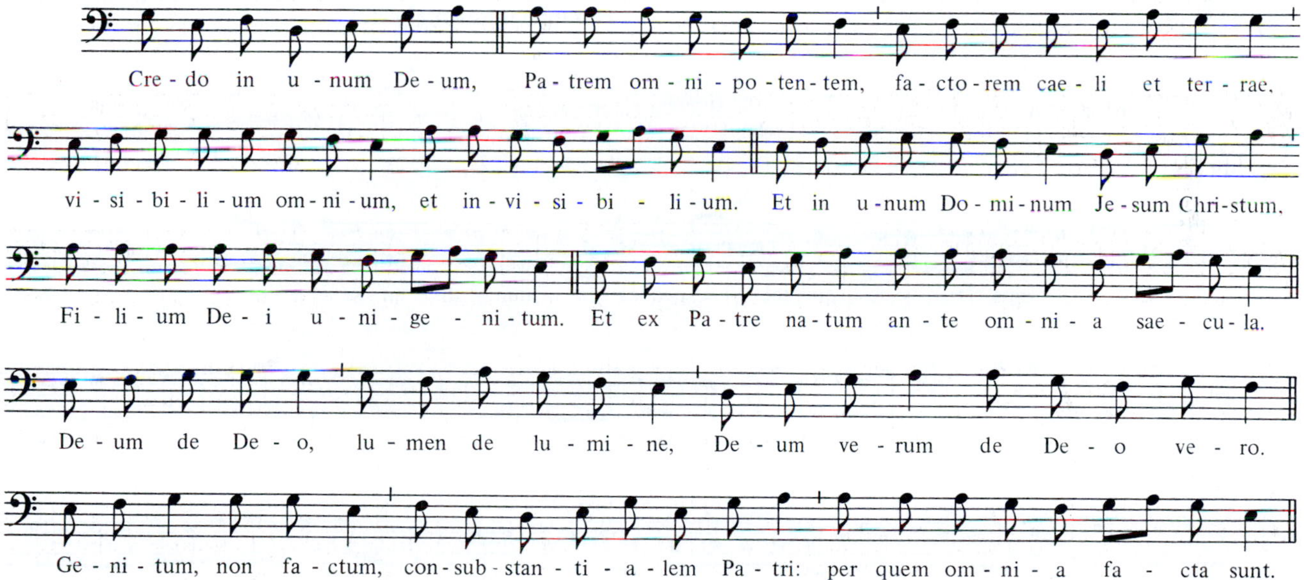

Liber Usualis p. 66

Credo in unum Deum,	I believe in one God,
Patrem omnipotentem, factorem caeli et terrae, visibilium omnium, et invisibilium.	The Father almighty, maker of heaven and earth, and of all things visible and invisible.
Et in unum Dominum Jesum Christum, Filium Dei unigenitum.	And in one Lord Jesus Christ, the only-begotten Son of God.
Et ex Patre natum ante omnia saecula.	Born of the Father before all ages.
Deum de Deo, lumen de lumine, Deum verum de Deo vero.	God of God, light of light, true God of true God.
Genitum, non factum, consubstantialem Patri: per quem omnia facta sunt.	Begotten not made; being of one substance with the Father; by whom all things were made.

Sanctus

Liber Usualis p. 38

Sanctus, Sanctus, Sanctus, Dominus Deus Sabaoth.
Pleni sunt caeli et terra gloria tua.
Hosanna in excelsis.
Benedictus qui venit in nomine Domini.
Hosanna in excelsis.

Holy, holy, holy, Lord God of hosts.
Heaven and earth are full of Thy glory.
Hosanna in the highest.
Blessed is He that cometh in the name of the Lord.
Hosanna in the highest.

Agnus Dei

Liber Usualis p. 39

Agnus Dei, qui tollis peccata mundi:
miserere nobis.
Agnus Dei, qui tollis peccata mundi:
miserere nobis.
Agnus Dei, qui tollis peccata mundi:
donna nobis pacem.

Lamb of God, who takest away the sins of the world:
have mercy on us.
Lamb of God, who takest away the sins of the world:
have mercy on us.
Lamb of God, who takest away the sins of the world:
grant us peace.

ON PAROLE DE BATRE/A PARIS/FRESE NOUVELE *Franconian motet*

Thirteenth-century composers centered in Paris used chants as the basis for compositions called *motets.* These involved one or two newly composed voices above a portion of an existing chant, which was placed in the lowest voice, called the *tenor.* The middle and upper voices, called the *duplum* (or *motetus*) and the *triplum,* were composed separately above the tenor, following certain rules governing the use of consonance and dissonance. In the earliest of these motets, the rhythm of all the voices was based on the rhythmic modes, a set of six metric patterns combining short and long values in different ways. Later motets, such as the following, display greater freedom from the rhythmic modes, an advance credited to the work of the theorist Franco of Cologne.

"On parole de batre" exhibits the gradual move toward secularization. The tenor is a street vendor's cry instead of a chant and the upper voices describe the delights of city living.

What repetitive features can you discover in the tenor? In the upper voices? Is there any sharing or exchange of melodic material? What are the phrase lengths and how are they articulated (i.e., how do they begin and end)? Do the phrases align with the text punctuations? On which rhythmic mode do you think the parts were based?

> *Composed c. 1260*
>
> Related reading: Jeremy Yudkin, *Music in Medieval Europe* (Englewood Cliffs, N.J.: Prentice-Hall, 1989), pp. 391–426. A discussion of the evolution of the motet from the clausula and its development during the thirteenth century.

Triplum:

They speak of threshing and winnowing,
of digging and ploughing.
I don't care at all for these tasks,
for nothing is so pleasurable
as partaking of good clear wine and capons,
and being with good companions strong and hearty,
singing, making merry, and in love,
and having the necessary talents
to attract beautiful ladies
to one's utmost pleasure.
This is all to be found in Paris.

Duplum:

In Paris, evening and morning,
good bread and good clear wine can be found,
good meat and good fish as well as all kinds of friends,
excellent jewels and fine ladies,
and in the meantime,
prices a poor man can afford.

Tenor:

Fresh strawberries! Good blackberries!
Blackberries, good blackberries!

Translation by Mary Schiller

Guillaume de Machaut

Guillaume de Machaut (ca. 1300–1377) was the leading composer of the *Ars Nova.* His motets, probably composed early in his career, are polytextual, some employing both French and Latin texts; most are in three voices and most are isorhythmic. In such structures, the tenor is set in a rhythmic pattern called a *talea,* which is repeated exactly or in diminution throughout the piece. A repeated melodic pattern *(color)* may also be employed which may or may not coincide with the length of the talea.

BONE PASTOR GUILLERME/BONE PASTOR, QUI PASTORES/ BONE PASTOR *Isorhythmic motet*

QUESTIONS FOR DISCUSSION

Formal Structure

1. This work has a highly organized isorhythmic structure. Describe this method of organization and explain its role in defining the overall form. Explain the relationship of the talea and color in the tenor voice. Then examine the other parts for the presence of a talea or color and discuss your findings.
2. Locate the main dividing point in the work and explain what it is that creates the division. In terms of length, what is the ratio of the first section to the second section? What feature of the musical organization causes this to be so?

Melodic/Rhythmic Structure

1. Show the range of each voice part as well as the combined range of all voices. How do the two upper voices compare in range and rhythmic activity? In what way do they complement each other? To what extent do they share melodic material?
2. Renotate the tenor in reduced note values (𝅝‿𝅗𝅥. = 𝅗𝅥.), choosing the more appropriate of these meters: 3/2 or 6/4. Then explain your choice.
3. Discover the meaning of the term *hocket.* Then locate one or two examples of hocket in this work.

Harmonic/Tonal Structure

1. Can you identify an overall tonal center in this work? What is the effect of the conflicting key signatures? Do the individual parts sound modal, and if so, what modes are suggested?
2. The most characteristic cadence of the fourteenth century involves a double leading tone above the tenor. Locate several examples in this work.
3. What are the most common three-note sonorities in this work? Which of these occur at cadences?

Texture/Articulation/Dynamics

1. Describe the overall texture of the work in terms of the spacing of individual voices and their degree of linear independence. Does the texture change significantly during the course of the work and if so, where and in what way?

Composed 1324

Related reading: Sarah Fuller, "On Sonority in Fourteenth-Century Polyphony: Some Preliminary Reflections," *Journal of Music Theory,* Vol. 30, No. 1 (Spring 1986), p. 35f. A discussion of sonority in Machaut's motets, using Bone Pastor as a primary example, with detailed examination of the work's cadences.

10
me non est ti - bi da - tum; fa - ven - te sed Mi - ner -
sto - res ce - te - ros vin - cis per mo -
19
va vir - tu - tum est ca - ter - va for - ti - ter ar - ma - tum.
res et per ge - nus et per
28
Por - tas ur - bis et po - stes tu - e mu - nis, ne ho - stes Ur - bem po -
fru - ctum stu - di - o - - rum tol -
37
pu - len - tur mon - dus, de - mon et ca - ro, mor -
len - tem men - tes y - mo - rum
46
su quo-rum a - ma - ro plu - ri - mi mor - den - tur. Mi - tra que ca -
ce - lo te - nus, O Gui - ller - me te

55
put cin-git bi- no cor- nu de- pin-git du-o te - sta - men - ta,
de - cen - ter Or - na - - tum
64
que mi-tri- fer ha-be-re de- bet tan-quam cin- ce-re
rex, qui po - ten - ter cunc - ta
73
men-tis or-na- men-ta. Et quo-ni-am im- bu-tus et to - tus in-vo-lu-
re - git su - e do - - mus ad
82
tus es im - pre - li-ba - tis, fer-re mi-tram est dig-na tu- a cer-vix, ut
de - co - rem Re-men-si - um in pa - sto -
91
si-gna sint e-qua si-gna- tis. Cu-ram ge-rens po-pu-li, vis
rem pre - e - le-git. E - le - git

100
ut que-ant sin-gu-li va-gos pro-fi-ce-re pri-ma par-te ba-cu-li at-tra-he-
te, vas ho-ne-stum, vas in-si-
106
re; par-te qui-dem a-li-a, que
gne, de quo ni-chil
112
est in-ter-me-di-a, mor-bi-dos re-ge-re, len-tos par-te ter-ci-a scis pun-ge-
sit e-ge-stum ni-si di-
118
re. O-ves pre-di-ca-mi-ne et
gne. De-dit te
124
cum con-ver-sa-mi-ne pa-scis lau-da-bi-li, de-mum e-ro-ga-mi-ne sen-si-bi-
vas spe-ci-a-le si-bi re-

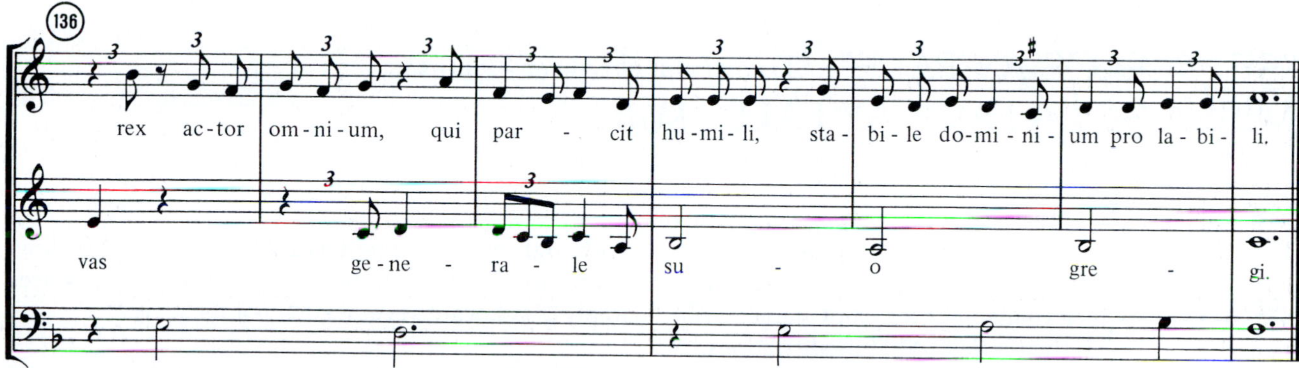

Superius:

Good shepherd Guillerme,
A breast that is unarmed
Is not given to you,
But with Minerva's help
You are armed with great virtue.

Fortify your city gates and doors
lest the enemy overrun the city,
the world, the devil and the lusts of the flesh,
of which multitudes have been smitten.

The mitre that surrounds your head
portrays with its two horns
the two testaments,
which its wearer must have
as ornaments of a pure mind.

And because you are imbued with
and totally committed to excellence,
your neck is worthy to bear the mitre,
that the symbol be equally dignified by its bearer.

You have concern for the people,
you hope that each tries to help the wayward.
You draw them to you
with a part of your staff.

But with another part,
you administer to the sick,
and with the third part
you will prod the tardy.

You preach to your sheep
and convert them
with nourishing praise
and understanding.

After this suffering
may the King who does all things,
who spares the humble,
grant stability for the inconstant.

Motetus:

Good shepherd, who surpasses others
in virtue and lineage
and in the fruits of study
which transports human thoughts heavenward,

O Guillerme, so aptly dressed,
the King, whose power rules all,
has selected you to adorn his house
as shepherd of Reims.

He chose you, honorable vessel,
distinguished conduit,
from which nothing without dignity issues.

He gave to you, special vessel,
to himself, the King.
He gave you, universal vessel,
his flock.

Tenor:

Good shepherd

Guillaume Dufay

Guillaume Dufay (1400–1474) was the outstanding figure of the Burgundian school, which established the techniques and norms that became the basis of polyphonic composition throughout the Renaissance. These included the practice of setting the five divisions of the polyphonic Ordinary in a unified manner, the regular use of a four-voice texture with the triad as the basic harmonic unit, and the development of voice-leading and doubling procedures that were to become standard.

"SE LA FACE AY PALE" *Tenor from three-voice chanson*
MISSA SE LA FACE AY PALE *Kyrie I*

This mass is a *cantus firmus* type, composed around 1450. The cantus firmus, which appears in the tenor, is from Dufay's own chanson of the same name. Only a portion is used in the Kyrie I. What modifications to it has Dufay made? Examine the harmonic structure. Are open-fifth sonorities or complete triads more abundant? In the complete triads, which chord member is most often in the bass? What generalizations can you make regarding doubling in the four-voice chords? Identify and describe the cadences. Is imitation featured prominently in this movement? Although the movement as a whole has a 3/2 feeling, there are several points where one or more voices imply 6/4. Locate several such points.

Composed ca. 1450

Related reading: Howard Mayer Brown, *Music in the Renaissance* (Englewood Cliffs, N.J.: Prentice-Hall, Inc., 1976), pp. 45–51. A discussion of this mass, including an outline of its structure showing use of the cantus firmus throughout the work.

If my face is pale
the cause is love,
It is the main reason.
And love is so much to me
That I gladly would drown
in the sea of love.

But O, she knows,
Whose slave I am,
That without having her
I can have nothing good.

Translation by Shara Turek

Ky - ri - e e - lei - son, Ky - ri - e e - lei - - - - -
Ky - - - - - - - - ri - e e - - - lei - - son,
Ky - - - - ri - - - - e e - lei - - - - - - - - - - - - - - - - - -
7
son,
son,
13
Ky - ri - e e - - - lei - - - son,
Ky - - ri - e e - lei - son,
Ky - - - ri - e e - lei - - - - - - - - - - - son,
20
Ky - - - - ri - - - -
26
e e - lei - - - - - - - - - - son,
Ky - ri - e e - lei - - - - son,
Ky - - - ri - - e e - - lei - - - - - - - - son.

Guillaume Dufay

"FRANC CUEUR GENTIL"

This chanson is one of Dufay's fifty-nine *rondeaux.* The nearly equal treatment of the voices reflects a general tendency that was to become the textural ideal in the music of the Renaissance. Diagram the form, using the letters "a" and "b" to symbolize the two musical phrases and using uppercase "A" and "B" to show text repetitions. Look up the term *rondeau* in the *Harvard Dictionary of Music* or other sources. Is this chanson written in a common form for a rondeau? How are the major points of punctuation in the text emphasized musically? Locate and describe each of the cadences. Identify all examples of imitation. Can you point to a passage that particularly illustrates the growing favor with which composers of the time regarded the triad? Although most of the piece fits easily into the 3/4 meter suggested by the editor's bar lines, several passages do not. For example, can you explain what is happening rhythmically at mm. 15–17, 23–24, and 37?

From *Dufay Opera Omnia,* Tom. VI, ed. Heinrich Besseler, 1964. Reprinted by permission of Arman Carapetyan, Director, American Institute of Musicology in Rome.

Noble charming heart, gracious above all others,
Rich in honor and supplied with all good things;
I give myself to you; to you I bind myself entirely,
No other will I ever want for a sweetheart.

Josquin Desprez

Josquin (ca. 1450–1521) was the greatest and most influential composer in the early part of the sixteenth century. His output consists mostly of Masses, motets and chansons, of which the motets form the largest single group. His Mass techniques include *cantus firmus*, parody and paraphrase. The motets are structured as series of imitative points, with a new melodic phrase for each text phrase. Josquin's settings range from two voices to six.

MISSA MATER PATRIS *Agnus Dei (excerpt)*

The Agnus Dei is the fifth division of the Mass Ordinary. Refer to page 10 and examine the Agnus Dei for the *Missa De Angelis*. Of how many sections is it composed? What part of the Agnus Dei from Josquin's *Missa Mater Patris* is given below? What special relationships do you observe among the voices? One can detect foreshadowings of the Baroque era in certain respects, such as the prominent use of sequences and the use of a complete triad at the important cadence in mm. 29–30. Regarding that cadence, how does it relate to the mode established at the beginning? What mode would you ascribe to the movement?

AGNUS DEI

16
- lis pec - ca - - - - ta mun - - - - - - - di, mun - - - - - - -
- ta mun - - - - - - - di,
- ca - - - - - ta mun - - - - - -
- lis pec - ca - - - - ta mun - - - - - di, mun - - - - - -

23
- di, mi - - se - re - - - - re no - - - - bis.
mi - - se - re - - re no - - - - bis.
- di, mi - - se - re - - re no - bis.
- di, mi - - se - re - - - - re no - - - - bis.

31
DUO
Superius
Altus
A - - gnus De - - - - - -
A - - gnus De - - - - - - i, qui

36
- i, qui tol - - - - - - lis pec - ca - -
tol - - - - lis pec - ca - - - ta mun - - - -

Josquin Desprez

"AVE MARIA . . .VIRGO SERENA"

Josquin's motets, for three to six voices, represent the motet style characteristic of the entire sixteenth century. The various text phrases are set to a series of imitative passages which are themselves grouped into larger units representing the major divisions of the work. In addition to these "points of imitation," there may be passages for paired voices, strictly chordal sections for all voices, or passages in strict canon. The four-voice motet "Ave Maria . . . virgo serena" develops freely, using points of imitation for each of the text phrases. This work depicts the stations in the life of Mary from the Nativity to Assumption.

QUESTIONS FOR DISCUSSION

General Question

1. Circle the descriptive adjectives in each category below which best describe this motet:
   a. prevailingly diatonic; prevailingly chromatic; equally diatonic and chromatic
   b. prevailingly conjunct; prevailingly disjunct; equally conjunct and disjunct
   c. prevailingly imitative; prevailingly non-imitative; equally imitative and non-imitative
   d. through-composed; repetitive; strophic
   e. prevailingly syllabic; prevailingly melismatic; equally syllabic and melismatic

Formal Structure

1. Structurally, this work can be divided into three, or possibly four sections. Identify them and explain which musical elements serve to distinguish one section from the next.
2. What smaller divisions are present in the first large section? What creates these divisions?
3. Locate the point of greatest contrast in the work and explain how this contrast is achieved.

Melodic/Rhythmic Structure

1. In general, would you say that the melodic phrases of this work are characterized by similarity or diversity with respect to their length, rhythmic activity and range?
2. Compare the superius at mm. 84–88 and mm. 78–81. How are the two phrases similar and how are they different? Are they sequential?
3. Locate an example of each of the following:
   a. a 4–3 suspension at a cadence
   b. a double suspension at a cadence
   c. voice pairing in parallel sixths
   d. melodic repetition in all voices simultaneously
   e. melodic sequence

Harmonic/Tonal Structure

1. Upon what mode is this work constructed? Do the principal cadences reinforce the mode or contradict it? If you are familiar with the cadential practice of later periods such as the Baroque era, explain how these cadences differ.
2. The two passages in this work which seem to be closest harmonically to the major-minor tonal system are similar to each other texturally. Can you identify these two passages?

Texture/Articulation/Dynamics

1. The first verse of the text consists of four two-word phrases. Describe the manner in which they are set. How many large musical gestures result? Describe the means by which a drive toward the cadence is created.
2. Describe the different textures employed in this work.

> *Composed 1497 (?)*
>
> Related Reading: Howard Mayer Brown, *Music in the Renaissance* (Englewood Cliffs, N.J.: Prentice-Hall, Inc., 1976), pp. 123–127. A discussion of this work. Additional resource: Irving Godt, "Motivic Integration in Josquin's Motets," *Journal of Music Theory*, Vol. 21, No. 2 (Fall 1977), p. 264f.

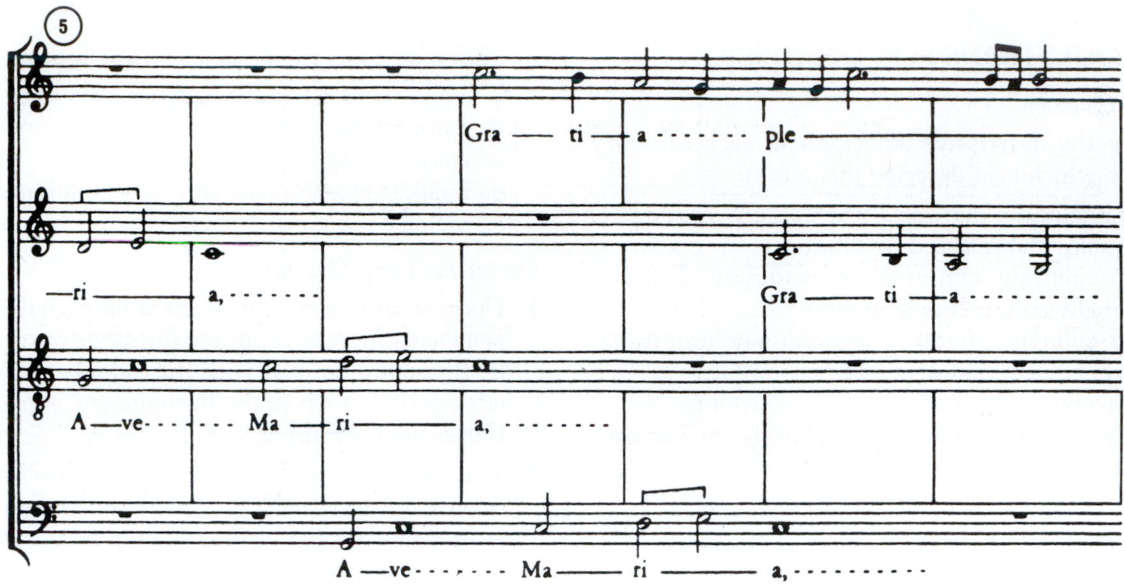
5
Gra — ti — a - - - - - - - ple —
— ri — a, - - - - - - -
Gra — ti — a - - - - - - - -
A — ve - - - - - Ma — ri — a, - - - - - - - -
A — ve - - - - - Ma — ri — a, - - - - - - - - -

12
— na, - - - - - - - - - - -
Do — mi-nus
ple — na, - - - - - - - - -
Gra — ti — a - - - - - - - - - - ple — na, - - - - - - -
Gra — ti — a - - - - - - - - - - ple — na, - - - - - - -

18
te — cum, - -
Do — mi — nus - - - - te — cum, - - - - - - - - - -
Vir —
Do — mi-nus - - - - te —
Do — mi — nus - - - - -

24
Vir — go se — re — na, - - - se —
—go se — re — na, - - -
— cum, - - Vir — go se — re —
te — cum, - - - Vir —

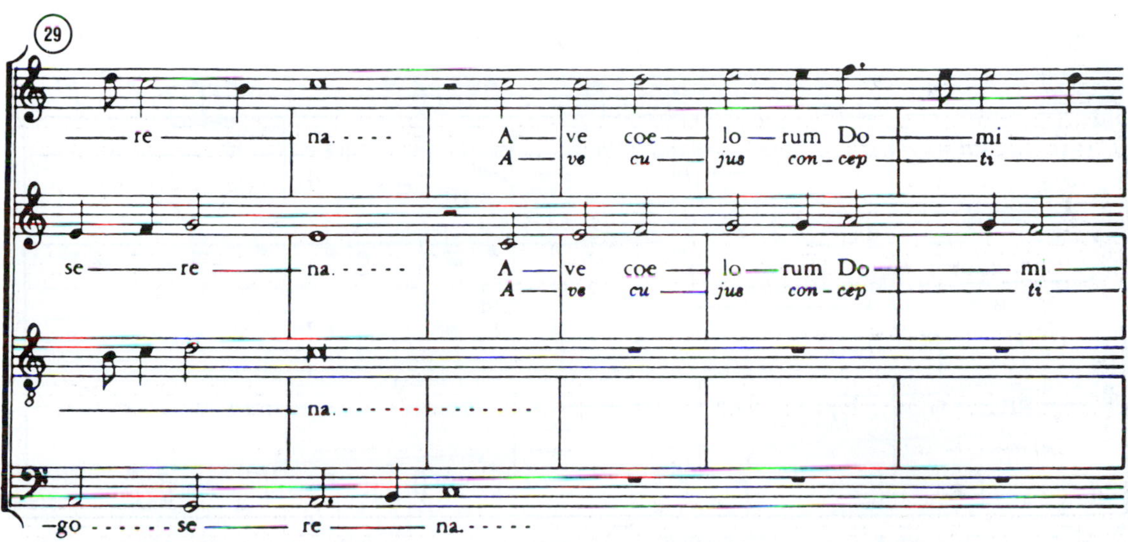
29
— re — na. - - - A — ve coe — lo — rum Do — mi —
A — ve cu — jus con – cep — ti —
se — re — na. - - - A — ve coe — lo — rum Do — mi —
A — ve cu — jus con – cep — ti —
— na. - - -
—go - - - se — re — na. - - -

35
— na, - - - Ma —
— o - - - So —
— na, - - - Do — mi — na, - - - Ma —
— o - - - con — cep — ti — o - - - So —
A — ve coe — lo — rum Do — mi — na, - - - Ma —
A — ve cu — jus con — cep — ti — o - - - So —
A — ve coe — lo — rum Do — mi — na, - - - Ma —
A — ve cu — jus con – cep — ti — o - - - So —

41
—ri— a ple—na gra—ti—a, Coe—le—sti—a, - - ter—
-lem—ni ple—na gau—di—o,
—ri—a ple—na gra—ti—a, - - - - - - - Coe-le—sti—a, - - ter—
-lem—ni ple—na gau—di—o, - - - - - - -
—ri—a ple—na gra—ti—a, Coe-le—sti—a, - - - ter—re-
-lem—ni ple—na gau—di—o,
—ri—a ple—na gra—ti—a, Coe—le—sti—a, - - - - - ter
-lem—ni ple—na gau—di—o,

47
—re—stri—a, - - - Mun—dum re—plens - - - - - - lae—ti—
No—va re—plet - - - - - - -
[T]
—re-stri—a, - - - Mun—dum - - - re—plens lae—ti—
No—va - - - re—plet
[A]
—stri—a, - - - - Mun—dum - - - re—plens - - - lae—ti—
No—va - - - - re—plet - - -
—re—stri—a, - - - - - - Mun—dum re—plens - - - - - - lae—ti—
No—va re—plet - - - - - - -

52
—ti— a. - - - - - - - - - - - - - A—ve - - - - - - - - - - - - cu—jus - - - - - - - -
[A]
—ti—a, - - - - lae—ti—ti—a - - - A—ve - - - - - - - - - - - - cu—jus - - - -
[T]
—ti—a. -
—ti—a. -

58
na — ti — vi — tas.
na — ti — vi — tas.
No — stra fu — it so — lem —
No — stra fu — it so —

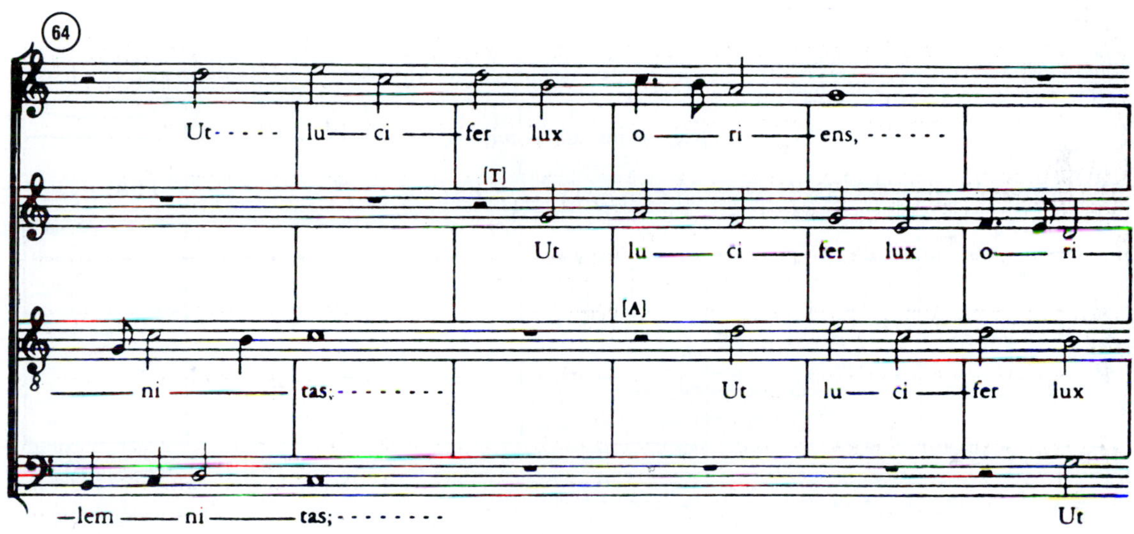
64
Ut lu — ci — fer lux o — ri — ens,
[T]
Ut lu — ci — fer lux o — ri —
[A]
— ni — tas;
Ut lu — ci — fer lux
— lem — ni — tas;
Ut

70
Ve — rum so — lem prae-ve —
— ens, Ve — rum so — lem prae — ve — ni — ens.
o — ri — ens, Ve — rum so — lem prae — ve —
lu — ci — fer lux o — ri — ens, Ve — rum so — lem prae —

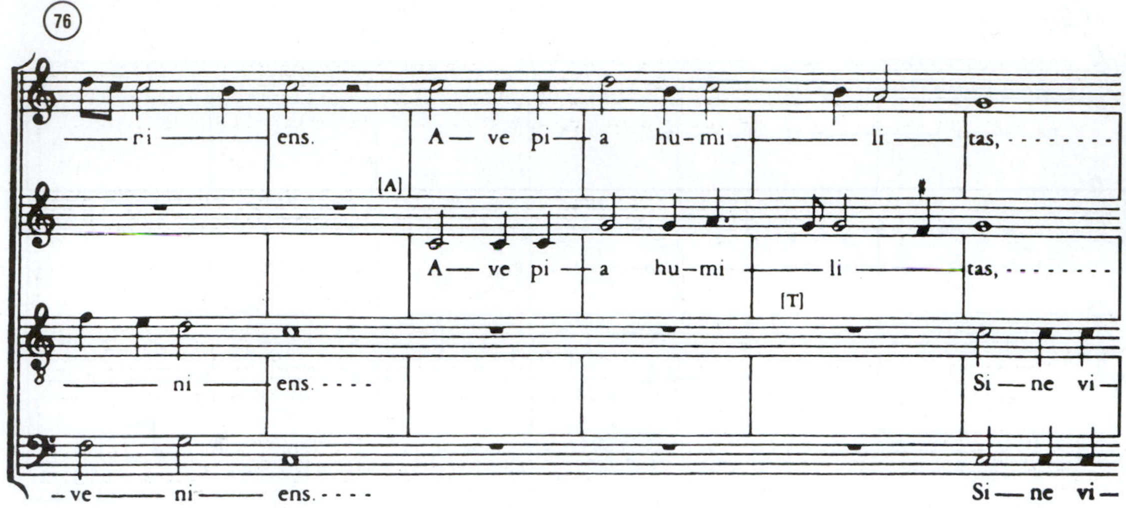
76
ri ens. A— ve pi— a hu–mi li tas,
[A]
A— ve pi— a hu–mi li tas,
[T]
ni ens. Si — ne vi—
–ve ni ens. Si — ne vi—

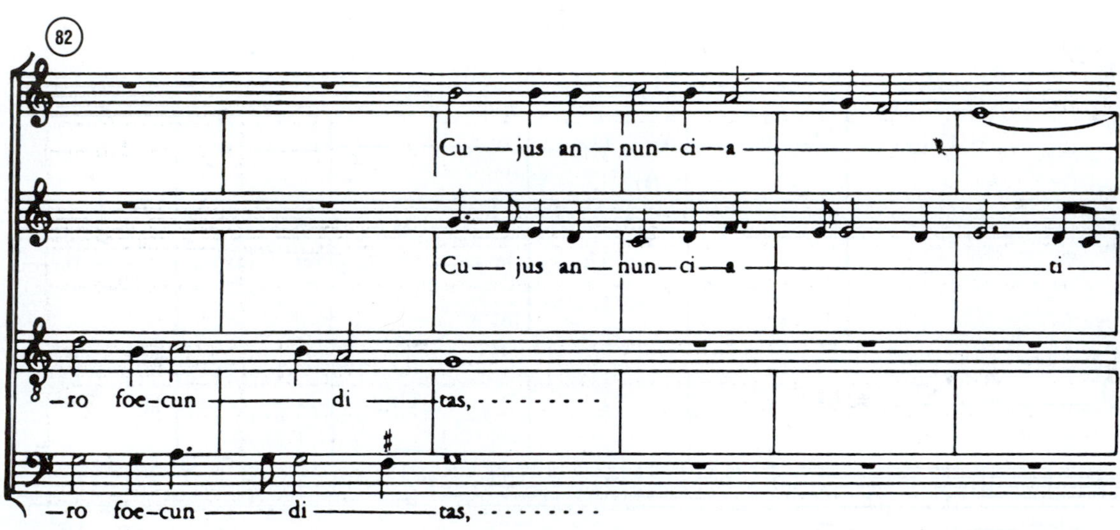
82
Cu—jus an—nun—ci—a
Cu— jus an—nun—ci—a ti—
–ro foe–cun di tas,
–ro foe–cun di tas,

88
ti— o
—o
No— stra--fu it-----sal va ti o.
No — stra---- fu it sal va ti — o.

94
A–ve ve– ra - - - - - - vir — gi — ni – tas, - - - - - Im–ma–cu— la — ta - - -
A–ve ve– ra - - - vir — gi — ni— tas, - - - - - Im–ma–cu – la — ta - - - - -
A – ve ve–ra - - - - - - - - - vir– gi — ni–tas, - - - - Im–ma — cu –la —
A–ve ve— ra - - - - - - vir — gi — ni — tas, - - - - - Im-ma–cu— la — ta - - -

100
ca — sti — tas, - - - Cu— jus - - - - pu — ri — fi — ca — ti — o - - - - - No—
ca — sti — tas, - - - Cu— jus - - - - pu — ri — fi — ca — ti — o - - - - - No—
–ta ca — sti –tas, - - - Cu–jus - - - - - pu – ri — fi– ca — ti — o - - - - - -
ca — sti — tas, - - - Cu— jus - - - - pu — ri — fi— ca — ti — o - - - - - No—

106
[o· – o]
–stra - - - - - - - fu — it pur — ga — ti — o. - - - - - - - - -
–stra - - - - fu — it pur – ga — ti — o. - - -
No – stra - - - - - - - - fu – it pur — ga — ti — o. -
– stra - - - - - - - - fu — it - - - - - pur — ga – ti — o. -

111
A ve prae cla ra o mni bus
A ve prae cla ra o mni
A ve prae cla
A ve prae cla ra

117
An ge li cis vir- tu
bus An ge li cis
ra o mni bus An
o mni bus An

123
ti bus, Cu jus fu
vir tu ti bus, Cu jus fu
ge li cis vir- tu ti bus,
ge li cis vir tu ti bus,

129
it ------ as sum pti o ------------ No stra glo
[T]
it ------ as sum pti o --- No stra
[A]
Cu jus fu it ------ as sum pti o --------
Cu jus --- fu it as sum pti o --------

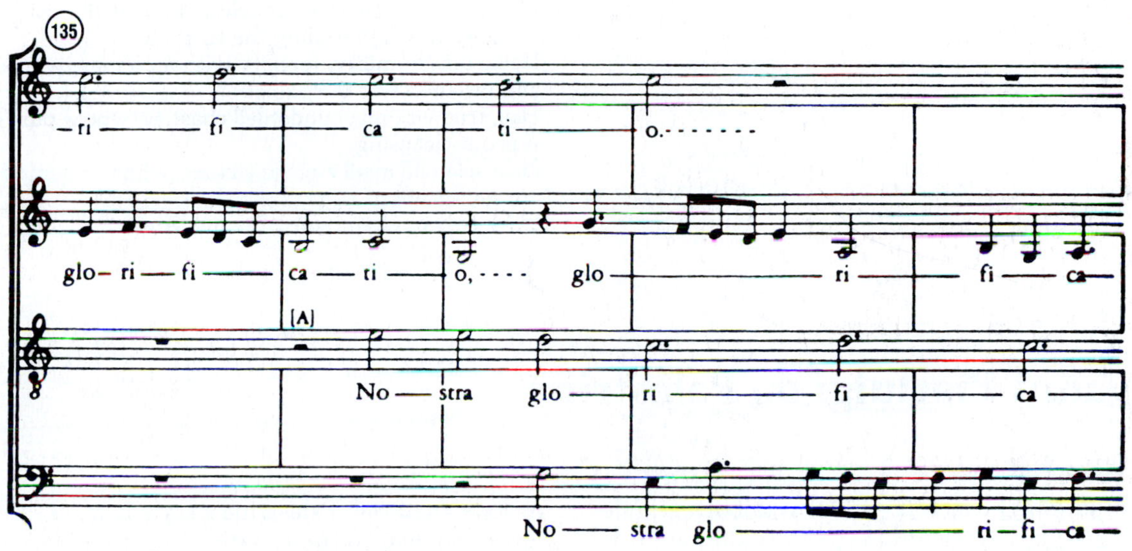
135
ri fi ca ti o. ------
glo- ri fi ca ti o, ---- glo ri fi ca
[A]
No stra glo ri fi ca
No stra glo ri fi ca

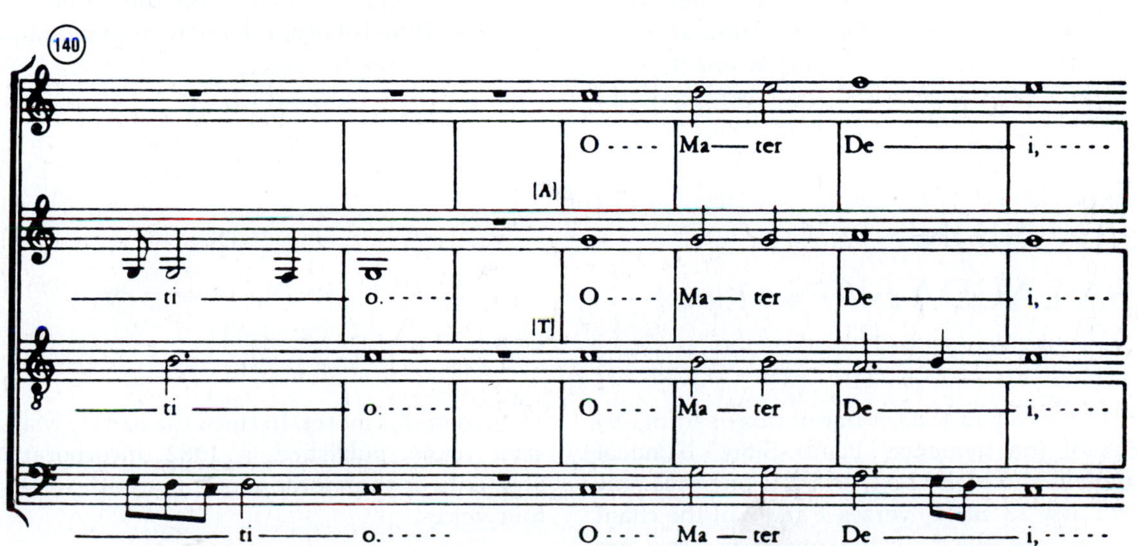
140
[A]
O ---- Ma ter De i, -----
ti o. ----- O ---- Ma ter De i, ----
[T]
ti o. ----- O ---- Ma ter De i, ----
ti o. ----- O ---- Ma ter De i, ----

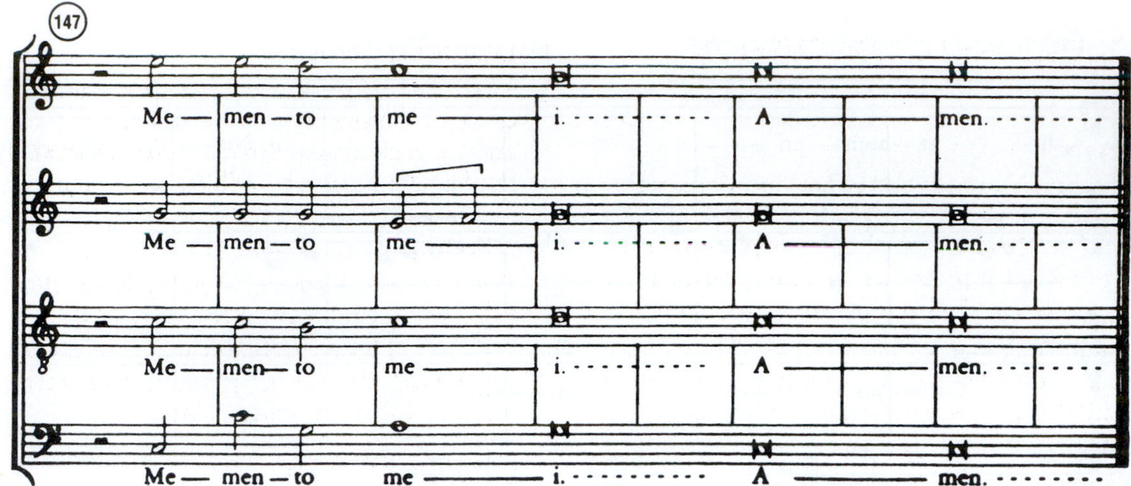

Hail Mary, full of grace, Lord (be) with you, serene Virgin.
Hail, whose conception, full of solemn joy, fills heavenly and earthly places with new delight.
Hail, whose birth was our celebration, as the rising light-bringing dawn, preceding the true sun.
Hail, pious humility, fertility without a man, whose annunciation was our salvation.
Hail, true virginity, undefiled chastity, whose purification was our cleansing.
Hail, splendid in all angelic virtues, whose assumption was our glorification.
O Mother of God, remember me, Amen.

Giovanni Pierluigi da Palestrina

Giovanni Pierluigi (ca. 1525–1594) was born at Palestrina, Italy. Due to his life-long association with the Church, Palestrina's sacred works are more numerous and more important than his secular. His 105 Masses represent all the important techniques of the time—*cantus firmus*, canon, free counterpoint, paraphrase and parody. Most of the Masses are based on chant, while most of the motets are based on freely invented melodic material. Palestrina's style is marked by conjunct and diatonic lines with gentle archlike contours moving mostly within the range of a tenth, carefully prepared and resolved dissonances, and imitative textures, with four to six voices the norm. His music is largely devoid of pronounced text- or mood-painting and other dramatic effects.

"LAUDA SION" *Motet*
MISSA LAUDA SION *Kyrie*

This motet, written in 1563, is one of three settings by Palestrina of the sequence "Lauda Sion." None of these employs the entire text, and this one uses only verses 1, 2 and 23. Study verses 1 and 2 of the chant (page 7) and observe how the music and text are adapted in this motet. In turn, the parody Mass of the same name, published in 1582, incorporates large segments of the motet. Note that both works are in four voices.

QUESTIONS FOR DISCUSSION

Motet

Formal Structure

1. Identify and describe the three large sections of this motet. How might the form be represented with letters? The first of the major sections may be further divided into *two* parts. Can you identify them and explain the basis for this division?
2. This motet employs a characteristic Renaissance procedure in which each text phrase is treated in turn imitatively. Identify these "points of imitation" in the first large section and explain how they differ from each other.

Melodic/Rhythmic Structure

1. What seems to be the purpose of the accidentals, both written and *musica ficta* (added by the performer), in this work?
2. Examine the cantus carefully. What observations can you make concerning:
   a. the interval structure in general;
   b. successive melodic leaps;
   c. tied note values;
   d. the smaller note values (quarter notes and eighth notes)?
3. Compare the four voices with respect to range, interval structure, rhythmic activity and contour. Are there any points at which the voices cross?

Harmonic/Tonal Structure

1. What is the pitch center of the work? Does it change? Palestrina's music contains both modal and tonal elements. Provide a harmonic analysis of the last six measures. Which of the harmonies fit logically into the tonality of G major and which reflect the older, modal system?
2. Describe the cadences employed in this work. Which type occurs most frequently? Comment on the final cadence. Can you make a generalization concerning the use of tones foreign to the harmonies at these cadence points?

Texture/Articulation/Dynamics

1. How many fundamentally different textures can you identify in this work? Give an example of each.
2. Comment generally on the setting of the text in this work. Can you find any instances of word-painting? One of the concerns of the Church at this time was that the words be clearly understandable. Do you feel that this has been accomplished here?

Mass: General Question

1. The *Missa Lauda Sion,* included in part in this anthology, is a parody Mass based upon the motet "Lauda Sion." Can you describe the way in which the motet is parodied in the Kyrie of the Mass?

Motet

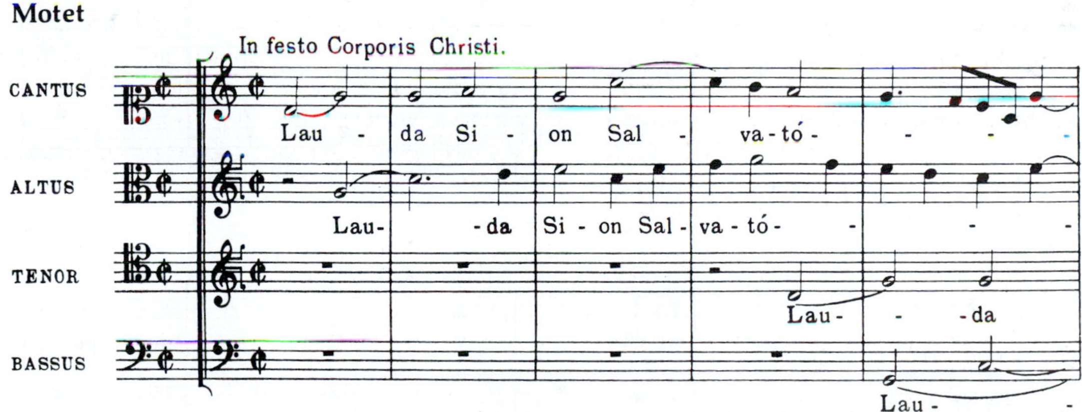

6
- rem, lau - da du - cem et pa - stó - -
- - - rem, lau - da du - cem et pa - stó - - -
Si - on Sal - va - tó - rem, lau -
- da Si - on Sal-va - tó - rem,

12
rem, in hy - mnis et cán - -
rem, in hy - mnis et cán -
da du - cem et pa - stó - - - rem, in hy - mnis et
lau - da du - cem et pa - stó - - -rem,

18
- ti - cis, in hy - mnis et cán - - ti - cis,
- - ti - cis, in hy - mnis et cán-ti - cis, et
cán - ti - cis, in hy - mnis, in hy -
in hy - mnis, in hy - mnis et cán - - ti - cis,

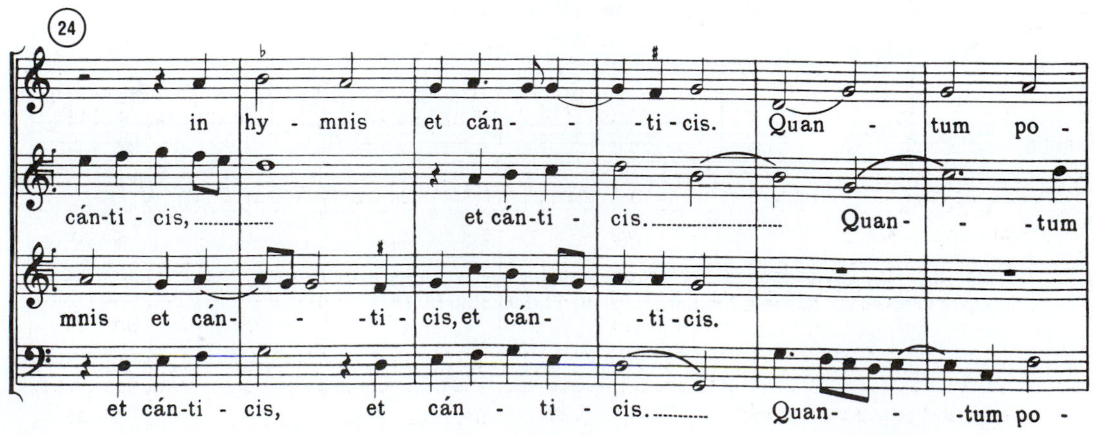
24
in hy - mnis et cán - - ti - cis. Quan - tum po -
cán-ti - cis, et cán-ti - cis. Quan - - - tum
mnis et cán - - ti - cis, et cán - - ti - cis.
et cán-ti - cis, et cán - ti - cis. Quan - - -tum po -

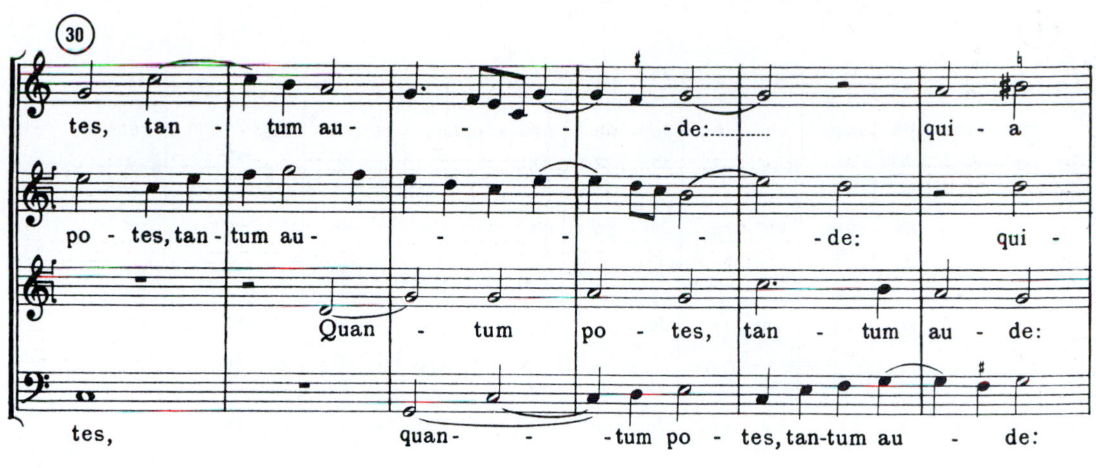
30
tes, tan - tum au - - - de: qui - a
po - tes, tan - tum au - - - - de: qui -
Quan - tum po - tes, tan - tum au - de:
tes, quan - - tum po - tes, tan-tum au - de:

36
ma - jor o - mni lau - de, o - - mni lau - de,
a ma - jor o-mni lau - - de, o - - - mni lau -
qui-a ma - jor o-mni lau - de, qui - a ma - jor o - mni
qui - a ma - jor o - mni lau -

42
nec lau - dá - re súf - - - fi - cis,
- - de, nec lau - dá - re súf - - - fi - cis, nec
lau - de, nec lau -
- de, nec lau - dá - re súf - fi - cis,

48
nec lau - dá - re súf - - - fi - cis. Bo - ne
lau-dá - re súf - fi - cis. Bo - ne
dá - re súf - - fi - cis, súf - - fi - - cis. Bo - ne
nec lau-dá - re súf - - fi - cis. Bo - ne

54
pa - stor, pa - nis ve - re, Je - su no - stri mi - se - ré - re:
pa - stor, pa - nis ve - re, Je - su no - stri mi - se - ré - re:
pa - stor, pa - nis ve - re, Je - su no - stri mi - se - ré - re:
pa - stor, pa - nis ve - re, Je - su no - stri mi - se - ré - re:

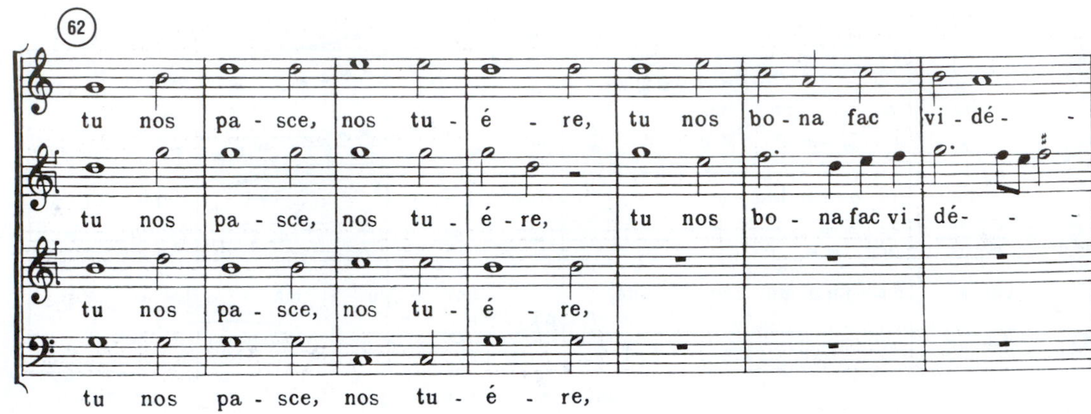
62
tu nos pa - sce, nos tu - é - re, tu nos bo - na fac vi - dé -
tu nos pa - sce, nos tu - é - re, tu nos bo - na fac vi - dé -
tu nos pa - sce, nos tu - é - re,
tu nos pa - sce, nos tu - é - re,

69
re in ter - - ra...
re in ter - - ra vi - -
tu nos bo - na fac vi - dé - re in ter -
tu nos bo - na fac vi - dé - re in ter - ra

75
vi - vén - ti - um. A - - -men, a - men.
- vén - ti - um. A - - -men, a - men.
ra vi - vén - ti - um. A - - -men, a - men.
vi - vén - ti - um. A - - -men, a - men.

Praise Sion the Savior,
Praise the leader and shepherd,
In hymns and singing.

As much as you can;
The greatest of all praise
Is not sufficient.

Good Shepherd, true bread,
Jesus have mercy on us:
Feed us, protect us,
Make us see the good things
In the land of the living.
Amen.

Reprinted by permission of the Istituto Italiano per la Storia della Musica, Roma. From *Palestrina Opera Complete,* ed. Raffaele Casimiri, Edizione Fratelli Scalera, 1939.

For translation: See *Missa De Angelis* (page 8).

Roland de Lassus

In the works of Roland de Lassus (1532–1594), one can find practically every compositional technique of the late sixteenth century. His forms are usually made up of small sections distinct in rhythm and texture. His music ranges from highly chromatic to completely diatonic, from purely chordal to highly polyphonic, and his use of imitation is generally less persistent and pervasive than Palestrina's. More than in Palestrina, emerging elements of functional harmony are evident. Modality is often undermined by chromaticism, and dominant-tonic chains through the circle of fifths are common.

"DEH, LASCIA, ANIMA"

"Deh, lascia, anima" is one of forty-one four-voice madrigals composed by Lassus. Published seven years before his death, it is an example of the spiritual madrigal—a type which he cultivated almost exclusively in his latest period. Setting the serious text in a reserved harmonic style, Lassus reflects the musical spirit of the Counter Reformation in a restrained but expressive, smoothly flowing polyphony, quite different from Gesualdo's highly chromatic "Occhi del mio cor vita," which you may wish to compare (page 50).

QUESTIONS FOR DISCUSSION

Formal Structure

1. Identify the various textual-musical phrases which make up this work. How are they distinguished musically one from another? Are they related, and if so, in what way? How would you describe the overall form?
2. Can you find any instances of substantial textual or musical repetition? Are the sections of this work characterized more by similarity or by contrast? Do you feel that the work as a whole has a continuous or sectional feeling? To what do you attribute this?

Melodic/Rhythmic Structure

1. Compare the four voices of this work with respect to range, intervallic structure and rhythmic activity.
2. Would you describe the melodic character of this work as diatonic or chromatic? What accidentals are employed? Can you make any generalizations concerning their use?
3. Label the suspensions that occur at m. 16, m. 17, m. 19, and m. 36 (beat three) and describe their preparation and resolution.

Harmonic/Tonal Structure

1. Assign a key or mode to this work and explain what factors influenced your decision. Does the music seem to "modulate" at any points and if so, to what key or mode?
2. Can you generalize concerning Lassus' preferences with respect to:
   a. position of chords (inversion structure);
   b. triad types (major, minor, augmented or diminished);
   c. doubling?
3. Identify the following cadences: mm. 8–9; mm. 19–20; mm. 30–31.
4. Identify the type of six-four chords (cadential, passing, or embellishing) which appear at the following points: m. 34; m. 37; m. 51.

Texture/Articulation/Dynamics

1. Describe Lassus' use of imitation in this work.
2. How would you describe the overall texture? Are there points of contrast in this respect, and if so, where are they?

Composed 1587

Related reading: Gustave Reese, *Music in the Renaissance* (New York: W.W. Norton & Co., 1959), pp. 690–695. A stylistic comparison of Lassus and Palestrina.

S.
A.
T.
B.
Deh, la - scia a -
Deh, la - scia a - ni -
Deh, la - - - scia a -
Deh, la - scia a -
4
- ni - ma ho - ma - i la - scia l'im - pre - se
- ma ho - ma - i la - scia l'im - pre - se
- ni - ma ho - ma - i la - scia l'im - pre - se
- ni - ma ho - ma - i la - scia l'im - pre - se
8
va - - - - ne, e le vo - glie mon - da - -
va - - - - ne, e le vo - glie mon - da - ne,
va - - - - ne, e le vo - - glie mon - da -
va - - - - ne, e le vo - glie mon - da - ne,

12
- ne, che t'han con - dot - ta in tan - ti a - - ma -
che t'han con - dot - ta in tan - - - ti a - ma - -
-ne, che t'han con - dot - ta in tan - - ti a -
che t'han con - dot - - ta in tan - - ti a - - ma - -

17
- ri gua - - - i: al - hor can-tar pot-
- ri gua - i: al-hor can - tar pot - ra -
- ma - ri gua - i: al-hor can-
- ri gua - - - i:

22
- ra - i, al - hor can - tar pot - ra - i de la ve - ra spe
- i, al - hor can - tar pot - ra - i de la ve - ra, de la ve -
- tar, al - hor can - tar pot - ra - i de la ve -
al - hor can - tar pot - ra - i de la ve -

26
-ran-za, de la ve - ra, de la ve-ra spe-ran - - -
-ra, de la ve-ra, de la ve - ra spe - ran -
-ra, de la ve-ra spe - ran-za, de la ve - ra spe-ran - za il
-ra, de la ve - ra, de la ve - ra spe - ran - za il
29
-za il pre-gio al - te - ro; el - la non
-za il pre - gio al - te - ro; el - la non a - ma il
pre-gio al-te - - - ro; el - la non
pre-gio al-te - ro; el - - la non a -
33
a - ma il can - to se non scor-ge il cor san - -
can - to se non scor - ge il cor
a - ma il can - to se non scor - ge il cor san -
- ma il can - to se non scor-ge il cor san -

37
- to: la - scia il tor - to, la - scia il
san - - to: la - scia il tor - - -
- - - to: la - scia il tor - - to sen - tie -
- to: la - scia il tor - to, la - scia il tor -
41
tor - to sen - tie - - - ro e po - scia a dir di
- to sen - tie - - - ro e po - scia a dir di
- - ro e po - scia a dir di
- - to sen - tie - - ro e po - scia a dir di
45
lei, e po - scia a dir di lei, vol - gi il pen - sie - - - - -
lei, e po - scia a dir di lei, vol - gi il pen - sie - ro, vol -
lei, e po - scia a dir di lei, vol - gi il pen - sie - - -
lei, e po - scia a dir di lei, vol - gi il pen - sie - - -

Ah, leave soul, henceforth leave the vain undertakings, and the mundane desires which have led you to so many bitter mishaps: then you will be able to sing the lofty merit of true hope: to her the song is not acceptable unless she perceives the pure heart: leave the crooked path and then turn your thoughts to speak of her.

Roland de Lassus

BEATUS HOMO and JUSTI TULERUNT CANTIONES DUARUM VOCUM *Nos. 2 and 7*

These works come from Lassus' *Magnum opus musicum,* a collection of 516 motets for two to twelve voices. In what ways do these works sound modal? What elements of major-minor tonality are present? Identify the pitch center on which each is based and also identify any secondary pitch centers. In No. 2, what governs the use of B-natural versus B-flat? In No. 7, where are the principal cadences and what distinguishes them? In both, what observations can you make regarding the treatment of dissonance (i.e., the most common kinds, where dissonance occurs, how long it lasts, how it is resolved)? Pay special attention to the suspensions. What types (9–8, 7–6, etc.) do you find? What further observations can you make regarding them? Imitation forms the very foundation of these motets. At how many different pitch intervals does imitation occur? Can you locate an example of imitation by inversion?

Beatus Homo

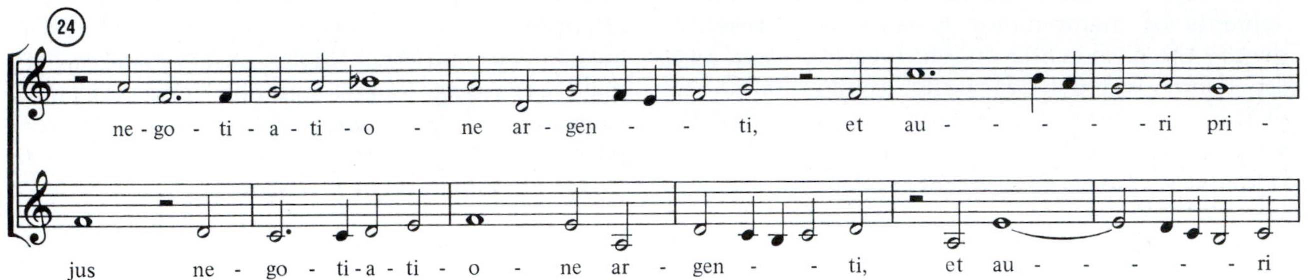

Blessed is the man that findeth wisdom and is rich in prudence: the purchasing thereof is better than the merchandise of silver, and her fruit than the chiefest and purest gold.

Justi Tulerunt

The just took the spoils of the wicked, and they sung to thy holy name, O Lord, and they praised with one accord thy victorious hand.

Carlo Gesualdo di Venosa

"OCCHI DEL MIO COR VITA"

In the sixteenth century, a growing interest in chromaticism led to the exploration of tuning systems that contained more than twelve pitches to the octave, the development of keyboard instruments capable of playing music based on such tuning systems, and the composition of intensely chromatic madrigals by composers such as Luca Marenzio (1554–1613) and Carlo Gesualdo (1561–1613). The following selection is typical of Gesualdo's style. The text deals with the pain of unrequited love. This anguish is expressed in music that alternates between an intensely chromatic chordal style and diatonic-imitative polyphony, a format that Gesualdo adopted in many of his madrigals. Can a central tonality be assigned to this piece, and if so, what is it? How do the changes in musical character reflect the text? Study the imitation that plays such a prominent role in this work. Other devices and techniques that deserve attention include melodic and harmonic sequences, chromatic third relationships between chords, cross-relations between voices, and the use of both functional and nonfunctional chromaticism.

9
- - te,oi - mè, l'u - sa-ta a - ì - ta! Tem - po è ben di mo - ri - re,
l'u - sa - ta a - ì - ta! Tem - po è ben di mo - ri - re, tem - po è
oi - mè, l'u - sa-ta a - ì - - ta! Tem - po è ben di mo - ri - re, tem - po è
l'u - sa-ta a - ì - ta! Tem - po è ben di mo - ri - re, tem - po è
mè, l'u - sa - ta a - ì - ta! tem - po è
16
a che più tar - do, a che più
ben di mo - ri - re, a che più tar - do, a che più
ben di mo - ri - re, a che più tar - - do, a che più tar -
ben di mo - ri - re, a che più tar - do, a che più
ben di mo - ri - re, a che più tar - do, a che più
21
tar - do? A che, a che
tar - do? A che ser - ba - te il guar - -
- do? A che, a che ser - ba - te il guar - - - -
tar - do? A che ser - ba - te il guar - - do
tar - do? A che ser - ba - te il guar - -

26
— ser-ba - te il guar - - - - - - do,
- - do, a che ser - - ba - te il guar - - -
do, a che ser-ba - te il guar - - - do, a che ser-
a che ser-ba - - te il guar - - - - - do?
- - do, a che ser - - - ba - te il guar -
31
il guar - - - - do? For - se per non mi - rar, per non mi-
- - do? For - - se per non mi-rar, per non — mi-rar,
ba - te il guar - - - do? For - se per non mi-rar, per non
For - se per non mi - rar, for - se
- - - do? For - - se per non mi - rar,
36
rar co - - me v'a - do - - - - - ro.
per non mi - rar co - me v'a - do - ro. Mi -
mi - rar co - me, co - me v'a - do - - ro. Mi - ra -
per non mi - rar co - - - me v'a - do - ro. Mi -
per non mi - rar co - - me v'a - do - - - - - ro. Mi -

Light of my life
You deny me, alas,
The help you usually give to me!
It is time [for me] to die,
Why wait any longer?
When you look at me
Can you not see how much I love you?
If not, just watch me die!

Translation by Clifford Billions

DER PRINZENTANZ; PROPORZ *Anonymous lute dances*

The pairing of dances was common in late-sixteenth-century instrumental music, and eventually led to the suite of the Baroque era. Many dance pairs such as the following were composed for the lute, a plucked-string instrument that was a favorite in Renaissance households. What relationship exists between the Prinzentanz and the Proporz? What is the form of each? What unifying motives are present? Is the work in a mode or in major-minor tonality? (Support your answer.) Take note of the melodic phrasing. How does it compare to that found in vocal works such as Josquin's "Ave Maria," Palestrina's motet "Lauda Sion," or Lassus' *Cantiones duarum vocum?*

Composed ca. 1550

Related reading: Edward E. Lowinsky, *Tonality and Atonality in Sixteenth-Century Music* (Berkeley and Los Angeles: University of California Press, 1962), pp. 62–71. A discussion of the emergence of major-minor tonality in sixteenth-century dance music.

Der Prinzentanz [Slow]
5
9
14
Proporz [Fast]
20

John Dowland

"FACTION THAT EVER DWELLS" *from Second Book of Songs and Ayres*

Lute ayres were popular in England during the first quarter of the seventeenth century. Dowland (1562–1626) was the leading composer in this genre. In this work, the lute tablature is exactly as it appears in the original edition. Above the tablature is a strictly literal transcription of the lute part. Can this piece be better analyzed in terms of modality or major-minor tonality? What reasons can you cite for your answer? Four additional verses of text are contained in the original. That being the case, how would you describe the form?

Composed 1597

Related reading: Edward E. Lowinsky, *Tonality and Atonality in Sixteenth-Century Music* (Berkeley and Los Angeles: University of California Press, 1962), pp. 54–61. A discussion of the emergence of major-minor tonality in the lute ayre.

VOICE

LUTE

Fac - tion, that ev - er dwells In Court where

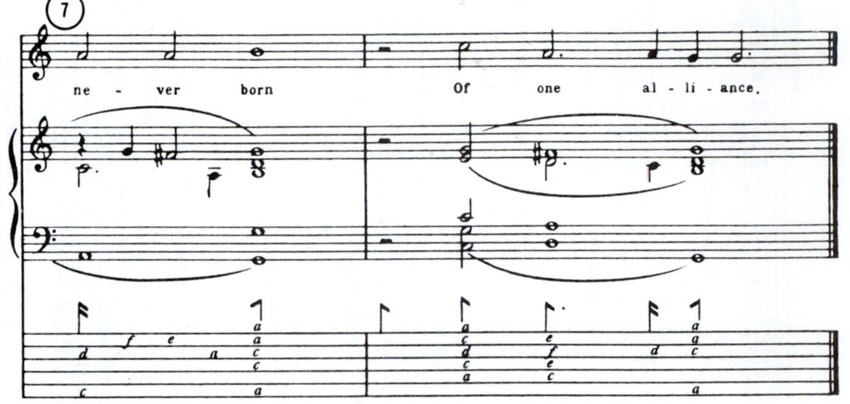

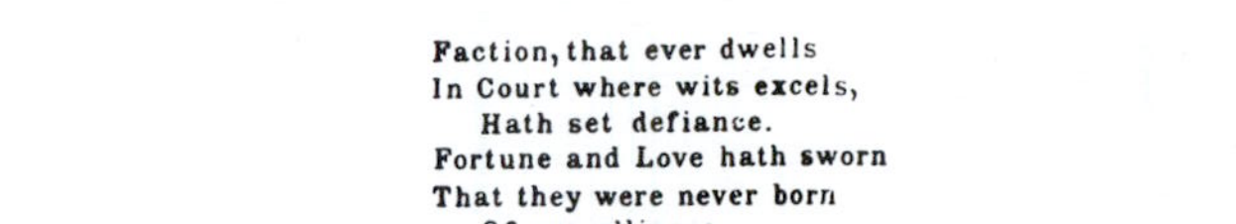

Faction, that ever dwells
In Court where wits excels,
Hath set defiance.
Fortune and Love hath sworn
That they were never born
Of one alliance.

Fortune swears weakest hearts
The book of Cupid's arts
Turn with her wheel.
Senses themselves shall prove
Venture her place in love
Ask them that feel.

This discord it begot
Atheist, that Honour, not
Nature, thought good.
Fortune should ever dwell
In Court where wits excel,
Love keep the wood.

So to the wood went I
With Love to live and die,
Fortune forlorn.
Experience of my youth
Made me think humble Truth
In desert born.

My saint is dear to me
And Joan herself is she,
Joan fair and true;
Joan that doth ever move
Passions of love with love.
Fortune adieu!

Fulke (Greville) Lord Brooke

William Byrd

THE CARMANS WHISTLE *from My Ladye Nevells Booke* (1591)

Between 1560 and 1620, a large corpus of music was composed for the virginal, an English keyboard instrument somewhat smaller than the harpsichord. This music played an important role in the development of keyboard style in general, in the development of the theme-and-variations form in particular, and in the gradual emergence of major-minor tonality. William Byrd (1543–1623) was the first, the most gifted and most influential of the English virginalists. *My Ladye Nevells Booke* contains forty-two of his works for virginal, in various forms, of which "The Carmans Whistle" is one of the best known.

QUESTIONS FOR DISCUSSION

Formal Structure

1. This work consists of a theme followed by eight variations. What measures actually constitute the theme? Describe its phrase-period structure and its overall form.
2. Which elements of the theme—form, melody, rhythm, harmony, modality, texture—are most clearly retained in the eight variations, and which are most freely treated?
3. Point to a variation which:
   a. makes most extensive use of sequential scale patterns
   b. is largely homophonic
   c. employs chain suspension figures in the accompaniment to the theme
   d. is highly imitative
   e. is largely a two-voice texture

   (You should be able to cite a different variation for each of the above.)
4. Is there an overall tendency toward greater or lesser complexity or intensity in this work? What features of the final variation may help to impart a climactic feeling?

Melodic/Rhythmic Structure

1. Make a reduction showing the basic contour of the theme. Include only those pitches which you feel serve to outline this contour. This melody was a very popular English folksong. What folklike elements do you observe?
2. Compare the right- and left-hand parts in the first four measures. How are they related? Identify the subtle rhythmic change which occurs in the right-hand part and speculate as to the possible reason for it.
3. Variation 4 begins with a sequential pattern. Notate this pattern, indicate how many times and at what interval it is repeated, and indicate whether the repetitions constitute real or tonal sequences.
4. a. The following figure appears in the right-hand part beginning at the end of m. 24:

   How much of the music in mm. 25–28 is related to this figure? Bracket or circle all similar figures.

   b. The following figure appears in the left-hand part at mm. 41–42:

   Find three more occurrences, either exact or sequential repetitions, of this figure.

Harmonic/Tonal Structure

1. Provide a Roman numeral analysis of mm. 5–16. Then bracket all chord successions which represent root movement by fourth or fifth. Approximately what proportion of the total root movement is by these intervals? How does this compare with earlier Renaissance pieces you have studied?
2. Of the nine cadences which close the theme and eight variations, how many may be classified as perfect authentic?
3. Locate, in the final variation, an example of each of the following: (a) a chromatic third relationship; (b) a cross-relation; (c) a secondary dominant.

Texture/Articulation/Dynamics

1. What is the term for a work such as this which employs a variable number of voices in the texture? How many, and how few, voices are present at various points in the work? Does a particular number of voices seem to predominate?
2. Do you feel that texture helps in any way to articulate the various sections of this work, and if so, how?

7
13
19
25

29
35
40
45
49

53
57
61
65
69
73

77
82
86
89
92
95
6

98
6
100
103
106
6
109
6

Unit

II

THE BAROQUE ERA

The Baroque era began in Italy in the late sixteenth century and ended in Germany around the middle of the eighteenth century. Elements of the Baroque style emerged gradually and evolved continuously. Among the important musical innovations were the birth of opera, the consolidation of major-minor tonality, the move toward equal temperament (late in the period), the *basso continuo* with figured bass notation, the change from an intervallic to a chordal conception of harmony, the rise of instrumental music to a level equal in quality and quantity to that of vocal music, and the birth of the large, heterogeneous instrumental ensemble (eventually to become the modern orchestra).

Characteristic genres include the continuo madrigal, chamber duet, opera, oratorio, cantata, trio sonata, concerto grosso, solo concerto, suite, and specific keyboard genres such as the toccata and variations. Fugal procedures evolved as the era progressed and were employed in many works, both vocal and instrumental.

Claudio Monteverdi

"DICE LA MIA BELLISSIMA LICORI" *from Madrigals Book VII*

Claudio Monteverdi (1567–1643) wrote nine madrigal books that span a 51-year period and clearly reveal the gradual changes in style that took place in the early part of the seventeenth century. The transitional nature of this continuo madrigal (also called a chamber duet), published in 1621, is reflected in its mixture of modal and tonal elements and combination of polyphonic and homophonic textures. Identify some examples. The short text is extended through considerable repetition. What happens *musically* at the repeated text phrases? Can you detect any obvious examples of text painting? What is the form? At a casual glance, one might think that the meter changes demarcate the formal divisions. However, the major dividing point in this work occurs earlier. Locate it and describe the important musical changes that it initiates. At least two important motives can be identified—one occurring in the earlier part of the work and the other occurring in the later part. (The latter's many occurrences are disguised rhythmically.) Identify both motives.

> *Composed 1619*
>
> Related reading: Richard L. Crocker, *A History of Musical Style* (New York: McGraw-Hill, 1966), pp. 232–243. A description of Monteverdi's madrigal books, including a discussion of portions of this work.

11
ch'Amor È un Spi-ri - tel - lo È un Spiri-tel - lo Che vaga e vola e non si
-tel - lo È un Spi-ri - tel - lo È un Spi-ri-
15
può te-ne-re È un Spi-ri - tel - lo Che vaga e vola e non si può te-ne-re
-tel - lo Che vaga e vola e non si può te-ne-re È un Spi-ri - tel - lo
18
È un Spi-ri - tel - lo È un Spi-ri - tel - lo Che va-ga e
È un Spi-ri - tel - lo È un Spi-ri - tel - lo Che va-ga e vo-la e non si
21
vo-la e non si può te-ne - re non si può te-ne-re non si può non si può
può te-ne - re non si può te - ne-re non si può te-ne-re non si può non si può

24
non si può te - ne - re nè toc - car nè ve - de - re nè toc - car nè ve - de - re
non si può te - ne - re nè toc - car nè ve - de - re nè toc - car nè ve - de - re nè toc -
3 6
27
nè toccar nè ve - de - re E pur se gl'oc - chi gi - ro ne suoi be -
- car nè ve - de - re
33
- gl'oc - - chi il mi - ro
il mi - ro ma nol pos - so toccar il mi - ro ma nol pos - so toc -
38
- car nol pos - so toc - car nol pos - so toc - car nol pos - so toc - car nol

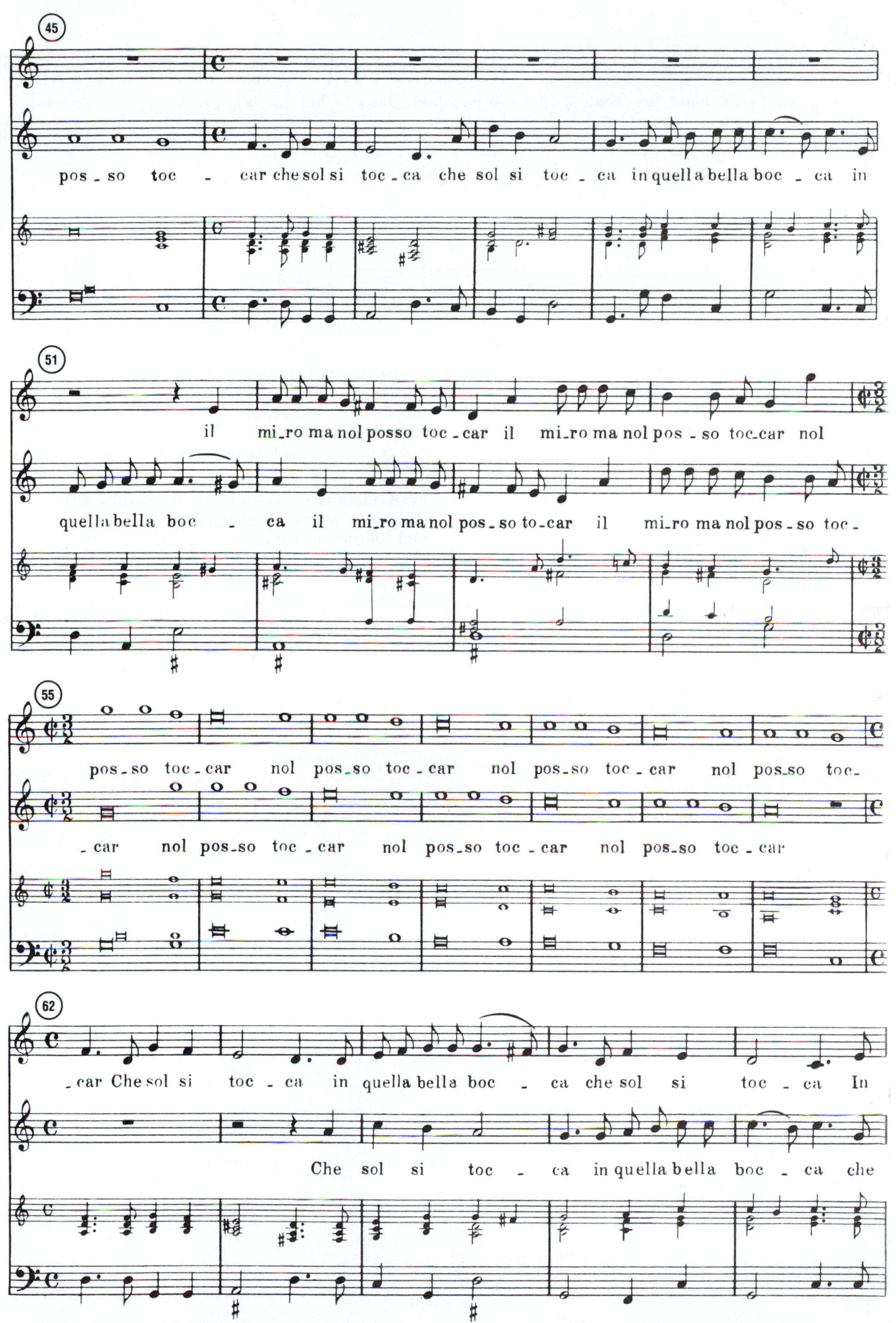
45
pos - so toc - car che sol si toc - ca che sol si toc - ca in quella bella boc - ca in
51
il mi-ro ma nol posso toc - car il mi-ro ma nol pos - so toc-car nol
quella bella boc - ca il mi-ro ma nol pos - so to-car il mi-ro ma nol pos - so toc -
55
pos - so toc - car nol pos-so toc - car nol pos-so toc - car nol pos-so toc-
- car nol pos-so toc - car nol pos-so toc - car nol pos-so toc - car
62
- car Che sol si toc - ca in quella bella boc - ca che sol si toc - ca In
Che sol si toc - ca in quella bella boc - ca che

Sometimes when I speak with her of love
my very beautiful Licori says
that Love is a small spirit
which wanders and flies
and cannot be held, touched or seen.

And even if my eyes turn to his beautiful eyes
I look, I look but I cannot touch [the small spirit]
Because in that beautiful mouth
One touches the sun.

Arcangelo Corelli

Arcangelo Corelli (1653–1713) was a highly skilled violinist, and he wrote primarily for violin. Solo sonatas, trio sonatas, and concertos form the bulk of his output. In the trio sonatas, two violins weave a counterpoint above a supporting *continuo* (keyboard part). Techniques associated with fully developed major-minor tonality are abundant in Corelli's music. These include modulations (usually short-lived), melodic and harmonic sequences, all diatonic seventh chords, and circle-of-fifths progressions.

TRIO SONATA OP. 4, NO. 3 *Prelude and Sarabande*

The trio sonata was by far Corelli's favorite medium; four of his six sets of compositions were written for this type of ensemble. This work was composed in 1695.

QUESTIONS FOR DISCUSSION

Formal Structure

1. Discuss the form of the Prelude in terms of the repetition and contrast of musical material, the cadences, and the unifying motives.
2. What formal similarities exist between the Prelude and Sarabande?
3. Identify the unifying motives present in the Sarabande.

Melodic/Rhythmic Structure

1. In the Prelude, locate an example of each of the following:
   a. an augmentation of the sixteenth-note figure appearing in the second half of m. 4;
   b. a phrase that is extended cadentially.
2. Corelli employed a particular cadential mannerism so frequently that it has become known as the "Corelli clash." Consult the Harvard Dictionary of Music or other sources for an exact description of this formula and locate examples of it in the Sarabande.
3. How many phrases do you hear in the Sarabande? How might they be symbolized using letters? Do they form periods? Explain your answer.

Harmonic/Tonal Structure

1. Does the key signature of this work reflect the actual tonality? Can you offer an explanation?
2. In the Prelude, compare the following cadence points with respect to type, relative strengths, and notable similarities: m. 4, mm. 7–8, mm. 11–12, mm. 17–18.
3. Reduce the harmonies of mm. 1–4 of the Prelude to their simplest three-voice structure in root position and label the quality of each chord.
4. Compare the Prelude and the Sarabande tonally.
5. Provide a complete harmonic analysis of the Sarabande.

Texture/Articulation/Dynamics

Compare the two movements from the standpoint of texture. Does the texture change within each movement and if so, in what way?

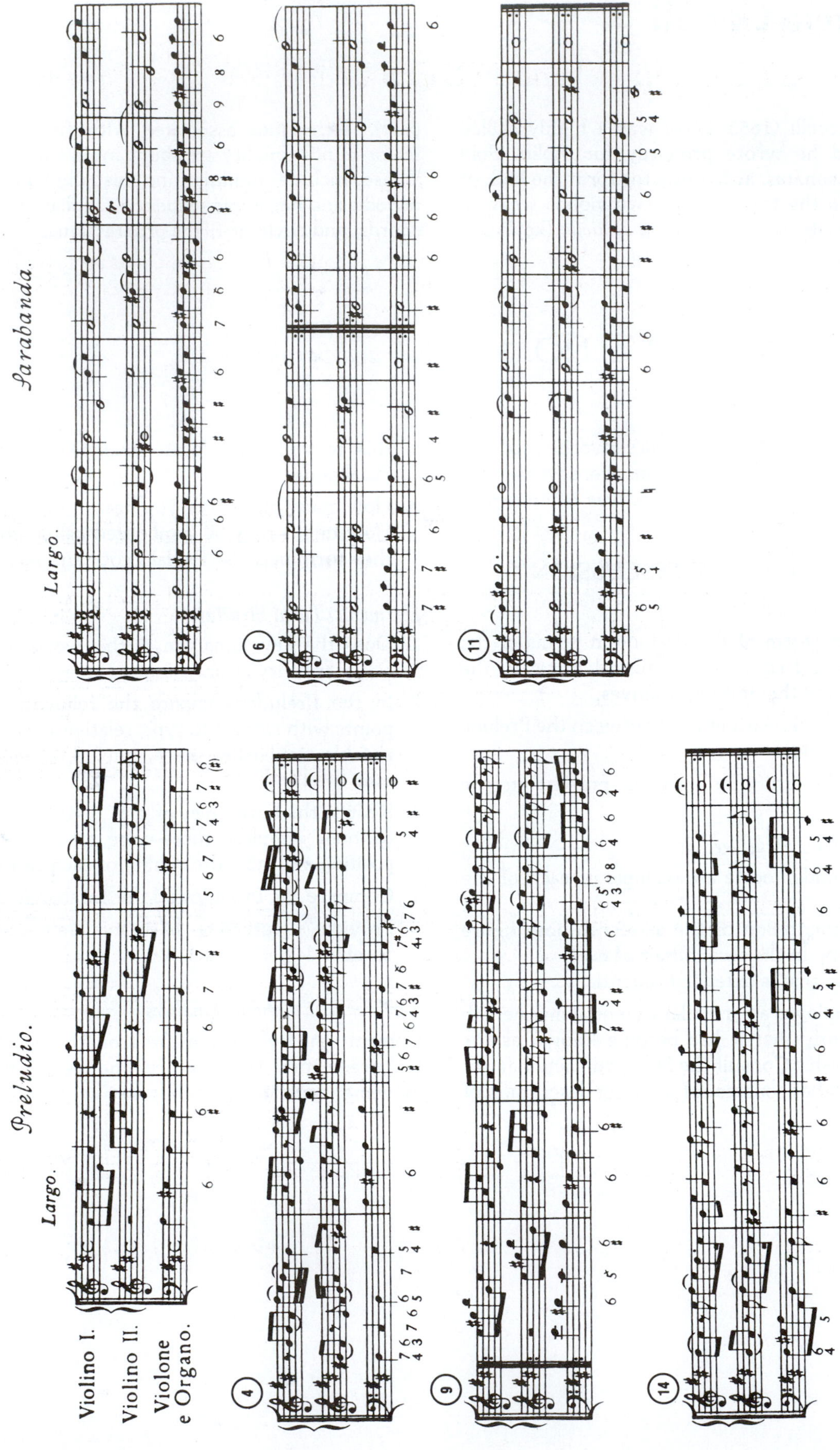
Preludio.
Largo.
Violino I.
Violino II.
Violone
e Organo.
Sarabanda.
Largo.

Henry Purcell

"THY HAND, BELINDA" and DIDO'S LAMENT *from Dido and Aeneas*

Henry Purcell (1659–1695) assimilated the various elements of the middle Baroque style and infused them with specifically English mannerisms. Although he is best known today for his theater music, he wrote only one true opera, *Dido and Aeneas.* The following selection is the final aria from that work, preceded by a short recitative. The aria can be viewed as a variation form. What serves as the theme? Which aspects of it remain the same throughout the composition and which aspects change? At this point in the opera, Dido has been left by her husband and prepares to die by her own hand. What musical elements help to portray this picture?

"Thy Hand, Belinda"

Dido's Lament

13
breast; When I am laid, am laid in earth, may my wrongs cre-
20
-ate No trou-ble, no trouble in thy breast; Re-member me, re-
27
-mem-ber me, but ah! for - get my fate. Re-mem-ber me, but

François Couperin

PASSACAILLE *from Pièces de Clavecin, Sixth Ordre*

As a court musician during the latter days of Louis XIV's reign, François Couperin (1668–1733) composed music that perfectly reflected the refined, decorative and sentimental character of the Rococo age. Most of his keyboard music is contained in four books of *Pièces de Clavecin,* composed in 1713, 1716, 1722, and 1730. Is the following Passacaille a *passacaglia,* as the term is usually defined? What other formal principle do you observe? The piece contains a degree of harmonic chromaticism not altogether common in Couperin's music. Analyze, for example, the first eight measures. Numerous suspensions embellish the music. The passages beginning at m. 28, m. 105, and m. 143 are worth analyzing in this regard. Identify the type of cadence at mm. 11–12. Every major cadence in this work is embellished in one of two ways. Explain. Identify all tonal centers that are established and explain their relationship to the home key.

Passacaille

29
tr
33
tr
3
37
42
48
p dolce
53

58
63
68
73
77
81

86
91
Mouvt marqué
96
102
108
113

118
mf
123
tr
f
3
128
133
tr
138
143

149
154
159
132
165
tr
170
f

THREE MENUETS *from the Notebook for Anna Magdelena Bach*

(BWV Anh. 115, BWV Anh. 116, BWV Anh. 121)

Below are three minuets from a 1725 collection of suites, fantasias, and miscellaneous single movements by J. S. Bach and others. Which two are most similar in form? What is different formally about the remaining one?

BWV Anh. 115: Describe the phrase relationships present in this minuet. Identify the tonal center, the secondary tonalities established, and the types of modulations that occur. Although the left hand of m. 14 suggests a single harmony for this measure, the first beat is better analyzed as a chord distinct from that of beats two and three. What is the chord and what reason can you give for analyzing it as such? What other works in this unit have a bass line similar to this one?

BWV Anh. 116: This minuet is the simplest of the three harmonically, establishing only one tonality outside of the home key. What is this tonality, where does it occur, and what types of modulation lead to it and from it? This minuet is also the easiest to analyze harmonically, due to the clear arpeggiations that occur in one hand or the other in practically every measure. Provide a complete analysis. Compare the phrasing to that in the preceding minuet. How is it similar and how is it different? Additionally, locate and describe all sequences.

Menuet

BWV Anh. 121: This minuet is the shortest of the three but also the most chromatic and harmonically complex. What three tonal centers can you identify? Keeping in mind that chromatically raised pitches often function as secondary leading tones (and thus as the third of a secondary dominant or dominant seventh chord), analyze harmonically the final eight-measure phrase. The second beat of m. 22 deserves special attention. What interval is formed by the two voices? What type of chord might this imply?

CHORALE HARMONIZATIONS *With text verse*

The chorale, a simple strophic hymn of limited pitch range with German text, originated in sixteenth-century Protestant Germany as a result of church reforms by Martin Luther (1483–1546). It is familiar today chiefly because of its importance in the church music of J.S. Bach, especially the cantatas. At some point in the majority of these elaborate vocal works (most often at the end), a single verse of a chorale, in four-part harmony, was sung by the choir. (See No. 7 of Cantata No. 78, on page 158.) These harmonizations exhibit the essence of Baroque harmonic practice and provide insight into part-writing techniques that remained fundamental to musical composition for generations.

A number of chorales are given here in two different harmonizations for comparison. Where the additional harmonization is by a composer other than Bach, it is always the simpler of the two, Bach's containing more non-chord tones, modulations and chromatic harmonies.

"Ach wie nichtig, ach wie flüchtig"

This chorale setting appears as the closing movement of Bach's Cantata No. 26, the title of which is changed to "Ach wie flüchtig, ach wie nichtig." It was composed in 1724. The hymn is by Michael Franck.

1. Oh, how fleeting, oh, how vain is the life of man!
   Our life is like a fog which rises and fades away again.

2. Oh, how fleeting, oh, how vain are the affairs of man!
   Everything that we see must fall and pass away;
   he who fears God will remain forever.

"Aus tiefer Not"

Two settings of this chorale are given. The first is by Johann Walther (1496–1570). The second is Bach's harmonization from Cantata No. 38, of the same name, where it appears as the final movement.

No. 1

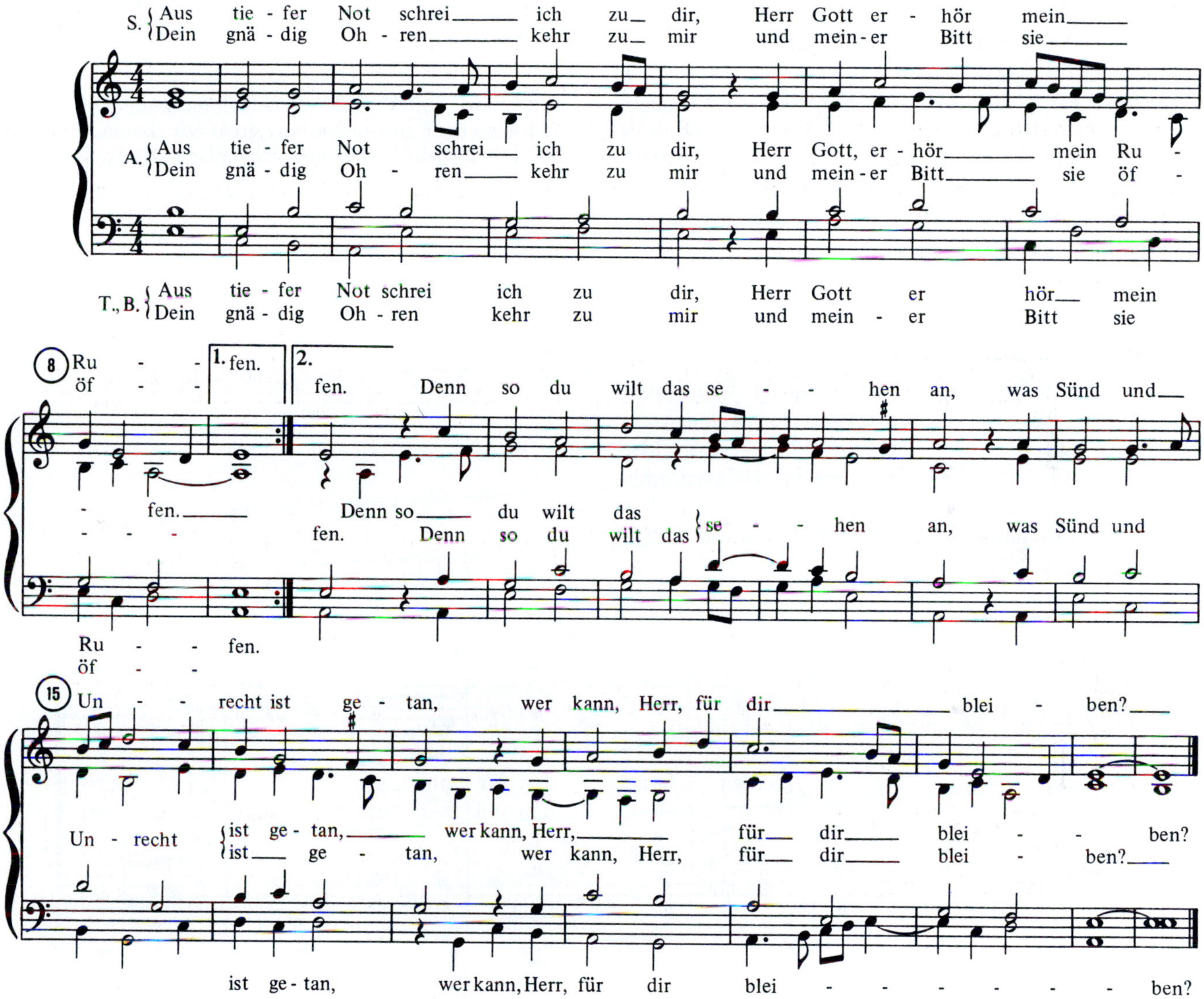

S. Aus tie - fer Not schrei ich zu dir, Herr Gott er - hör mein
Dein gnä - dig Oh - ren kehr zu mir und mein - er Bitt sie
A. Aus tie - fer Not schrei ich zu dir, Herr Gott, er - hör mein Ru -
Dein gnä - dig Oh - ren kehr zu mir und mein - er Bitt sie öf -
T., B. Aus tie - fer Not schrei ich zu dir, Herr Gott er hör mein
Dein gnä - dig Oh - ren kehr zu mir und mein - er Bitt sie
8
Ru - - 1. fen.
öf - - 2. fen. Denn so du wilt das se - - hen an, was Sünd und
- fen. Denn so du wilt das
- - - fen. Denn so du wilt das se - - hen an, was Sünd und
Ru - - fen.
öf - -
15
Un - recht ist ge - tan, wer kann, Herr, für dir blei - ben?
Un - recht ist ge - tan, wer kann, Herr, für dir blei - - ben?
ist ge - tan, wer kann, Herr, für dir blei - ben?
ist ge - tan, wer kann, Herr, für dir blei - - - - - - - ben?

No. 2

Ob bei uns ist der Sün - den viel, bei Gott ist viel mehr Gna - de;
sein Hand zu hel - fen hat kein Ziel, wie gross auch sei der Scha - de.
Er ist all -

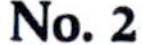

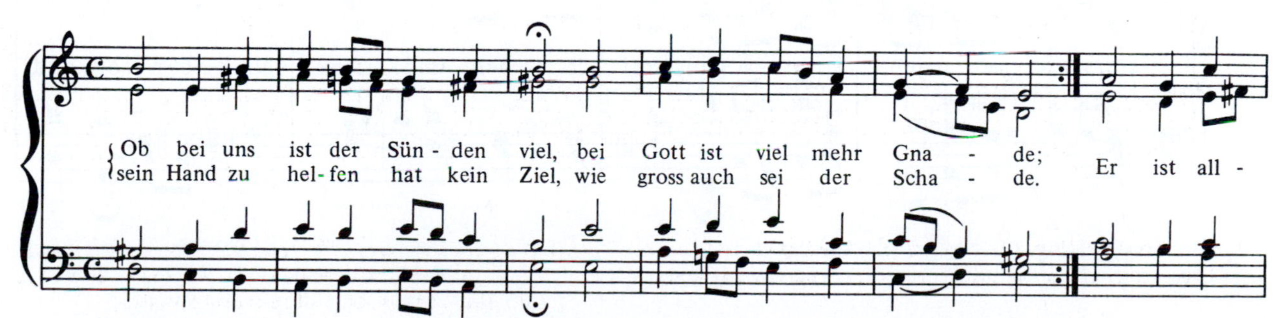

Though our sins be many, with God there is much more mercy;
His helping hand has no limit, no matter how great our shame.
He alone is our good shepherd, He who shall deliver Israel from all its sins.

"Christ lag in Todesbanden"

Two harmonizations of this chorale have been included for the purpose of comparison. You may refer also to Chorales No. 15 and 371 of the *Bach-Riemenschneider 371 Harmonized Chorales* for two additional harmonizations. The chorale closes Cantata No. 4 of the same name, using the seventh stanza of the text.

No. 1

9
sin - gen Hal - le - lu - - ja, Hal - le - lu - - ja!
(7 Str.)

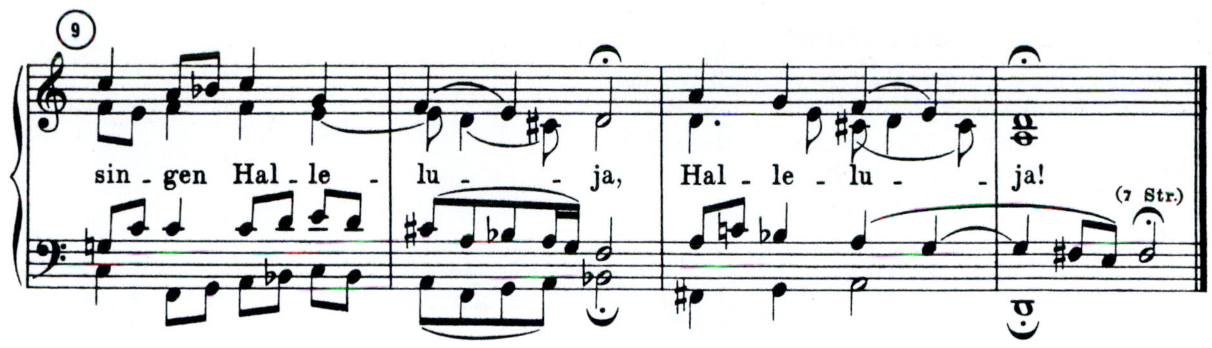

No. 2

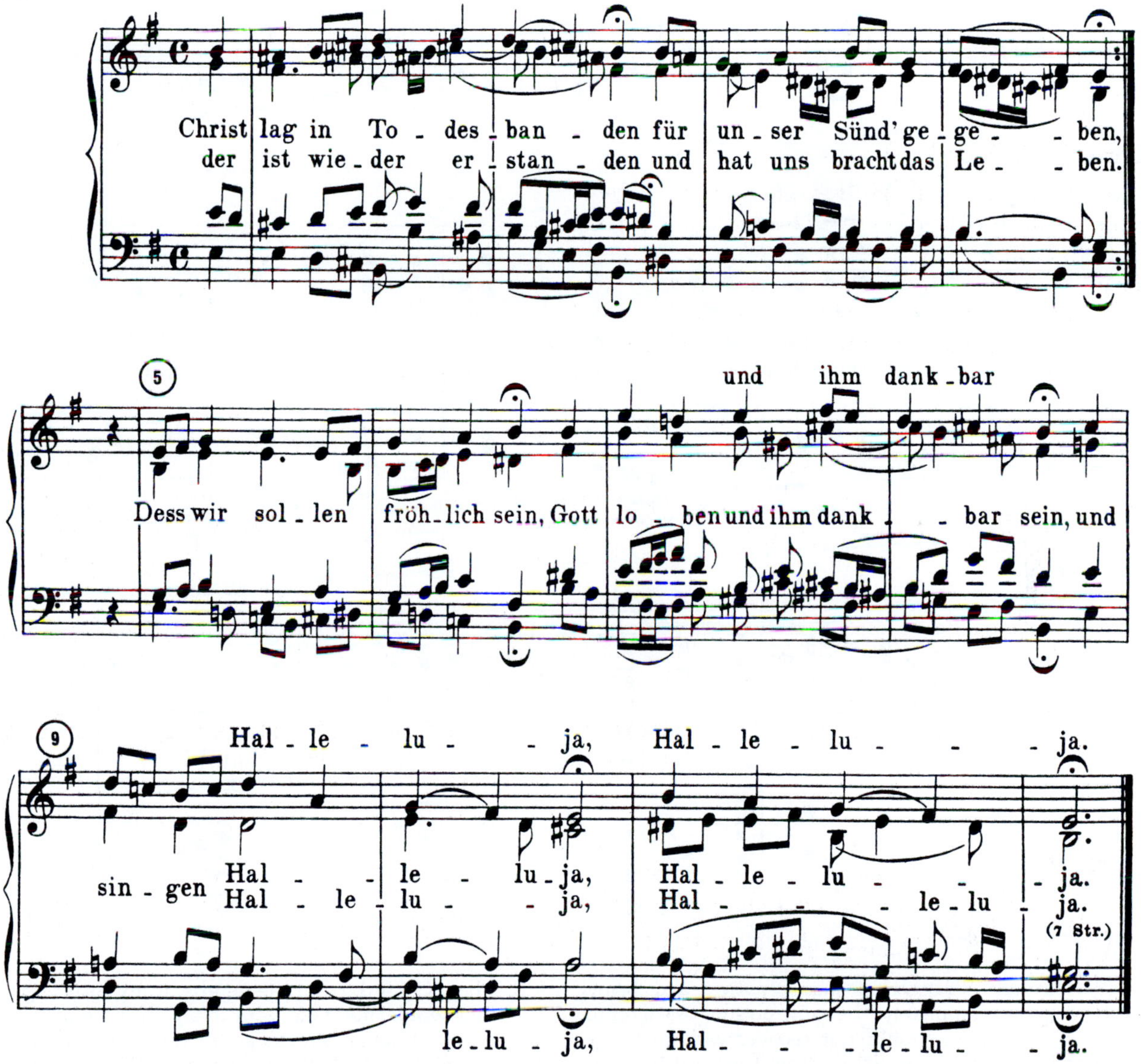

Christ lag in To - des - ban - den für un - ser Sünd' ge - ge - - ben,
der ist wie - der er - stan - den und hat uns bracht das Le - - ben.
5
und ihm dank - bar
Dess wir sol - len fröh - lich sein, Gott lo - ben und ihm dank - - bar sein, und
9
Hal - le - lu - - ja, Hal - le - lu - - - ja.
sin - gen Hal - - le - lu - ja, Hal - le - lu - - ja.
Hal - le - lu - - ja, Hal - - - le - lu - ja.
(7 Str.)
le - lu - ja, Hal - - - le - lu - - ja.

Christ lay in the chains of death, given for our sin,
he who has risen again and has brought us life.
For that we should be happy, praise God and be thankful
to him, and sing Hallelujah!

"Durch Adams Fall ist ganz verderbt"

This chorale closes Cantata No. 18 ("Gleich wie der Regen und Schnee von Himmel fällt"), which was composed in Weimar in 1714. Bach used the eighth stanza of the text by L. Spengler (1524).

1. Through Adams fall man's nature and being perished completely, the same poison passed on to us so that we might not recover without God's solace. This has saved us from the great harm in which the serpent forced Eve to take God's wrath upon herself.

8. I beg, O Lord, from the depths of my heart, that you would not take your Holy Word from my mouth; thus my sin and guilt won't shame me, for I place all my trust in your grace. Whoever relies firmly on your grace will not see death.

"Freuet euch, ihr Christen"

This is one of three chorales (the closing one) which are found in Cantata No. 40 ("Dazu ist erschienen der Sohn Gottes"), composed in 1723. The hymn is by Christian Keimann (1646).

1. Be happy all you Christians, be happy, all of you, who can!
God has done much for us. Rejoice with a great sound,
because he freed us from the power of death through his dying.
Joy, joy and more joy! Christ keeps back all tribulation.
Delight, delight and more delight! He is our heavenly blessing.

2. Jesus, in your mercy, care for your members;
grant what one may request to refresh your brothers;
give all of Christendom peace and a blessed year!
Joy, joy and more joy! Christ keeps back all tribulation.
Delight, delight and more delight! He is our heavenly blessing.

"In allen meinen Taten"

In everything I do I seek guidance from the highest one [God] who has and can do all things;
he himself must give counsel in all things if they are to succeed.

"Nun preiset alle"

Let's all now extol God's charity,
praise Him with sounds, dear Christendom.
He is sending you a friendly invitation to Himself.
Rejoice in His favor, Israel!

"Wer nur den lieben Gott lässt walten"

This chorale ends Cantata No. 88 ("Siehe, ich will viel Fischer aussenden, aspricht der Herr"), composed in 1726. The melody was composed by Georg Neumark in 1657. Two harmonizations—one in A minor and one in B minor—are given here for comparison.

No. 1

No. 2

Whoever gives God a free hand and relies entirely on him,
God will preserve him marvelously in all need and grief.
Whoever trusts in God the Almighty has not built on sand.

CHORAL HARMONIZATIONS *Without text verse*

The following harmonizations are presented in compact format without text, as they appear in the Bach-Riemenschneider *371 Harmonized Chorales and 69 Chorale Melodies.* The first, "Es ist genug," is by far the most complex of the chorale harmonizations in this anthology. It was later used by Alban Berg (1885–1935) in the second movement of his Violin Concerto.

"Es ist genug, so nimm, Herr"

"Gott lebet noch"

"Herr, Ich habe missgehandelt"

Harmonization by Johann Cruger (1598–1662).

"Herr, Ich habe missgehandelt"

Harmonization by J. S. Bach.

"O Gott, du frommer Gott"

"Sei gegrüsset, Jesu gütig"

"Wach' auf, mein Herz"

"Wachet auf, ruft uns die Stimme"
Harmonization by Otto Nicolai (1810–1849).

"Wachet auf, ruft uns die Stimme"
Harmonization by J. S. Bach.

CHORALE MELODIES WITH FIGURED BASS

To a number of chorale melodies, Bach added only a figured bass, leaving the complete realization to the improvisatory skills of the organist. The five examples that follow can be used as exercises in figured bass realization and part writing. You may wish to compare your realizations of "Ermuntre dich," "Gott lebet noch," and "Sei gegrüsset, Jesu gütig" with Bach's own, which appear on pages 93, 94, and 96.

"Ermuntre dich"

"Eius ist noth! ach Herr, dies eine"

"Gott lebet noch"

"Meines Lebens letzte Zeit"

"Sei gegrüsset, Jesu gütig"

Johann Sebastian Bach

With J. S. Bach (1685–1750), practically every genre of the late Baroque era reached an artistic peak. His forms include variations, binary, ritornello, ternary, and through-composed. His long and aperiodic phrases have well-defined rhythms that tend to be independent of the bar lines. His masterful use of the late Baroque harmonic vocabulary encompasses all diatonic triads and seventh chords, secondary function, and a few additional altered chords such as augmented sixth and Neapolitan sixth chords. Bach's textures are saturated with counterpoint. His command of fugal and canonic techniques established him as a contrapuntist without peer in the history of music.

TWO-PART INVENTIONS NOS. 1, 6, 9, and 13

In 1723, just prior to his move to Leipzig, Bach composed two sets of keyboard studies in double and triple counterpoint, called Inventions and Sinfonias, intended both as finger exercises and as a stimulant to the pupil's artistic sense and latent compositional talents. Each set is arranged in the following ascending order of keys from C major to B minor (those with more than four sharps or flats were excluded): C major, C minor, D major, D minor, E-flat major, E major, E minor, F major, F minor, G major, G minor, A major, A minor, B-flat major, B minor. In each invention, a short subject serves as the basis for the entire composition.

Related reading: Thomas Benjamin, *Counterpoint in the Style of J. S. Bach* (New York: Schirmer Books, 1986), pp. 142–164. A discussion of Bach's Two-Part Inventions, with attention to No. 1 and No. 13 and a model analysis of No. 4.

Invention No. 1

Which of the following transformations of the principal motive can you find: transposition; melodic inversion; diminution; augmentation; fragmentation; sequence; inverted (exchanged) counterpoint; combinations of these techniques? Locate the first important cadence and describe its relationship to the music that precedes and follows it.

Invention No. 6

Discuss this invention from the standpoint of form. In addition, examine carefully the distribution of the musical material between the two hands.

Invention No. 9

How long is the principal melodic idea here? How many complete statements of it occur? Describe the accompanying voice at these points. How many tonal centers are clearly established? What tonal centers are more briefly touched upon?

Invention No. 13

What are the primary contrapuntal devices employed in this invention? Harmonic analysis is relatively uncomplicated because most of the material involves arpeggiated harmonies. What is the prevailing harmonic rhythm? Identify the most important cadences and indicate the tonality at those points.

Inventio 13.
4
8
11
14
18
22

Johann Sebastian Bach

BRANDENBURG CONCERTO NO. 2 *Third Movement*

Perhaps the most important instrumental genre of the late Baroque era was the concerto. Its major composers were Corelli, Giuseppe Torelli (1658–1709), Antonio Vivaldi (1669?–1741), and J.S. Bach. The six concertos dedicated to Christian Ludwig, the Margrave of Brandenburg, were composed at Cöthen between 1719 and 1721. Bach employed the three-movement order (fast-slow-fast) and the *ritornello* form (alternating solo and *tutti*), adding his own consummate contrapuntal skill, to bring this Baroque form to its artistic peak. A comparison with Handel's Concerto Grosso Op. 6, No. 1 (first and second movements) on page 163 will be instructive.

QUESTIONS FOR DISCUSSION

Formal Structure

1. In this movement, Bach has skillfully interwoven two common Baroque formal processes. Can you identify them?
2. Having identified the two formal processes in Question 1, describe the movement from the standpoint of each.
3. Bach makes use of a limited number of melodic ideas in this movement. Identify the most important of these.

Melodic/Rhythmic Structure

1. Locate within the movement three clear examples of melodic sequences and describe them, using terms such as real, tonal, modified, partial, and so on.
2. Identify and describe the chain suspension that occurs beginning at m. 97.
3. Discuss the use of imitation in mm. 85–96.
4. Locate a passage that is clearly based on melodic minor scale principles.

Harmonic/Tonal Structure

Four tonalities are clearly defined in this movement. Identify them and indicate where each occurs.

Texture/Articulation/Dynamics

1. Invertible counterpoint is the source of much of this movement's textural and timbral variety. Locate and describe some notable examples of this technique.
2. Locate and describe two passages of highly contrasting texture in the movement. The passages for full ensemble exhibit varying degrees of contrapuntal complexity. Locate one such passage that can be described as highly contrapuntal and another that can be described as homophonic or almost so.

Allegro assai.
Tromba.
Flauto.
Oboe.
Violino.
Violino I. di ripieno.
Violino II. di ripieno.
Viola di ripieno.
Violone di ripieno.
Violoncello e Cembalo.
8

16
24

32
40

48
55

63
71

78
tr
85

cade

109
tr
117

124
132
Coda

Johann Sebastian Bach

DAS WOHLTEMPERIERTE CLAVIER, BOOK I

Prelude and Fugue No. 1 in C major; Fugue No. 11 in F major; Fugue No. 16 in G minor; Fugue No. 21 in B-flat major; Prelude and Fugue No. 22 in B-flat minor

Bach completed the two books of *The Well-Tempered Clavier* (WTC) in 1722 and 1744 respectively. The purpose of the collections was twofold: to demonstrate the practical advantages of well-temperament, a tuning system which permitted excursions to the most remote key areas without retuning, and to provide an organized body of material for students to practice and study. Each volume covers the entire cycle of twenty-four major and minor keys beginning with C and moving up the scale chromatically. Each piece is a concise and self-contained composition of utmost harmonic and contrapuntal sophistication. A recommended order of study, based on the relative complexity of the fugues, is: No. 21, No. 11, No. 16, No. 1, and No. 22.

Prelude and Fugue No. 1

This fugue is one of the most "subject-centered" fugues of the WTC. How many entrances of the subject can you locate? Locate the strongest cadences. Is it possible to speak of a coda in this fugue? Explain why or why not. What fugal techniques are most used?

Composed 1722

Related reading: Felix Salzer, ed., *Five Graphic Music Analyses* (New York: Dover, 1969), pp. 36–37. Heinrich Schenker's analysis of this Prelude.

Prelude No. 1

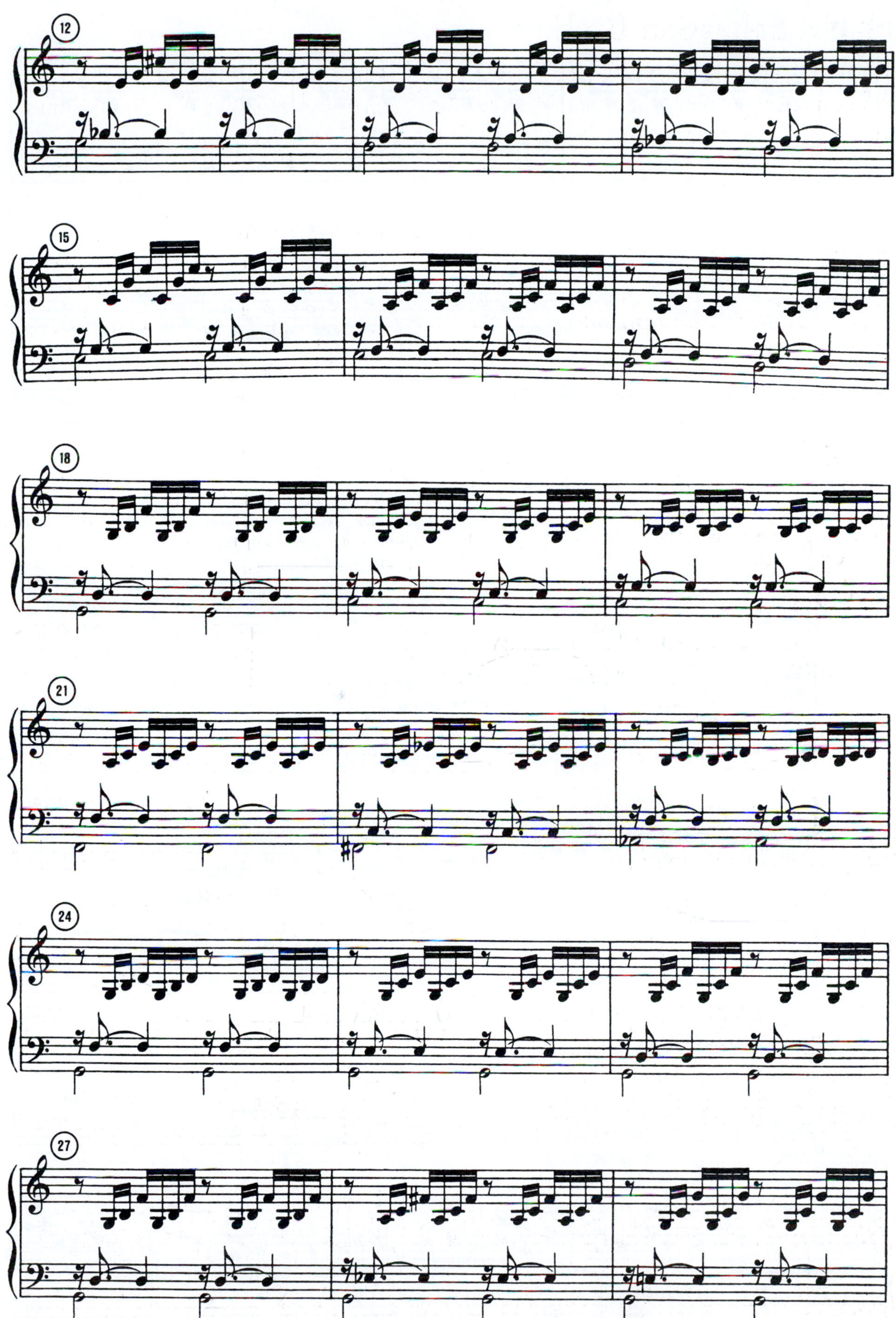
12
15
18
21
24
27

Fugue No. 1

8
10
12
14
17
19

Fugue No. 11

Which of the following features can be found in this three-voice fugue: countersubject; counterexposition; tonal answer; invertible counterpoint; stretto; partial entries; sequence; imitation; melodic inversion; augmentation; fragmentation; coda? Explain how some of the entrances of the subject are modified in this fugue.

18
24
30
36
42
48

Fugue No. 16

This is a four-voice fugue. Locate all entrances of the subject and describe the material in the accompanying voices. Of what material are the episodes (those passages separating statements of the subject) composed? What tonal centers are clearly established?

7
10
14
17
20
23

Fugue No. 21

Does this fugue contain one or two countersubjects? Explain your answer. Invertible counterpoint plays a major role in this work. Locate and describe some prominent examples.

9
13
17
21
25
29

QUESTIONS FOR DISCUSSION

Prelude and Fugue No. 22 in B-Flat Minor

Formal Structure

1. What seems to be the most important unifying element in Prelude No. 22?
2. Locate the first decisive cadence in the prelude.
3. As defined by cadence, tonality, and gesture, this prelude can be considered a binary form. Where would you locate the divisions and why? What element(s) of return can you discover toward the end of the piece?
4. Locate the four areas of the fugue that contain appearances of the subject (or answer). Although each succeeding area is shorter than the previous, the number of subject/answer entrances does not decrease, but in fact, increases. How is this explained?

Melodic/Rhythmic Structure

1. The melodic line of mm. 1–2 is stated three more times during the course of the prelude, albeit with some variation. Locate these other statements and describe how each differs from the original.

2. Locate an example of imitation in mm. 15–16 of the prelude.
3. Compare carefully the first two voices to enter in the fugue through m. 11. Be especially attentive to imitative and sequential aspects as well as extrametrical rhythmic implications. Then trace the first voice as far as the end of the exposition and comment on its overall structure.
4. Upon what material are the episodes of this fugue based?

Harmonic/Tonal Structure

1. Locate the three instances of pedal point which occur in the prelude and analyze the harmonic structure at those points.
2. At what point in the prelude does the music begin to move away from the tonic? What is the first new tonality to be established and where does it occur? At what point is the tonic reestablished?
3. At m. 38 of the fugue the music is in the key of D-flat. What is the key of the preceding measure and how is the movement to D-flat accomplished?

Texture/Articulation/Dynamics

1. Does any significant change of texture occur during the course of the prelude? In general, how many voices make up the texture? Locate a point at which the number of voices gradually but significantly increases and describe the effect.
2. How do the passages containing appearances of the subject compare texturally with the episodes in this fugue?

Prelude No. 22

9
11
13
15
17
19

21
23
Fugue No. 22
Tonal
S1
A2
b♭ minor
W
W W W
1/2
7
1/2
W
W
1/2
13
V7/iv
19

25
31
37
44
49
55

Johann Sebastian Bach

FRENCH SUITE NO. 6 IN E MAJOR, BWV 817 *Sarabande and Menuet*

The six *French Suites* were composed at Cöthen, sometime between 1717 and 1723. Each suite contains the usual four movements—*Allemande, Courante, Sarabande* and *Gigue*—with simpler, more modern dances inserted between the *Sarabande* and *Gigue.* Given here are one standard and one optional dance. Both are twenty-four measures long. What is different about them formally? What is similar about them tonally? The Sarabande contains numerous references to tonalities other than the home key. Some of these are mere tonicizations (secondary dominants) and others may be heard as modulations. Identify all tonicizations and modulations and justify your explanation of each. Measure 17 presents an interesting analytical problem. Though it appears to be in the principal tonality, the measures immediately preceding and following are not. In what key should this measure be analyzed? Both movements are unified by recurring motives. Identify all occurrences. In the Menuet, look for examples of the motive in augmentation, diminution and inversion.

10
15
20
Menuet.
7
13
19

Johann Sebastian Bach

GOLDBERG VARIATIONS *Aria, and Variations 1, 12, 18, and 27*

Bach's Goldberg Variations is a set of thirty variations on a sarabande-like aria. All the variations adhere to the form of the aria and to its general harmonic structure, giving the work the character of a *chaconne.* The aria and Variations 1, 12, 18, and 27 are given here.

First, identify the form of the aria and represent it symbolically, using uppercase letters for sections and lowercase letters for phrases. How many phrases are there? What are their lengths? Do they form periods? Add a basic tonal plan to your diagram. Three of the four variations share a common technique. Identify it and also explain how the technique is employed differently in each of these variations. Beyond retaining the harmonic structure of the aria, certain of the variations retain its distinctive bass line as well (with slight modifications). Which of the variations given here do so? Variation 1 is perhaps the easiest to analyze harmonically because at least one hand arpeggiates the harmonies in each measure. Provide a complete harmonic analysis of this variation.

ARIA

Reproduced by kind permission of Gregg International from the 1968 reprints of the original Breitkopf & Härtel Bach-Gesellschaft 1851–99 editions.

18
23
28
Variatio 1
4

8
12
16
20
23

Variatio 12

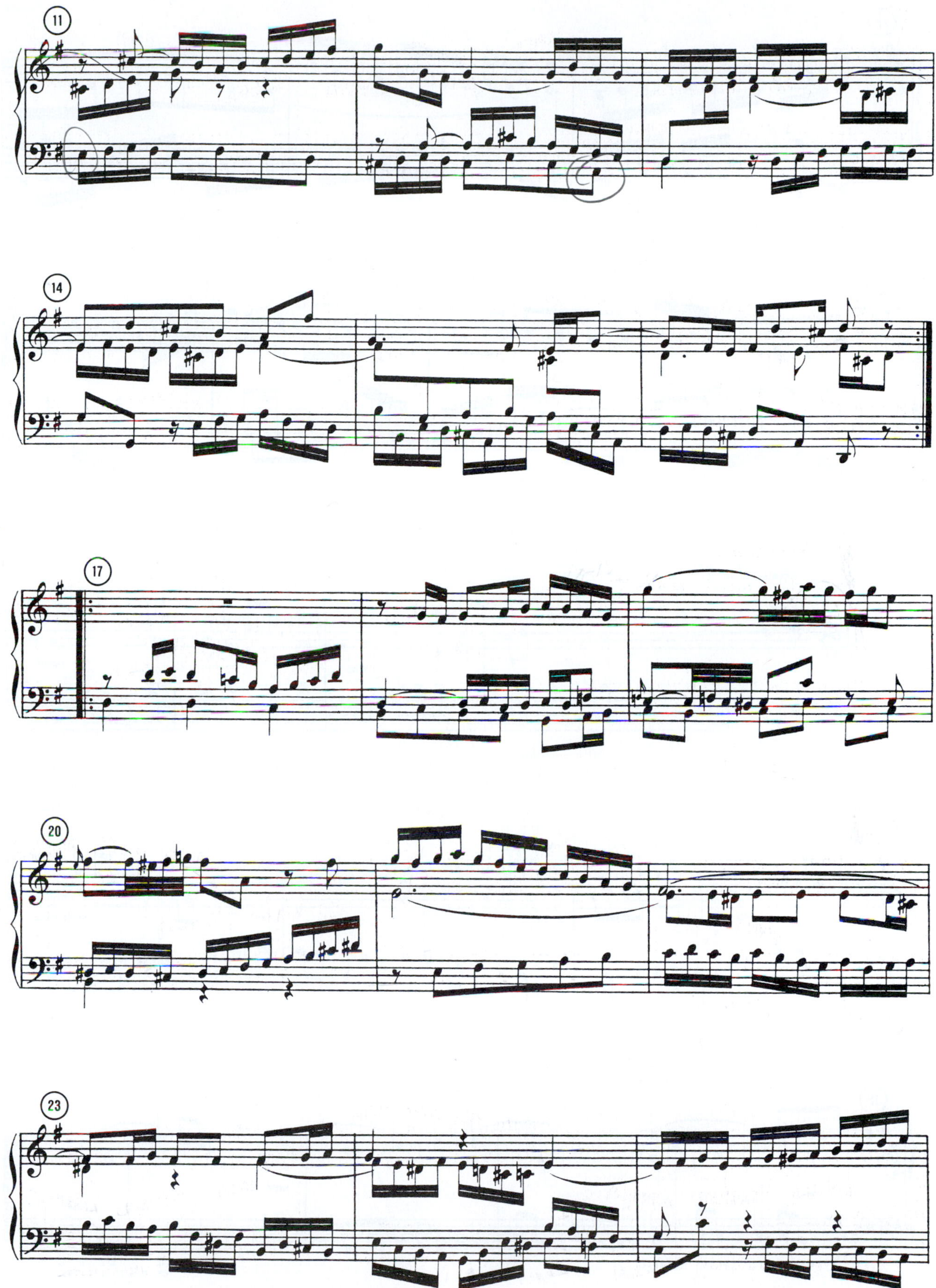
11
14
17
20
23

26
29
Variatio 18
6
12

17
23
28
cannon at 9th
Variatio 27
5

9
13
17
21
25
29

Johann Sebastian Bach

CANTATA NO. 78 *"Jesu, der du meine Seele"*

Chorus (No. 1), Tenor recitative (No. 3), Tenor aria (No. 4), Chorale (No. 7)

The church cantata of the late Baroque era was a large, multi-movement vocal-instrumental composition—a synthesis of Italian operatic elements and German Protestant church music that formed a musical framework for the sermon. Cantata No. 78 is of a type developed by Bach in which the entire cantata text is based on the words of a chorale. This particular chorale deals with Jesus as helper and savior of the soul. Since you may wish to focus on all questions pertaining to a given movement at one time, the following reference list is provided:

MOVEMENT	PERTINENT QUESTIONS
Chorus (No. 1)	F1, 2, 3; H/T 1, 2, 3; T/A/D 1,2
Tenor recitative (No. 3)	F4, M/R 1, H/T 4
Tenor aria (No. 4)	M/R 2, 3; H/T 5, 6
Chorus (No. 7)	H/T 7

QUESTIONS FOR DISCUSSION

Formal Structure

1. No. 1: Notate the melodic pattern that serves as the foundation for the movement. Notate the various transpositions of this pattern that occur. Also, locate an instance in which the pattern appears inverted.
2. No. 1: Where does the principal point of division occur in this movement? How do tonality and melodic/rhythmic elements help to create the division? How does the division reflect the meaning of the text? What are the relative proportions of the parts of the movement?
3. No. 1: The chorale for this cantata appears as the final choral movement. How is it employed in the first chorus? Look especially for a recurring pattern in the way the several chorale phrases are preceded, presented and accompanied.
4. No. 3: Recitatives are important elements in the musical scheme of the cantatas, providing a deviation from strict rhythm and tempo, a change to a purely homophonic texture, and an effective means of setting portions of the text that are less suitable for arias or choruses. Discuss the tenor recitative in the following respects: melody and rhythm, harmony and tonality, accompaniment, and overall form.

Melodic/Rythmic Structure

1. No. 3: Study the translation for this recitative. In what ways, both general and specific, does the music reflect the text?
2. No. 4: In mm. 1–12, locate, describe and explain the following:
   a. a passage displaying melodic minor scale principles;
   b. a melodic sequence;
   c. a large-scale tonic arpeggiation;
   d. a Neapolitan sixth chord, implied melodically.
3. No. 4: Upon what material are the instrumental passages separating the vocal phrases based?

Harmonic/Tonal Structure

1. No. 1: Identify the important tonal centers established in this movement.
2. No. 1: Identify the harmonic pattern that occurs in mm. 103-117. Then, locate another passage in the movement based on the same type of harmonic motion.
3. No. 1: The sequences of mm. 103–106 and mm. 125–128 appear to contain similar melodic material. Compare the harmonic structure of each and explain the fundamental difference.
4. No. 3: Realize, in simple block chords, the figured bass for this highly chromatic recitative, through m. 12 (the first cadence). Does the melody seem to determine the harmonies or do the harmonies seem to be controlling the melody here? Can you discover a logic to the unusual harmonic successions?
5. No. 4: Identify the tonal center of mm. 21–30. Then identify two examples of secondary function that occur within this tonality in these measures.
6. No. 4: Name the tonalities established in this movement, giving inclusive measure numbers.
7. No. 7: Provide a harmonic analysis of this chorale.

Texture/Articulation/Dynamics

1. No. 1: Measures 37–68 are a musical repetition of which measures? What is new here? The repetition is not without some variation. Discuss this.
2. No. 1: Can you discover any textural pattern that seems to repeat itself throughout this movement?

1.
Corno
Flauto traverso
Oboe I
Oboe II
Violino I
Violino II
Viola
Soprano
Alto
Tenore
Basso
Continuo
Organo (bez.)
Organo
piano
tr

8
forte

15
tr
piano
piano
Je - su, der du mei - ne See - -
Je - su, der du mei - ne
piano
21
forte
forte
tr
piano
piano
Je - su, der du mei - - ne See - le
- - le, Je - su, der du mei - ne See - le hast durch dei - nen bit - tern
See - le, Je - su, der du mei - ne See - le hast durch dei - nen
Je - su, der du mei - ne See - - le
forte
piano

28
forte
forte
hast durch dei - nen
Tod , hast durch dei - nen bit - tern Tod , hast durch dei - nen
bit - tern Tod, durch dei - nen bit - tern Tod , hast durch dei - nen
hast durch dei - nen bit - tern Tod , hast durch dei - nen
forte
35
tr
piano
forte
bit - tern Tod
bit - tern Tod
bit - tern Tod
bit - tern Tod
piano

43
piano
forte
aus des
piano
50
forte
forte
piano
forte
forte
aus des Teu - fels fin - stern
Teu - fels fin - stern Höh - - le, aus des Teu - fels fin -
aus des Teu - fels fin - stern Höh - le, aus des Teu - fels fin -
aus des Teu-fels fin-stern
forte

56
piano
piano
piano
Höh - - le
- stern Höh - le und der schwe-ren See - len - not ___, und der ___ schwe -
stern Höh - le und der schwe-ren See-len - not, der schwe - ren
Höh - - le und der schwe-ren
63
forte
forte
forte
forte
forte
forte
und der schwe - ren ___ See-len - not
- ren ___ See - len - not, und der schwe-ren ___ See - len - not
See - len - not ___, und der schwe - ren ___ See - len - not
See - len - not ___, und der schwe-ren See - len - not

70
piano
piano
tr
tr
piano
piano
piano
kräf - tig - lich her-aus - ge -
kräf - tig - lich her-aus - ge - ris - - -
kräf - tig -
piano
76
forte
forte
ris - - - - - sen, her-aus - - ge-ris - - sen, her-aus - -
- sen, kräf-tig-lich her - aus - - - - ge-ris - - sen, her-aus -
lich her - aus - ge - ris-sen, kräf - tig - lich her-aus-ge - ris - sen, her - aus-ge -

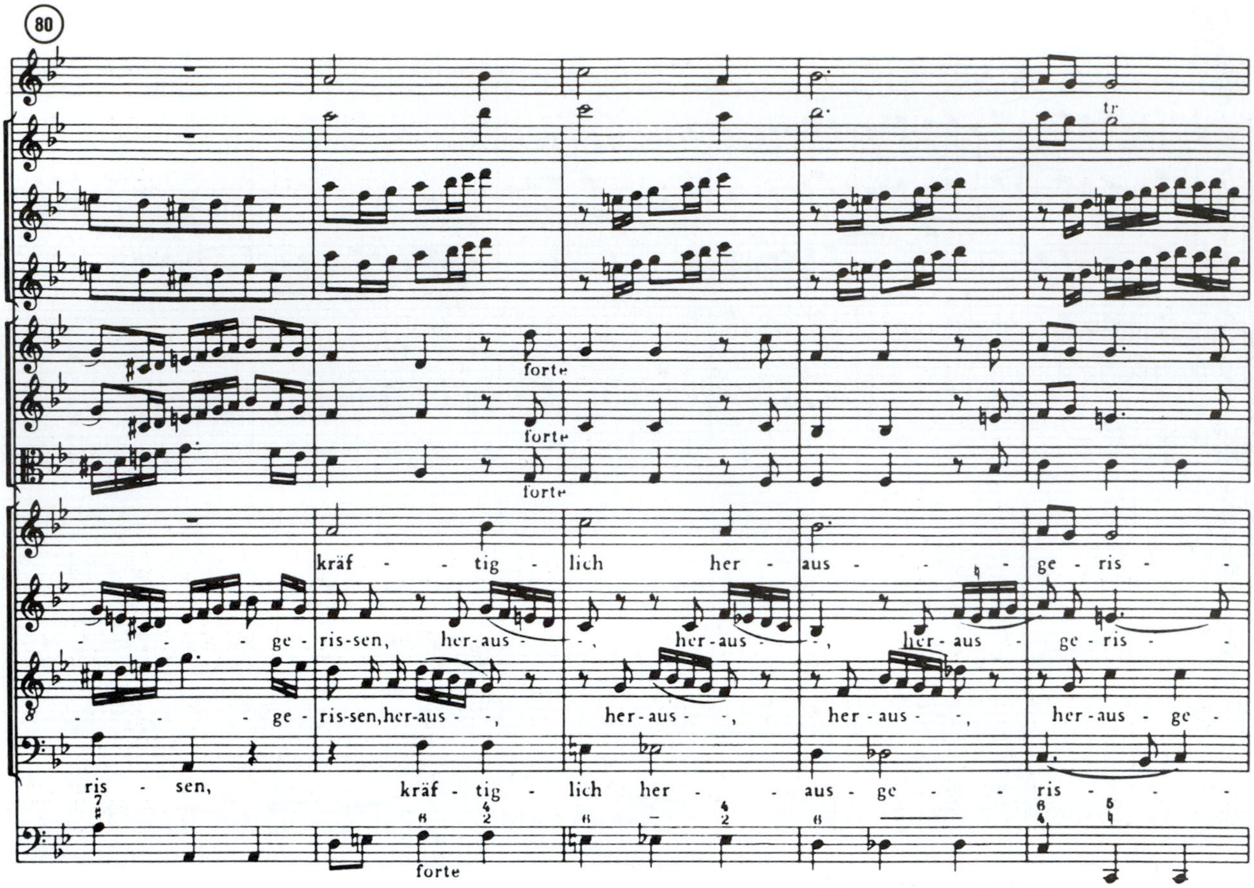

80

tr

forte

forte

forte

kräf - tig - lich her - aus - - - ge - ris -

- - - ge - ris-sen, her-aus - -, her-aus - -, her - aus - ge - ris - -

- - ge - ris-sen, her-aus - -, her - aus - -, her - aus - -, her - aus - ge -

ris - sen, kräf - tig - lich her - - aus - ge - - ris - - -

forte

91
tr
- - ches las-sen wis - - sen, mich sol - - - ches las-sen wis - - - - -
wis-sen, mich sol - - - - - - - - ches las-sen wis - - - - - - sen, und mich
und mich sol-ches las-sen wis-sen, mich sol - - - - - - ches las-sen wis - - - -
95
forte
forte
forte
piano
piano
piano
piano
piano
und mich sol - - ches las - - - - sen wis - - sen
- sen, mich sol-ches las-sen wis - - - - - - - - - - sen
sol - - ches las-sen wis - - sen, und mich sol-ches las - sen wis - sen
- sen, und mich sol - ches las - sen wis - - - - sen
forte
piano

100
tr
forte
forte
tr
forte
forte
forte
forte
106
piano
piano
piano
durch dein an - - ge -
durch dein an - - ge - neh - - mes Wort, durch dein
piano

111
forte
forte
forte
forte
forte
tr
neh - mes Wort, durch dein an - ge - neh - mes Wort, durch dein
an - ge - neh - mes Wort, durch dein an - ge - neh - mes
durch dein an - ge - neh - mes Wort, durch dein an - ge -
116
tr
tr
forte
durch dein an - ge - neh - mes Wort,
an - ge - neh - mes Wort, durch dein an - ge - neh - mes Wort,
Wort, durch dein an-ge-neh - mes Wort, durch dein an - ge - neh - mes Wort,
neh - mes, dein an-ge-neh - mes Wort, durch dein an - ge - neh - mes Wort,
forte

122
127
tr
piano
sei doch itzt, o
sei doch itzt, o Gott, mein Hort, o Gott

132
piano
piano
forte
forte
forte
forte
forte
tr
Gott, mein Hort, o Gott, mein Hort, o Gott, mein Hort, sei doch itzt, o
tr
, mein Hort, sei doch itzt, o Gott, o Gott, mein Hort, Gott, mein Hort, sei doch itzt, o
tr
sei doch itzt, o Gott, mein Hort, Gott, mein Hort, sei doch
forte
137
piano
piano
piano
piano
piano
sei doch itzt, o Gott, mein Hort!
Gott, o Gott, mein Hort, o Gott, mein Hort!
Gott, mein Hort, o Gott, mein Hort, o Gott, o Gott, mein Hort!
itzt, o Gott, o Gott, mein Hort!
piano

3. Recitativo
Tenore
Continuo
Organo (teilw. bez.)
Organo
piano
Ach! ich bin ein Kind der Sün-den, ach! ich ir - re weit und breit. Der Sün-den Aus-satz,
4
so an mir zu fin-den, ver - läßt mich nicht in die-ser Sterb-lich - keit. Mein Wil - le trach-tet nur nach
7
Bö-sen. Der Geist zwar spricht: ach! wer wird mich er - lö - sen? A - ber Fleisch und Blut zu
10
zwin-gen und das Gu-te zu voll-brin-gen, ist ü-ber al - le mei-ne Kraft. Will ich den Scha-den nicht ver-heh-len, so kann ich
14
nicht, wie oft ich feh-le, zäh-len. Drum nehm ich nun der Sün-den Schmerz und Pein und mei-ner Sor-gen
18
Bür-de, so mir sonst un - er - träg-lich wür-de, ich lief-re sie dir, Je - su, seuf - zend ein. Rech-ne
a tempo
21
nicht die Mis-se-tat, die dich, Herr, er - zür - - - - - - - net hat!

4. Aria

Solo
Flauto traverso
Tenore
Continuo
Organo (bez.)
Organo
pizzicato
Das Blut, so mei - ne
Schuld durch-streicht,
das Blut, so mei - ne Schuld durch-streicht, macht mir das Her-ze

22
wie - der leicht, macht mir das Her - ze wie - der leicht und spricht mich frei, und spricht
26
mich frei. Ruft
31
mich der Höl - len Heer zum Strei - te, zum Strei - te, zum Strei - te, zum
35
Strei - - - - - - - te, so ste - het Je - sus mir zur Sei - te, daß
39
ich be-herzt, be-herzt, be-herzt und sieg - - - haft, be-herzt und sieg - haft sei.
43
Ruft mich der Höl - len Heer zum Strei - te, zum

47
Strei - te, zum Strei - te, zum Strei - te, zum
51
Strei - te, so ste -
55
het Je - sus, so ste - het Je - sus mir zur Sei - te, daß
59
ich be-herzt, be-herzt, daß ich be - herzt, ich be-herzt und sieg - haft sei.
63
69

7. Choral

Flauto traverso
Soprano Corno Oboe I Violino I
Sopr.
Alto Oboe II Violino II
Alto
Tenore Viola
Viola Ten.
Basso
Continuo Organo (bez.)
Organo
Herr, ich glau-be, hilf mir Schwa-chen, laß mich ja ver - za-gen nicht;
5
du, du kannst mich stär-ker ma-chen, wenn mich Sünd und Tod an-ficht. Dei-ner Gü-te will ich trau-en,
11
bis ich fröh-lich wer-de schau-en dich, Herr Je-su, nach dem Streit in der sü-ßen E-wig-keit.
tr

1. Jesus, through your bitter death
   you have mightily snatched my soul
   from the devil's dark lair and from its deep despair,
   and you have made this known to me through your comforting word.
   Be now, O God, my refuge.

3. I am a child of sin, alas! I go far astray.
   The wickedness of my sin which courses through me stays with me in my mortality.
   My will desires only evil even as my spirit says:
   Ah! who will deliver me?
   But to conquer flesh and blood and achieve good,
   is beyond all my strength.
   I don't want to hide my sins, but I cannot count how often I fail.
   So now I take the burden of the pain
   and anguish of my sins and my cares
   which are beyond endurance, and with a sigh I give them to you, Jesus.
   Don't count up the sins, O Lord, which have angered you!

4. The blood which wipes out my guilt
   makes my heart light again and acquits me.
   Even if the host of hell call me to battle, Jesus stands at my side,
   and I am heartened and victorious.

7. Lord, I believe, help my weakness and don't let me lose heart;
   you can make me stronger when sin and death attack me.
   I want to trust in your goodness until I shall see you with joy,
   Lord Jesus, in sweet eternity after the struggle.

George Frideric Handel

Although they both were born in Germany in 1685 and they died within nine years of one another, George Frideric Handel (1685–1759) and Bach probably never met or exerted much musical influence upon one another. Handel spent the greater part of his career in London, writing secular music, while Bach lived mainly in Leipzig, writing music for the church. Handel composed in practically all current genres, with particular emphasis on opera and oratorio. His melodies tend to be rhythmically simple and more diatonic than Bach's, and they rarely exhibit a connection with the German chorale. Likewise, his harmonic usage is generally more diatonic than Bach's. Handel's music is less consistently and rigorously polyphonic than Bach's, while dramatic textural contrast is more pronounced. His scores show more attention to dynamic detail, tempo indications, and special effects such as pizzicato.

PIÈCES POUR LE CLAVECIN *Suite No. 4 in D minor*

This composition is taken from the second of two collections of harpsichord suites. The date of composition is not known, but it was published (without Handel's permission) in 1733. The Sarabande is a concise example of the Baroque variation technique. Determine which elements of the theme are retained and which are changed in the two variations. Of additional interest is the close relationship between two of the other movements. Determine the nature of this relationship.

Allemande
3
6
9
12
16

Courante
8
18
26
34
Sarabande
9

17
Var. 1.
25
33
Var. 2.
41
Gigue
4
8

George Frideric Handel

CONCERTO GROSSO OP. 6, NO. 1 *Prelude and Allegro*

Written eighteen years after Bach's *Brandenburg Concertos*, the twelve concertos of Handel's *Opus 6* represent his most significant contribution to the field of instrumental music and stand alongside the *Brandenburg Concertos* as the highest achievements in the form. A detailed comparison of this work with Bach's *Brandenburg Concerto No. 2* (see page 106) will reveal much concerning the differences between the two composers, both in general and in their approaches to the concerto genre.

QUESTIONS FOR DISCUSSION

Formal Structure

1. A concerto grosso sets a small group of instruments (the *soli*, or *concertino*) against a larger group (the *tutti*, or *ripieno*). Identify each of these groups in the two movements. Then, make a diagram showing how the two groups alternate. (You may use R_1, R_2, R_3, and so on for the *ripieno* passages and S_1, S_2, S_3, and so on for the solo, or *concertino*, passages.)
2. In the first movement, identify a motive that is consistently associated with the *tutti* passages.
3. Relate mm. 11–18 of the first movement as precisely as you can to preceding material.
4. If you have studied sonata form, explain how the second movement can be viewed as an early example. You should be able to identify an exposition containing tonic and dominant theme areas with a transition between the two and a codetta, a development, and a recapitulation with a coda.

Melodic/Rhythmic Structure

1. In the second movement, locate an example of each:
   a. a real (exact) melodic sequence with an interval of repetition a second higher;
   b. a tonal sequence repeated a second lower;
   c. a real sequence repeated a fifth higher;
   d. a restatement of a melodic idea an octave higher;
   e. an exact restatement of a melodic idea.
2. Describe the melodic structure of the second movement in terms of phrase lengths, presence or absence of cadences, diatonic or chromatic content, rhythmic complexity, and the degree of similarity or contrast in melodic ideas. Then, if you have studied a quantity of J.S. Bach's music at this point, compare the melodic styles of Bach and Handel.

Harmonic/Tonal Structure

1. Name the tonal centers established in the first movement at m. 13, m. 19, m. 22 and m. 27. Which one of these tonal centers is *not* among the keys closely related to G major (the home key)? Exactly what is its relationship? Explain precisely how the modulation from the key of m. 22 to the key of m. 27 is accomplished.
2. In the first movement, provide a complete harmonic analysis of mm. 29–34.
3. In the second movement, locate the following:
   a. a cadential extension that is a prolongation of dominant harmony;
   b. a succession of dominant seventh chords;
   c. a cadential six-four chord;
   d. a deceptive cadence.
4. In the second movement, locate and compare two different passages containing a series of V_7–I motions.

Texture/Articulation/Dynamics

1. Describe the following points in the second movement as homophonic, polyphonic but non-imitative, or polyphonic and imitative:
   a. mm. 3–4;
   b. mm. 5–8;
   c. mm. 13–14;
   d. mm. 15–18;
   e. mm. 19–21;
   f. mm. 29–32.
2. Compare this concerto with Bach's *Brandenburg Concerto No. 2* (see page 106) in terms of texture, use of dynamics, and orchestration.

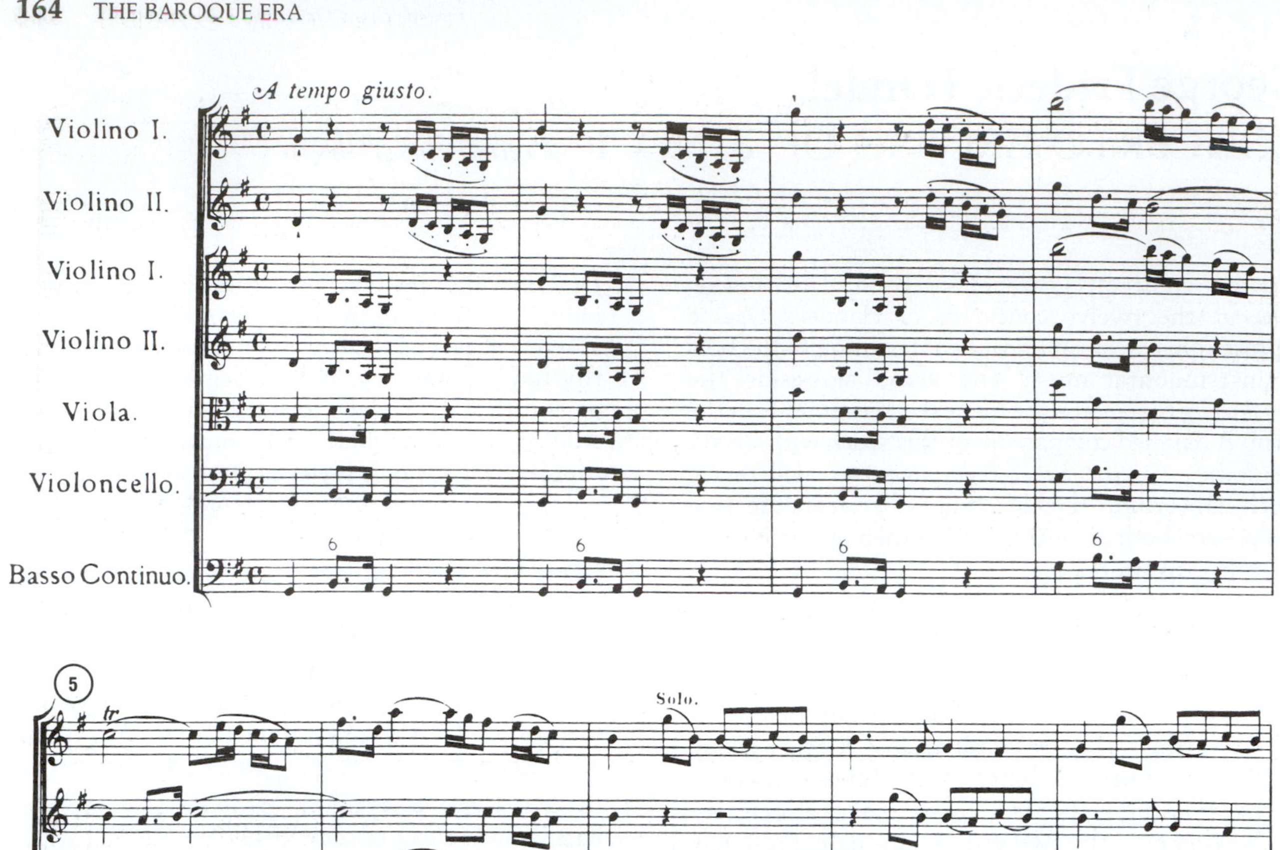
A tempo giusto.
Violino I.
Violino II.
Violino I.
Violino II.
Viola.
Violoncello.
Basso Continuo.

5
Solo.

10
Tutti.
Solo.

16
Tutti.
Solo.
22
Tutti.
Solo.
Tutti.
tr
p
pp
28

Allegro.
Solo.
Tutti.
Solo.
Tutti.
5
9

15
p
p
p
p
p
p
5
6
#
5
6
6
5
6
19
f
f
f
f
f
f
6
4
#
6
4
#
6
4
#
6
4
6
#
6
6
23
6
5
6
5
6
#
#
#
#
#
4
2
6
6
5
6
#
#
#
#
#

27
31
Solo.
36
Tutti.

41
45
49
p
f

Unit III

THE CLASSICAL PERIOD

Important aesthetic ideals of the Classical period (ca. 1750–1825) were clarity of thought and balanced formal proportions. This demanded an approach to composition that paid careful attention to details of organization. The musical forms of the period reflect these concerns. Important genres include the symphony, sonata, and concerto, and chamber music genres—string quartet, piano trio and so on. Though less numerous, vocal works, in the form of the Mass, oratorio, and opera, were also produced. Most of these works consist of multiple movements, three or four being the most common number in the instrumental genres. Individual movements generally fall into one of the following formal categories: theme and variations, ternary, binary, strophic, rondo, or sonata form. Sonata form is by far the most characteristic Classical form for instrumental music, and its influence can be seen in most of the other forms of the period.

The long, spun-out melodic lines of the Baroque era were replaced in the Classical period by shorter, clearly punctuated phrases and periods, often of four or eight measures' length. Harmonic rhythm tended to be slower, and rigorous counterpoint was favored less often than more homophonic textures. The Classical period saw the disappearance of the *basso continuo* as a harmonic support and the replacement of the harpsichord by the piano as the preferred keyboard instrument. The size of the orchestra became fairly standard by the end of the century—pairs of woodwinds, horns and trumpets; timpani; and strings; and composers became increasingly conscious of the coloristic possibilities of different instrumental combinations, coupled with dynamics and articulation.

The following chronological chart is for your reference. You may wish to check the box most closely representing the formal process as you complete your study of each work. This will aid you in future reference to the music of this unit. An additional space is provided for further comments or information.

S.F. = sonata form
R = rondo
V = theme and variations
B = binary
T = ternary
F = fugue
S = strophic
TC = through-composed

YEAR	COMPOSER	WORK/KEY	FORM/PROCESS								COMMENTS AND FURTHER INFORMATION
			S.F.	R	V	B	T	F	S	TC	
1742	C.P.E. Bach	*Prussian Sonata No. 1* I: F major									
1772	Haydn	*String Quartet* Op. 20, No. 5 I: F minor IV: F minor									
1778	Mozart	*Piano Sonata* K. 332 I: F major II: B-flat major									
1780	Haydn	*Sonata* H. XVI: 37 I: D major II: D minor III: D major									
1782	Mozart	*Die Entführung aus dem Serail* No. 5: C major No. 8: A major									
1787	Mozart	*Eine kleine Nachtmusik* I: G major III: G major									

YEAR	COMPOSER	WORK/KEY	FORM/PROCESS								COMMENTS AND FURTHER INFORMATION
			S.F.	R	V	B	T	F	S	TC	
1791	Mozart	*Concerto for Clarinet and Orchestra* K. 622 I: A major									
1794	Haydn	*Symphony No. 102* IV: B-flat major									
1797	Haydn	*String Quartet* Op. 76, No. 3 II: G major									
1797	Beethoven	*Piano Sonata* Op. 7 III: E-flat major									
1798	Beethoven	*String Quartet* Op. 18, No. 1 I: F major									
1798	Beethoven	*Piano Sonata* Op. 10, No. 1 III: C minor									
1799	Beethoven	*Piano Sonata* Op. 13 II: A-flat major									
1801	Beethoven	*Piano Sonata* Op. 26 III: A-flat minor									
1804	Beethoven	*Piano Sonata* Op. 53 I: C major Adagio: F major									
1812	Beethoven	*Symphony No. 7* Op. 92 II: A minor									

C.P.E. Bach

PRUSSIAN SONATA NO. 1 *First Movement*

C.P.E. Bach (1714–1788) figured prominently in the development of the Classical style. His *Prussian Sonatas* (1742) are important predecessors of the Classical keyboard sonata, containing outer movements that may be regarded as early examples of sonata form. Although the movement that follows does not contain the clearly articulated themes to be found in later sonata-form expositions, it does exemplify the basic tonal motion, along with a clear development and recapitulation. Stylistically, however, the movement evidences the linear-contrapuntal texture of the Baroque era.

Can you point to a passage that might be considered transitional between the two tonalities of the exposition? At what point is the second tonal area stabilized? Can you point to a passage that might be regarded as a codetta? A number of soon-to-be standard developmental techniques (as well as some traditional contrapuntal techniques) are applied beginning at m. 32. Can you identify them? In what ways does the recapitulation differ from the exposition? Although the piece has a two-voice texture for the most part, the harmonies are rather clearly implied. What sequence of harmonies is suggested in mm. 10–13? What occurs melodically at this point?

Composed 1742

Related reading: Philip Barford, *The Keyboard Music of C.P.E. Bach* (New York: October House Inc., 1966), pp. 50–61. A summary of the process by which sonata form developed from binary form, followed by a short discussion of this movement and its emerging sonata-form features.

19
forte
25
f
forte
32
38
44
50

Franz Josef Haydn

The creative career of Franz Josef Haydn (1732–1809) encompassed the greater part of the Classical period. Most numerous among his compositions are the piano sonatas, string quartets, and symphonies, and he played a prominent role in the development of the last two genres. Haydn's phrases are terse and clearly articulated, often containing elements of folk music. He was fond of third-related and parallel major-minor key relationships, especially between movements. His textures are prevailingly homophonic, with sections of contrapuntal development, fugato, or canon providing contrast. Haydn's orchestration was frequently experimental for the time, with soloistic use of woodwinds and strings, double stops and occasional *divisi* in the strings, and dramatic timbral and dynamic contrasts.

STRING QUARTET OP. 20, NO. 5, H. III: 35 *First and Fourth Movements*

The six "Sun" quartets of Op. 20 were composed in 1772, during Haydn's *Sturm und Drang* ("Storm and Stress") period. Compared to his earlier quartets, these display, on the whole, a more contrapuntal conception, greater dynamic and expressive detail, and more thorough and pervasive development of thematic material. The *Questions for Discussion* that follow refer to the first movement, which is in sonata form. In addition, consider the fourth movement—a fugue with two subjects. Which of the subjects is given the more thorough treatment? Where does the section containing the initial group of entrances end? What material forms the basis for the first episode? For succeeding episodes? What is the significance of the term *al rovescio*, at m. 92? Describe the canon that begins at m. 145 (instruments involved, pitch interval, time interval, duration, and so on). What are the most important tonal areas in the movement?

You may wish to compare Bach's Fugue No. 4 from *The Well-Tempered Clavier* Book I. Which of the two works is the more rigorously contrapuntal?

QUESTIONS FOR DISCUSSION

First Movement

Formal Structure

1. In the exposition, where exactly does the transition between tonal areas begin? Where does it end? To what tonality does it progress?
2. How many distinct thematic passages do you find within the second tonal area? Might one of these be called a codetta? Explain your answer.
3. Locate the beginning and end of the development. Then identify all material from the exposition that appears in this section. What developmental techniques—fragmentation, sequence, imitation, registral changes, melodic or rhythmic variation, and so on—are applied to this material?
4. At what point in the recapitulation (give the measure number) does the music first begin to differ from its presentation in the exposition? At what point (give inclusive measure numbers) is the music the same except for tonality and voicing? At what point (give inclusive measure numbers) is the music identical in *all* respects except tonality?
5. Locate the coda. In it, how does Haydn achieve a union of material originally heard separately?

Melodic/Rhythmic Structure

1. Describe the melodic structure of the first thirteen measures, addressing such matters as phrase lengths and relationships, and phrase extension techniques.
2. Between m. 60 and m. 68, a melodic (and harmonic) sequence takes place. Identify precisely the material that is repeated, locate all sequential repetitions, indicate the pitch level of those repetitions, and indicate whether the sequences are real or tonal.

Harmonic/Tonal Structure

1. To what tonality does Haydn briefly allude as he moves toward the second tonal area of the exposition?
2. Describe, using an appropriate Roman numeral, the following chromatic harmonies found in the exposition:

   a. m. 9; c. m. 34;
   b. m. 14, beat 4; d. m. 46, beat 4.

3. Name the tonal center implied at the following points:

   a. m. 49; d. m. 69;
   b. m. 52; e. m. 77.
   c. m. 57;

   Which of these is not closely related to the principal tonality of F minor?

4. The most harmonically complex passage of the movement occurs at mm. 142–146. Through enharmonic respelling, however, the passage can be analyzed fairly easily in a single key. Provide such an analysis.

Texture/Articulation/Dynamics

Locate a passage at least two measures in length—*if one exists*—illustrating each of the following textures:

a. viola and cello in parallel motion;
b. melody in first violin, three lower instruments homorhythmic;
c. all four instruments rhythmically independent;
d. outer voices paired rhythmically against inner voices;
e. three-voice texture;
f. violins and viola homorhythmic, cello independent;
g. first violin and viola paired rhythmically against second violin and cello.

Which of these textures appears to be the most common in this movement?

I
Allegro moderato
Violino I
Violino II
Viola
Violoncello
poco p
cresc.

36
cresc.
cresc.
cresc.
cresc.
42
decresc.
decresc.
decresc.
decresc.
46
1.
2.
cresc.
cresc.
cresc.
cresc.
cresc.
cresc.
cresc.
cresc.
49
54
59
62

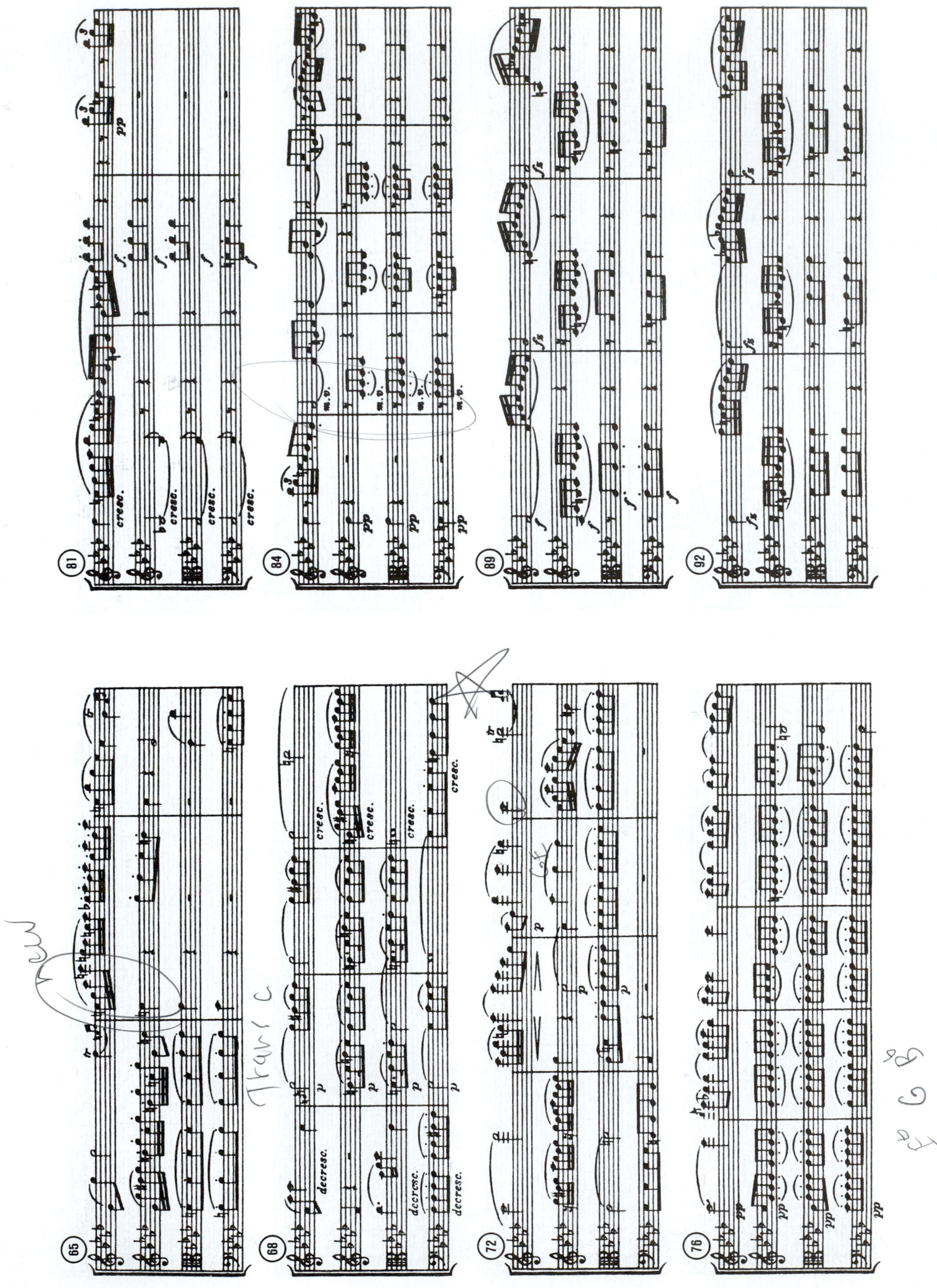
65
68
decresc.
p
cresc.
72
p
76
pp
81
cresc.
fz
84
pp
m.v.
89
f
92
fz

95
fz
m.v.
98
102
105
109
p
pp
114
cresc.
118
f
123

127
131
134
138
143
149
153
156

Finale
Fuga a due Soggetti
IV
sempre sotto voce
8
14
21
28
34
40
46

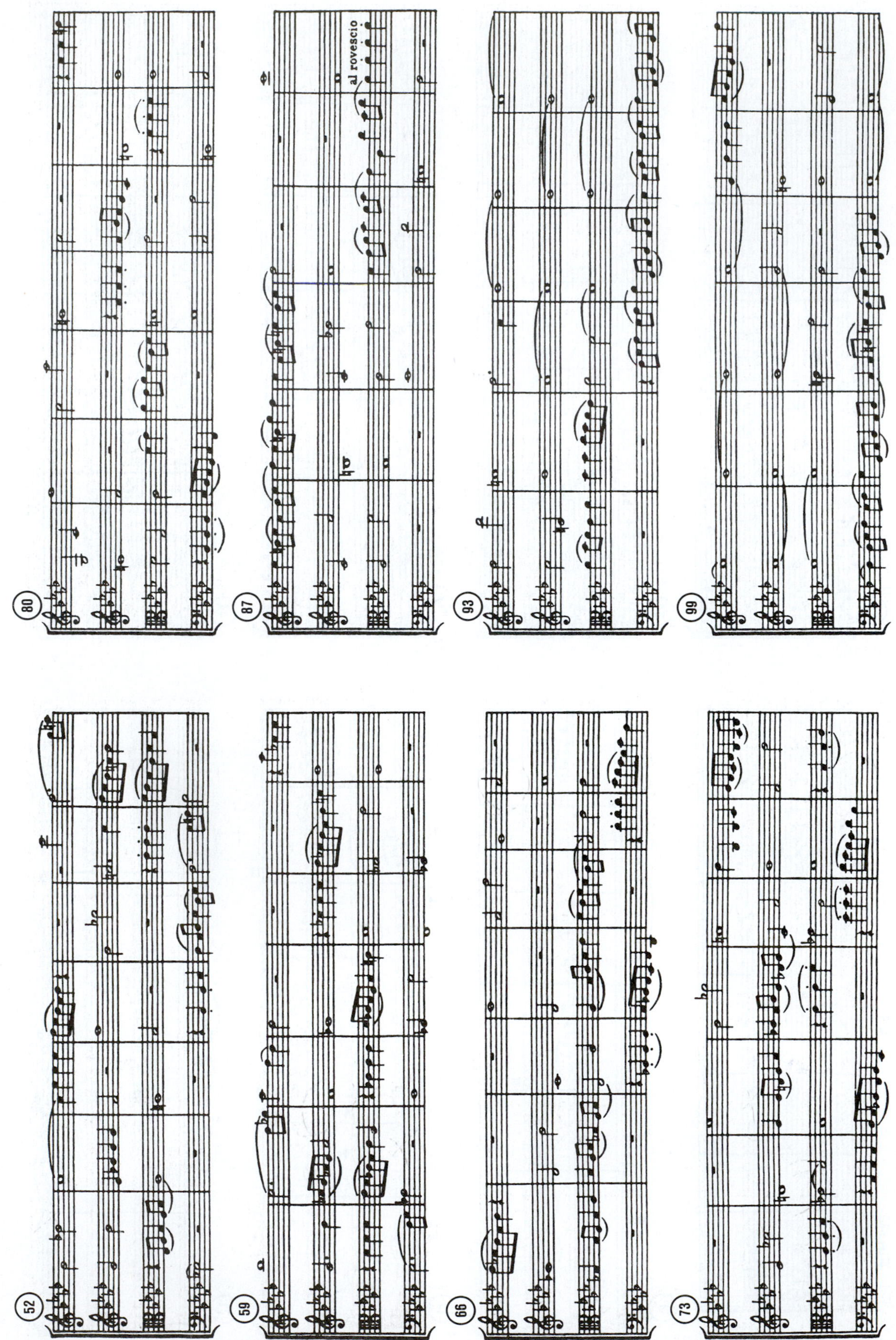
52
59
66
73
80
87
al rovescio
93
99

105
112
m.v.
m.v.
m.v.
m.v.
118
124
130
136
144
ff in canone
ff
ff
ff
150

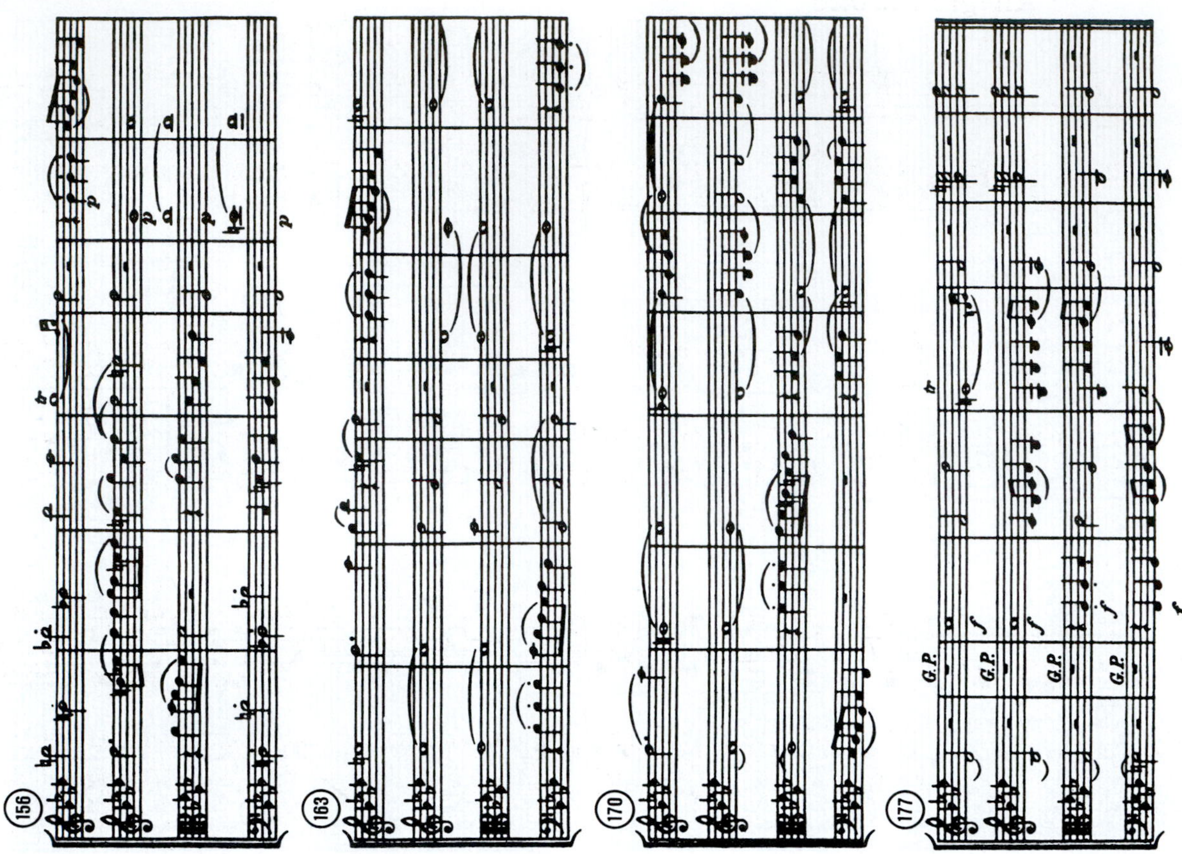

Franz Josef Haydn

PIANO SONATA H. XVI: 37

Haydn's piano sonatas span thirty-four years—from 1760 to 1794—and thus display considerable stylistic growth. This sonata is one of his earlier works. The three movements provide succinct examples of three of the most popular forms of the day. Can you identify them? Study the movements from the standpoint of balance and symmetry (regarding phrase/period structure and larger formal matters). Then identify some prominent examples of these Classical ideals. Haydn was fond of using folk material. Are any folk elements present in this work? Also worth studying are the tonal plans of the movements. Does Haydn move beyond the circle of closely related keys that so often defined the tonal boundaries of Baroque movements? Change of mode—the shift from a major key to the parallel minor or the reverse—was common in Classical music. Can you identify examples of this procedure? A harmonically restless passage begins after the double bar in the first movement. Can you identify the tonalities either established or suggested here? What thematic elements in this passage have been introduced earlier?

Composed 1780

Related reading: Allen Forte, *Introduction to Schenkerian Analysis* (New York: W.W. Norton and Company, 1982), pp. 376–381. Voice-leading graphs of the third movement, with explanations and a summary of the form and tonal plan.

From Edition Peters No. 713a. Used by permission.

21

f

24

meno f

cresc.

27

f

p

30

f

ff

33

tr

p

f

37

p

f

41
f
tr tr
p
f
tr tr
p
45
cresc.
f
48
51
f
54
meno f
f
57
tr
p
61
f
tr tr
tr tr

65
meno f
68
cresc.
71
f
dim.
74
mf
77
cresc.
f
p
81
cresc.
84
f

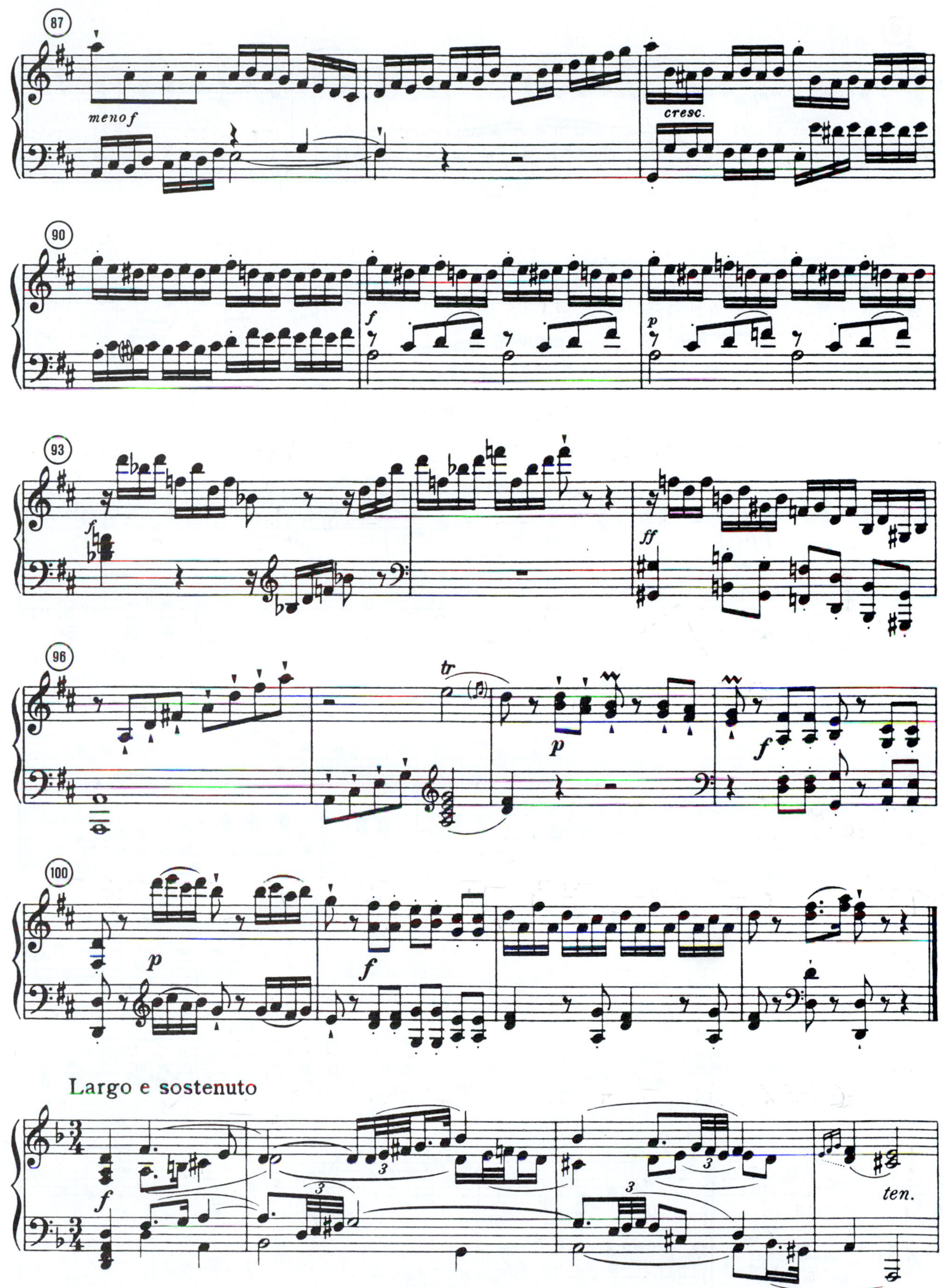
87
meno f
cresc.
90
f
p
93
f
ff
96
tr
p
f
100
p
f
Largo e sostenuto
f
ten.

mf
ten.
pp
ff
p
Attacca subito il Finale
Finale
Presto, ma non troppo
pinnocentemente
f

29 *f* *p* *f*

36 *p* *p*

44

52 *f*

61 *mf*

69 *p* *mf*

75 *cresc.*

84

f *decresc.* *p*

94

f

102

108

p *f*

115

p

122

f

128

Franz Josef Haydn

STRING QUARTET OP. 76, NO. 3 *Second Movement*

Haydn's so-called "Emperor Quartet" derives its name from the fact that the second movement is a set of variations on Haydn's song, "God Save the Emperor Franz." (This song served for many years as the Austrian national anthem.) In any variation form, a useful procedure is to identify thematic elements that are retained and changed in each of the variations. Generally speaking, as the form developed over the years, composers took ever greater liberties with the theme as they sought to vary it in imaginative ways. To test the truth of this statement, compare this work with such earlier examples of the form as Purcell's Dido's Lament or the Sarabande from Handel's Suite No. 4. Analyze the melodic form of the theme. Given its chorale-like four-voice setting, it provides a worthwhile means to observe how Haydn applied the voice-leading procedures of the Baroque era.

Composed 1797

Related reading: Douglass M. Green, *Form in Tonal Music* (New York: Holt, Rinehart and Winston, 1979), p. 109f. Discussion of the overall plan of this movement with a diagram of its textural complexity.

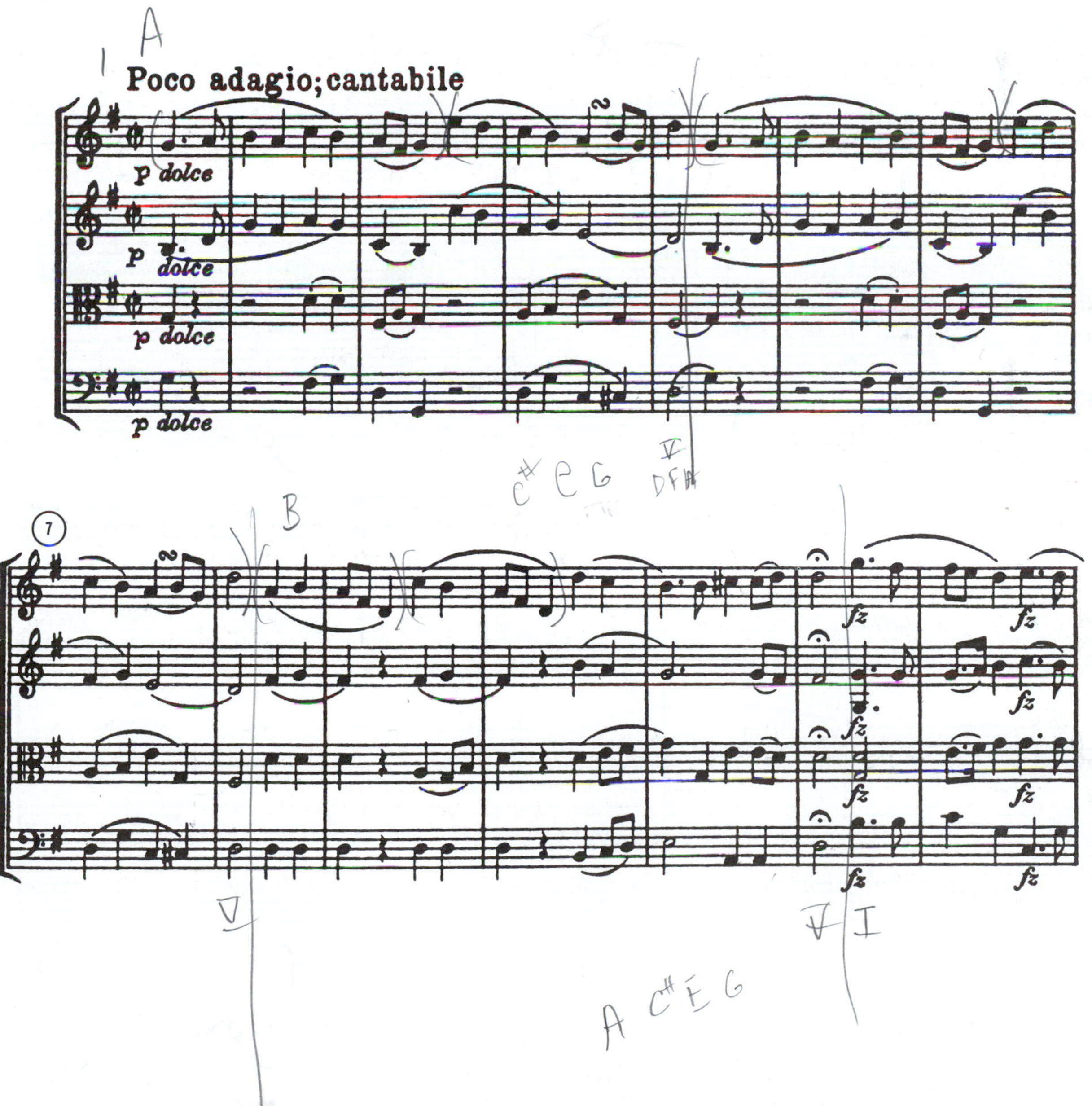

14
p
fz
Var. I
21
sempre piano
23
26

29
32
fz
fz
p
p
35
6
fz
fz
38
p
p

Var. II
41
p
p
p
p
44
48
51

54
fz
fz
57
fz
fz
Var. III
61
p
p
p
65
p

69
73
77
Var. IV
81
p

87
92
96
100
pp
pp
pp
pp
pp
pp
pp
pp

Franz Josef Haydn

SYMPHONY NO. 102 *Fourth Movement*

During the 1790s, Haydn was invited by impresario J. P. Salomon to compose two sets of six symphonies for a concert series in London. These *London Symphonies* reveal Haydn's mature genius in such matters as form, orchestration and harmonic means. Symphony No. 102 in B-flat major was first performed in 1795 by an orchestra of approximately forty strings, twenty winds and timpani.

QUESTIONS FOR DISCUSSION

Formal Structure

1. Although this movement has the repetitive structure of a rondo (alternating episodes and refrains), it also embodies characteristics of sonata form. Illustrate, using letters and measure numbers, the rondo structure, and then show the way in which the sections in combination resemble the larger divisions of a sonata-form movement.
2. Within the exposition, which of the following are present and where are they located: tonic theme group; transition to the dominant; dominant theme group; codetta?
3. What common small form can be found within the exposition?

Melodic/Rhythmic Structure

1. What is the prevailing phrase length in this movement?
2. It is possible to speak of two types of melodic chromaticism—one in which the chromatics reflect, or are a consequence of, chromatic harmonies, and one in which the chromatics oppose the harmonic structure (as in non-chord tones). In this movement, both types can be found. Locate a good example of each.
3. As in many of his finales, Haydn built this movement upon a folk melody. Examine the first twelve measures, and describe them from the standpoint of phrasing, rhythm, pitch structure and repetition. In what ways is this melody similar to folk songs that you know?
4. Describe the way in which the melodic material is manipulated in mm. 187–202 to achieve a sense of gathering momentum.

Harmonic/Tonal Structure

1. What tonal areas are suggested in mm. 1–12?
2. Describe by Roman numeral each of the following:
   a. the chord outlined by the first violins in mm. 60–63;
   b. the chord at mm. 176–177;
   c. the chord that is prolonged at mm. 182–185.
3. The music is in B-flat prior to m. 166 and in D minor at m. 174. Describe precisely how the movement to D minor is accomplished.
4. Identify the most harmonically unstable section of the movement and list the tonalities that are briefly encountered, indicating the location of each by measure number.

Texture/Articulation/Dynamics

1. The second episode (rondo section C) exhibits six major changes of texture. Locate these changes and describe them.
2. Would you say this movement is characterized by strong dynamic contrast? Locate the most dynamically active section.
3. Discuss in general terms the orchestration of this movement from the following standpoints: violin range; number of independent string parts; special string techniques; brass and woodwind functions.

Presto
Flauti
Oboi
Fagotti
Corni in B
Trombe in B
Timpani in B-F
Violino I
Violino II
Viola
Violoncello e Basso
8
Fl.
Ob.
Fg.
Cor. (B)
Tbe. (B)
Timp.
Vl.
Vla.
Vc. Cb.
a 2.
15
Fl.
Ob.
Fg.
Cor. (B)
Tbe. (B)
Timp.
Vl.
Vla.
Vc. Cb.
23
Fl.
Ob.
Fg.
Cor. (B)
Tbe. (B)
Timp.
Vl.
Vla.
Vc. Cb.

30
Fl.
Ob.
Fg.
Cor. (B)
Tbe. (B)
Timp.
Vl.
Vla.
Vc. Cb.
1.
44
Fl.
Ob.
Fg.
Cor. (B)
Tbe. (B)
Timp.
Vl.
Vla.
Vc. Cb.
a 2.
38
2.
a 2.
Fl.
Ob.
Fg.
Cor. (B)
Tbe. (B)
Timp.
Vl.
Vla.
Vc. Cb.
49
Fl.
Ob.
Fg.
Cor. (B)
Tbe. (B)
Timp.
Vl.
Vla.
Vc. Cb.

56
Fl.
Ob.
Fg.
Cor. (B)
Tbe. (B)
Timp.
Vl.
Vla.
Vc. Cb.
68
Fl.
Ob.
Fg.
Cor. (B)
Tbe (B)
Timp.
Vl.
Vla.
Vc. Cb.
62
Fl.
Ob.
Fg.
Cor. (B)
Tbe. (B)
Timp.
Vl.
Vla.
Vc. Cb.
76
a 2.
Fl.
Ob.
Fg.
Cor. (B)
Tbe. (B)
Timp.
Vl.
Vla.
Vc. Cb.

84
Fl.
Ob.
Fg.
Cor. (B)
Tbe. (B)
Timp.
Vl.
Vla.
Vc. Cb.
98
92
106

112
Fl.
Ob.
Fg.
Cor. (B)
Tbe. (B)
Timp.
Vl.
Vla.
Vc. Cb.
118
Fl.
Ob.
Fg.
Cor. (B)
Tbe. (B)
Tmp.
Vl.
Vla.
Vc. Cb.
124
Fl.
Ob.
Fg.
Cor. (B)
Tbe. (B)
Timp.
Vl.
Vla.
Vc. Cb.
132
Fl.
Ob.
Fg.
Cor. (B)
Tbe. (B)
Timp.
Vl.
Vla.
Vc. Cb.

140
Fl.
Ob.
Fg.
Cor. (B)
Tbe. (B)
Timp.
Vl.
Vla.
Vc. Cb
155
148
162
II.
a 2.

169
Fl.
Ob.
Fg.
Cor. (B)
Tbe. (B)
Timp.
Vl.
Vla.
Vc. Cb.
a 2.
182
176
189

196
Fl.
Ob.
Fg.
Cor. (B)
Tbe. (B)
Timp.
Vl.
Vla.
Vc. Cb.
a 2.
Cello.
Bassi.
209
203
216

224
Fl.
Ob.
Fg.
Cor. (B)
Tbe. (B)
Timp.
Vl.
Vla.
Vc. Cb.
240
sf
(sf)
f
232
a 2.
sf
p
248

256
Fl.
Ob.
Fg.
Soli
Cor. (B)
Tbe. (B)
Timp.
Vl.
Vla.
Vc. Cb.
269
pizz.
pizz.
pizz.
262
Soli
278
a 2
arco
arco
arco

288
Fl.
Ob.
Fg.
Cor. (B)
Tbe. (B)
Timp.
Vl.
Vla.
Vc. Cb.
302
Fl.
Ob.
Fg.
Cor. (B)
Tbe. (B)
Timp.
Vl.
Vla.
Vc. Cb.
298
Fl.
Ob.
Fg.
Cor. (B)
Tbe. (B)
Timp.
Vl.
Vla.
Vc. Cb.
306
Fl.
Ob.
Fg.
Cor. (B)
Tbe. (B)
Timp.
Vl.
Vla.
Vc. Cb.
Bassi
Fine Laus Deo

Wolfgang Amadeus Mozart

The style of Wolfgang Amadeus Mozart (1756–1791) is a synthesis of Italian lyrical-dramatic and German contrapuntal-developmental elements. He excelled in both symphonic (German) and operatic (Italian) composition, creating masterworks in two genres for which Haydn is not particularly well known—opera and concerto. His melodies are usually lyrical, graceful and symmetrical, without the obvious folk elements found in Haydn's music. His choices for principal keys usually involve no more than three sharps or three flats, with C, D and E-flat particular favorites. Mozart's early works are highly homophonic, but increased contrapuntal interest can be noted during the 1780s. Although he was not as given to orchestrational experimentation as was Haydn, he used the woodwinds, especially the clarinet, more freely and with greater variety then did Haydn.

PIANO SONATA K. 332 *First and Second Movements*

Among Mozart's best-known and most often played piano sonatas are those which he composed while in Paris in 1778. What is the form of the first movement of K. 332? How is it conditioned by Mozart's inspired gift for melody? Analyze mm. 23–40 from the standpoint of tonality, sequences and chromatic harmonies. What role do these measures fulfill in the form? Plot the tonal progress of the music between m. 94 and m. 131. How does it represent a continuation of the tonal motion begun earlier in the movement? As with the Haydn Piano Sonata, H. XVI: 37, you should study this movement from the standpoint of melodic and formal balance and symmetry.

The second movement contains considerable chromaticism as well as some interesting mode changes (parallel major-minor relationships). Of particular interest is the manner in which the move to the dominant is accomplished. At the most basic formal level, how many sections does this movement comprise? How would you symbolize the form using letters? What similarities to sonata form exist? What primary difference can you cite?

Composed 1778

Related reading: James P. Fairleigh, "Transition and Retransition in Mozart's Sonata-Type Movements," *College Music Symposium,* Vol. 26 (1986), pp. 14–26. A general perspective on Mozart's use of sonata form, with a closer look at the transitional and retransitional passages. (The first movement of K. 332 is used as an example.) Consideration is given to the ways in which the transition may differ at its reappearance in the recapitulation.

19
(sf)
(sf)
27
(sf)
(sf)
33
38
46
(cresc.)
(p)
53
(cresc.)
(f)
60

67
(cresc.)
76
84
88
94
105
113

119
125
133
142
150
158
163
(cresc.)

168
173
179
185
(cresc.)
(p)
(cresc.)
191
(f)
197
204
(cresc.)
(p)

212
220
224
Adagio.
4
7
10

13
sfp
sfp
sfp
sf
tr
p
p
16
3
3
tr
tr
(f)
(p)
18
3
(sfp)
tr
(f)
tr
tr
(p)
21
(Nach den ältesten Ausgaben.)
p
cresc.
p
(Nach dem Autograph Mozart's.)
p
24
sfp
sfp
3
p

26
cresc.
sf
p
28
p
sfp
31
sfp
sfp
sfp
p
tr
3
3
34
f
p
tr

Wolfgang Amadeus Mozart

EINE KLEINE NACHTMUSIK *First and Third Movements*

Mozart composed this serenade for strings in 1787 for an occasion which is not known. Although somewhat lighter in style than his symphonic works of the same period, it follows the same four-movement plan. What is the form of the first movement? What is the form of the third movement and what musical elements serve to create this structure? Note especially the ways in which the Trio contrasts with the Menuetto. What are the forms of the Menuetto and Trio *individually?* What other works in the anthology have you studied that have a similar structure?

7
tr
p
p
p
p
14
tr
tr
sf
p
sf
p
cresc.
tr
tr
sf
p
sf
p
cresc.
sf
p
sf
p
cresc.
sf
p
sf
p
cresc.
21
(f)
(f)
(f)
(f)
28
3
p
3
p
p
p
3
3
3
35
tr
tr
tr
tr
3
3
f
f
f
f

42
p
tr
f
3
49
tr
p
56
f
p
64
tr
71

79
86
94
101
108
tr
p
sf
cresc.
(f)
f

115
122
129
MENUETTO.
Allegretto.
9
cresc.
Fine

Wolfgang Amadeus Mozart

DIE ENTFÜHRUNG AUS DEM SERAIL *Act I, No. 5; Act II, No. 8*

The *Singspiel*, a German form of comic opera with German libretto and spoken dialogue, developed in the early part of the eighteenth century and reached an artistic peak with this work. The plot concerns a Spanish lady, Kostanze, who is sold by pirates along with her servants, Blonde and Pedrillo, to the Pasha Selim, who hopes to win her affection. The man with whom she is in love, Belmonte, comes to her rescue and with Pedrillo arranges a midnight escape.

Act I, No. 5 (Chorus of the Janissaries)

This is ceremonial music by the Pasha's escort, heralding his return from a day of boating. The formal divisions are clearly distinguished by short instrumental punctuations and by changes in the choral texture. Equally clear are the modulations. Locate each of these, and describe the modulation in each case. To gain a sense of the overall structure of this movement, you may wish to construct a formal/tonal diagram that identifies by measure numbers the instrumental passages, the choral passages, and the tonalities.

Allegro
G. Orch. f
9
Chor der Janitscharen
Sopran
Alt
Singt dem gro - ßen Bas - sa Lie - der, dem gro - ßen Bas - sa Lie - der,
Tenor
Singt dem gro - ßen Bas - sa Lie - der, dem gro - ßen Bas - sa Lie - der,
Baß
17
tö - - ne, feu - ri - ger Ge - sang, und vom U - fer hal - le
tö - - ne, feu - ri - ger Ge - sang, und vom U - fer hal - le

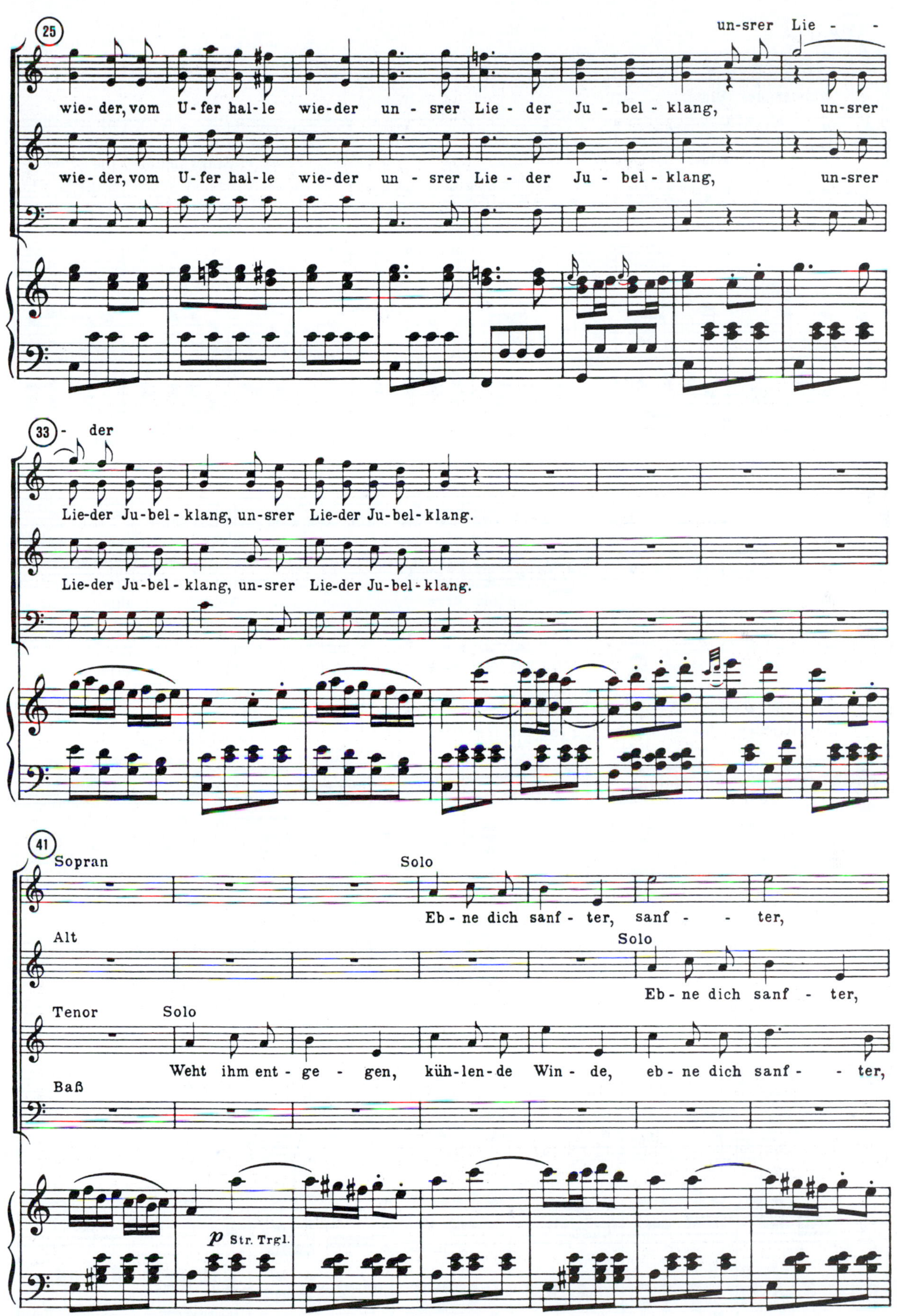
25
un-srer Lie - -
wie-der, vom U-fer hal-le wie-der un - srer Lie - der Ju - bel - klang, un-srer
wie-der, vom U-fer hal-le wie-der un - srer Lie - der Ju - bel - klang, un-srer
33
- der
Lie-der Ju-bel - klang, un-srer Lie-der Ju-bel - klang.
Lie-der Ju-bel - klang, un-srer Lie-der Ju-bel - klang.
41
Sopran
Solo
Eb - ne dich sanf - ter, sanf - - ter,
Alt
Solo
Eb - ne dich sanf - ter,
Tenor
Solo
Weht ihm ent - ge - gen, küh-len-de Win - de, eb - ne dich sanf - - ter,
Baß
p Str. Trgl.

48
wal-len-de Flut.
wal-len-de Flut. Singt ihm der Lie - be
wal-len-de Flut.
Solo
Singt ihm ent - ge - gen, flie-gen-de Chö - re,
Bläs.
Str.
55
Weht ihm ent -
Freu - - - - - den ins Herz. Weht ihm ent -
Singt ihm der Lie - be Freu-den ins Herz. Singt ihm ent -
singt ihm der Lie - - be Freu-den ins Herz.
Bläs.
Str.
62
ge - - gen, küh - - len-de Win - - de, eb - -
ge - - gen, küh - - len-de Win - - de, eb - -
ge - - gen, flie - - gen-de Chö - - re, singt
Bläs.
Str.

69
ne dich sanf - - - - - - - - - - - ter, wal - len - de Flut.
ne dich sanf - - - - - - - - - - - ter, wal - len - de Flut.
ihm der Lie - - be, der Lie - - - be Freu - den ins Herz.
f G. Orch.
76
Sopran
Alle
Alt
Singt dem gro - ßen Bas - sa Lie - der, dem gro - ßen Bas - sa
Tenor
Singt dem gro - ßen Bas - sa Lie - der, dem gro - ßen Bas - sa
Baß
83
Lie - der, tö - - ne, feu - ri - ger Ge - sang, und
Lie - der, tö - - ne, feu - ri - ger Ge - sang, und

89
vom U - fer hal - le wie - der, vom U - fer hal - le wie - der un - srer
vom U - fer hal - le wie - der, vom U - fer hal - le wie - der un - srer
96
un - srer Lie - - - der
Lie - der Ju - bel - klang, un - srer Lie - der Ju - bel - klang, un - srer
Lie - der Ju - bel - klang, un - srer Lie - der Ju - bel - klang, un - srer
102
Lie - der Ju - bel - klang.
Lie - der Ju - bel - klang.
(Janitscharen ab)
108

Sing to the great Pasha songs,
Let fiery songs ring out,
Echoing from the shore
Our joyous songs ring.

Blow gently against him, breezes,
Be calm, flowing torrent.
Greet him with song,
Lyric voices,
Sing to him with love
And heartfelt joy.
Blow gently, cooling breezes,
Be calm, flowing torrent.

Sing to the great Pasha songs,
Let fiery songs ring out.
Echoing from the shore
Our joyous songs ring.

Translation by Mary Schiller

Act II, No. 8 (Aria)

Blonde, who has been rebuffing the advances of the slavemaster Osmin, sings a short aria concerning the treatment of women. In what popular Classical form is this song cast? The melodic phrasing is typical Mozart. Study the song from this standpoint.

18
Bl.
leicht. Doch mür - ri - sches Be - feh - len und
Vl.I.
mf
p
mf
21
Bl.
Pol - tern, Zan - ken, Pla - gen, und Pol - tern, Zan - ken, Pla - gen macht,
p
mf
cresc.
f
p
25
Bl.
daß in we - nig Ta - gen so Lieb als Treu ent - weicht, macht,
29
Bl.
daß in we - nig Ta - gen so Lieb als Treu ent - weicht,
fp
34
Bl.
so Lieb als Treu ent-weicht. Durch Zärt-lich-keit und

39
Bl.
Schmei-cheln, Ge-fäl-lig-keit und Scherzen er-o-bert man die Her-zen der
44
gu-ten Mäd-chen leicht, der gu-ten Mäd-chen leicht. Doch mür-ri-sches Be-
cresc.
p
sf
48
feh-len und Pol-tern, Zan-ken, Pla-gen, und Pol-tern, Zan-ken, Pla-gen macht,
sf p
sf p
cresc.
f
51
daß in we-nig Ta-gen so Lieb als Treu ent-weicht,
p
sf
p
fp
56
so Lieb als Treu ent-weicht.
fp

Through tenderness and flattery,
and pleasantry and little jokes,
one conquers the heart of a maiden easily.
But rude orders and blustering,
quarreling and tormenting,
make both love and faithfulness quickly slip away.

Translation By Mary Schiller

Wolfgang Amadeus Mozart

CONCERTO FOR CLARINET AND ORCHESTRA K. 622

First Movement

Of Mozart's concertos, those for the piano are the best known and most frequently performed. However, he also composed concertos for other instruments, including violin, flute, horn, and clarinet. The *Clarinet Concerto,* K. 622, was composed in 1791, toward the very end of his life. Although one may argue that there is no such thing as a "typical" Mozart concerto, this movement displays a number of features that are highly representative, including the ordering and reordering of a large number of themes, the equality and complementarity of the solo and orchestral parts, and the synthesis of the Baroque ritornello principle with the Classical sonata form.

QUESTIONS FOR DISCUSSION

Formal Structure

1. The first movement of a Classical concerto can often be viewed as a sonata form with added orchestral material—before and perhaps after the soloist's exposition, and perhaps preceding and following the soloist's recapitulation. Frequently, the term *double exposition* is used because the opening orchestral *tutti* itself resembles the first part of a sonata-form movement. Locate and compare the orchestral and solo expositions in terms of tonalities and thematic content. What key sonata-form element is lacking in the orchestral exposition?
2. Locate the development section, identify the principal subdivisions within it, and identify the material that is treated in this part of the movement. Is it drawn from the orchestral exposition, the solo exposition, or both? Is new (previously unheard) material used and if so, where?
3. Provide a thematic and tonal diagram of the recapitulation (including the coda). Which previous section does the recapitulation (*excluding* the coda) most closely resemble? What differences exist? Upon what material is the coda based?

Melodic/Rhythmic Structure

1. Locate in either the orchestral or solo exposition a clear example of each of the following:
   a. A modulating phrase;
   b. A repeated phrase;
   c. A double period;
   d. Two successive phrases that *do not* form a period;
   e. A cadential extension.
2. Describe the following sequential passages, identifying: the melodic pattern that is repeated in sequence; each sequential statement of the pattern; the pitch interval of repetition. Also identify the sequence as real or tonal.
   a. mm. 20–24
   b. mm. 227–239
3. What do you find to be common phrase lengths in the exposition? Cite some examples.
4. Discuss in detail the phrase structure of mm. 31–49.

Harmonic/Tonal Structure

1. In the solo exposition, the move to the second tonal area is accomplished in a thematic passage that emphasizes three different tonalities. Locate this passage and identify the tonalities suggested, indicating where each begins.
2. Besides the dominant and the three tonalities you have identified in answer to H/T 1, what other tonality is heard in the solo exposition? Indicate its location.
3. List the tonalities that are heard in the development section and locate each by measure numbers.
4. Locate an example of:
   a. change of mode from major to parallel minor or the reverse;
   b. a Neapolitan sixth chord;
   c. a tonic prolongation.
5. Name the tonality in effect at m. 192; at m. 200. Provide a Roman numeral analysis of the intervening measures (mm. 193–199), explaining precisely the modulation between the two tonal centers.

Texture/Articulation/Dynamics

1. Discuss the changes in orchestration that accompany repeated material in the recapitulation.
2. Discuss some of the elements of textural variety to be found in the development.

Allegro
Tutti
2 Flauti
2 Fagotti
2 Corni in A
Clarinetto principale in A
Violino I
Violino II
Viola
Violoncello
Contrabasso
5
Fl.
Fg.
Cor (A)
Cl.pr. (A)
Vl.
Vla.
Vc. e Cb.
10
zu 2
Fl.
Fg.
Cor. (A)
Cl.pr. (A)
Vl.
Vla.
Vc. e Cb.
14
zu 2
Fl.
Fg.
Cor. (A)
Cl.pr. (A)
Vl.
Vla.
Vc. e Cb.

17
Fl.
Fg.
Cor. (A)
Cl. pr. (A)
Vl.
Vla.
Vc. e Cb.
zu 2
21
Fl.
Fg.
Cor. (A)
Cl. pr. (A)
Vl.
Vla.
Vc. e Cb.

24
Fl.
Fg.
Cor. (A)
Cl. pr. (A)
Vl.
Vla.
Vc.
Cb.
29
Fl.
Fg.
Cor. (A)
Cl. pr. (A)
Vl.
Vla.
Vc.
Cb.

33
37
41
44
Fl.
Fg.
Cor. (A)
Cl.pr. (A)
Vl.
Vla.
Vc. e Cb.
zu 2
tr
f
p

56
Solo
Fl.
Fg.
Cor. (A)
Cl.pr. (A)
Vl.
Vla.
Vc. e Cb.
p
61
Fg.
Cl.pr. (A)
Vl.
Vla.
tr
65
Fg.
Cl.pr. (A)
Vl.
Vla.
Vc. e Cb.

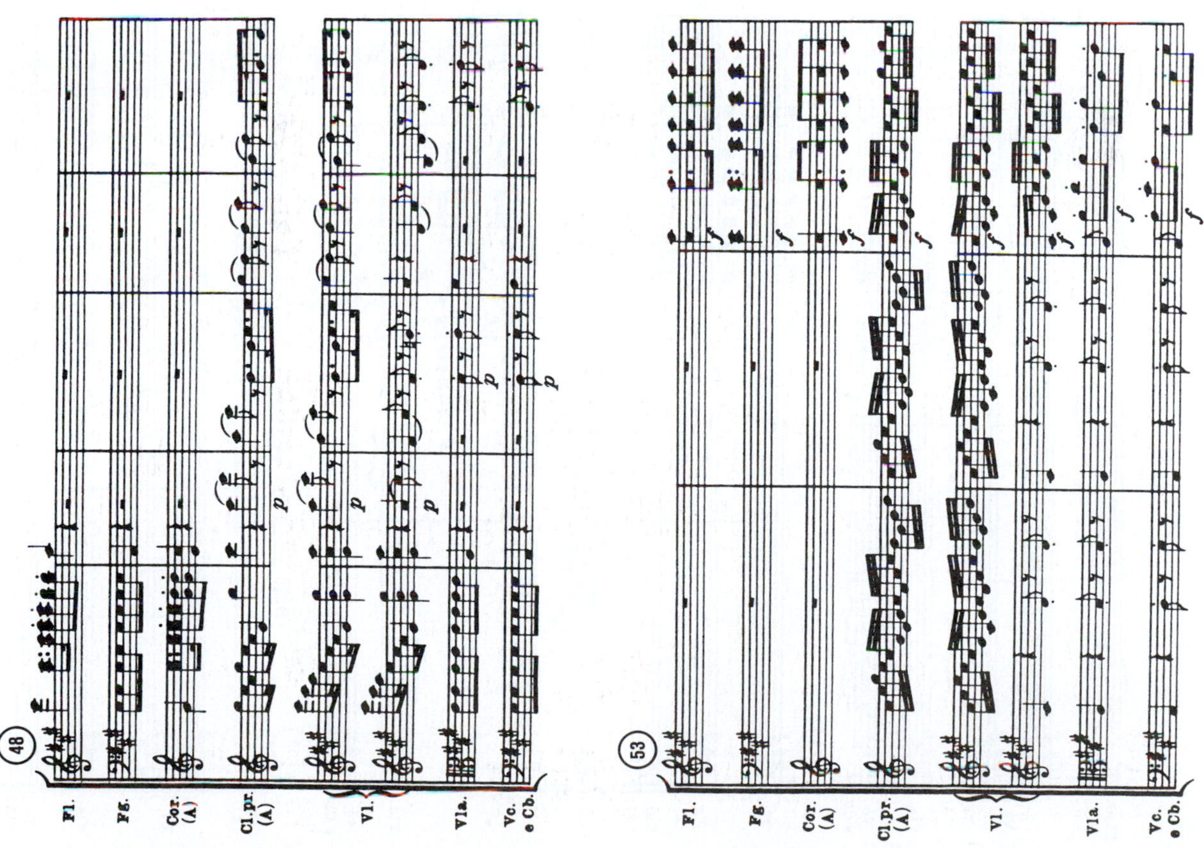
48
Fl.
Fg.
Cor. (A)
Cl.pr. (A)
Vl.
Vla.
Vc. e Cb.
p
53
Fl.
Fg.
Cor. (A)
Cl.pr. (A)
Vl.
Vla.
Vc. e Cb.
f

68
Cl.pr. (A)
Vl.
Vla.
Vc. e Cb.
73
Tutti
Fl.
Fg.
Cor. (A)
Cl.pr. (A)
Vl.
Vla.
Vc. e Cb.
77
Solo
Cl.pr. (A)
Vl.
Vla.
Vc. e Cb.
82
Cl.pr. (A)
Vl.
Vla.
Vc. e Cb.
86
Cl.pr. (A)
Vl.
Vla.
91
Cl.pr. (A)
Vl.
Vla.
Vc. e Cb.

96
Fl.
Fg.
Cor. (A)
Cl.pr. (A)
Vl.
Vla.
Vc. e Cb.
Tutti
zu 2

99
Fl.
Fg.
Cor. (A)
Cl.pr. (A)
Vl.
Vla.
Vc.
Cb.
Solo

104
Cl.pr. (A)
Vl.
Vla.
Vc. e Cb.
108
Cl.pr. (A)
Vl.
Vla.
Vc. Cb.
111
Cl.pr. (A)
Vl.
Vla.
Vc.
Cb.
116
Cl.pr. (A)
Vl.

121
Cl. pr. (A)
Vl.
Vla.
Vc.
126
Cl. pr. (A)
Vl.
Vla.
Vc.
Cb.
131
Cl. pr. (A)
Vl.
Vla.
Vc.
Cb.
135
Cl. pr. (A)
Vl.
Vla.
Vc. e Cb.
138
Cl. pr. (A)
Vl.
Vla.
Vc. e Cb.
141
Cl. pr. (A)
Vl.
Vla.
Vc. e Cb.

144
Cl.pr. (A)
Vl.
Vla.
Vc. e Cb.
147
Cl.pr. (A)
Vl.
Vla.
Vc. e Cb.
150
Cl.pr. (A)
Vl.
Vla.
Vc. e Cb.
153
Tutti
zu 2
Fl.
Fg.
Cor. (A)
Cl.pr. (A)
Vl.
Vla.
Vc. e Cb.
cresc.
157
zu 2
Fl.
Fg.
Cor. (A)
Cl.pr. (A)
Vl.
Vla.
Vc. e Cb.

160
Fl.
Fg.
Cor. (A)
Cl. pr. (A)
Vl.
Vla.
Vc. e Cb.
zu 2
163
168
zu 2
172
Solo
177

181
Cl. pr. (A)
Vl.
Vla.
Vc. e Cb.
184
Cl. pr. (A)
Vl.
Vla.
Vc. e Cb.
188
Fl.
Fg.
Cor. (A)
Cl. pr. (A)
Vl.
Vla.
Vc. e Cb.
Tutti
zu 2
193
Fl.
Fg.
Cor. (A)
Cl. pr. (A)
Vl.
Vla.
Vc. e Cb.
Solo
zu 2
199
Fl.
Fg.
Cor. (A)
Cl. pr. (A)
Vl.
Vla.
Vc. e Cb.
204
Cl. pr. (A)
Vl.
Vla.
Vc.
Vcllo.

209
Cl.pr. (A)
Vl.
Vla.
Vc. e Cb.
212
Fl.
Fg.
Cl.pr. (A)
Vl.
Vla.
Vc. e Cb.
zu 2
216
Fl.
Fg.
Cl.pr. (A)
Vl.
Vla.
Vc. e Cb.
222
Fl.
Fg.
Cor. (A)
Cl.pr. (A)
Vl.
Vla.
Vc. e Cb.
zu 2
cresc.
227 Tutti
Fl.
Fg.
Cor. (A)
Cl.pr. (A)
Vl.
Vla.
Vc.
Cb.
zu 2

231
Fl.
Fg.
Cor. (A)
Cl. pr. (A)
Vl.
Vla.
Vc.
Cb.
zu 2
235
240
244
Vc. e Cb.

247
Solo
Fl.
Fg.
Cor. (A)
Cl. pr. (A)
Vl.
Vla.
Vc. e Cb.
a 2
250
255
259
262
267
Tutti

270
Solo
Fl.
Fg.
Cor. (A)
Cl. pr. (A)
Vl.
Vla.
Vc. e Cb.
277
Cl. pr. (A)
Vl.
Vla.
Vc. e Cb.
283
Fl.
Cl. pr. (A)
Vl.
286
Tutti
Solo
zu 2
Fl.
Fg.
Cor. (A)
Cl. pr. (A)
Vl.
Vla.
Vc. e Cb.
290
Cl. pr. (A)
Vl.
Vla.
Vc.
Cb.
294
Cl. pr. (A)
Vl.
Vla.
Vc. e Cb.

298
Cl. pr. (A)
Vl.
Vla.
Vc.
Cb.
301
Cl. pr. (A)
Vl.
Vla.
Vc.
Cb.
p
306
Cl. pr. (A)
Vl.
Vla.
Vc.
Cb.
311
Cl. pr. (A)
Vl.
Vla.
Vc.
Cb.
315
Cl. pr. (A)
Vl.
p
p
Vla.
p
Vc. e Cb.
321
Cl. pr. (A)
Vl.
tr
tr
tr
Vla.
Vc. e Cb.

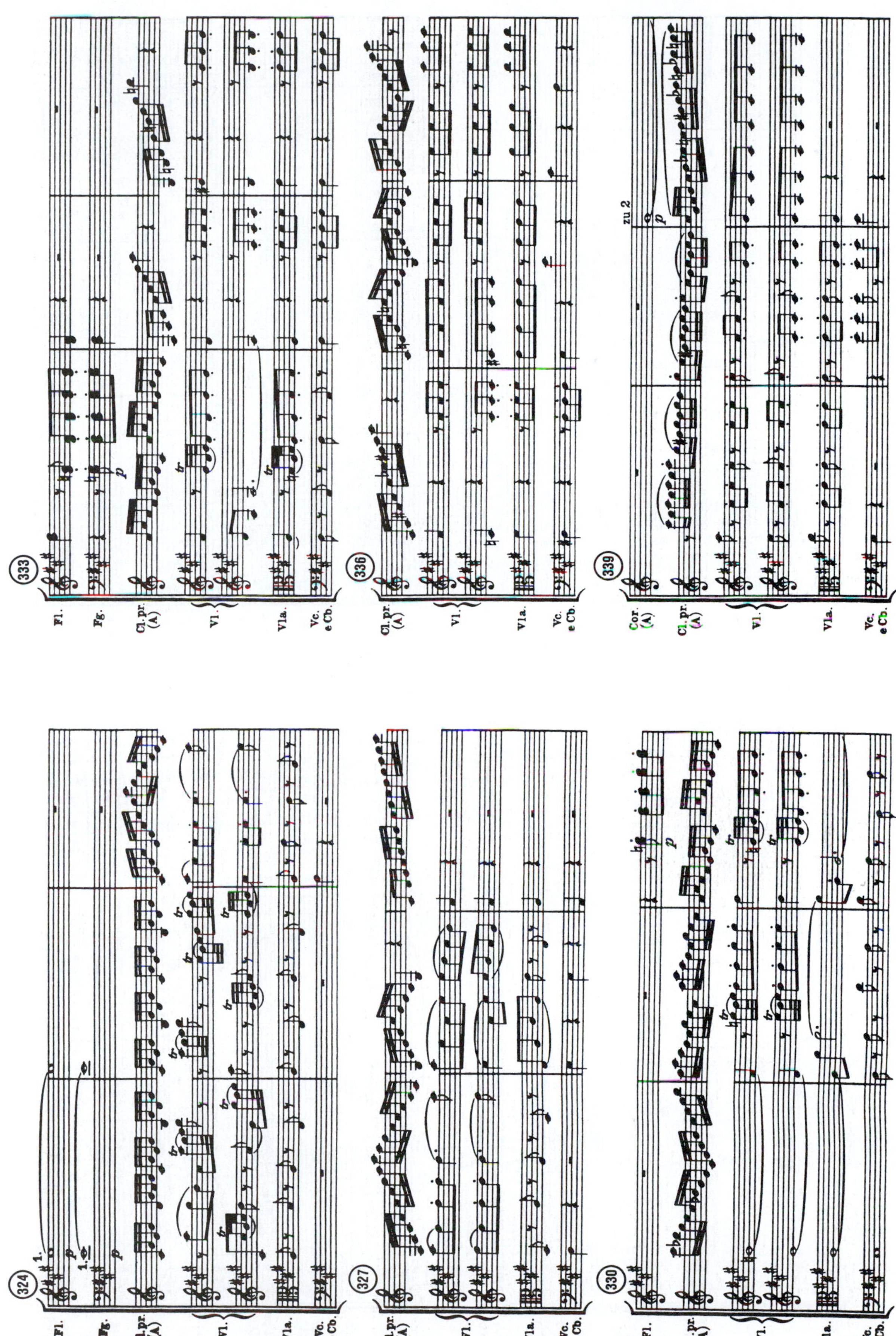
324
Fl.
Fg.
Cl. pr. (A)
Vl.
Vla.
Vc. e Cb.
327
330
333
336
339
Cor. (A)
zu 2

342
Tutti
zu 2
cresc.
Fl.
Fg.
Cor. (A)
Cl.pr. (A)
Vl.
Vla.
Vc. e Cb.
351
347
356

Ludwig van Beethoven

The transition from the Classical to the Romantic period can be seen in the works of Ludwig van Beethoven (1770–1827). In his music, sonata-form dimensions are expanded, and dividing lines between sections are often blurred. Beethoven's rhythms are often highly motivic—that is, they pervade his music. His melodies often contain sudden halts, tempo changes and extended syncopations. His harmonies may involve abrupt and sometimes distantly related tonal shifts, chromatic third relationships, changes of mode and enharmonic modulations. Beethoven's textures are predominantly homophonic in the early works, highly contrapuntal by the last period. Abrupt and extreme dynamic contrasts are common. His orchestral and piano textures are generally thicker than Haydn's or Mozart's and darker, owing to greater use of the lower register. His orchestration features greater soloistic use of the woodwinds.

PIANO SONATA OP. 7 *Third Movement*

Although the third movement of Op. 7 follows tradition in its overall structure, some unusual departures may be cited. Can you discover them? Likewise, this movement foreshadows in its harmonic language some of the bold experimentation that was to characterize much of Beethoven's later music. Plot the tonal plan of the Allegro. In what way is it tonally similar to Baroque examples of this form that you have studied? In what ways is it different? What time-honored compositional technique does Beethoven employ after the double bar? What is the most remote tonal region of the Allegro, where does it occur, how does Beethoven arrive at it, and how does he return to the home tonality? Can you discover the melodic line in the Minore section? It may aid your understanding of the phrase structure here if you renotate this part of the movement as a single-line melody with block chord accompaniment (or simply letter names for the underlying harmonies).

27
tr
37
mancando
pp
dolce.
47
pp
56
64
decresc.
pp
cresc.
73
f
ff
80
sf
sf
sf
sf
sf

87
Minore.
96
pp
ffp
101
ffp
106
p
decresc.
pp
112
p
ffp
117
ffp
122
f
p
ffp

Ludwig van Beethoven

PIANO SONATA OP. 10, NO. 1 *Third Movement*

The three piano sonatas of Opus 10, written between 1796 and 1798, were dedicated to the wife of a Viennese aristocrat, who, in appreciation, presented Beethoven with a magnificent horse (which Beethoven later sold!). It may suprise you to learn that certain features of Op. 10, No. 1 caused a contemporary reviewer to criticize the work for its abundance and "piling up" of musical ideas.

QUESTIONS FOR DISCUSSION

Formal Structure

1. This movement is in sonata form. There is one feature of the exposition that creates a sense of abruptness that may have led to the critic's remark mentioned in the introductory paragraph. Can you identify this feature?

2. Locate by measure number the beginnings of each of the sonata-form features present in this movement.
3. Upon what material from the exposition is the development based? the coda?

Melodic/Rhythmic Structure

1. Examine the rhythmic motive of mm. 55–57. Can you find an earlier precedent for this motive in the movement? Where else does it occur? Can you think of another work in which Beethoven employed this motive?
2. Describe the phrase-period structure of the first sixteen measures.
3. Discuss the means by which the four-measure phrase in mm. 28–32 is extended to become, instead, a ten-measure unit. Mention also any elements of repetition which exist in this passage.

Harmonic/Tonal Structure

1. Identify by Roman numeral the chords which occur at the following points: m. 3, first quarter; m. 7, first and second quarters; m. 38, fourth quarter; m. 39, second quarter; m. 41, fourth quarter.
2. Provide a Roman numeral analysis of the following passages:

   a. mm. 8–11;
   b. mm. 47–57.

3. Identify the tonality at the following points in the movement and describe the means by which Beethoven arrives at these tonalities:

   a. m. 17;
   b. m. 74;
   c. m. 86;
   d. m. 103;
   e. m. 115.

Texture/Articulation/Dynamics

1. Would you describe the overall texture of this movement as:

   a. highly homophonic;
   b. highly polyphonic;
   c. alternately homophonic and polyphonic?

   Support your answer.

2. Describe the contrapuntal techniques employed at mm. 22–26.
3. How would you characterize Beethoven's use of dynamics in this movement? Is there any point at which the dynamics strike you as unusual? Explain.

Composed 1798

Related reading: Allen Forte, *Introduction to Schenkerian Analysis* (New York: W.W. Norton and Company, 1982), pp. 280–293. An extensive and detailed examination of this movement, with numerous voice-leading graphs and a formal/tonal summary.

16
ff
p
ffp
fp
24
fp
31
ff
3
ff
35
3
ff
sf
p
40
ff
sf
ff
p
sf
47
p
sf
p
sf
52
cresc.
ff
sf
sf
p

58
64
69
cresc.
f
sf
73
ff
p
ffp
80
fp
cresc.
86
sf
ff
91
ff
sf
p

Ludwig van Beethoven

PIANO SONATA OP. 13 *Second Movement*

The second movement of Beethoven's well-known *Pathétique Sonata* is structured in such a way that certain musical material recurs at various points. Locate each of these "refrains." Are they identical or are they different, and if so, in what ways? What happens *between* the refrains? Using letters to identify the sections, provide a diagram of the form. What is the name of this form? Plot the tonal plan of the movement, paying particular attention to the means by which the modulation is accomplished between m. 41 and m. 44. What is the true relationship between the tonalities at these points? What is the relationship between these tonalities and the home key? Renotate the first eight measures of the movement in a four-voice chorale style (the range is slightly lower than that of a normal SATB setting, but the individual voice motion is clearly implied). What voice-leading principles from the Baroque era remain in evidence?

Adagio cantabile.
p
5
9
13
17
21
cresc.

25
cresc.
pp
p
30
35
pp
39
cresc.
42
sf
sf
sf
fp
decresc.
45
pp

48
rf
rf
cresc.
51
p
55
59
63
66
pp
69
rf
rf
rf
pp

Ludwig van Beethoven

PIANO SONATA OP. 26 *Third Movement*

This movement, a funeral march, has its counterpart in the slow movement of the Eroica symphony, composed two years later, in 1803. What is its form? Compare it formally to the *Piano Sonata Op. 7* on page 255. Do you observe any similar harmonic/tonal processes? This movement contains an abundance of nineteenth-century harmonic techniques. Look for such things as changes of mode disguised by enharmonic spellings, unusual chromatic third relationships, harmonies "borrowed" from the parallel key, and Neapolitan chords. What instrument is suggested by the passage in mm. 31–38?

22
tr
sf
p
26
cresc.
f
ff
30
p
cresc.
f
ff
Ped.
32
p
cresc.
f
ff
Ped.
sf
sf
34
p
cresc.
f
ff
Ped.
36
p
cresc.
f
ff
Ped.
sf
sf
38
1.
2.
p

41
cresc.
p
46
sf
p
51
cresc.
p
pp
55
sf
ff
sf
p
60
cresc.
tr
sf
p
cresc.
65
f
ff
p
cresc.
70
p
cresc.
p
sf
decresc.
pp
𝄮.
*

Ludwig van Beethoven

PIANO SONATA OP. 53 *First Movement and Adagio Introduction to the Rondo*

This sonata, written in 1804, was dedicated to Count Ferdinand von Waldstein, one of Beethoven's earliest patrons. Like the *Eroica Symphony*, written a year earlier, it exhibits expanded formal dimensions and pitch range (reflecting, perhaps, the composer's acquisition in 1803 of a new piano with a larger keyboard). Its unusual key relationships, its careful instructions regarding pedaling, phrasing and dynamics, and its virtuoso elements reflect a conception of piano music that was to dominate the medium for generations. The *Questions for Discussion* that follow pertain to the first movement. In addition, there is much of interest in the short Adagio that serves as a link to the Rondo finale. Consider its form and also how it, like the first movement, appears to begin "out of the key." The first phrase is saturated with harmonic chromaticism and invites careful study.

QUESTIONS FOR DISCUSSION

Formal Structure

1. Label the principal divisions of this movement and the smaller areas within those divisions.
2. Are all the features commonly found in a full-blown sonata-form movement present here? How many themes do you hear after the arrival at the second tonal area? Might any be considered a codetta?
3. Opinions may differ as to the precise beginning of the transition between the first and second tonal areas. Name at least two possible locations and discuss the merits of each point of view.
4. Into how many subsections does the development divide and what is the basis for the divisions?
5. Discuss the major differences between the exposition and the recapitulation.

Melodic/Rhythmic Structure

1. Identify some large-scale stepwise patterns that appear within the first tonal area of the exposition. At least two considerably longer step progressions appear early in the development. Identify them.
2. To what previous material might the theme of the second tonal area be related? Describe the phrase-period structure of this theme.
3. The material of mm. 92–95 is given elaborate sequential treatment in subsequent measures. Determine precisely the length of the pattern(s) that is (are) stated sequentially, identify the repetitions, and classify the sequences as real or tonal.
4. The melodic material of mm. 249–252 is compressed and repeated sequentially in subsequent measures. Describe precisely this compression and also identify the sequences.

Harmonic/Tonal Structure

1. Although the home key is C major, little actual reference to this key is made at the beginning of the movement. Give an account of the various tonalities suggested in the first thirty measures of music.
2. Describe the harmonic relationships between the first and second tonal areas of the exposition. How is this relationship different in the recapitulation?
3. The most remote tonal region of the movement is reached in m. 124. What is it? What is its relationship to the home key? Explain the logical method by which Beethoven arrives at this tonality.
4. Provide a harmonic analysis of mm. 124–136. Be sure to explain the logic of the seemingly remote relationship between the harmonies of m. 125 and m. 126. What type of modulation is involved here?
5. At what point in the development does the music clearly become a harmonic preparation for the recapitulation? Describe this passage from both a melodic and a harmonic standpoint.
6. Beethoven employs a change of mode several times in the recapitulation. Locate and describe these occurrences.

Texture/Articulation/Dynamics

1. Describe precisely the role of texture in defining the subsections of the development.
2. Within this prevailingly homophonic movement, a few polyphonic passages can be found. Locate them.
3. Cite a few instances where Beethoven uses dynamics to presage or to underscore an important musical change.

Composed 1804

Related reading: David Beach, Donald Mintz, Robert Palmer, "Analysis Symposium," *Journal of Music Theory*, Vol. 13, No. 2 (1969), p. 186f. Detailed discussion of the *Introduzione*. The first and third articles apply differing analytical methods to the movement and the second essay considers its relationship to the preceding and following movements.

Allegro con brio.
pp
4
pp
8
cresc.
f
sf
sf
12
decresc.
p
pp
16
pp
19
cresc.
22
p

25
cresc.
28
f
sf
sf
sf
31
decresc.
decresc.
p
p
35
dolce e molto ligato.
cresc.
sf
p
41
cresc.
3
p
dolce
44
cresc.
sf
3
47
p
cresc.

50
53
56
decresc.
cresc.
59
62
65
68
decresc.

71
pp
cresc.
tr
74
fp
fp
79
cresc.
p
84
cresc.
p
1.
pp
2.
cresc.
p
88
cresc.
p
pp
93
97
cresc.
f

100
p
cresc.
103
f
pp
106
109
cresc.
112
f
116
120

123
126
129
132
135
f
p
138
f
p
f
decresc.
141
pp

144
cresc.
147
150
f
153
sf
sf
ff
A' Recapitulation 1st period area
156
pp
159
pp
163
cresc.

166
f
sf
sf
decresc.
p
pp
171
pp
174
f pp
177
pp
180
cresc.
183
transition
p

185
188
cresc.
f
sf
sf
sf
190
decresc.
decresc.
193
p
p
dolce
198
cresc.
sf
p
cresc.
p
3
204
dolce
cresc.
sf

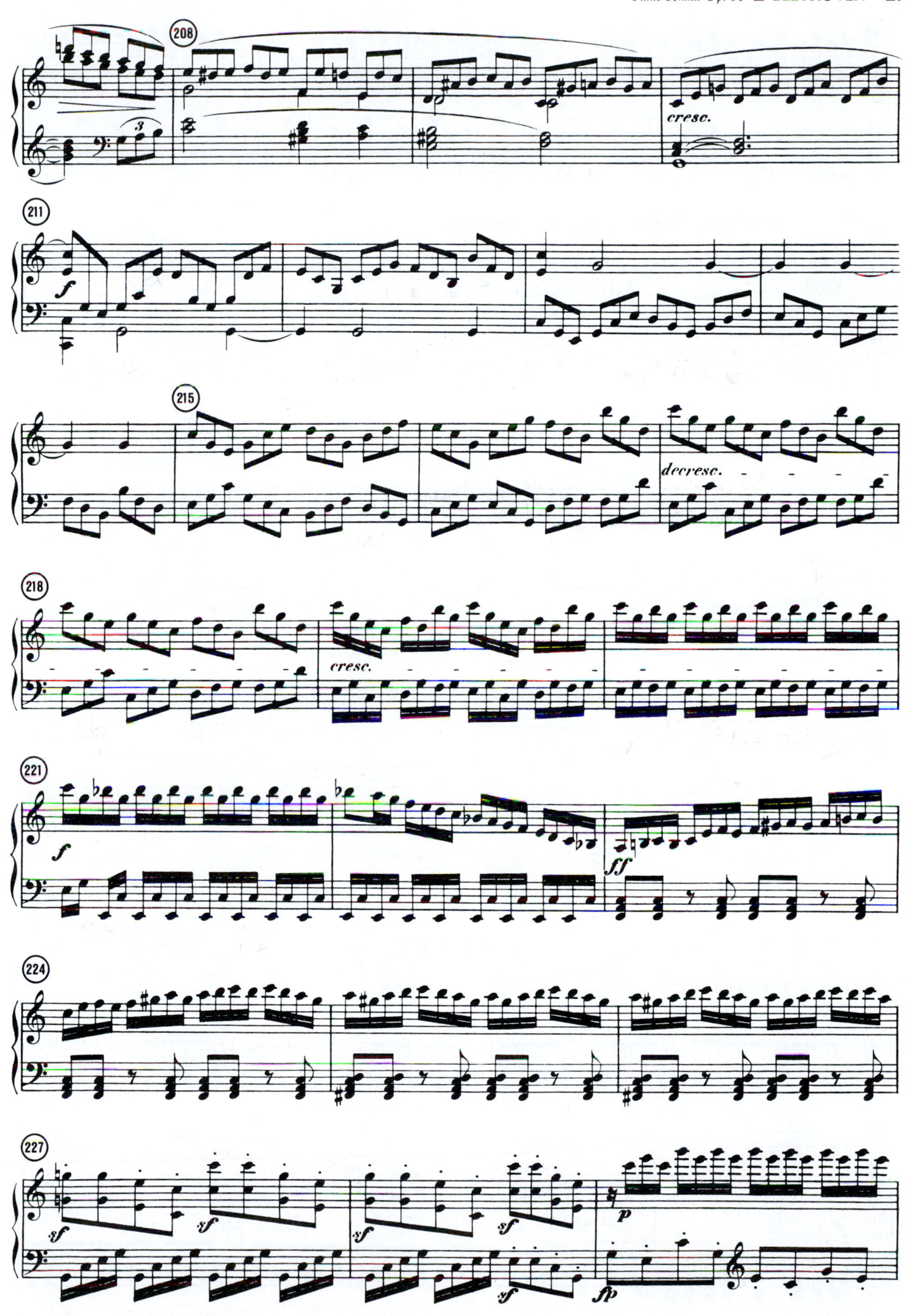
208
cresc.
211
f
215
decresc.
218
cresc.
221
f
ff
224
227
sf
sf
sf
sf
sf
p
fp

230
decresc.
pp
233
cresc.
tr
fp
237
fp
241
cresc.
p
245
cresc.
p
cresc.
p
pp
250
f
p
254
f
sf
sf
sf
sf
ff

258
f p
cresc.
pp
262
pp
266
269
cresc.
272
f
sf
275
ff
3
f
sf
278
fp

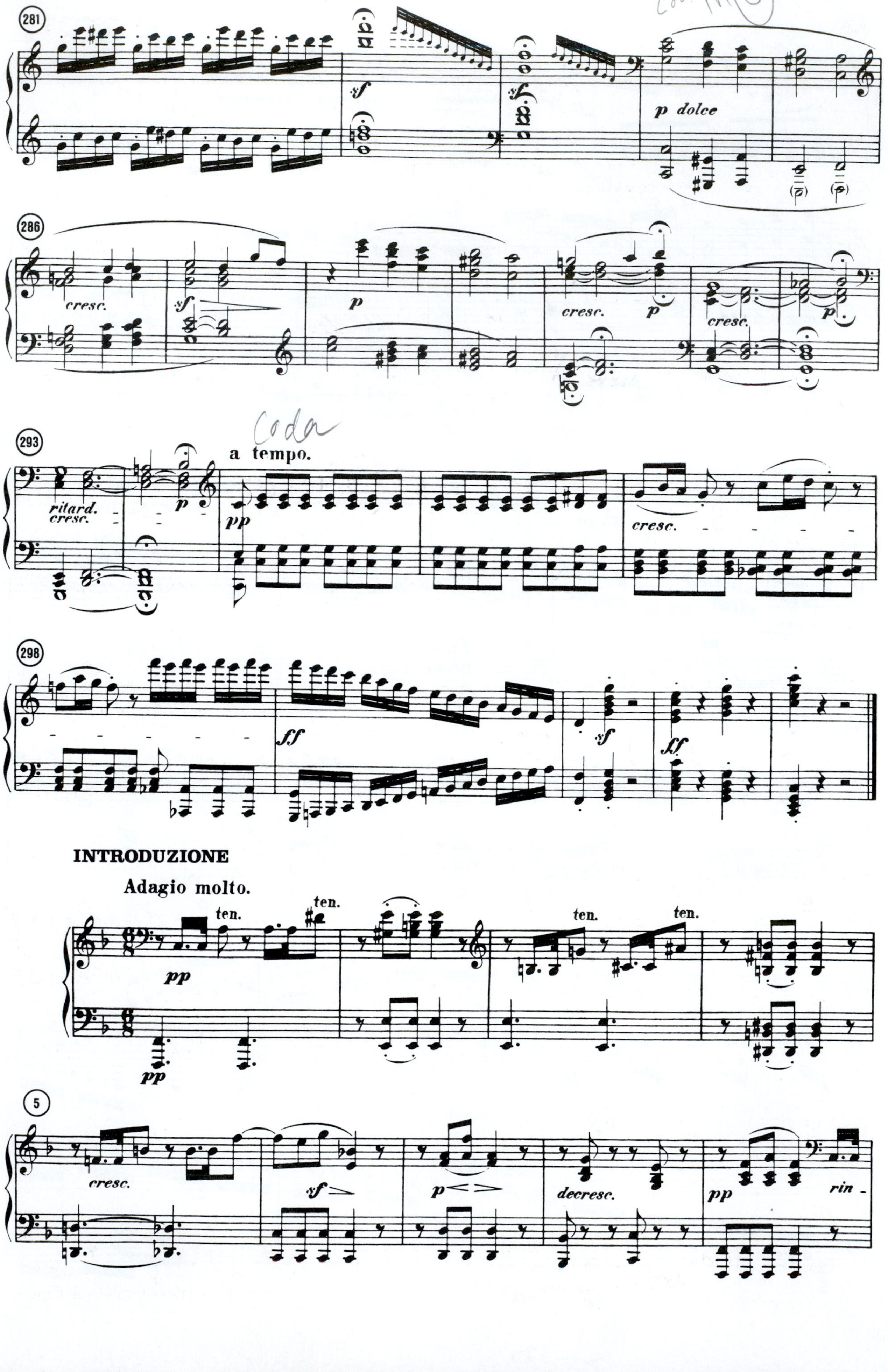

281
sf
sf
p dolce
286
cresc.
sf
p
cresc.
p
cresc.
p
293
a tempo.
ritard.
cresc.
p
pp
cresc.
298
ff
sf
ff
INTRODUZIONE
Adagio molto.
ten.
ten.
pp
ten.
ten.
pp
5
cresc.
sf
p
decresc.
pp
rin -

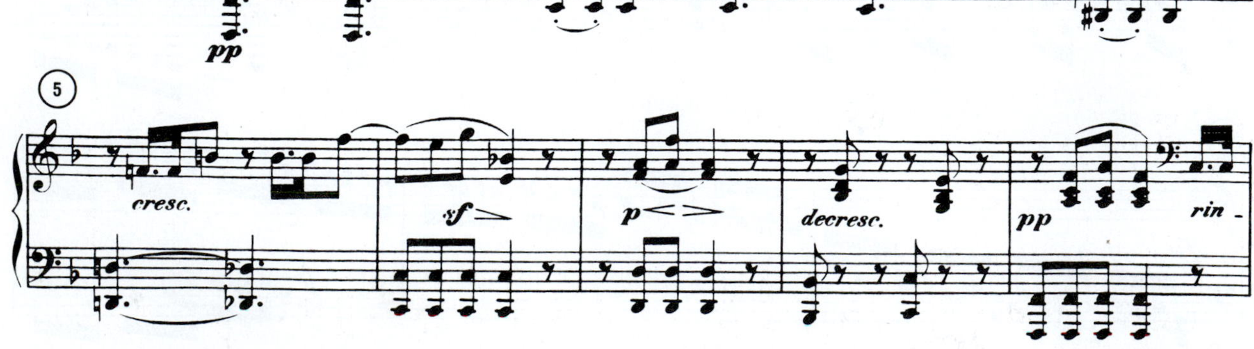

10
forzato
sf
sf
decresc.
p
rinf.
sf
sf
decresc.
13
p
cresc.
sf
cresc.
sf
16
decresc.
pp
cresc.
pp
20
cresc.
pp
cresc.
23
sf
sf
sf
sf
decresc.
26
pp
pp
sf
attacca subito il Rondo.

Ludwig van Beethoven

STRING QUARTET OP. 18, NO. 1 *First Movement*

Opus 18 comprises six string quartets written between 1798 and 1800. The first movement of No. 1 is intensely motivic. Trace, for example, the melodic-rhythmic figure of m. 1 throughout the movement. Intense motivic organization of this sort, however, is not the only Beethoven hallmark. Formally and harmonically, the movement foreshadows the bold experimentation which was to characterize Beethoven's later work. Where, exactly, does the transition to the second tonal area begin? Through what distant tonality does it pass on its way? How many themes are present in the second tonal area? The development is harmonically restless, imitative and, at one point, intensely contrapuntal. What is the harmonic relationship between its beginning and the end of the exposition? At one point in the development, the harmonic rhythm slows dramatically. Locate this point. Explain the logic of the ensuing chord succession with respect to the movement's home key. In a sonata-form recapitulation, the second tonal area material typically reappears in the home key. Does it do so in this movement? How is the transition affected? In Beethoven's later sonata-form movements, the coda was substantially expanded. How is the coda in this early work prophetic in that regard?

28
37
44
52
59
f
p
pp
cresc.
sf
ff
decresc.
tr

68
cresc.
sf
p
77
f
fp
83
fp
p cresc.
95
1
sf
ff
106
cresc.

112
f
f
f
f
f
f
f
f
119
fp
f
p
pp
pp
pp
fp
fp
pp
fp
fp
pp
129
f
sf
sf
f
f
sf
sf
f
f
f
sf
sf
f
f
sf
sf
138
sf
sf
f
sf
sf
sf
sf
f
sf
sf
sf
sf
f
sf
sf
f
sf
sf
147
sf
sf
sf
sf
fp
sf
sf
sf
sf
fp
sf
sf
sf
sf
fp
sf
sf
fp

155
fp
fp
fp
fp
164
sf
sf
sf
sf
171
sf
sf
177
sf
cresc.
ff
p
187
p
p
p
p
cresc.

199
tr
tr
tr
cresc.
f
cresc.
f
cresc.
f
cresc.
f
209
p
p
p
p
cresc.
cresc.
cresc.
cresc.
215
ff
ff
ff
ff
decresc.
p
p
p
p
224
cresc.
sf
cresc.
sf
cresc.
sf
233
p
cresc.
f
fp
cresc.
p
cresc.
f
fp
p
cresc.
f
fp
p
cresc.
f
fp

241
250
263
270
279
cresc.
f
fp
pp
sf
ff
p
tr

Ludwig van Beethoven

SYMPHONY NO. 7 IN A MAJOR OP. 92 *Second Movement*

Beethoven completed his Seventh Symphony, which Richard Wagner (1813–1883) called the "apotheosis of the dance," in 1812. The second movement was encored at the first performance and has since been a favorite among audiences. In this movement, two important compositional processes—variation and recurrence—are integrated. As a result, formal analysis can take place at two levels. Note the simplicity of the theme heard in mm. 3–26. How would you describe its form? What elements from it are retained as the movement progresses?

Beethoven liked nothing better than to take the most elementary of materials and construct a highly sophisticated piece of music from it. Describe the way in which the music gradually builds from a modest beginning to a full orchestral texture. Consider also the strong musical contrast that is present at the broadest formal level in this movement. Note not only the precise means by which this contrast is achieved but also the method by which the sections are unified.

Beethoven was highly skilled in the art of counterpoint and incorporated fugal writing in many of his works, especially late in his career. Locate and analyze a passage in this movement that illustrates his contrapuntal skill.

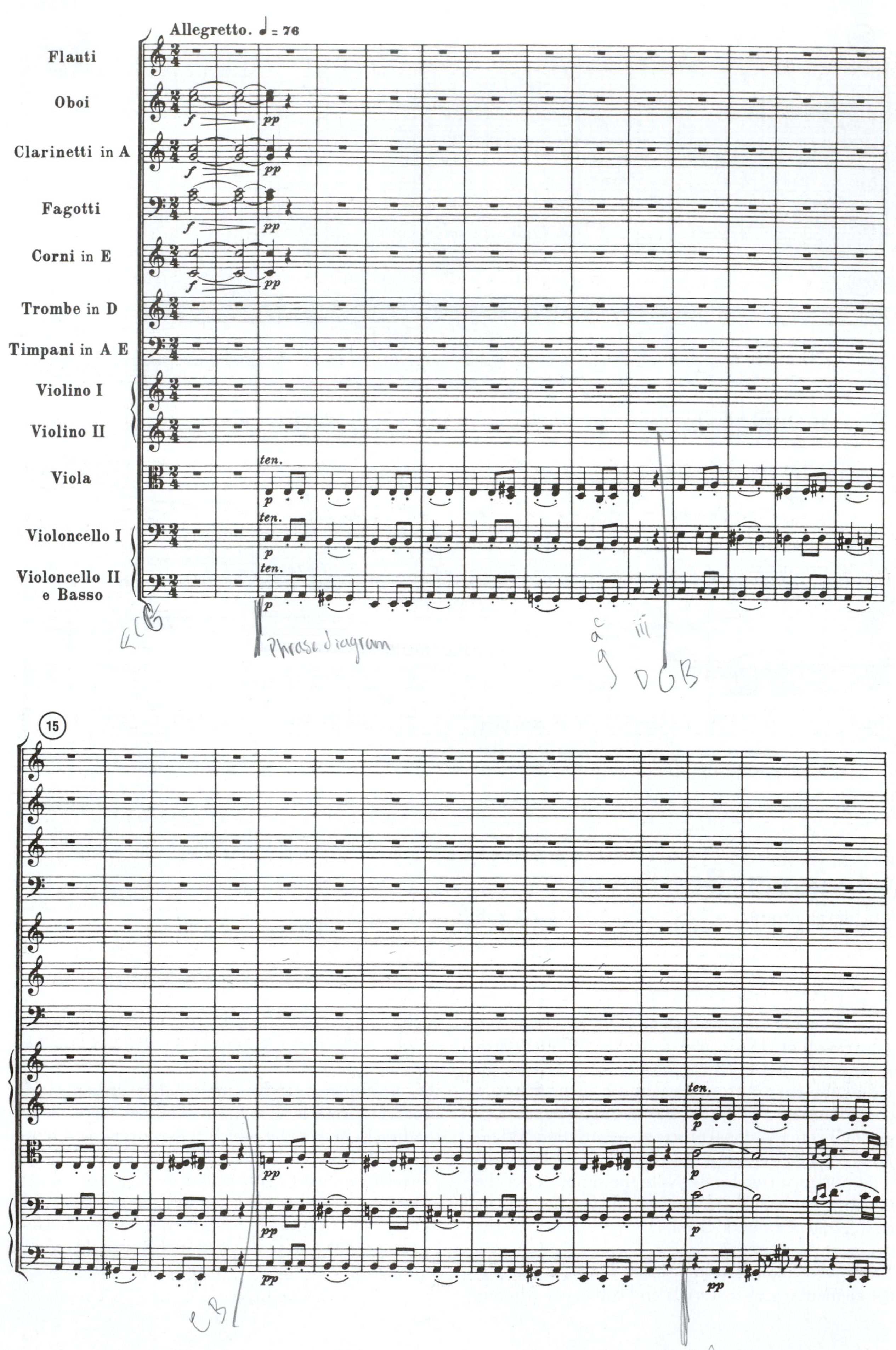
Allegretto. ♩ = 76
Flauti
Oboi
Clarinetti in A
Fagotti
Corni in E
Trombe in D
Timpani in A E
Violino I
Violino II
Viola
Violoncello I
Violoncello II e Basso
ten.
15

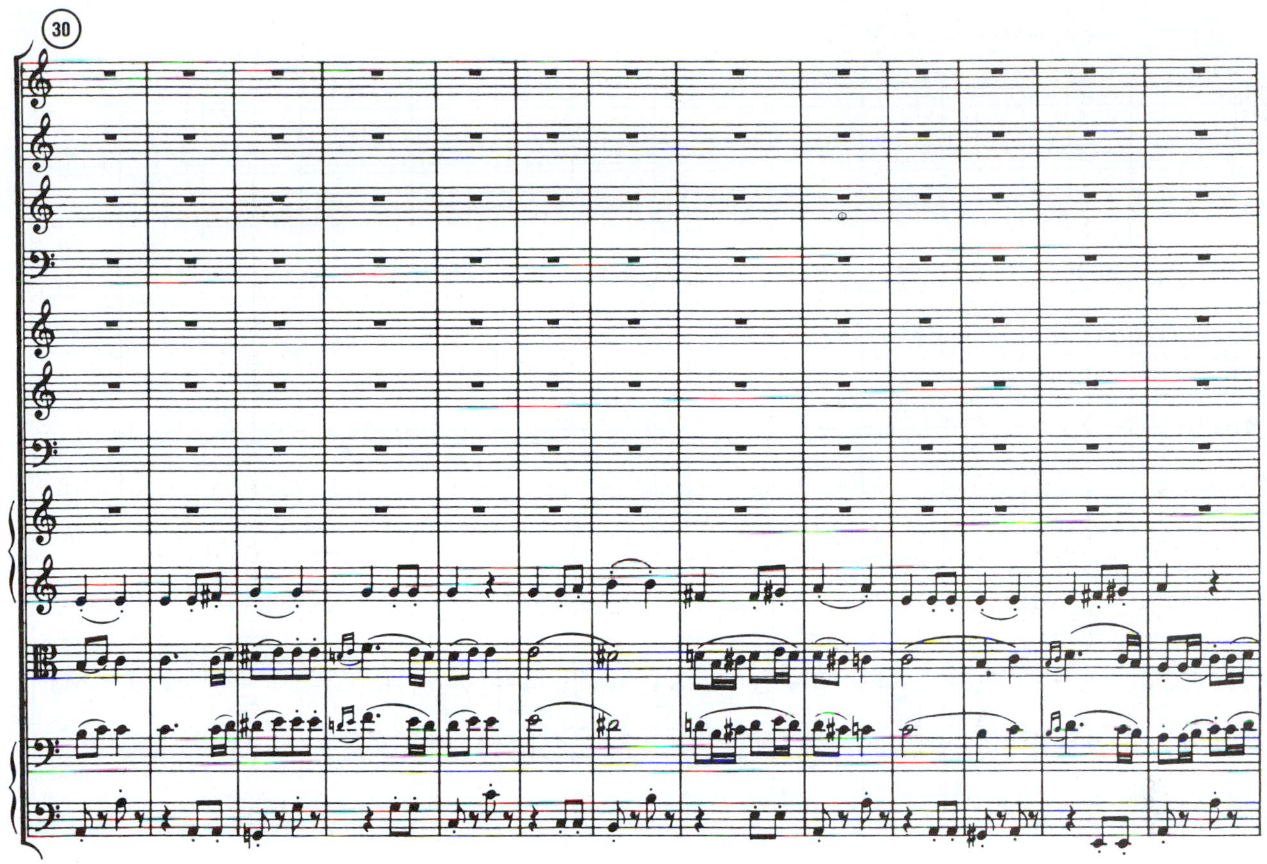

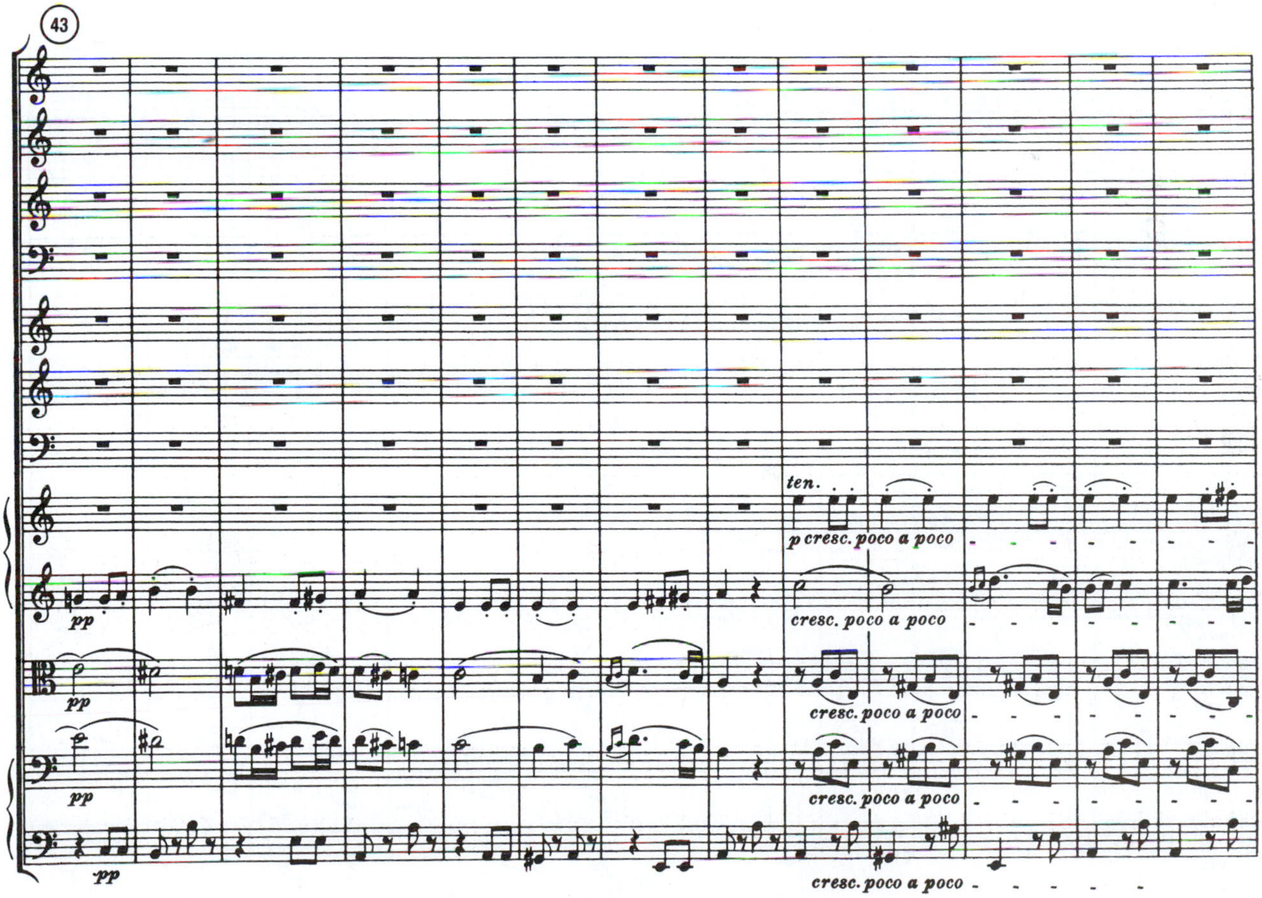

43

ten.

p cresc. poco a poco

pp

cresc. poco a poco

pp

cresc. poco a poco

pp

cresc. poco a poco

pp

cresc. poco a poco

56
cresc.
cresc.
f
f
f
f
f
69
cresc.
ten.
ff
ten.
ff
ten.
ff
ten.
ff
ten.
cresc.
ff
ff
ff
più f
ff
più f
ff
più f
ff
più f
ff
più f
ff

80
ten.
90
dim.
dimin.
sempre dim.
p

101
dolce
dolce
p
p
p
p
pizz.
pizz.
p
p
112
p
II.

123
cresc.
dimin.
p
133
dolce dim.
pp

143
cresc.
cresc.
cresc.
cresc.
p dolce
p dolce
p dolce
cresc.
sempre stacc.
pizz.
cresc.
cresc.
arco
arco
pizz.
cresc.
pizz.
cresc.
153
sempre stacc.
sempre p
sempre p

161

169
p
p

177
cresc.
dimin.
pp
arco.

185
sempre pp
pp
arco.

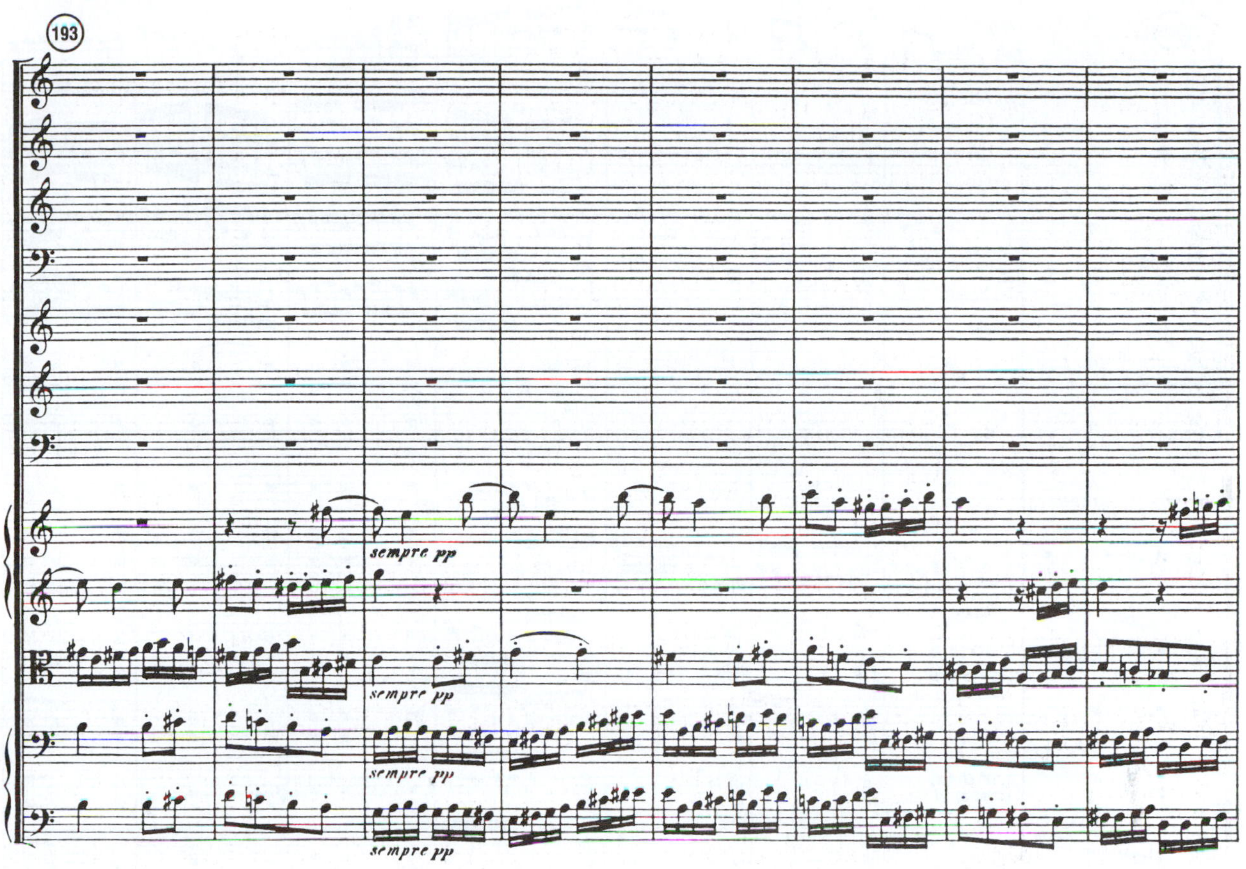
193
sempre pp
sempre pp
sempre pp
sempre pp

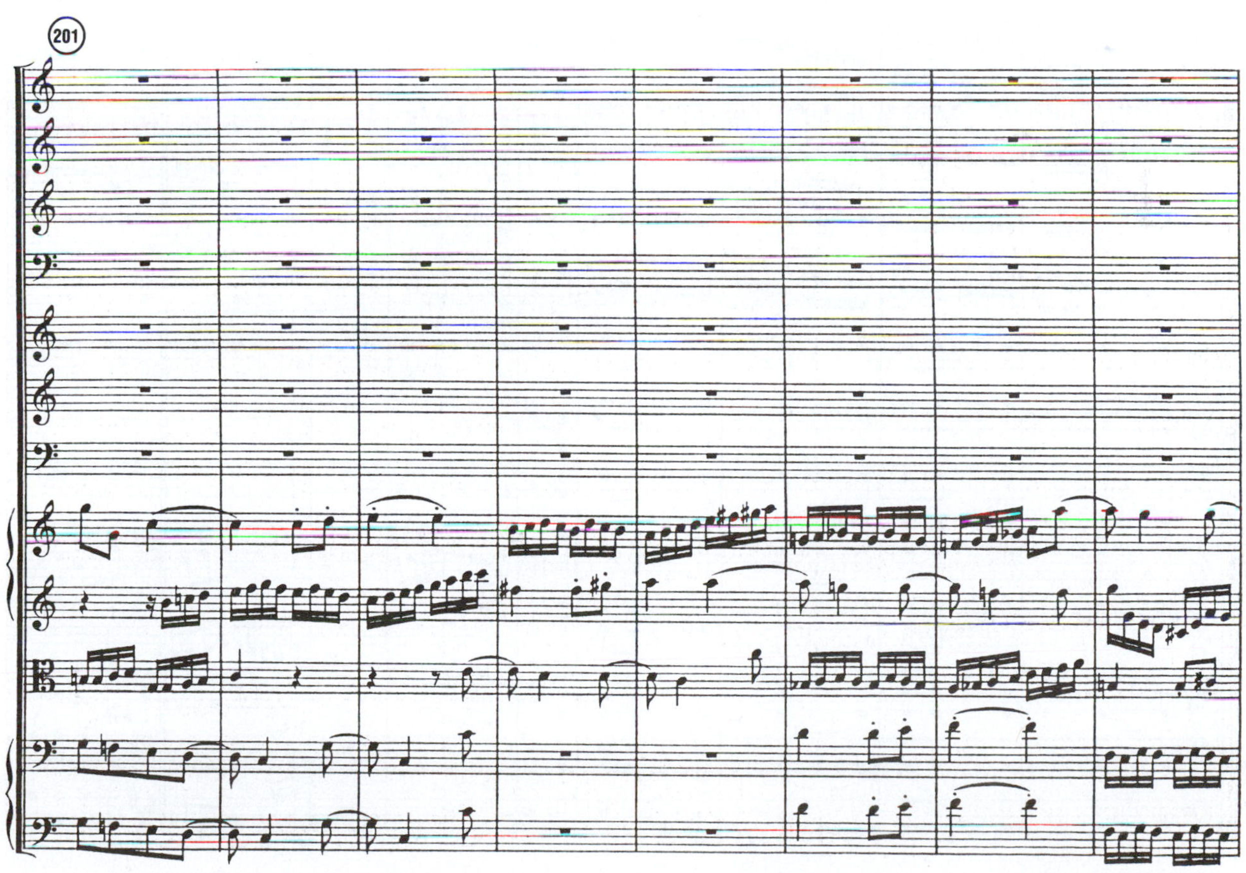
201

209
ten.
p cresc.
pp
cresc.
a 2
ten.
p cresc.
a 2
ten.
cresc.
ff
a 2
cresc.
a 2
cresc.
cresc.
ten.
cresc.
cresc.
cresc.
cresc.
217
ten.
p
ten.
dolce
p
ten.
dolce
p
ten.
ten.
ten.
ten.
ten.
p
pizz.
p
pizz.
p

226
p
p
p
237
dimin.
ten.
pp
ff
arco

249
ten.
ff
pp
p
pizz.

264
pp
ten.
f
arco.

Unit IV

THE ROMANTIC PERIOD

The music of the Romantic period (ca. 1815–1900) was characterized by unprecedented diversity. Emphasis was on both the very large and the very small, from the lengthy tone poems of Liszt and Strauss and the music dramas of Wagner to the intimate songs and piano miniatures of Schubert and Schumann. The Classical concern for clarity and balance was subordinated to the desire for freedom of expression and dramatic contrast. Major genres and their most important composers were:

Song:
Schubert, Schumann, Brahms, Wolf, Mussorgsky, Fauré, Mahler

Piano music:
Schubert, Mendelssohn, Schumann, Chopin, Liszt, Brahms

Chamber music:
Schubert, Schumann, Brahms, Franck, Dvořák

Orchestral music:
Schubert, Mendelssohn, Schumann, Berlioz, Liszt, Brahms, Dvořák, Bruckner, Tchaikovsky, Mahler, Strauss

Opera:
Weber, Berlioz, Verdi, Wagner

Romantic melodies were generally more expansive and flowing than those of preceding and following eras. Increased chromaticism both reflected and influenced the expanding harmonic vocabulary. In order to convey emotional extremes, composers called for tempos both faster and slower than previously.

In the nineteenth century, chromatic third relationships and mode mixture rivaled the tonic-dominant polarity that had dominated Classical music. Abrupt modulations to remote keys became commonplace, and a new vocabulary of altered chords was created through extensive melodic chromaticism. Late in the period, composers produced passages that at times eluded tonal identification. In short, the resources of functional harmony were explored to their fullest.

Although polyphonic textures may readily be found in nineteenth-century music, they rarely approach the complexity and rigor of Baroque counterpoint. Orchestral color, a prime means of expression, is manifest in generous use of expressive markings, string instrument effects such as tremolando, pizzicato, and harmonics, use of solo instruments in unusual combinations, and the addition to the orchestra of such instruments as the harp, English horn, trombone, tuba and contrabassoon. These last two instruments, along with the practice of subdividing the string section, impart a darker tone and thicker texture to the Romantic orchestra.

The following chronological chart is for your reference. You may wish to check the box most closely representing the formal process as you complete your study of each work. This will aid you in future reference to the music of this unit. An additional space is provided for further comments or information.

R = rondo
B = binary, rounded binary or binary variant
T = ternary or compound ternary
S = strophic or modified strophic
TC = through-composed
O = other

YEAR	COMPOSER	WORK/KEY	FORM/PROCESS						COMMENTS AND FURTHER INFORMATION
			R	B	T	S	TC	O	
1816	Schubert	*Originaltänze* Op. 9, No. 3 A-flat major							
1816	Schubert	*Originaltänze* Op. 9, No. 23 B major							
1822	Schubert	"Die Liebe hat gelogen" C minor							
1823	Schubert	"Ungeduld," from *Die Schöne Müllerin* A major							
1823	Schubert	"Pause," from *Die Schöne Müllerin* B-flat major							
1827	Schubert	*Impromptu* Op. 142, No. 2 A-flat major							
1829	Chopin	*Valse* Op. 69, No. 2 B minor							
1831	Chopin	*Nocturne* Op. 9, No. 2 E major							
1833	Chopin	*Mazurka* Op. 17, No. 2 E minor							

YEAR	COMPOSER	WORK/KEY	FORM/PROCESS						COMMENTS AND FURTHER INFORMATION
			R	B	T	S	TC	O	
1833	Chopin	*Mazurka* Op. 17, No. 4 A minor							
1835	Schumann	"Valse noble," from *Carnaval* Op. 9 B-flat major							
1838	Schumann	"Curious Story," from *Kinderscenen* Op. 15 D major							
1838	Schumann	"An Important Event," from *Kinderscenen* Op. 15 A major							
1838	Schumann	"By the Fireside," from *Kinderscenen* Op. 15 F major							
1839	Chopin	*Prelude* Op. 28, No. 4 E minor							
1839	Chopin	*Prelude* Op. 28, No. 9 E major							
1839	Chopin	*Prelude* Op. 28, No. 20 C minor							
1839	Chopin	*Prelude* Op. 28, No. 21 B-flat major							
1840	Schumann	"Wenn ich in deine Augen seh," from *Dichterliebe* Op. 48 G major							
1840	Schumann	"Ich will meine Seele tauchen," from *Dichterliebe* Op. 48 B minor							
1840	Schumann	"Das ist en Flöten und Geigen," from *Dichterliebe* Op. 48 G minor							

YEAR	COMPOSER	WORK/KEY	FORM/PROCESS						COMMENTS AND FURTHER INFORMATION
			R	B	T	S	TC	O	
1848	Schumann	"Soldier's March," from 43 *Klavierstücke für die Jugend* Op. 68 G major							
1848	Schumann	"Nordic Song," from 43 *Klavierstücke für die Jugend* Op. 68 F major							
1848	Liszt	"Il Pensieroso," from *Années de Pèlerinage* Bk. II C-sharp minor							
1859	Wagner	*Prelude* from *Tristan und Isolde* A minor*							
1859	Wagner	*Liebesnacht* from *Tristan und Isolde* A-flat major							
1882	Fauré	"Chanson d'Amour" Op. 27, No. 1 G major							
1888	Wolf	"Gebet," No. 28 from *Mörike Songs* E major							
1888	Wolf	"Wer sich der Einsamkeit ergiebt," No. 1 from *Goethe Songs* A minor							
1892	Brahms	*Ballade* Op. 118, No. 3 G minor							
1895	Brahms	*Sonata No. 1 for Clarinet and Piano* Op. 120 II: A-flat major							
1896	Brahms	"O Tod, wie bitter bist Du," from *Vier Ernste Gesänge* E minor							
1904	Mahler	"Nun will die Sonn' so hell aufgeh'n," from *Kindertotenlieder* D minor							

*Refer to page 358 regarding the tonality of this excerpt.

Franz Peter Schubert

Franz Schubert (1797–1828) produced an amazingly large output during his short life, much of it vocal music. His *Lieder* are primarily strophic, modified strophic, or through-composed, the form generally reflecting the text. His melodies range from lyrical and expansive to simple and folklike. His harmonies range from completely diatonic to richly chromatic. Remote and complex modulations, mixture of major and minor modes, use of all types of third relationship, and abundant Neapolitan and augmented sixth chords (often enharmonic) characterize his style. Schubert's normally homophonic textures often involve a syncopated, repeated chord accompaniment that can almost be regarded as a trademark.

ORIGINALTÄNZE OP. 9, NOS. 3 and 23

Schubert wrote numerous short dances for the piano. The two examples that follow have much in common. Can you identify their similar features? How long are the phrases in these works? Do they combine to form periods, and if so, what kind—parallel or contrasting? Examine each work for sequences (both melodic and harmonic) and tonicizations. Also, consider the form of each.

Franz Peter Schubert
"DIE LIEBE HAT GELOGEN"

This short song contains within its eighteen bars a wealth of nineteenth-century harmonic devices, including augmented sixth chords, the Neapolitan sixth chord, chromatic third relationships, and mode mixture of all sorts. A first step toward harmonic analysis might be to identify the rapidly changing references to different tonalities. Some of these tonal references can only be completely understood by recognizing how certain chords function enharmonically. An example is the first chord of m. 16. In addition to making a detailed harmonic study, you should seek to understand how the various musical elements serve to create the form of this piece.

Composed 1822

Related reading: Deborah Stein, "Schubert's 'Die Liebe hat gelogen': The deception of mode and mixture," *Journal of Musicological Research,* Vol. 9 (1989), pp. 109–131. A study of Schubert's use of harmonic deception and metric ambiguity in this work to portray the poetic idea of betrayal and deception. Includes a voice-leading graph of the song.

"DIE LIEBE HAT GELOGEN"

Love has been untrue,
Sorrow weighs heavy,
Everyone around me has been deceptive!

Hot [tear] drops flow
Steadily down my cheeks,
Stop, my heart, your beating,
Poor heart, Stop!

Love has been untrue,
Sorrow weighs heavy,
Everyone around me has been deceptive!

Franz Peter Schubert

DIE SCHÖNE MÜLLERIN *"Ungeduld" and "Pause"*

Among the best known of Schubert's *Lieder* are those contained in the cycle, *Die schöne Müllerin* ("The lovely miller woman"), composed on the poetry of Wilhelm Müller in 1823. The two selections that follow illustrate different formal principles. What are they and what features of the text might have prompted Schubert to use these forms? Each song contains other special features worth studying. "Ungeduld"("Impatience") contains sequences and a variety of secondary harmonic functions, including a *secondary* augmented sixth chord. (Identify these.) "Pause" ("Interlude") contains modulations to both closely related and remote tonalities. Consider, for example, the modulations that occur at m. 33 and m. 56 as well as the means by which Schubert returns to the home key from both of these tonalities. A particularly poignant passage occurs at mm. 63–77. What common nineteenth-century harmonic technique initiates this passage? Although these measures seem to move far afield, everything can be explained in functional harmonic terms. Both songs contain short piano introductions and postludes, typical of many Schubert songs.

"Ungeduld"

12
Kie_selstein, ich möcht' es sän auf je_des fri_sche Beet, mit Kres_sen_sa_men, der es
rein und klar, bis er sie spräch mit mei_nes Mun_des Klang, mit mei_nes Her_zens vol_lem,
16
schnell ver_räth, auf je_den weissen Zet_tel möcht' ich's schrei_ben: Dein ist mein
hei_ssem Drang, dann säng' er hell durch ih_re Fen_ster_schei_ben: Dein ist mein
20
Herz, dein ist mein Herz und soll es e - - wig,
Herz, dein ist mein Herz und soll es e - - wig,
24
e - - wig_ blei - - - ben. ben.
e - - wig_ blei - - - ben.
1.2.3.
4.
f

"UNGEDULD"

I would fain carve it on the bark of every tree,
I would fain engrave it on every pebble,
I would like to sow it in every fresh garden bed
With seeds of cress that would quickly tell the tale;
On every white sheet of paper I would like to write it:
"Thine is my heart, and will stay thine forever!"

I would like to train a young starling
Till it could speak the words pure and clear,
Till it could speak them with the sound of my voice,
With the warm passion of my heart:
Then it would sing clearly through her window panes:
"Thine is my heart, and will stay thine forever!"

I would like to breathe it into the morning breezes,
And whisper it through the busy woodland;
O, could it radiate from every flower chalice!
Could their fragrance bear it to her from near and far!
O waves, can you set nothing but mill-wheels going?
"Thine is my heart, and will stay thine forever!"

I thought it must be there in my eyes,
That one could see it burning in my cheeks,
That it could be read from my silent mouth,
That very breath of mine would tell it clearly to her;
Yet she notices nothing of all my anxious longing:
"Thine is my heart, and will stay thine forever!"

"Pause"

Composed 1823

Related reading: "Schenker and chromatic tonicization: A reappraisal," in *Schenker Studies,* ed. Hedi Siegel (Cambridge: Cambridge University Press, 1990), pp. 138–145. A discussion of this song's pivotal position in the cycle and the relationship of its chromatic passages to the text, including a middle ground (Schenkerian) graph of the entire song.

12
hab' sie umschlungen mit einem grü - nen Band; ich kann nicht mehr singen, mein Herz ist zu voll,
17
weiss nicht, wie ich's in Rei - me zwingen _ soll. Mei - ner Sehn - sucht
pp
22
al - ler - hei - ssesten Schmerz durft' _ ich aus - hauchen in Lie - der - scherz, und wie ich klagte
28
so süss und fein, _ glaubt' ich doch, mein Lei - den wär' nicht klein. Ei, wie
ff
34
gross ist wohl meines Glückes Last, dass kein Klang auf Er - den es in _ sich fasst, dass kein Klang auf
pp

39
Er-den es in sich fasst?
pp
45
Nun, lie-be Lau-te, ruh' an dem Na-gel hier! und weht ein
50
Lüft-chen ü-ber die Sai-ten dir, und streift ei-ne Bie-ne mit ih-ren Flü-geln dich, da
54
wird mir so bange, und es durchschauert mich. Warum liess ich das Band auch
pp
59
hän-gen so lang? Oft fliegt's um die Sai-ten mit seuf-zendem Klang.

"PAUSE"

I have hung my lute on the wall,
And wound a green riband about it,
I can sing no more, my heart is so full,
That I know not how to contain it in rhyme.
The burning pain of my desire
I dared to breathe forth in light song;
And though my plaints were soft and gentle
I knew well that my sorrow was not a trifle.
Oh, how great then is the burden of my happiness,
Since no sound on earth can express it!

Now, dear lute, rest here on your nail!
And if a light breeze passes over your strings,
Or if a bee brushes against you,
I shall tremble, and a thrill will pass through me.
Why did I leave the riband, too, hanging for so long?
Often it flutters around the strings with a sighing sound.
Is it the echo of my love pangs?
Will it be the prelude to new songs?

Franz Peter Schubert

IMPROMPTU OP. 142, NO. 2, D. 935

Schubert's two sets of *Impromptus* are among the best known of his character pieces for piano. Although the word "impromptu" suggests a casual, extemporized style, the following work is a carefully planned and organized musical structure, worthy of detailed study.

QUESTIONS FOR DISCUSSION

Formal Structure

1. Describe this work's overall form. Can you name another work you have studied—perhaps in Unit III—that has a similar form?
2. List as many ways as you can in which the Trio provides contrast to the Allegretto.
3. Describe the role that the passage at mm. 91–98 plays in the form.

Melodic/Rhythmic Structure

1. Describe the phrase-period structure of the Allegretto.
2. Locate an example of a cadential extension.
3. Precisely where is the melodic line in the Trio section?
4. Although the Trio is composed entirely of arpeggiations, a long scalar passage can be found at one point. Locate this passage.

Harmonic/Tonal Structure

1. The passage at mm. 17–30 is among the most interesting of the work from the harmonic standpoint. Contained within these measures are a tonicization (or perhaps modulation), augmented sixth chords, harmonies belonging to the parallel minor key, and harmonic sequence. Identify each of these.
2. Describe the tonal changes that take place between: m. 58 and m. 59; m. 66 and m. 67; m. 76 and m. 77. What harmonic process is involved at each of these points?
3. Provide a complete tonal diagram of the work, showing all tonal centers, their location by measure number, and their precise functional relationship with the home key.

Texture/Articulation/Dynamics

1. Which term—homophonic or polyphonic—better describes the texture of this work?
2. Locate and describe precisely the textural variations that exist within this work. (Such variations may have to do with register, number of voices, spacing, or rhythmic differentiation among the voices.)

28
37
Trio.
47
53
decresc.
59
65
cresc.
70

75
p
decresc.
80
86
decresc.
pp
92
decresc.
99
sempre ligato
pp
107
115
f
ff

Robert Schumann

Robert Schumann (1810–1856) wrote largely for one genre at a time. Thus, his first twenty-three opus numbers are solo piano music, followed by a large number of songs (in 1840), symphonic works (in 1841), and chamber music (in 1842). The piano and song cycles are in ternary, strophic and other small forms. Schumann's phrasing is generally symmetrical, and his melodies display a fondness for dotted rhythms and dance rhythms, and for frequent tempo changes.

Schumann's harmonies are, like Schubert's, full of chromaticism. His music is generally more contrapuntal than Schubert's or Chopin's, and the piano usually assumes a more varied role in his songs than in Schubert's.

CARNAVAL OP. 9 *"Valse noble"*

Carnaval, written in 1834–35, is one of Schumann's early cycles for the piano, its individual pieces depicting various characters in Schumann's life and times. "Valse noble" is fourth in the cycle. Which term—rounded binary or ternary—would be the more appropriate description of its form and why? What elements play a role in defining the form? Study the piece harmonically, considering the possibilities of both modulation and tonicization. Measures 5–6, while melodically identical to mm. 1–2, are harmonized differently. What is the reason?

Un poco maestoso.
f
sf
p
molto teneramente
molto teneramente
ff
f

Robert Schumann

KINDERSCENEN OP. 15, NOS. 2, 6, and 8

Kinderscenen ("Scenes of Childhood") is a set of thirteen short piano pieces selected by Schumann from a group of about thirty which he wrote in 1838. Three are reproduced below. The subtly different realizations of the binary and ternary principles in the three works invite careful comparison. Also consider how each represents tonally the principle of statement-departure-return. What formal feature present in No. 8 is lacking in Nos. 2 and 6? Consider how No. 2 would appear if the written-out repetitions were replaced by repeat signs. Study these songs also for their melodic and harmonic structure. All three are mildly chromatic, No. 6 offering the best examples of secondary function.

No. 2: "Curious Story"

No. 6: "An Important Event"

No. 8: "By the Fireside"

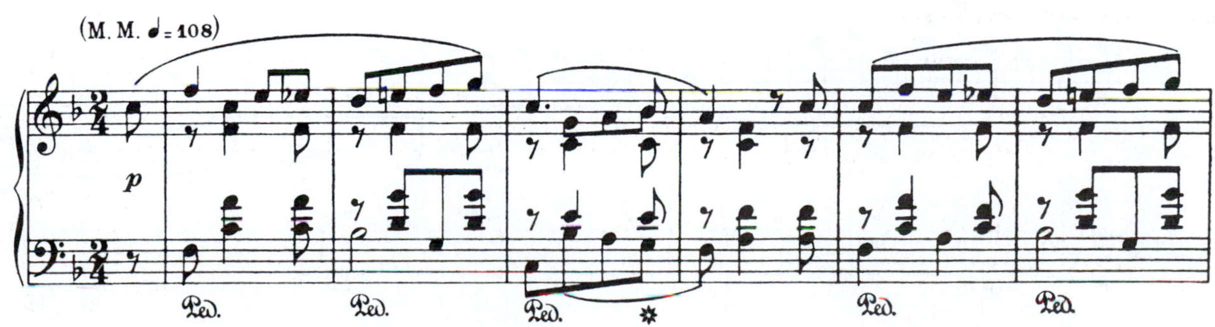

7
mf

14
rit.
sf
p

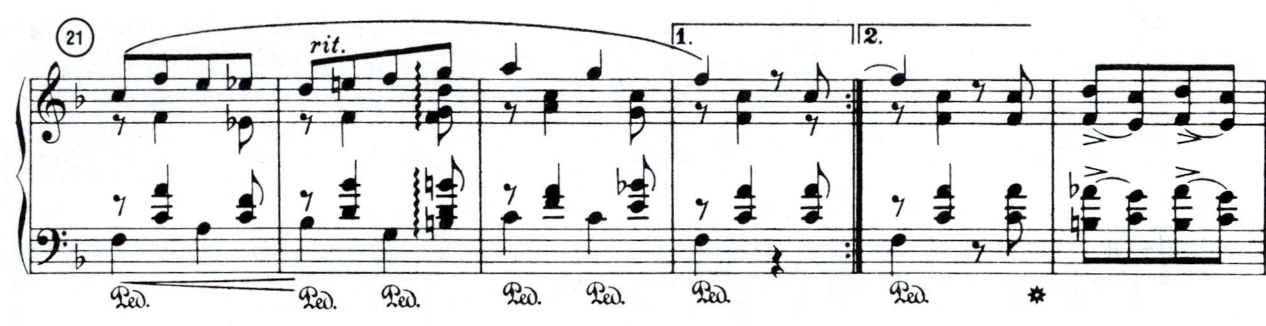
21
rit.
1.
2.

26
ritardando

Robert Schumann
DICHTERLIEBE OP. 48, NOS. 4, 5, and 9

Schumann composed his song cycle *Dichterliebe* ("A Poet's Love") in 1840, the year during which he wrote over one hundred songs. Widely varied in mood, color, rhythmic and dynamic character, the songs nevertheless produce an overall sense of unity and interdependence, and performances of the entire cycle are common. Like Schubert, Schumann used a variety of forms, of which strophic, ternary and through-composed are quite common. Identify the form for each of these songs and explain what features of the text may have prompted their use. Song No. 4, while only twenty-one measures long, makes clear references to three different tonal centers, and additional secondary functions can be found. Although Song No. 5 remains in a single tonality, a tonicization is present. What is the melodic form (i.e., the phrase-period structure)? Song No. 9 moves through four tonalities, two of these more clearly established than the others. Both pivot-chord and chromatic (direct) modulations are present.

Composed 1840

Related reading: Arthur Komar, "The music of *Dichterliebe:* The whole and its parts," *Norton Critical Scores* (New York: W.W. Norton & Company, 1971), p. 63f. An analytical essay on the cycle, including a voice-leading graph of Song No. 4 (p. 75) and discussions of Song No. 5 (p. 75f) and Song No. 9 (p. 84f).

No. 4, "Wenn ich in deine Augen seh' "

"WENN ICH IN DEINE AUGEN SEH"

When I look into your eyes,
my sorrow and woe fade away;
and when I kiss your mouth,
I am completely well again.

When I am against your breast
the pleasure of heaven sweeps over me;
but when you speak: "I love you!"
I must cry bitterly.

No. 5, "Ich will meine Seele tauchen"

"ICH WILL MEINE SEELE TAUCHEN"

I want to dip my soul
into the depths of the lily;
and with a tinkling sound the lily will whisper
a song about my beloved.

The song is to shake and tremble
like the kiss from her mouth,
which once she gave me
in a wonderfully sweet moment!

No. 9, "Das ist ein Flöten und Geigen"

28
die Herz - al - ler - lieb - ste mein.
p
35
p
Das ist ein Klin - gen und Dröh -
42
f
nen, das ist ein Klin - gen und Dröh - nen, ein Pau - ken und ein Schal -
f
49
p
mein;
dazwi - schen
p

"DAS IST EIN FLÖTEN UND GEIGEN"

There is fluting and fiddling
and loud trumpeting throughout.
My dearest and most beloved is dancing
in the wedding dance.

There is ringing and droning,
drumming and blowing;
and in the midst of it all
the dear little angels are sobbing.

Robert Schumann

43 KLAVIERSTÜCKE FÜR DIE JUGEND OP. 68

No. 3 Soldier's March, No. 41 Nordic Song

Schumann is said to have remarked that, whereas the *Kinderscenen* (see page 323) represents the "reminiscences of an older person," the *Album for the Young* represents "the anticipations and experiences of young people." Compare the two selections given below in terms of form, tonal plan, harmonic material and melodic structure. What similarities do you observe?

No. 3: Soldier's March

No. 41: Nordic Song

Frédéric François Chopin

Frédéric Chopin (1810–1849) is unique among major composers in that his compositions are almost exclusively for the piano. His melodies, composed mostly of four- and eight-measure phrases, often contain elaborate and highly chromatic embellishments, and his rhythms are often derived from dances. His music contains the full range of nineteenth-century chromatic harmonies. A particularly interesting and individual technique is sometimes termed "chordal mutation"—a process wherein harmonies change by one chord member at a time, producing interesting (and often non-functional) harmonic successions. Chopin's textures are prevailingly homophonic, and his wide-ranging broken-chord accompaniments, imaginative use of the pedals, and registral extremes provide a wealth of pianistic colors.

VALSE OP. 69, NO. 2

This work is the earliest of the Chopin selections in this anthology and it is also harmonically the most diatonic. Likewise, the tonal plan is fairly conservative. (Identify the tonal relationships.) Offsetting this are melodically chromatic passages. Identify some of these. Describe the phrase structure. Many of Chopin's works can be viewed as expansions of the ternary principle. Can this work be so regarded?

33
con anima
39
rit.
a tempo
45
f
50
sf
sf
56
61
f
poco rit.
dim.
1. a tempo
2. a tempo

65
mf dolce
72
poco cresc.
79
dim.
mf
86
cresc.
93
dimin.
sf
p
f
99
p

106
poco rit.
a tempo
cresc.
dim.
Ped. * Ped. * Ped. * Ped. * Ped. *
113
con anima
Ped. * Ped. * Ped. * Ped. * Ped. * Ped. * Ped. *
120
rit.
a tempo
Ped. * Ped. * Ped. * Ped. * Ped. * Ped. * Ped. *
127
f
sf
sf
Ped. * Ped. * Ped. * Ped. * Ped. * Ped. *
133
rit.
Ped. * Ped. * Ped. * Ped. * Ped. * Ped. *
139
f
calando e dimin.
Ped. * Ped. * Ped. * Ped. *

Frédéric Chopin
NOCTURNE OP. 9, NO. 2

This well-known nocturne exemplifies Chopin's fondness for symmetrical phrasing and melodic embellishment. Repetition, varied repetition and contrast are all instrumental in creating the form. How would you describe this form? What is the formal and harmonic function of the final ten measures? Although this early work is not as chromatic as the later *Preludes Op. 28*, Nos. 4, 9, 20 and 21, it contains an abundance of secondary functions, which you should seek to identify and understand. Particularly characteristic in this regard is m. 12.

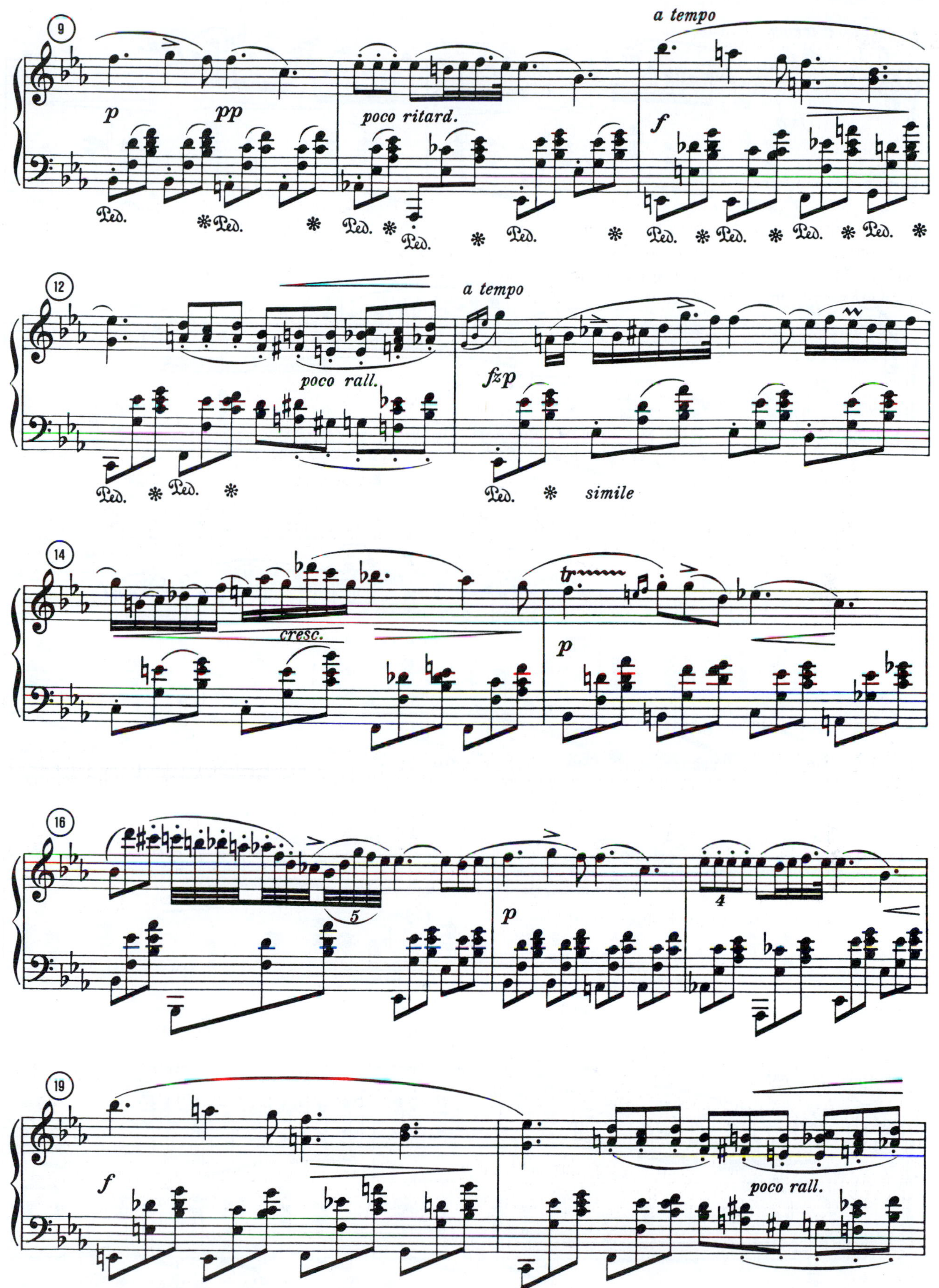
9
a tempo
p
pp
poco ritard.
f
Ped.
12
a tempo
poco rall.
fzp
simile
14
cresc.
p
16
5
p
4
19
f
poco rall.

21
a tempo
fzp
23
tr
p
5
5
25
p
pp
poco rubato
sempre pp
dolciss.
Ped.
28
8
p
30
8
con forza
stretto
f

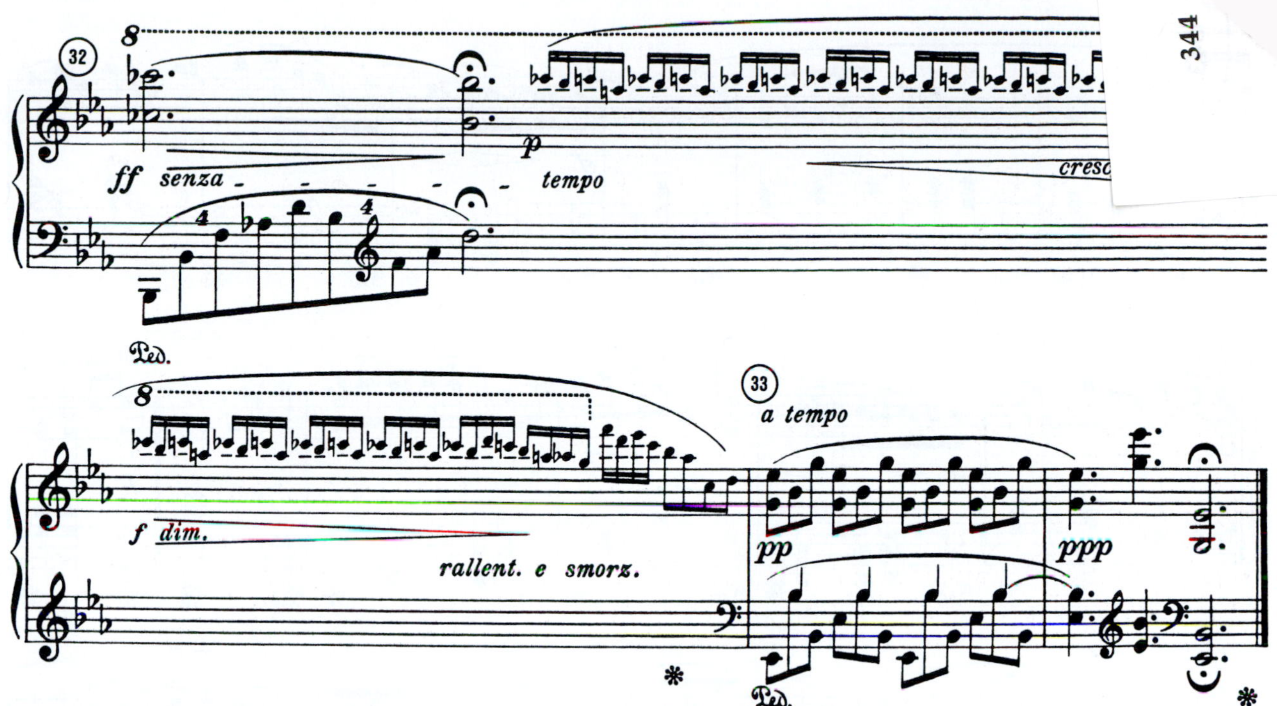

Frédéric Chopin

MAZURKAS OP. 17, NO. 2 and OP. 17, NO. 4

Terry Fam.

Chopin, who found in the Polish mazurka a source of musical inspiration, published fifty-one piano works under that title. These works are *stylizations*—refinements, not intended for dancing but still capturing the rhythmic, harmonic and melodic essence of the dance.

Op. 17, No. 2 in E Minor

13
sf
20
sf
leggiero
dolce
p
26
34
42
pp
50
stretto
cresc.
a tempo
f
sf

QUESTIONS FOR DISCUSSION

Mazurka Op. 17, No. 4

Formal Structure

1. Describe the overall form of this work and identify the various sections, noting their respective lengths. Can any section be further subdivided?
2. Of the elements listed below, select those that define the form and explain the role of each. Which, in your opinion, provides the single most important element of contrast in the work?
   - a. rhythmic figures;
   - b. phrase length;
   - c. contour;
   - d. harmonic structure;
   - e. tonality or modality;
   - f. texture;
   - g. dynamics;
   - h. register;
   - i. accompaniment;
   - j. articulation.
3. Explain how mm. 1–4 serve to introduce the work melodically, texturally and tonally.

Melodic/Rhythmic Structure

1. Discuss the melodic line of mm. 5–20 with respect to phrase-period structure, motivic content and overall shape (contour).
2. Outline the most important melodic pitches (the structural melody) of mm. 109–124. Does this line, or a variation of it, appear at any other point in this work?
3. Analyze and compare the melodic ornaments of mm. 15, 18, 31 and 103.
4. Measure 37 contains a dominant seventh chord on E and m. 38 contains an A minor triad. What types of non-chord tones are represented by:
   - a. the D-sharp in m. 37;
   - b. the D in m. 38?

Harmonic/Tonal Structure

1. Chopin frequently employs prolonged pedal points. Locate some examples in this work and identify them as tonic, dominant or other.
2. Discuss the tonal ambiguity at the beginning of this work. At what point does the tonic clearly emerge?
3. Name the important tonal centers and give locations.
4. Locate the simplest section from a harmonic standpoint and describe it generally.
5. Provide a harmonic analysis of mm. 29–36. Include a reduction showing all voice leading.
6. Provide a reduction of mm. 109–116 that shows all important voice leading.

Texture/Articulation/Dynamics

1. Describe the texture of this work and explain how textural variety is achieved.
2. Describe the registral contrast present.

Composed 1833

Related reading: Joel Lester, *Harmony in Tonal Music,* Vol. II (New York: Alfred A. Knopf, 1982), p. 181f. An examination of voice leading and its impact on the harmonic aspect of this work.

Op. 17, No. 4 in A Minor

43
a tempo
poco riten.
ten.
50
56
ten.
ten.
dol.
p
Ped.
*
Ped.
*
62
69
77

85
ff
ten.
93
p
ten.
101
ten.
Ped.
107
Ped.
114
sotto voce
122
sempre più piano
calando
Ped.
perdendosi

Frédéric Chopin

PRELUDES OP. 28, NOS. 4, 9, and 20

In its systematic progression through all twenty-four major and minor keys, this set of preludes resembles in format J. S. Bach's *Das Wohltemperierte Clavier.* However, Bach preludes, which are followed by fugues, move upward chromatically from the key of C, whereas Chopin's progress through the circle of fifths in the following manner: C major-A minor-G major-E minor and so on.

In *Prelude* No. 4, the principal element of interest is harmony. Functional chord progressions can be found to form the basis, especially if you view the prelude as alternating between the tonal centers of E minor and A minor. However, a great many chords occur as the result of another process. Can you determine what that process is? What is this work's form and how is it created? A very clear dramatic peak occurs. Locate it and describe how it is achieved. A curious harmony occurs three measures from the end. Can you explain this chord in the context of the three harmonies that follow?

Prelude No. 9 is also a succession of fast-moving harmonies. Between m. 5 and m. 8, the music makes reference to at least four different tonalities. Can you name them? Although the endpoint of this passage constitutes the most remote tonal region of the work, Chopin quickly—almost casually—returns to the principal tonality through a deft stroke. Explain this.

Prelude No. 20 is *monomotivic.* Identify the unifying motive and note its many appearances. Again, a number of nineteenth-century harmonic practices may be cited, including rapid successions of tonicizations, Neapolitan chords, and augmented sixth chords. A complete harmonic analysis will be worthwhile.

Composed 1839

Related reading: Richard S. Parks, "Voice leading and chromatic harmony in the music of Chopin," *Journal of Music Theory,* Vol. 20, No. 2 (Fall 1976), p. 189f. Examination of Prelude No. 4 and other selected Chopin works from the standpoint of voice leading and the creation of "parenthetical harmonies."

12
p
16
stretto
f
dim.
p
20
smorz.
pp

Largo
No. 9
f
3
f
p
cresc.

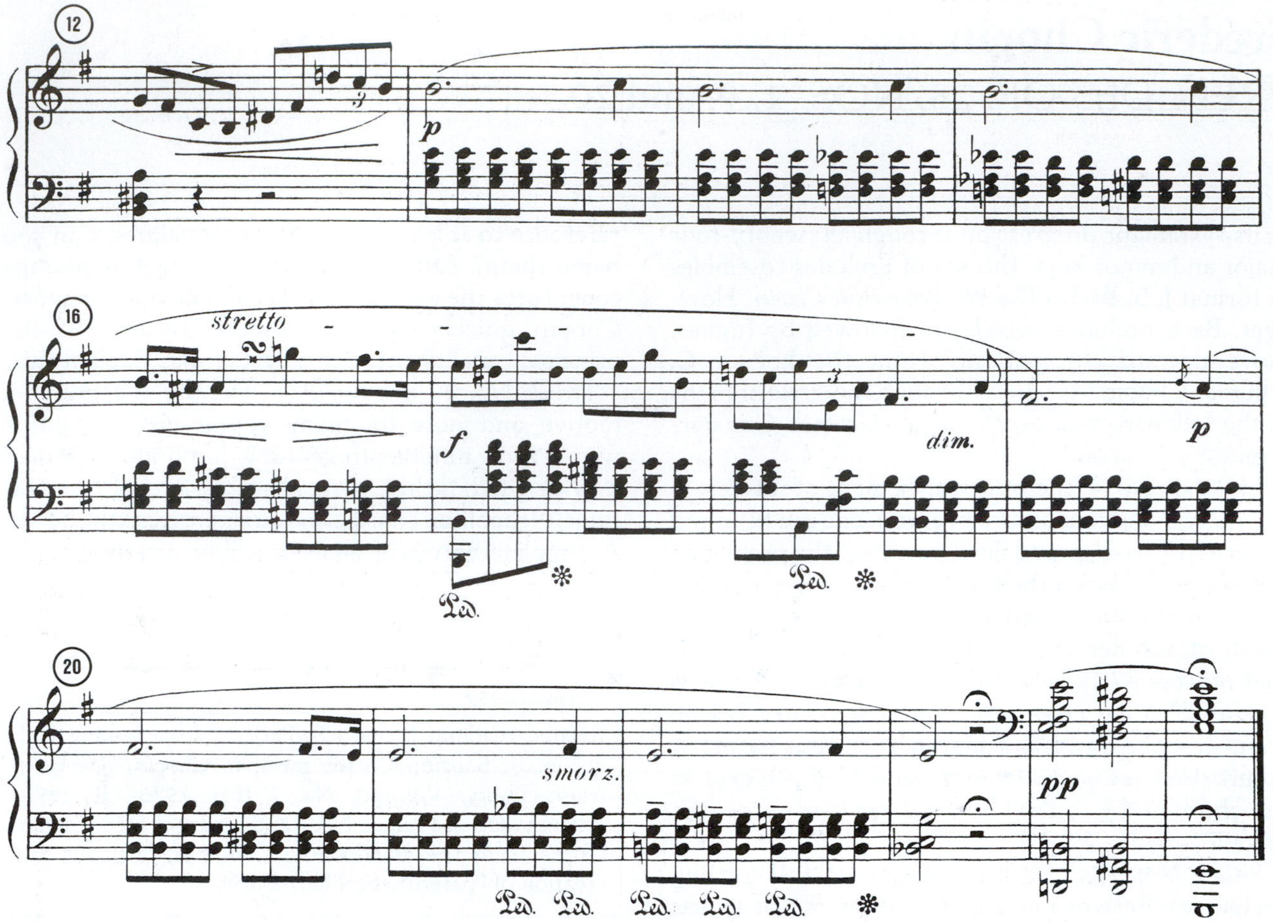

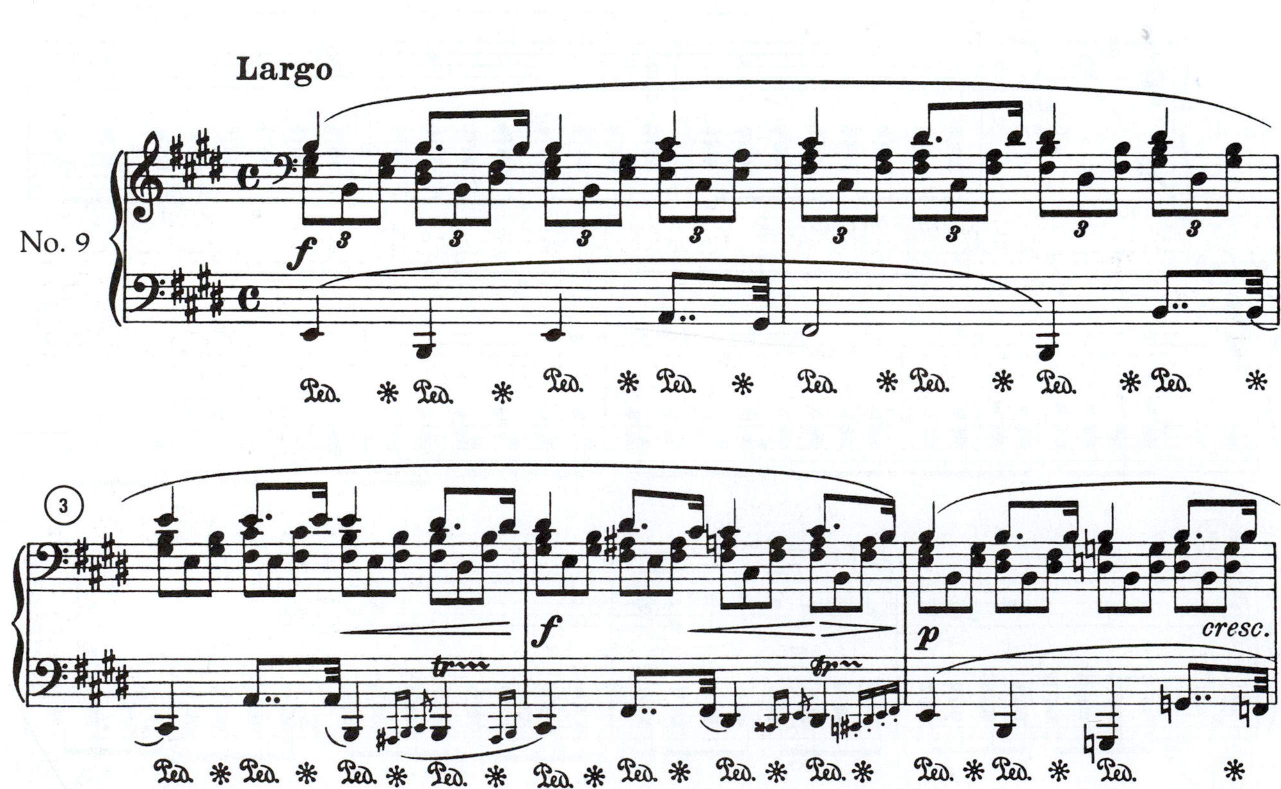

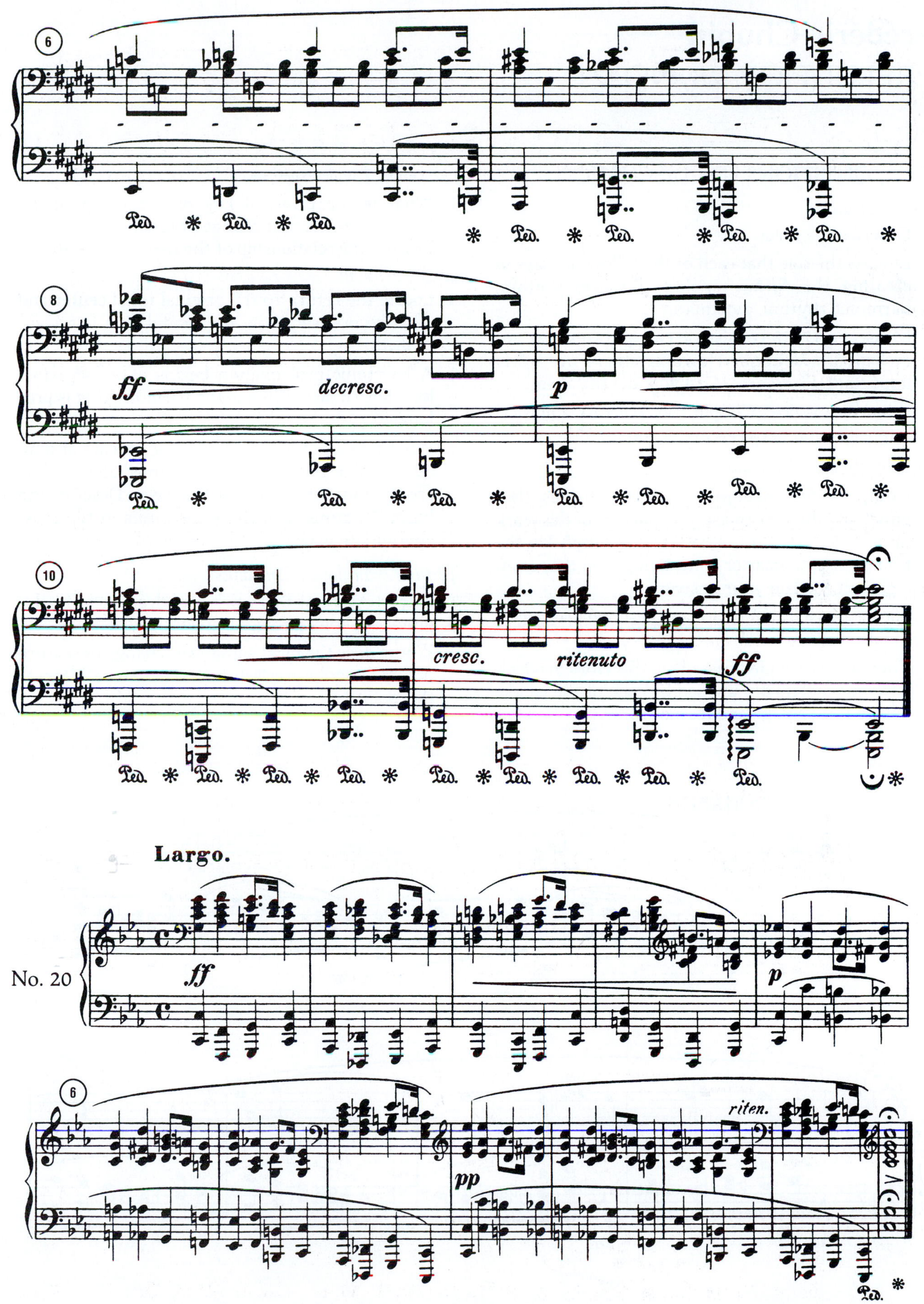
6
Ped.
8
ff
decresc.
p
10
cresc.
ritenuto
ff
Largo.
No. 20
ff
p
6
pp
riten.

Frédéric Chopin

PRELUDE OP. 28, NO. 21

QUESTIONS FOR DISCUSSION

Formal Structure

1. Describe the form.
2. Discuss the role that each of the following plays in creating the form: tonality, texture, rhythm, harmonic rhythm, dynamics.
3. Measures 17–32 consist of two phrases that are melodically identical. However, there are other important differences. Can you identify them?
4. What means does Chopin use to create a musical intensification between m. 33 and m. 39?

Melodic/Rythmic Structure

1. Compare the strength of the cadences that punctuate the first and second phrases of this work (mm. 1-16). Which is stronger and why? Are the two phrases similar or contrasting? Do they form a period? Explain your answers.
2. Locate a melodic sequence and describe it as real or tonal.
3. There is an extended passage in this work in which different meters are implied by each of the hands. Locate this passage and discuss it.

Harmonic/Tonal Structure

1. What is the principal key of the composition? Where does the first change of tonal center occur? Discuss the relationship of the new tonal center to the original.
2. Locate the return to the original tonal center and describe precisely how the modulation is accomplished.
3. A harmonic prolongation begins at m. 45. How long does it last? What is the harmony that is prolonged?
4. What type of chromatic harmony appears at mm. 39–40? The measures which immediately follow are the most chromatic of the piece. Describe the harmonic content of these measures in the most appropriate way.

Texture/Articulation/Dynamics

1. Is the texture of this work best described as polyphonic or homophonic? Support your answer.
2. Where does the most significant change of texture occur? Describe precisely how the texture differs at this point.

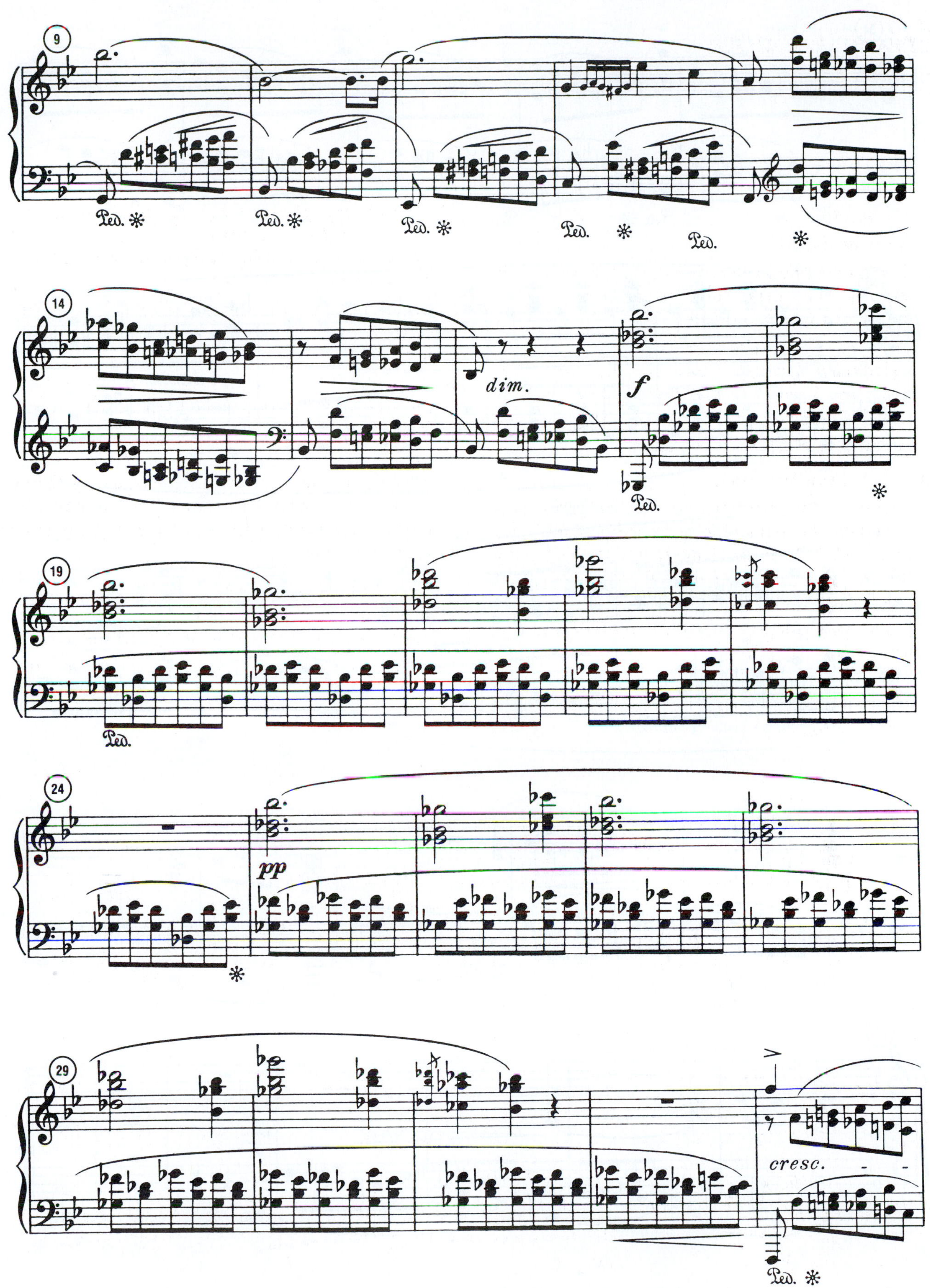

9
Ped. ✻
Ped. ✻
Ped. ✻
Ped. ✻
Ped. ✻
14
dim.
f
Ped. ✻
19
Ped.
24
pp
✻
29
cresc.
Ped. ✻

34
Ped.
39
ff
dimin.
43
47
52
cresc.
f

Franz Liszt

"IL PENSIEROSO" *from Années de Pèlerinage, Bk. II*

Franz Liszt (1811–1886) was a Hungarian pianist of unmatched virtuosity and a composer whose highly chromatic music perfectly embodied the restless, Romantic spirit of the middle nineteenth century. His "Years of Pilgrimage" consists of twenty-six descriptive pieces in three volumes. "Il Pensieroso" ("The Thinker") depicts his impression of Rodin's famous sculpture. Pensive, austere, devoid of embellishment and harmonically advanced, it provides an excellent example of middle-to-late-nineteenth-century harmony. Consider, for example, the reasons behind the enharmonic respelling of the chords of m. 9 at m. 11, or of m. 14 at m. 16. To what extent are the harmonies in this section melodically generated? A passage of quite different harmonic character begins in m. 33. Analyze the passage harmonically and melodically. At the larger level, examine the tonal scheme. What kind of relationships exist between the tonal centers? Identify the most remote tonal region of the first section. How is it reached and how is the return to tonic effected? (The two harmonic processes are quite different.) Finally, examine the overall form, describe it and explain which elements play a role in its definition.

Composed 1848

Related reading: David Allen Damschroder, "Structural levels: A key to Liszt's chromatic art," *College Music Symposium*, Vol. 27 (1987), p. 46f. An examination of voice leading and other linear factors that generate much of the non-functional harmonies in selected examples.

Howard Cinnamon, "Tonic arpeggiation and successive equal third relations as elements of tonal evolution in the music of Franz Liszt," *Music Theory Spectrum*, Vol. 8 (1986), p. 1f. Examination of Liszt's voice leading and equal division of the octave (into successive minor thirds and major thirds), including two works from this collection.

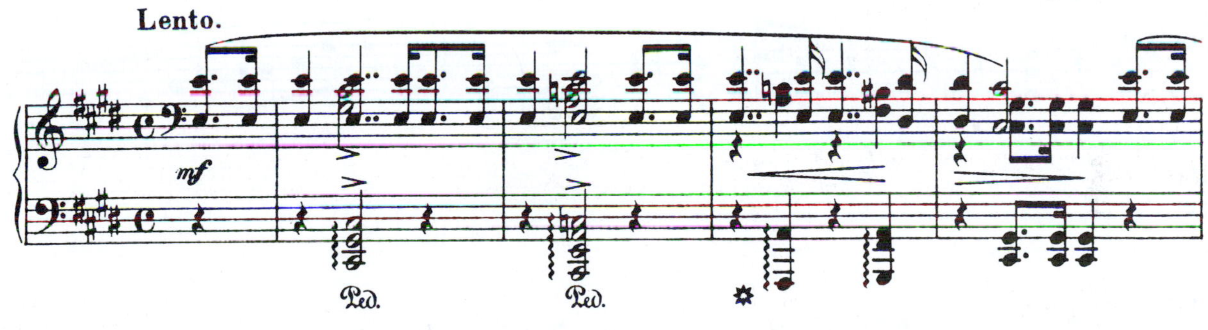

10
sf
Ped.
14
sf
Ped.
sf
Ped.
18
23
sotto voce
pesante
Ped.
Ped.
Ped.

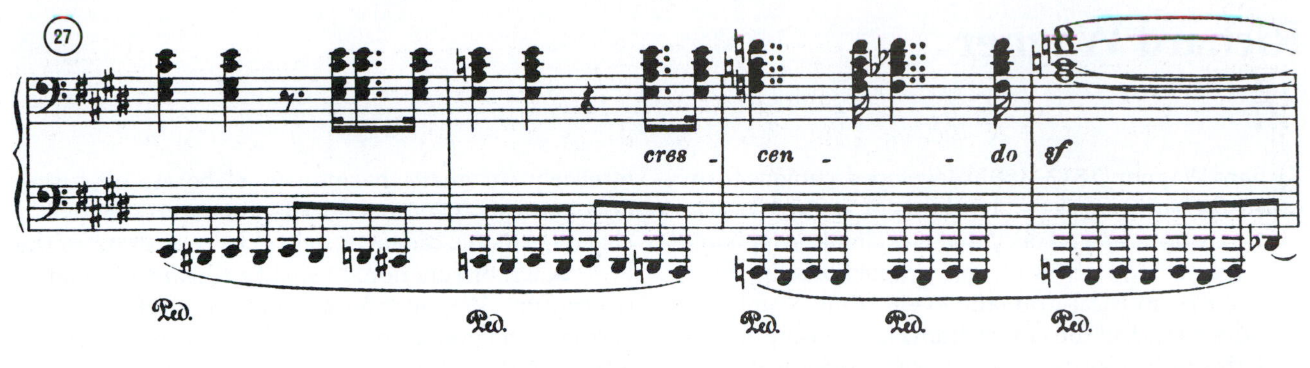
27
cres - cen - - do sf
Ped.
Ped.
Ped.
Ped.
Ped.

31
rit.
dim.
p espressivo
Ped.
Ped.

36
rinf.
p
Ped.

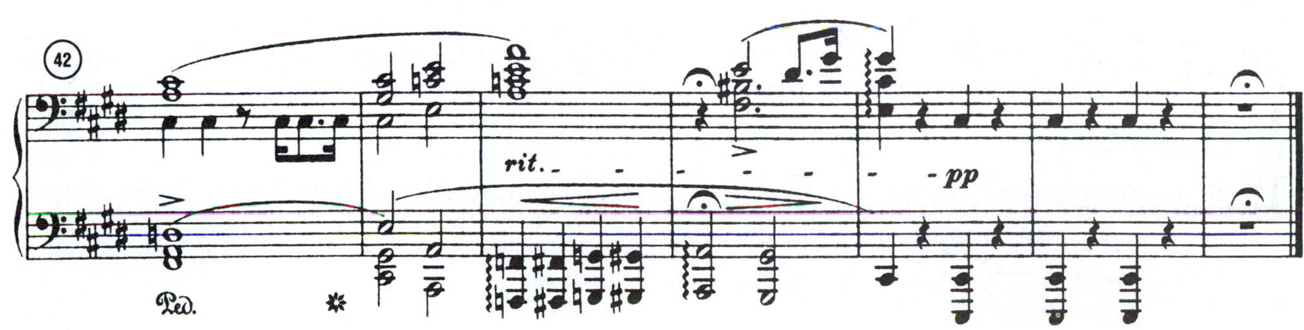
42
rit.
pp
Ped.

Richard Wagner

Richard Wagner (1813–1883) developed a unique form called the *music drama*—a synthesis of acting, poetry, music, costume and scenery that was almost symphonic in character and often of epic proportions. In these works, one musical-dramatic event leads seamlessly into the next, and the entire drama is intensely organized through a system of *leitmotifs*—musical figures usually related to a specific person, thought or feeling.

Wagner's "endless melody" comprises long, lyrical, expansive melodic lines with infrequent cadences. His intensely chromatic harmonies, elaborate obscuring dissonances, rapid tonal fluctuations, and deceptive or elided harmonic cadences helped to contribute to the breakdown of functional tonality toward the end of the century. Wagner's scores contain colorful soloistic passages and impressive massed choral and orchestral effects. Although not contrapuntal in the traditional sense of a fixed number of independent voices, his music has considerable polyphonic substance.

TRISTAN UND ISOLDE *Prelude to Act One and the opening of Act One, Scene One; Liebesnacht (mm. 46–67 of Act Two, Scene Two)* Piano reduction

A system of *leitmotifs* exists in *Tristan und Isolde*, Wagner's most influential work. Completed in 1859, this work is cast in a highly chromatic idiom in which identifiable tonal centers are frequently absent for extended periods. The Prelude to Act One introduces several of the *leitmotifs*. These motives have been named in accordance with their first appearance in the drama proper, but their significance is generally broader than the names would suggest.

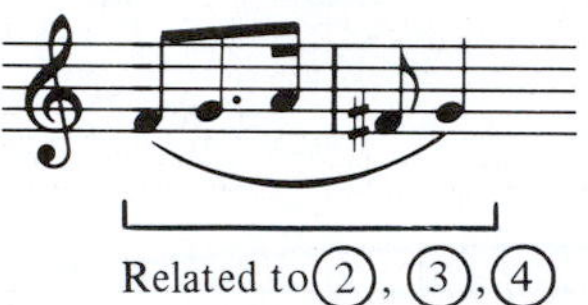

Can you locate their first, as well as later, appearances in the Prelude?

Harmonic analysis of the Prelude poses special problems. Much of it can be analyzed with respect to one of three different tonal centers. Can you identify them? Does any one tonal center predominate? (There is considerable debate as to the overall tonality of the Prelude.) While much of the music is characterized by dominant-sounding sonorities, there are relatively few points where these decisively resolve to the expected chord. Furthermore, the key signature appears to have little relevance to the music.

The Prelude leads directly into Scene One, of which only the opening measures are given. Two more important motifs are introduced here. One is associated with Isolde's anger at the young sailor's song, which she misconstrues as a slighting reference to herself:

Can you identify the other motif, which first appears in the sailor's song? Note the deceptive resolution at the very end of this excerpt. Such "resolutions" are typical of the entire drama.

The second excerpt is from the love duet "Liebesnacht," sung by Tristan and Isolde in Act Two. Although it is less chromatic than the Prelude, this passage contains sequences, chromatic modulations and numerous chromatic third relationships. Can you discover a pattern to the rapid succession of tonal centers implied at mm. 46–62?

Wagner was one of the most skillful orchestrators of his day. Although the music is presented here in piano reduction to facilitate harmonic analysis, it will be instructive for you to examine these excerpts in full orchestral score as well.

Completed 1859

Related reading: William Mitchell, "The Tristan Prelude: Techniques and structure," *The Music Forum,* Vol. I (1967), pp. 162–203. A detailed examination of the Prelude.

Roland Jackson, "Leitmotive and form in the Tristan Prelude," *The Music Review,* Vol. 36, No. 1 (February 1975), pp.42–53. The author identifies seven basic motives and examines their manipulation and combination in the Prelude.

Prelude to Act I and Beginning of Act I, Scene 1

21
poco rall.
riten.
dim.
p
cresc.
f
25
tempo
zart
dolce
dim.
p
cresc.
f
30
espress.
p
f
cresc.
35
zart
dolce
ten.
belebt
animato
f
dim.
p
40
Belebend.
Animando.
sf
cresc.
molto cresc.

44
rallent.
ff
dim.
a tempo
zart
dolce
dim.
p
p
49
sf
p
cresc.
f
f
p
53
cresc.
57
f
61
più f
ff
meno f
5
espress.
Ped.

64
sempre più f
marcato
67
f
69
f
71
più f
più f
73
molto espress.
ff
Ped.
Ped.
Ped.

76
sempre f
79
più f
più f

Allmählich im Zeitmass etwas zurückhaltend.
Il tempo poco a poco ritenuto.

espress.

dim.

87

p

zart
dolce

93

cresc.

f

p

Scene I.

A marquee, richly hung with rugs, on the forward deck of a sailing-ship, at first entirely closed at the back; on one side a narrow companion-way leads to the cabin below.

Isolda on a couch, her head buried in the cushions. Brangæna, holding back a curtain, looks out over the side of the ship.

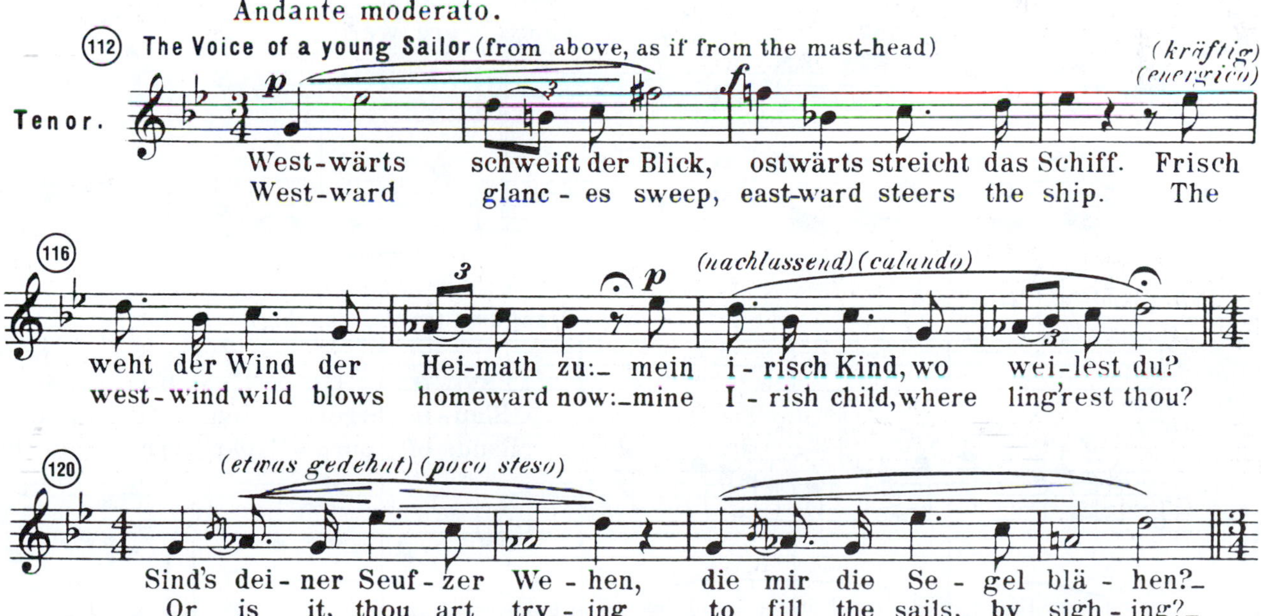

124
We - he, we - he, du Wind! Weh, ach we - he, mein Kind!
Blow then, wind fresh and wild! Woe, ah! woe is my child!
132
(feurig)
(con fuoco)
I - ri - sche Maid, du wil - de, min - ni - ge
Mine I - rish maid, my wild and am - o - rous
135
Lebhaft.
Vivace.
Isolda (starting up quickly)
(She looks round disturbed)
Maid! Wer wagt mich zu höh-nen?
maid! Who dares thus to mock me?
dim.
140
Mässig.
Moderato.
Brangä - ne, du? Sag', wo sind wir?
Brangæ - na, ho! Say, where are we?
147
Brangæna (at the opening)
Blau - e Strei - fen stie - gen im
Bands of pur - ple rise in the

153
B.
We - sten auf; sanft und schnell se - gelt das Schiff; auf
west - ern sky; soft and swift forg - es the ship; and
3
3

159
B.
ru - hi-ger See vor A- bend er - rei - chen wir si - cher das
holds it out calm, ere eve - ning we'll reach of a sure - ty the
3
3
3

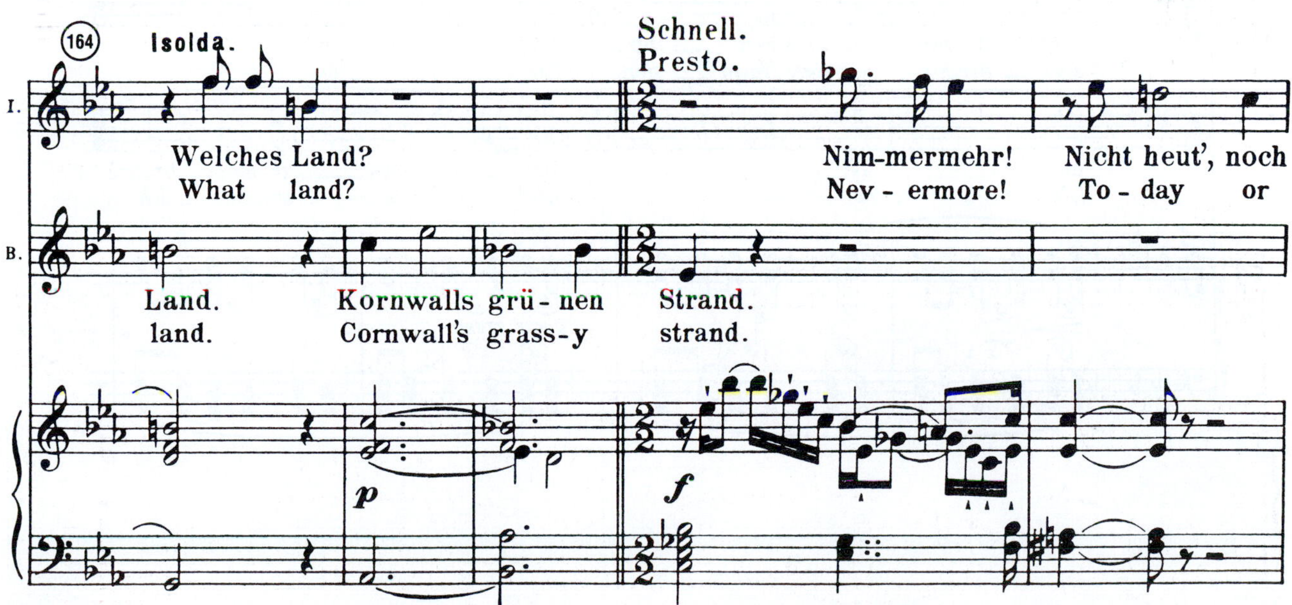
164
Isolde.
I.
Welches Land?
What land?
Schnell.
Presto.
Nim-mermehr! Nicht heut', noch
Nev - ermore! To - day or
B.
Land. Kornwalls grü - nen Strand.
land. Cornwall's grass - y strand.
p
f

Act II, Scene 2: "O sink' hernieder" (Liebesnacht)

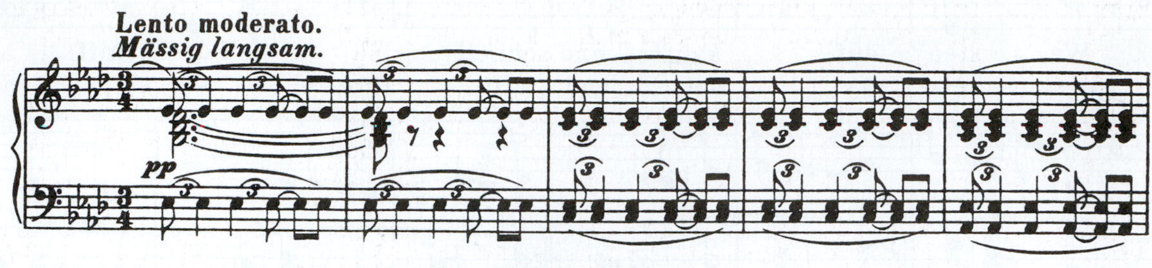

14
lift our lives' re-mem-brance from us,
gieb Ver-ges-sen, dass ich le-be,
from us,
le-be,
let us but a-bide with
nimm mich auf in dei-nen
dim.
18
let us but a-bide with thee;
nimm mich auf in dei-nen Schoss,
p
from the world, oh set us
lö-se von der Welt mich
thee;
Schoss,
p
from the world, oh set us free!
lö-se von der Welt mich los!
più p
pp
22
TRISTAN.
TRISTAN.
free!
los!
Ex-tin-guished in the twi-light's stream-ing
Ver-lo-schen nun die letz-te Leuch-te;
(dolce)
pp (sart)
26
ISOLDA.
ISOLDE.
all our doubt-ing, all our dream-ing,
was wir dach-ten, was uns däuch-te;
(dolce)
p (sart)
più p

30
ISOLDA.
ISOLDE.
all our fan - - cies,
all' Ge - mah - - nen,
TRISTAN.
TRISTAN.
all our mem' - ries,
all' Ge - den - - ken,
p espress.
poco cresc.
34
sa - cred twi - light's soft ad -
heil' - ger Dämm' - rung heh - res
sa - cred twi - light's soft ad - van - ces
heil' - ger Dämm' - rung heh - res Ah - nen
p
poco cresc.
poco f
38
p
van - ces bid vain fears to cease,
Ah - nen löscht des Wäh - nens Graus
bid vain fears to cease, from
löscht des Wäh - nens Graus welt -
cresc.
molto cresc.

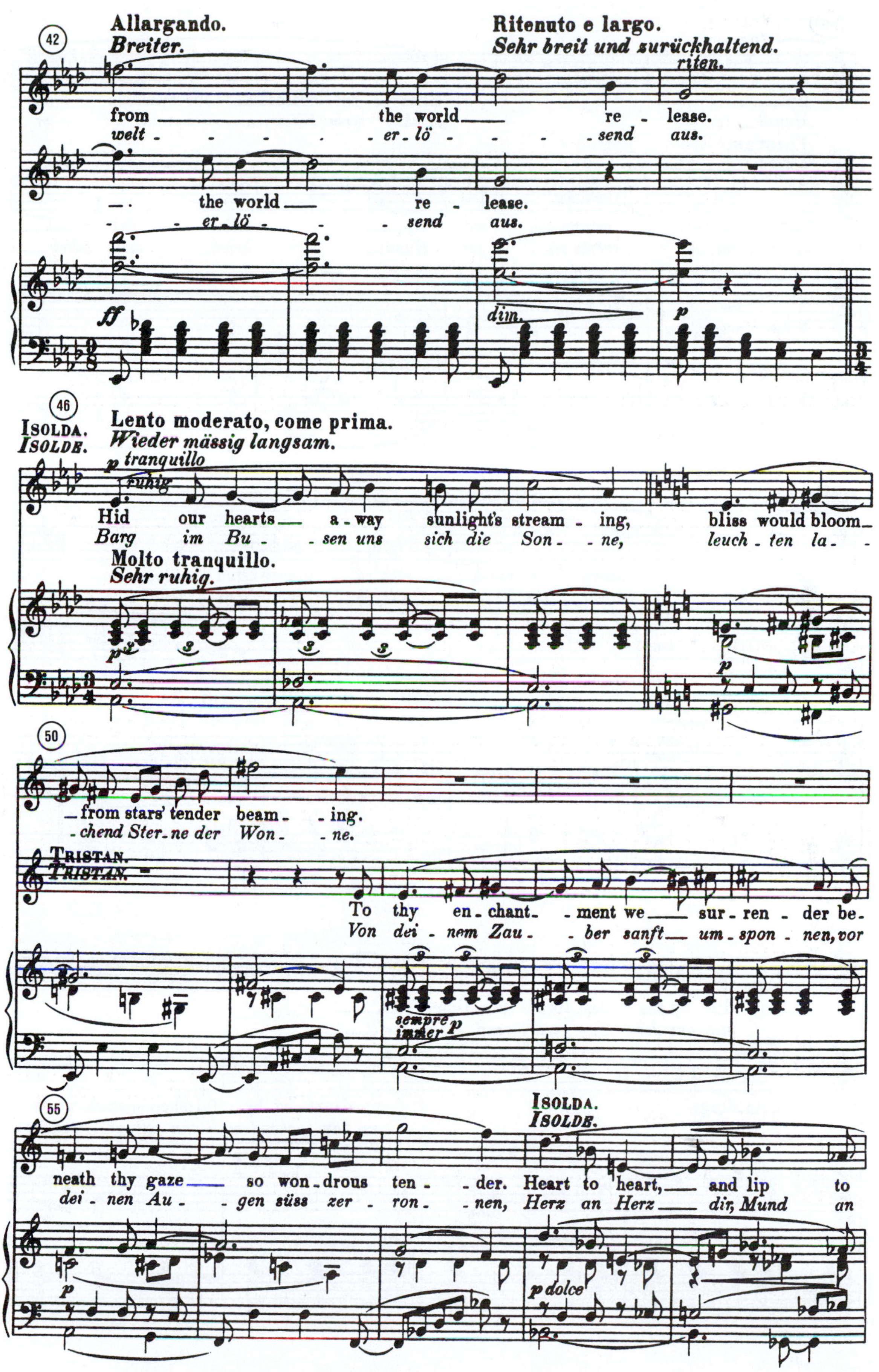
42
Allargando.
Breiter.
Ritenuto e largo.
Sehr breit und zurückhaltend.
riten.
from the world re - lease.
welt - - - - - - er - lö - - - - - send aus.
- the world re - lease.
- - er - lö - - - send aus.
ff
dim.
p
46
Isolda.
Isolde.
Lento moderato, come prima.
Wieder mässig langsam.
p tranquillo
ruhig
Hid our hearts a - way sunlight's stream - ing, bliss would bloom
Barg im Bu - sen uns sich die Son - ne, leuch - ten la -
Molto tranquillo.
Sehr ruhig.
50
from stars' tender beam - ing.
- chend Ster - ne der Won - ne.
Tristan.
Tristan.
To thy en - chant - ment we sur - ren - der be -
Von dei - nem Zau - ber sanft um - spon - nen, vor
sempre p
immer
55
neath thy gaze so won - drous ten - der.
dei - nen Au - gen süss zer - ron - nen,
Isolda.
Isolde.
Heart to heart, and lip to
Herz an Herz dir, Mund an
p dolce

60
lip. Bliss - ful beams our eyes are
Mund; bricht mein Blick sich wonn' - - er -
TRISTAN.
TRISTAN.
Each the oth - er's breath we sip. Bliss - ful beams
ei - nes A - thems ein' - ger Bund; bricht mein Blick
p dolce
p dolce
64
più p
bind - ing, a - bashed is earth with ra - diance blind - ing:
blin - det, er - bleicht die Welt mit ih - rem Blen - den:
p
our eyes are bind - ing, a - bashed is earth with ra - diance
sich wonn' - er - blin - det, er - bleicht die Welt mit ih - rem
più p
pp
68
lit by the day - light's dazz - ling lie,
die uns der Tag trü - gend er - hellt,
p
blin - ding: un - daunt - ed by falsehoods which we de -
Blen - den: zu täu - schendem Wahn ent - ge - gen - ge -
p
p
cresc.

72
accel.
thou'rt my world, thine am I
selbst dann bin ich die Welt:
fy, thou'rt my world, thine am I
stellt, selbst dann bin ich die Welt:
accel.
ff
77
Tempo primo.
Erstes Tempo.
Won - drous rap - ture
Won - ne - hehr - stes
Won - drous rap - ture
Won - ne - hehr - stes
Tempo primo.
Erstes Tempo.
dim.
80
weav - ing,
We - ben,
weav - ing,
We - ben,
p
molto cresc.

82
rallent.
dim.
che - rish'd vi - sions a - chiev - ing,
Lie - be - hei - lig - stes Le - ben,
dim.
che - rish'd vi - sions a - chiev - ing,
Lie - be - hei - lig - stes Le - ben,
rallent.
ff (molto espress.)
(sehr ausdrucksvoll)
dim.
p
più p
86
a tempo
p
ne'er daunt - ed by day - light's beam be
Nie - wie - der - er - wa - chens wahn - los
p
ne'er daunt - ed by day - light's beam be
Nie - wie - der - er - wa - chens wahn - los
a tempo
pp
più p
92
morendo
ersterbend
our un - dy - ing dream.
hold be - wuss - ter Wunsch.
morendo
ersterbend
our un - dy - ing dream.
hold be - wuss - ter Wunsch.
(Tristan and Isolda sink down on the flowery bank completely carried away by passion and remain reclining thus with heads in contact.)
(Tristan und Isolde versinken in gänzliche Entrücktheit, in der sie, Haupt an Haupt auf die Blumenbank zurückgelehnt, verweilen.)
pp

Johannes Brahms

The Classical sympathies of Johannes Brahms (1833–1897) are revealed in his choice of forms, in his interest in chamber music, in his tight control of all musical elements, and in his preference for Classical developmental procedures. Rhythmic variety is the essence of his style, and cross-rhythms, hemiola and syncopation (prolonged to create metric shifts) are abundant. Brahms's harmonies are unmistakably of the nineteenth century. Favored chordal and tonal relationships are the chromatic mediant and submediant and the minor subdominant. His penchant for doubling melodic lines in thirds and sixths and his use of cross-rhythms in his arpeggiated accompaniments impart a thick texture to his music. His orchestration has a warm, dark, sonorous quality, owing to his generous use of the horns and frequently divided lower-register strings.

BALLADE OP. 118, NO. 3

This piece is one of a number of short piano works that Brahms composed late in his life. Regarded by many as the culmination of his output for piano, most are in a ternary form and contain pervasive motivic relationships, rich, nineteenth-century chromatic harmonies, full textures, and many cross-rhythms and hemiola effects.

QUESTIONS FOR DISCUSSION

Formal Structure

1. Using appropriate letters, diagram the overall form, including both principal divisions and subdivisions, and list the elements that help to create this form, especially the elements that create the contrast between sections.
2. List important motives and note especially any melodic elements from one section that appear in another section. Describe the differences that exist in this recurring material.
3. In this work, passages can be identified that are *cadential* (essentially tonic prolongations that add a sense of finality to a passage), or *transitional* (leading to a new section). Locate and describe examples of each type.

Melodic/Rhythmic Structure

1. Locate an example of a four-measure phrase, a five-measure phrase, and a six-measure phrase. What role, if any, do phrase lengths play in defining the form of this work?
2. Locate an example of two phrases forming a period. Describe this period as parallel or contrasting.
3. Large-scale stepwise motion and large-scale arpeggiation can be found among the melodies of this work. Identify some examples.
4. In characterizing the melodic structure of this work *very generally,* which term of each pair is the more appropriate?
   a. conjunct or disjunct;
   b. rhythmically uniform or rhythmically diverse;
   c. wide range or narrow range.

Harmonic/Tonal Structure

1. Name the most important tonal centers in this work, give by measure number their locations, and describe their relationships with the principal tonality.
2. Several passages in the first major section of this work consist of circle-of-fifths progressions. Identify these passages.
3. The modulation in m. 41 is accomplished through the enharmonic treatment of the chord in m. 40. Explain the enharmonic function of this chord.
4. The music at m. 53 is in D-sharp minor. What is the tonal center in effect prior to this measure? Describe the role of the chord in m. 51 in the modulation. At m. 57, the music returns to the tonal center in effect prior to m. 53. Explain how this is accomplished.

Texture/Articulation/Dynamics

1. Describe the role of texture, articulation and dynamics in creating contrast among and within the sections of this work.
2. Locate some examples of Brahms's favorite device of melodic doubling in thirds or sixths.

Allegro energico
f
rit.
ten.
p
poco cresc.
cresc.

22
sf
f
27
32
p
dim.
37
dim. molto
41
pp una corda

45
49
53
espress.
dolce
57
pp
61

65
dolce
69
rit.
dim.
poco sosten.
p
73
poco
cresc.
a
f
poco
77
in tempo
f
81

85
rit.
ten.
p
Ped.
Ped.
89
93
poco cresc.
97
cresc.
sf
f
101

Johannes Brahms

SONATA NO. 1 FOR CLARINET AND PIANO OP. 120

Second Movement

This concise, eloquent Andante, from Brahms's final period, contains long, lyrical melodic lines supported by a wealth of late-nineteenth-century harmonic relationships. Brahms's masterful handling of his material is worth careful study. Note especially how the musical repetitions are varied at each recurrence. The passage at mm. 23–30 should be analyzed harmonically in detail. What is the formal role of the passage beginning at m. 41? Where does this passage end? The coda has a curiously modal quality. Elaborate on this. (Note: The clarinet part sounds a major second lower than written.)

Andante un poco Adagio
poco f
poco f
Ped.
7
espress.
p
dolce
p
dolce
Ped.
14
f
Ped.
21
p
p
pp
dim.
pp
p dolce
pp

26
p
p
p
p
p
30
dolce
dolce
pp
pp
35
p
cresc.
p
p
40
p
p espress.
dim.
dim.

45
più p
49
p espress.
dolce
53
espress.
57
sf
p dolce
p

61
pp leg. e dolce
65
f
69
p
dim.
pp
73
f
pp
dim.
Ped.

Johannes Brahms

VIER ERNSTE GESÄNGE *No. 3: "O Tod, wie bitter bist Du"*

Brahms's *Lieder,* which number over 260, come from every period of his career. Composed in 1896, the *Vier Ernste Gesänge* represent his final contribution to the genre. The texts—all taken from the Bible—deal with death, a subject that increasingly preoccupied the terminally ill composer. No. 3 begins with a descent of thirds that has been called Brahms's "death motive." This succession of descending thirds permeates the song. Look for it not only in the voice part but also embedded in the piano part. Note how it relates to the tonal centers established in the music up to the key change. The text is a prime determinant of form at the broadest level in this song. Careful study will also reveal correspondences at a more detailed level as well as numerous subtle examples of text painting.

10
und dem es wohl geht in al - len Din - gen und noch wohl es - sen mag! O
poco cresc.
f
13
Tod, o Tod, wie bit - ter, wie bit - ter bist du.
p
18
O Tod, wie
p
21
wohl ___ tust du ___ dem

23
Dürf - - - ti - gen, der da schwach und alt ist,
26
der in al - len Sor - gen steckt, und nichts Bes - sers
p
28
zu hof - fen, noch zu er - war - - - - ten hat! O
f
31
Tod, o Tod, wie wohl tust du,
p
p

"O TOD, WIE BITTER BIST DU"

O death, how bitter you are,
when someone thinks of you
who has good days and enough and lives without care,
and who has it well in all things and can enjoy his food!
O death, how bitter you are.

O death, how good you are to the needy
who are weak and old,
who are immersed in all cares
and have nothing better to hope for or to expect!
O death, how good you are.

Hugo Wolf

"GEBET" *(No. 28 from Mörike Songs)*
"WER SICH DER EINSAMKEIT ERGIEBT" *(No. 1 from Goethe Songs)*

Hugo Wolf (1860–1903) brought to the German solo song an intense harmonic chromaticism, high literary standards, a fluid, aperiodic and frequently declamatory melodic style, and imaginative pictorialism. These traits are exemplified in the two selections that follow, settings of texts by Eduard Mörike (1804–1875) and Johann Wolfgang von Goethe (1749–1832). In what popular forms are they cast? In what ways is the music reflective of the text? To what extent is the vocal line duplicated in the piano part? How does this compare with the piano accompaniments in the Schubert and Schumann songs in this anthology? To what extent do the tonic and dominant play important tonal roles in these songs?

"Gebet" contains numerous chromatic harmonies. Locate examples of altered dominants, mode mixture (minor-mode harmonies in a major context) and chromatic third relationships. Assuming a move to the dominant in the prelude, identify the chord on the last beat of m. 6.

"Gebet"

Sostenuto
(Getragen)
VOICE
PIANO
p
mf
6
with devotion and fervor
(fromm und innig)
Herr, schi - cke was du willst, ein
f
ff
p
pp
11
Lie - bes o - der Lei - des; ich bin ver - gnügt, dass Bei - des aus dei - nen
f
16
Hän - den quillt. Wol - lest mit Freu - den und wol - lest mit Lei - den mich
pp
mf
sf

"GEBET" ("Prayer")

Lord, send what you will,
Joy or suffering,
I can accept both from your hand.
Let neither joy nor grief overwhelm me!
Indeed, between the two lies the purest truth.

Translation by Clifford Billions

In "Wer sich der Einsamkeit ergiebt," discuss how the five-measure prelude is integrated within the body of the song. Aside from the principal tonality, three other tonalities are suggested in this passage. What are they? What modal characteristics are present in the song? Also to be found are Neapolitan sixth chords, dominant ninth chords, mode mixture, and augmented sixth chords.

"Wer sich der Einsamkeit ergiebt"

13
Ja! lasst mich mei-ner Qual! Und kann ich nur ein-mal recht
p
mf
p
16
p
tenderly
(zart) 3
very softly
(sehr leise)
ein - sam sein, dann bin ich nicht al - lein. Es schleicht ein
dim.
pp
ppp
19
Lie - ben-der lau-schend sacht, ob sei-ne Freun - - din al -
22
lein? so ü - ber-schleicht bei Tag und Nacht mich
f

25
Ein - - sa-men die Pein, mich Ein - sa-men die
dim.
28
Pein.
Ach, werd' ich erst ein -
poco rit.
a tempo
p
pp
p
31
dying away
(ersterbend)
mal ein - sam im Gra - be sein, da lässt sie mich al -
pp
35
lein.
p
più p
p
pp

"WER SICH DER EINSAMKEIT ERGIEBT"
("He who embraces loneliness")

He who embraces loneliness,
Ah! he is soon alone;
Everyone lives, everyone loves,
And leaves him [to his] sorrow.
Yes! leave me to my suffering!
And if I seek solace in my solitude,
Then I am not alone.

Did ever a lover steal softly,
[To see] whether his loved one is alone?
In this way both day and night
The pain of my solitude overcomes me.
Ah, I will at last be alone in my grave,
There [sorrow] will leave me.

Translation by Clifford Billions

Gabriel Fauré

"CHANSON D'AMOUR" OP. 27, NO. 1

Gabriel Fauré (1845–1924) composed nearly one hundred songs over the course of his career, and it is by these works, primarily, along with his *Requiem,* that he is known today. "Chanson d'Amour" is an early work. Try to understand it in functional harmonic terms, paying particular attention to the means by which modulations are accomplished. As many as five tonal centers are clearly established. Identify them. In addition, at least three more transient tonal centers are suggested. Identify these as well. The song is cast in a popular instrumental form. What is it? Finally, describe the melody in terms of phrase lengths and relationships.

10
-ront.
a tempo
marcato
14
p
J'ai - me ta voix, j'ai - me l'é-tran-ge grâ - ce de tout ce que tu
p
17
poco a poco cresc.
dis, Ô ma re-bel - - le, ô mon cher an - - ge,
cresc.
20
f
Mon en-fer et mon pa-ra - dis!
p
J'ai - me tes yeux,
mf
p

23
j'ai - me ton front, O ma re-bel-le, ô ma fa - rou - - che,
26
pp
senza rigore
J'ai - me tes yeux, j'ai - me ta bou - che Où mes bai-sers s'é-pui-se-
pp
29
- ront.
a tempo
marcato
33
p
J'ai - me tout ce qui te fait bel - - le, De tes pieds jus-qu'à tes che-
p

36
cresc. poco a poco
mf
-veux, Ô toi vers qui mon - tent mes voeux, Ô ma fa-
cresc. poco a poco
39
p
-rouche, ô ma re-bel - - le, J'ai - me tes yeux, j'ai-me ton front,
p
43
pp
Ô ma re-belle, ô ma fa - rou - che, J'ai-me tes yeux, j'ai - me ta bou - che
pp
47
p poco rit.
Où mes bai-sers s'é-pui-se - ront, Où mes baisers s'é-pui-se-
p poco rit.

"CHANSON D'AMOUR"

I love your eyes, I love your face,
Oh my rebellious one, Oh my shy one,
I love your eyes, I love your lips
Upon which my kisses will exhaust themselves.
I love your voice, I love the strange
Elegance of all that you say,
Oh my rebellious one, Oh my dear angel
My torment and my paradise!
I love your eyes, I love your face,
I love everything that makes you beautiful,
From your feet to your hair,
Oh you to whom all my desires ascend.

Translation by Mary Schiller

Gustave Mahler

"NUN WILL DIE SONN' SO HELL AUFGEH'N" *from Kindertotenlieder*

Gustave Mahler (1860–1911) pursued a dual career as composer and conductor. As a composer, he was primarily concerned with song and symphony, his orchestral songs representing a synthesis of the two genres. This selection is the first of five pieces contained in his cycle, *Kindertotenlieder* ("Songs on the death of children"). The chamber-like orchestration and small dimensions make it fairly accessible for analysis. How many principal melodic phrases can you find? Locate all variants of these phrases, in both the vocal and instrumental parts. Can you identify a fragment from one of these phrases that assumes a motivic function throughout the movement? Discuss the harmonic character of the passage beginning at m. 59. Note the orchestration in these same measures, particularly the way in which the lines are continuously shifting in color. Mahler was one of history's most meticulous orchestrators. Notice the very carefully calculated and explicit expressive and dynamic markings. Finally, what large-scale repetition do you observe? What aspects of the music are varied during these repetitions? Describe the overall form.

Composed 1904

Related reading: Felix Salzer, *Structural Hearing* (New York: Dover Publications, 1952), pp. 202–203. A voice-leading graph of the first twenty measures of this work.

Langsam und schwermütig; nicht schleppend
2 Flauti
2 Oboi
2 Clarinetti in B
Clarinetto basso in B
2 Fagotti
2 Corni in F
Arpa
Campanelle
Voce
klagend
sempre p
Nun will die Sonn' so
Langsam und schwermütig; nicht schleppend
Violino I
Violino II
Viola
Violoncello
Contrabasso
7
Ob.
Cl. b. (B)
Fg.
Cor. (F)
Arp.
Voce
Vla.
Vcl.
p espress.
klangvoll
mit verhaltener Stimme
hell auf-geh'n, als sei kein Unglück, kein
con sord.
con sord.
sempre pp
13
Cl. (B)
Cl. b. (B)
Cor. (F)
Arp.
Voce
Vla.
Vcl.
molto espress.
Un-glück die Nacht ge-scheh'n!
sempre pp

18
Ob.
Cl. (B)
Cl. b. (B)
Cor. (F)
Arp.
Camp.
klagend
pp subito
p subito
pp ausdrucks
24
Fl.
Ob.
Cl. (B)
Fg.
Cor. (F)
Voce
drucklos
p express.
a 2
Das Unglück ge-schah nur mir al - lein!
31
Ob.
Cl. (B)
Cl. b. (B)
Cor. (F)
Arp.
Voce
Vl. II
Vla.
Vcl.
sempre marcato
Die Son - ne, die Son-ne, sie schei - net all - ge-
con sord.
pp aber ausdrucksvoll
sempre con sord.
pp ohne Ausdruck

36
heftiger
sehr hervor-
Ob.
Cl. (B)
Cl. b. (B)
Fg.
a 2
espress.
sehr ausdrucksvoll
Cor. (F)
p espress.
Arp.
Voce
mein!
Vl. II
Vla.
Vcl.
Cb.
42
Fl.
Ob.
tretend
Cl. (B)
Cl. b. (B)
Fg.
Cor. (F)
Camp.
Voce
Du
48
Fl.
Ob.
Arp.
Voce
mußt nicht die Nacht in dir ver - schränken, mußt sie ins ew' - ge
senza sord.
Vl. I
pp mit großem Ausdruck
senza sord.
pizz.
Vcl.

54
nicht schleppend
Cl. (B)
Fg.
Cor. (F)
Arp.
Voce
Licht, ins ew' - - - - ge Licht ver - sen -
nicht schleppend
Vl. I
Vcl.
Cb.
pizz.
59
Etwas bewegter (Rubato)
Mit leidenschaftlichem Ausdruck
Fl.
a 2
Ob.
1.
Cl. (B)
a 2
Cl. b. (B)
Fg.
a 2
Cor. (F)
Arp.
Voce
ken!
Etwas bewegter (Rubato)
Mit leidenschaftlichem Ausdruck
Vl. I
Vl. II
con sord.
Vla.
Vcl.
arco
Cb.

63
zurückkehrend zum
Fl.
Ob.
Cl. b. (B)
Fg.
Cor. (F)
Arp.
Camp.
Voce
Ein
zurückkehrend zum
Vl. I
Vl. II
Vcl.
Cb.
1. Solo
68
Ob.
Cl. b. (B)
Fg.
Cor. (F)
Voce
Lämp-lein ver-losch in mei-nem Zelt!
con sord.
Vl. I
73
Tempo I
Cl. b. (B)
Cor. (F)
Arp.
mit Erschütterung
Voce
Heil! Heil sei dem Freu-den-licht der Welt.
Tempo I
molto espr.
Vl. I
con sord.
Vl. II
Vla.
senza sord.
Vcl.
arco
Cb.

"NUN WILL DIE SONN' SO HELL AUFGEH'N"

Now the sun will rise as brightly
As if no grief had occurred in the night!
The misery came to me only!
But the sun shines on all!

You must not be a victim of the night,
But immerse your grief in eternal light.
A small lamp has been extinguished in my tent!
Hail to the friendly light of the world!

Unit V

THE TWENTIETH CENTURY

Much of this century's music reflects a reassessment concerning the nature and function of melody, harmony, rhythm, form, and even sound itself. Perhaps no period in the history of Western music has seen such a sweeping re-examination of traditional values. The result has been a stylistic diversity greater than at any time in the past. The seeds of this diversity were sown in France and Germany and can be found in the aesthetic attitudes of two very different composers whose influences have been profound—Claude Debussy and Arnold Schoenberg. Many, if not most, of the composers in this unit can be traced to one or the other of these sources. A line of development less rooted in tradition can be seen in the music of Charles Ives, Edgard Varèse, Henry Cowell and John Cage, to mention only the best-known composers of this group. The music in this unit has been chosen to represent these and other lines of development in the most succinct yet comprehensive way.

Claude Debussy

Claude Debussy (1862–1918) composed his most important works between 1893 and 1913. Sharply critical of the Germanic tradition and Richard Wagner, he avoided traditional contrapuntal-developmental techniques. He based his fragmentary melodies on Church modes, whole-tone scales and pentatonic scales more often than on the traditional major and minor scales. Using the late-nineteenth-century harmonic vocabulary in a non-functional way, he augmented it with quartal harmonies, added-tone harmonies, modal successions and *planing* (parallel motion of chords). His colorful, widely spaced orchestral sonorities employ instruments in unusual registers and combinations, emphasizing solo woodwinds, muted brass, and subtle, quiet percussive effects.

POUR LE PIANO *Sarabande*

In this movement, Debussy pays homage to the French clavecinists of the Baroque era. What similarities in formal structure exist between Baroque suite movements you may have studied and this one? Look up the term "sarabande" and cite any characteristics of that Spanish dance form that can be found in this music. Beyond these similarities, there is little to relate this work to its Baroque predecessors. Rather, Debussy introduces many new and original techniques.

The motive that first appears in m. 5 has many interesting variants. Identify and explain all appearances. What kinds of harmonic structures appear in this work? Can you locate a point at which a distinct change in harmonic structure occurs? Is a single tonal center established? What is the principal tonality and how is it created? Does this work relate more to major-minor tonality or to the modal system? Explain.

9
p
p
13
plus p
retenu
pp
Au mouvt
p
3
3
3
3
18
mf
retenu
dim.
p
pp
23
pp
28
mf
p
pp

Animez un peu
mp
p très soutenu
p
Au mouvt
f
f
p
p
plus p
cresc.
mf
f

Claude Debussy

NOCTURNES *"Nuages"*

"Nuages" captures, in Debussy's words, "the slow, solemn motion of the clouds, fading away in grey tones tinged with white." Notice how the music's non-pulsatile, ametric feeling convincingly captures this image. Reflecting the sky's ever-changing appearance, the musical patterns come and go, one idea following another, familiar patterns re-emerging amidst new and changing ones. The fragmented, elusive ideas lack strongly defined rhythms and contours, remaining identifiable largely because of their orchestration. Note, for example, the various appearances of the English horn motive of mm. 5–8, or the horn figure of m. 23, or the opening two-measure woodwind pattern. Though musical continuity is strong, a large interior section is suggested by tonal, melodic and harmonic means and through orchestration. Explore this matter. Does any element from this section reappear near the end of the work? Specific techniques that you should identify include open-fifth harmonies, planing (involving various harmonic structures), pentatonicism, modality and chord mutation.

Composed 1899

Related reading: Richard S. Parks, *The Music of Claude Debussy* (New Haven: Yale University Press, 1989), pp. 243–248. A discussion of form and harmonic resources in "Nuages." The work's formal proportions are shown to conform to the Lucas and Fibonacci summation series. Harmony is discussed in terms of pitch class sets.

1. NUAGES
(Clouds)

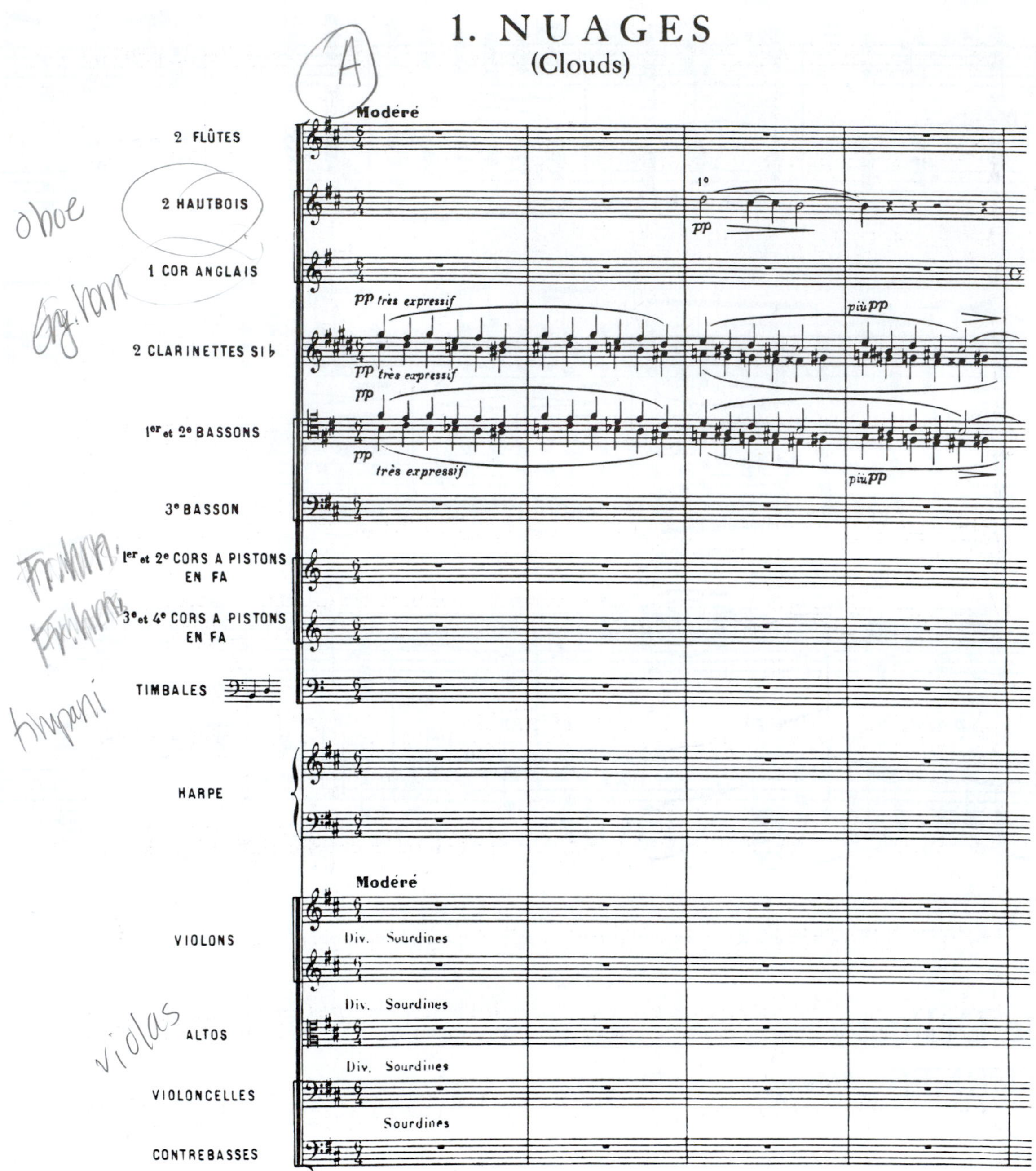

5
FL.
COR ANG.
expressif
CL.
1er et 2e Bons
1o
CORS
3o
TIMB.
Div. en 6
1
pp
p
ppp
pppp
tr
harp
violin
viola
cello
bass

11
TIMB.
2
pp
1ers vons
à 3
pp
à 2
2ds vons à 3
pp
ALTOS
pizz.
16
COR ANG.
très expressif
(un peu en dehors)
velles
Div.
sub p.

22
Eng. horn
COR ANG.
p
1°
p
CORS
3°
p
2ds vons
ALTOS
pp
velles
pp
pp

27
COR ANG.
3
CORS
3

32
HAUTB.
1°
CL.
Bons
CORS
Fr. hrns.

37
HAUTB.
à 2
p
p
cre . . scen . . do
CL.
B^{ns}
mf cresc.
à 4

42
4
HAUTB
COR ANG
CL
BONS
CORS
pizz.
Div.

46
COR ANG.
5
1er COR sourdines
p
5
pizz.
pizz.
arco
pizz.
arco
pp

50
COR ANG.
1er et 2e Bons
1er COR
pp
p
più p
54
HAUTB.
COR ANG.
6
p expressif
ALTO SOLO
sans sourdines
ppp
bog like beg.
melody in 2nd part

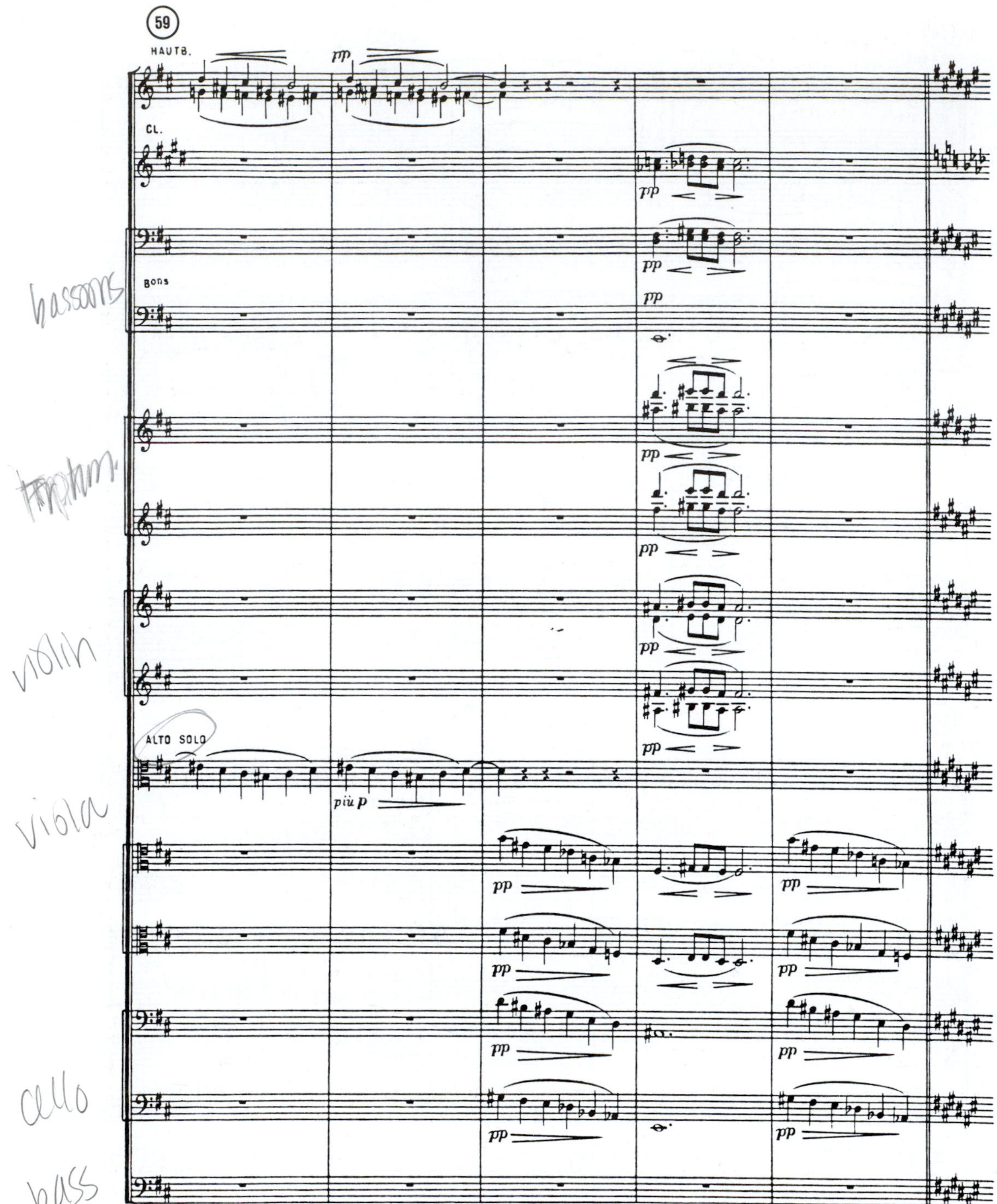
59
HAUTB.
pp
CL.
pp
BONS
pp
ALTO SOLO
più p
bassoons
French horn
violin
viola
cello
bass

64
7 Un peu animé
1re Fl.
1°
très expressif
Cl.
pp
1er et 2e Bons
pp
pp
Harpe
(Sol♭, Ré♭, La♭, Mi♭, Si♭)
7 Un peu animé
pp
pp
pp
pp
pp
pp
pp
pp
pp

69
1re FL.
CL
1o sourdines
CORS
3e sourdines
HARPE
1 Von SOLO (sans sourdines)
très expressif et très soutenu
ALTO SOLO
très expressif et très soutenu
velle SOLO
sans sourdines
très expressif et très soutenu
pizz.
arco

74
1re Fl.
Cl.
1er et 2e Bons
Cors
1o
3o
Harpe
8
Von solo
Alto solo
Velle solo
p
pp
ppp

79
1re FL.
1° tempo
più p molto dim.
pp
COR ANG.
sfz > p
p
CL.
pp
1er et 2e Bons
sf > p
1°
CORS
3°
piu p > pp
HARPE
sur la touche

85
HAUTB.
1°
p
più p
pp
9
R ANG.
p molto dim.
CL.
p
più p
pp
CORS
3°
p
più p
pp
TIMB.
tr
ppp
pp
9
pp
pp
pp
pp
pp
à 4
sur la touche
pp

91
COR ANG.
1er et 2e Bns
TIMB.
Plus lent
10
pp
ppp
à 8
à 4
97
1re FL.
Encore plus lent
SOLO
CORS
Sourdines
TIMB
pizz.
più pp

Claude Debussy

PRELUDES, BOOK I *No. 4 "Les sons et les parfums tournent dans l'air du soir"*

Debussy's two books of *Preludes* were composed between 1909 and 1913. In this piece, a succession of musical ideas appears in much the same way as one might imagine that "the sounds and scents wind through the night air" along a Parisian boulevard.

QUESTIONS FOR DISCUSSION

Formal Structure

1. The succession of key signatures suggests an ABA form. Is this analysis justified by other musical factors? What musical elements return along with the return of the original key signature?
2. It is tempting to find *within* the initial "A-major" key section a three-part form. How could this be justified? (Consider how tonal centers are created here, how musical contrast is achieved, and how cadential punctuation may contribute.)
3. In your opinion, does this piece contain a coda?
4. Discuss the role of the perfect fourth as a unifying interval.

Melodic/Rhythmic Structure

1. Discuss melodic repetition in this piece. Is any one phrase length especially common?
2. Debussy directs that the left hand at mm. 34–36 be "slightly stressed and sustained." Does this line or a variant appear elsewhere in the work?
3. Identify the principal melodic idea.
4. Speculate on the origin of the ostinato that begins at m. 15.

Harmonic/Tonal Structure

1. What is the principal tonality and how is it established?
2. What mode is suggested at mm. 1–2? mm. 50–53?
3. What scale forms the basis of the material of mm. 46–48?
4. Locate several examples of:
   a. planing;
   b. harmonies with added tones;
   c. pure triads;
   d. functional dominant seventh chords;
   e. non-functional dominant seventh chords.

Texture/Articulation/Dynamics

Describe the texture and overall dynamic character of this work.

En animant un peu
9
m.d.
p
expressif
m.d.
p
mf
p
14
En retenant
8
a Tempo
égal et doux
p dim.
pp
en dehors
19
Serrez un peu
Retenu
p
p
24
a Tempo
pp
pp
pp
m.d.
27
Plus lent
En animant
pp
p
mf

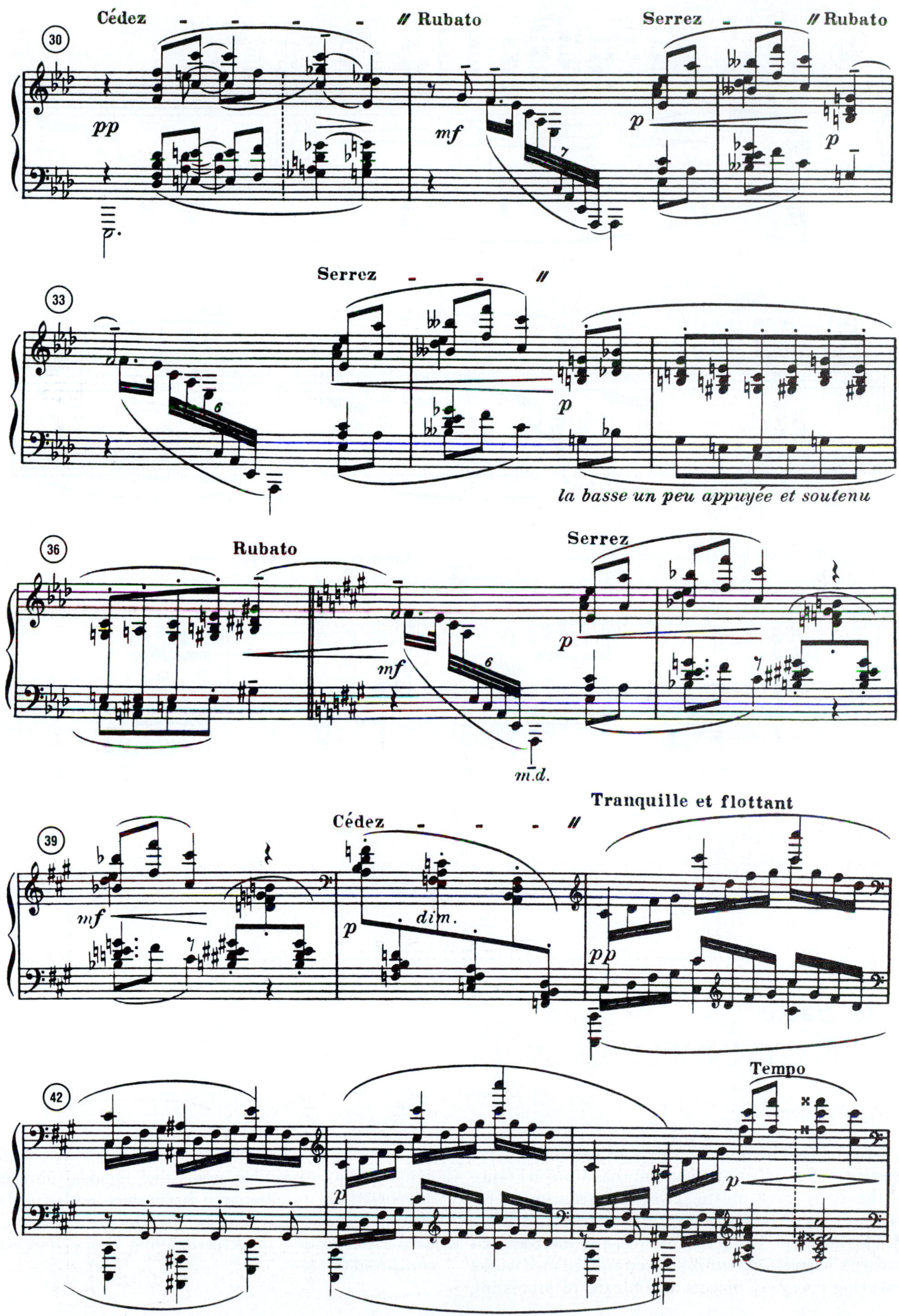
30
Cédez
Rubato
Serrez
Rubato
pp
mf
p
p
33
Serrez
p
la basse un peu appuyée et soutenu
36
Rubato
Serrez
mf
p
m.d.
39
Cédez
Tranquille et flottant
mf
p
dim.
pp
42
Tempo
p
p

Erik Satie

TROIS GYMNOPEDIES *No. 1*

In Erik Satie (1866–1925), one can see the musical precursor of an artistic movement that arose in France in the early part of the twentieth century. This movement, called "Dadaism," was a reaction against the seriousness of art. One of the best-known Dadaists, Marcel Duchamp, painted and sculpted works featuring everyday objects as a means of protesting the "profundity" of high art. In a like manner, Satie often employed simple, repetitive melodic phrases supported by rudimentary harmonies and chordal textures. These traits can be seen in the first of his *Trois Gymnopedies* (Greek ceremonial choral dances), composed in 1887.

Lent et douloureux (slowly and mournfully)
Piano
pp
pp
6
f
ped. simile
11
pp
16

21
p

26

31

36
pp

41
pp
ped. simile

46
f

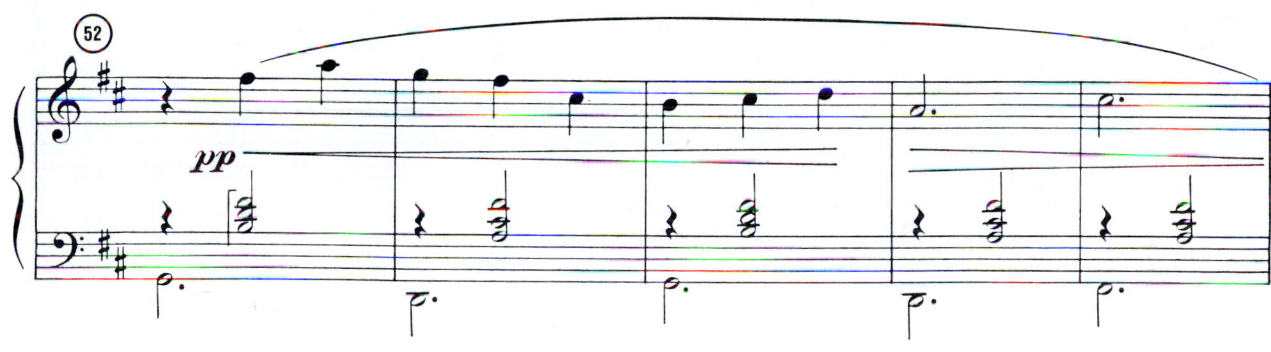
52
pp

57
p

Arnold Schoenberg

Arnold Schoenberg (1874–1951) began composing in the highly chromatic idiom of Wagner but abandoned traditional tonal principles by 1908 in favor of an atonal style tightly unified by recurrent melodic-harmonic motives or *cells.* This style in turn evolved into the twelve-tone method, which Schoenberg first used in 1923. Some of his "expressionistic" works of the pre-twelve-tone period are through-composed, while most of the twelve-tone works employ classical forms with readily identifiable themes and traditional proportions. However, despite the external form and particular method of pitch organization, the principle of perpetual variation pervades practically all of Schoenberg's music.

SECHS KLEINE KLAVIERSTÜCKE OP. 19, NO. 6

This short work, composed in 1911, is similar in its brevity, sparse texture, quiet dynamic level and motivic intensity to many of the works of Schoenberg's one-time pupil, Anton Webern. It is possible to view the piece as an elaboration of four related elements—two of them harmonic (i.e., chords) and two of them melodic (i.e., intervals). *One* of the melodic elements is contained in *both* of the harmonic elements and also occurs as a harmonic unit itself. The other melodic element appears at one point in the piece simultaneously with its inversion. Using these "clues," can you identify the four elements? Having done so, it will be possible to account for almost all the notes in this piece. You should be aware, however, that other analyses are possible and other relationships can be found, suggesting different interpretations for the tonal coherence of this work.

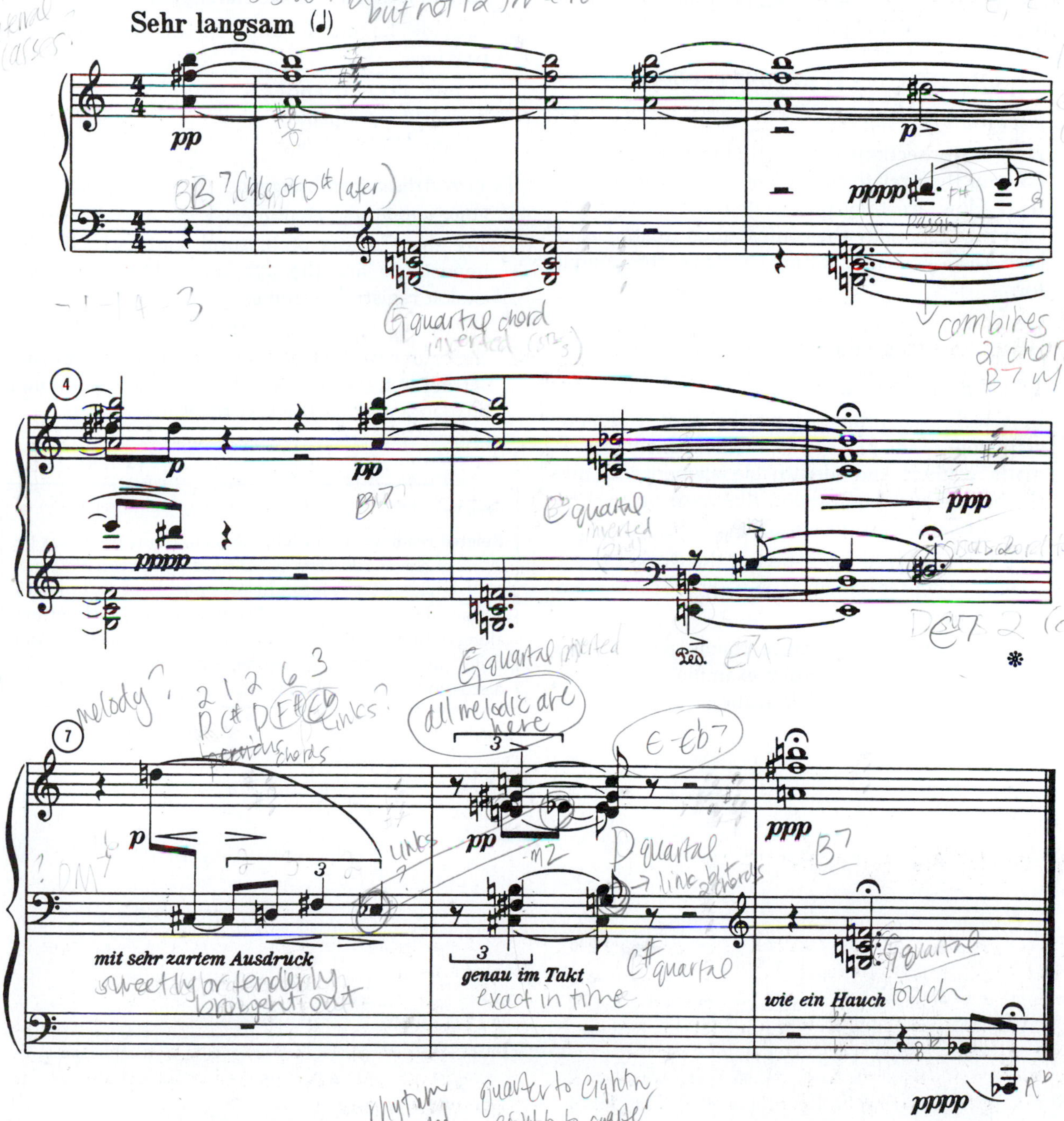

Sehr langsam (♩)

pp p ppppp

4

p pp ppppp ppp

Ped. *

7

p pp ppp

mit sehr zartem Ausdruck

3

genau im Takt

wie ein Hauch

pppp

Arnold Schoenberg

PIERROT LUNAIRE *No. 8 "Nacht"*

Pierrot Lunaire was written in 1912, almost coincident with another revolutionary work—Stravinsky's *Le Sacre du Printemps. Pierrot* consists of settings of twenty-one poems in German translation from Albert Giraud's cycle of the same name, divided into three parts of seven poems each. Different combinations of the five instruments that accompany the voice are employed in each song of the cycle. "Nacht," a passacaglia which begins the second part, is scored for bass clarinet, cello and piano.

QUESTIONS FOR DISCUSSION

Formal Structure

1. How many sections do you find in this piece and how do they relate to the verse structure of the text? How are they punctuated and contrasted? Compare especially the contrapuntal treatment in each section. Using letters, describe the overall form.
2. Generally speaking, how does the musical setting reflect or enhance the meaning of the text?

Melodic/Rythmic Structure

1. In which instrument does the first complete statement of the passacaglia theme occur? Of how many distinct and identifiable elements is this theme composed? Examine the voice part. How does it relate to the passacaglia?
2. Consider the rhythmic aspect of the work. Does it change or does it remain essentially the same from beginning to end?
3. Elements of the passacaglia theme pervade the entire movement. Carefully examine every measure and note its musical derivation. Then list a few of the more subtle manipulations of the opening three-note motive from the theme.

Harmonic/Tonal Structure

1. Do melodic or harmonic considerations seem to be more important in this piece? Support your answer with examples from the music.
2. Analyze the first three measures from both a harmonic and a melodic standpoint.
3. Provide harmonic analysis of the following passages:
   a. mm. 11–12 (piano);
   b. mm. 14–15 (piano);
   c. mm. 17–18 (piano).

Texture/Articulation/Dynamics

1. How would you characterize the overall texture? Are there points of textural contrast? Of what importance are the dynamics? Does this piece exploit registral extremes?
2. Locate the text phrases that are repeated during the course of the piece. Then examine the musical setting at those points. What musical repetition, if any, accompanies the text repetitions?

Composed 1912

Related reading: Alan Philip Lessem, *Music and Text in the Works of Arnold Schoenberg* (UMI Research Press, 1979), p. 120f. Chapter Five gives a history of this work, provides a chart showing the order of composition of each setting along with its instrumentation, date of composition, and order in the final grouping, and includes a short discussion of each movement.

Gehende (ca 80)
Baß-Klarinette in B.
Violoncell.
pp
Gehende (ca 80)
Rezitation.
p
Finstre, schwarze Rie-senfal-ter tö-tetender
Gehende (ca 80)
Klavier.
pp

6
B-Kl. (B)
Vcl.
Son-ne Glanz.
Ein ge-schloß-nes Zau-ber-buch,
pp
8

9
B-Kl. (B)
Vcl.
am Steg
(pp aber deutlich hörbar)
Etwas rascher.
Flag.
p
gesungen (womöglich die tieferen Noten)
Etwas rascher.
ruht der Ho-ri-zont,
ppp
verschwie-gen.
gesprochen
Aus dem Qualm ver-lor-ner
Etwas rascher.
pp

12
B-Kl. (B)
Vcl.
Flatterzunge
am Steg
pp
cresc.
pp dim.
ppp
f
Tie - fen steigt ein Duft, Erinnrung mordend! Fin - stre, schwar - ze
stacc.
ohne Ped.
15
I. Tempo
am Griffbrett
ff
fff
dim.
Rie - senfal - ter tö - te - ten der Sonne Glanz.
18
espress.
Flag.
p
Und vom Him - mel er - denwärts sen - ken sich mit schwe - ren Schwin - gen
molto legato

Ominous, black giant moths
Obliterate the glow of the sun.
The horizon lies as a sealed
magic book—silent.

From the smoke of lost depths
Rises a fragrance, annihilating memory!
Ominous, black giant moths
Obliterate the glow of the sun.

And from heaven towards earth
The horrors drop down invisibly
With heavy wings
Upon our hearts—
Ominous, black giant moths.

Arnold Schoenberg

THREE SONGS OP. 48 *No. 2 "Tot"*

In this song from 1933, Schoenberg has composed the piano accompaniment in such a way that certain members of the twelve-tone row are consistently heard together or adjacently. These pairings, which seem to be more important than the actual ordering of the row, produce an intervallic consistency that is audible both in the harmonies and in the melodic lines. Identify the row. Where can you find clear, linear statements? How many forms of the row does Schoenberg use? In addition to the pairing just mentioned, what larger segmentation of the row is employed? Also, how does Schoenberg insure that pitch duplication does not occur between the voice and piano parts? Two important points in this song—the piano prelude and the piano postlude—are emphasized in a way that has to do with the segmentation of the row. Explain this.

If all is one, what does it matter?
This one is happy, that one is mad.
What does it matter? All is one,
He has found happiness, and I have found none.

Arnold Schoenberg

VARIATIONS FOR ORCHESTRA OP. 31 *Introduction, Theme, and Variation II*

This is one of Schoenberg's few purely orchestral works and the first twelve-tone composition for a full orchestra. Here, he uses the large ensemble sparingly but coloristically, avoiding octave doublings, which he considered inconsistent with the twelve-tone premise.

The Introduction serves to "introduce" the row—gradually. Where might be a logical place to find a *complete* statement? In the Theme, what is the relationship between the melody and the accompanying chords? Variation II begins in intensely canonic fashion. Locate and describe the canons and discover their duration. How are the row forms distributed among the instruments involved? Schoenberg paid tribute to J. S. Bach in several of his works by incorporating the BACH motive (B-flat–A–C–B-natural).* Although the motive will not be found in a *strict* ordering of this row, it can be formed from four adjacent row members. Can you locate prominent examples of the BACH motive in the music? What row forms and transpositions does Schoenberg appear to favor?

*(H = B-natural in German musical scores.)

9
etwas drängend
Fl 1.2.
Ob 1.
Kl 1.
Bs Kl
Fg 1.
Hr 2. m Dpf
m Dpf
Hrf
etwas drängend
I. Gg
II. Gg
Br
Vcl
Kbs
pizz
(pizz)
arco
14
a 3
Fl 1.2.3.
Ob 1.2.3.
E H
Es Kl
Kl 1.
Fg 1.2.3.
a 4
Hr 1.2.3.4. m Dpf
o Dpf
m Dpf
Trp 1.
o Dpf
Hrf
Cel
I. Gg
II. Gg
Br
Vcl
Kbs
pizz
arco

𝅗𝅥. = 𝅗𝅥 (des 2/2) und = 𝅗𝅥. (des 12/8)
19 steigernd
pesante
Pic
Fl 1.2.3.
1.2.
Ob
3.
E H
Es Kl
Kl 1.2.3.
Bs Kl
Fg 1.2.3.
KFg.
1.3.
Hr.
o Dpf
2.4.
Trp 1.2.
o Dpf
1.2.
Pos
3.4.
Tª
Tamt
gestopft
gestopft
pizz
I. Gg
II. Gg
Br
Vcl
Kbs

rit . . . . Tempo I; wieder ruhig
des Tempo I = 60
23
Fl
p leicht
pp
fp
Ob 2.3.
E H
pp
sfp
f
Kl
p
pp dolce
a 2
Bs Kl
Fg 1.
offen
Hr
Pos 1.
pp dolce
Cel
I. Gg
m Dpf
3 fach get
II. Gg
Br
arco
Vcl
pizz
p dolce

29
Pic
Fl 1. 2. 3.
a 3
Ob 1.
E H
Es Kl
Hr 1. 2.
m Dpf a 2
o Dpf
Trp 1.
m Dpf
Hrf
I. Gg m Dpf
(m Dpf)
II. Gg m Dpf
Br
pizz
arco
Vcl
Flag
Kbs
THEMA
34 Molto moderato (♩= 88)
Ob 1.
E H
Kl 2.
Fg 3.
Hr 2. o Dpf
Hrf
Molto moderato (♩= 88)
Vcl
p zart
Kbs

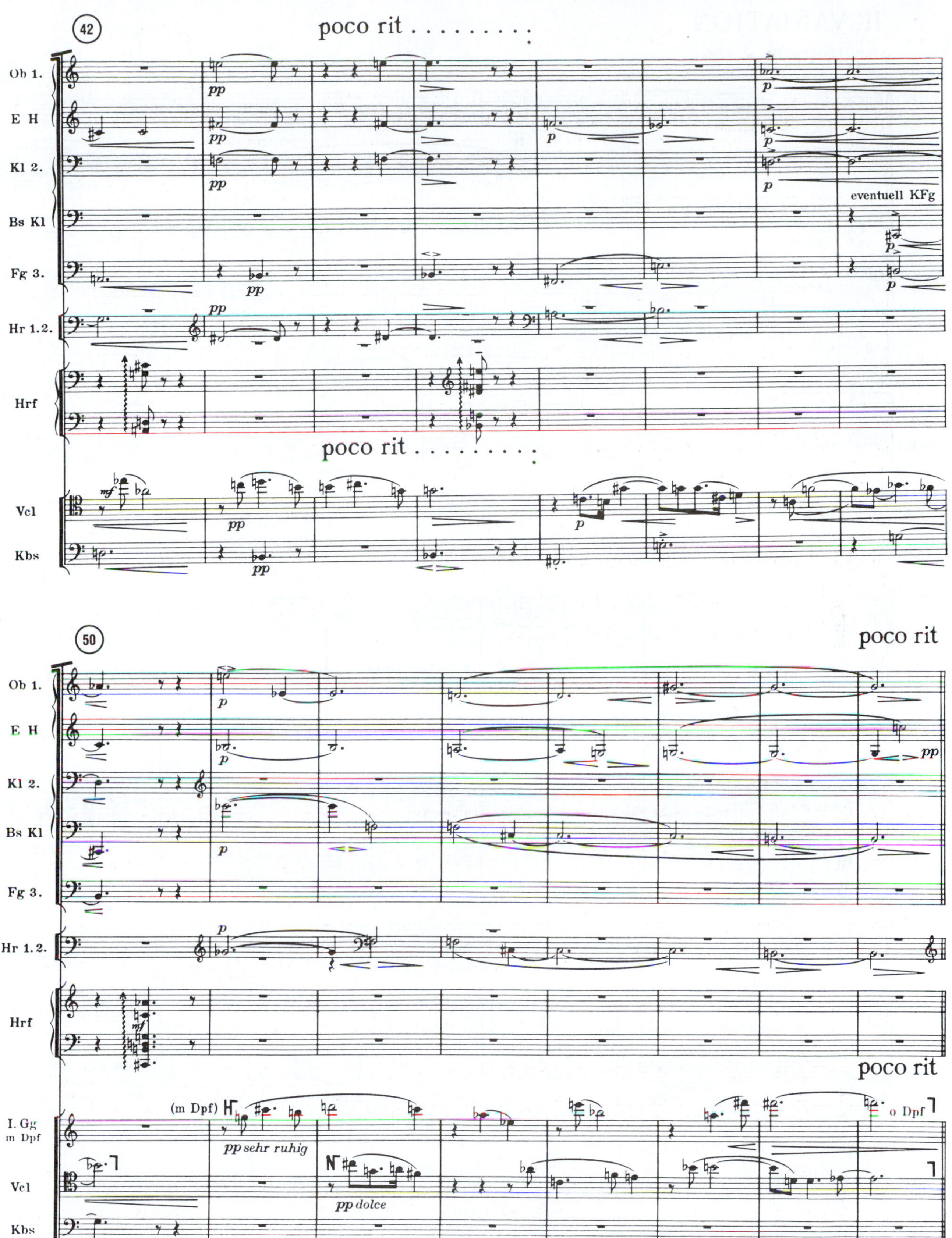
42
poco rit . . . .
Ob 1.
E H
Kl 2.
Bs Kl
Fg 3.
Hr 1.2.
Hrf
poco rit . . . .
Vcl
Kbs
pp
p
mf
eventuell KFg
50
poco rit
poco rit
I. Gg m Dpf
(m Dpf)
pp sehr ruhig
pp dolce
o Dpf

II. VARIATION

10
Fl 1.
Ob 1.
Kl 1.
Bs Kl
1.
Fg
2.
Hr 2.
Pos 3.
Solo Gg
m Dpf
Solo Vcl
mf
f
p
pp
14
Fg 1.2.
Hr
Solo Kbs
pizz
arco
espr

17
poco calando
Fl 1.
Ob 1.
E H
Es Kl
Kl 1.
Bs Kl
Fg 1.
Hr 1.
Pos 1.
p cantabile
pp dolce
poco calando
Solo Gg m Dpf
Solo Vcl
pizz
arco
mp espress
21
Fl 1.
Fl 2.3.
Ob 1.
Kl 1.
Bs Kl
Fg 1.
Fg 2.3.
Solo Gg m Dpf
Solo Vcl
Dpf weg
o Dpf

Charles Ives

Charles Ives (1874–1954) was perhaps the most important American composer (though unrecognized as such at the time) in the early twentieth century. Writing only to please himself, he composed a brand of distinctly American music that reflected the musical influences of his rural New England childhood. In the process, he anticipated most of the important developments of the century. These included cluster chords, polytonality, atonality, polyharmony, polytempo, quartal harmonies, microtonal harmonies, serial principles, aleatoric principles and spatial effects. Ives's musical conception was broad enough to permit the coexistence in his works of seemingly unrelated musical elements and techniques, and this is perhaps one of the most difficult aspects of his music.

114 SONGS *No. 2 "Evening" and No. 57 "Mists"*

Ives's songs span his creative career, from 1887 to 1926, and reflect his output as a whole. Most are contained in the collection entitled *114 Songs,* from which the following selections have been chosen.

"Evening"

This song, from 1921, is a rather straightforward setting of a portion of Milton's *Paradise Lost.* The song may be seen as divided into sections according to the changes in melodic and harmonic character that occur (although other factors coincide with these changes as well). Pursuing the matter on a smaller scale, note how the vocal line of mm. 7–10 seems to imply a different harmonic structure in each bar. Ives's belief in a unity that underlies all diversity may account for the unusual mixture. At what point in the song does the tonality seem to stabilize? Can you identify a tonal center for the work? In this regard, what is unusual about the ending? Although the harmonic organization appears to be based on diverse ideas, the melodic organization is quite motivic. For example, what aspects of the material heard in the opening measure recur? Of additional interest is the relationship between the voice and piano parts from m. 11 to the end.

4
and Twi-light gray had in her so-ber liv-ery all things— clad;
l.h.
r.h.
l.h.
r.h.
l.h.
l.h.
l.h.
r.h.

7
pp
Si - lence ac-com-pan - ied;— for the beast and bird— They to their grass-y couch,
ppp

10
a little faster
these to their nests were slunk, but the wake - ful night - in -
più moto

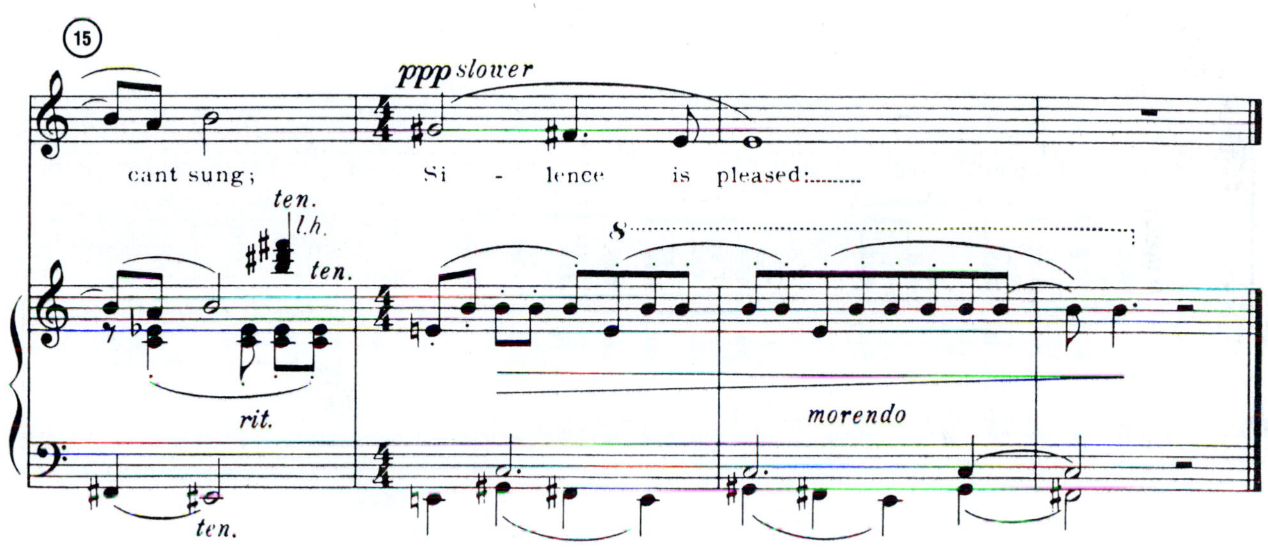

"Mists"

The introductory first measure of this song from 1910 seems somewhat inconsistent harmonically with what immediately follows. What might be its purpose? Can you cite some other examples of seemingly unrelated elements either juxtaposed or superimposed? Musical contrast is the key to this song's form as well. Identify the form and list the elements that define it. Prominent techniques include planing and polytonality, of which you should seek to identify all examples. The high register piano part is conceived as a "shadow" of the middle register and is to be "scarcely audible" (see the footnote to the score). How are the two parts related musically?

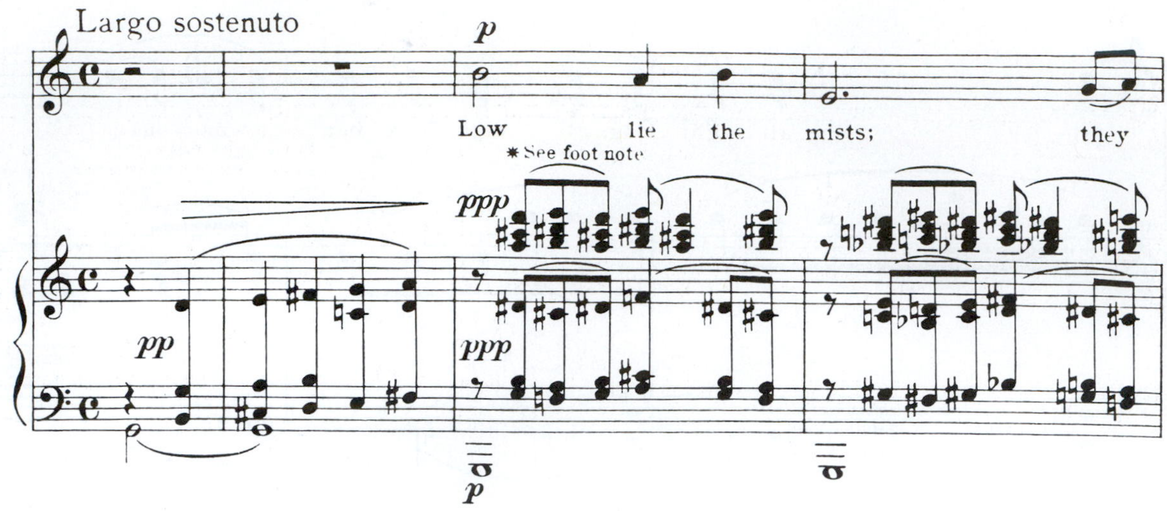

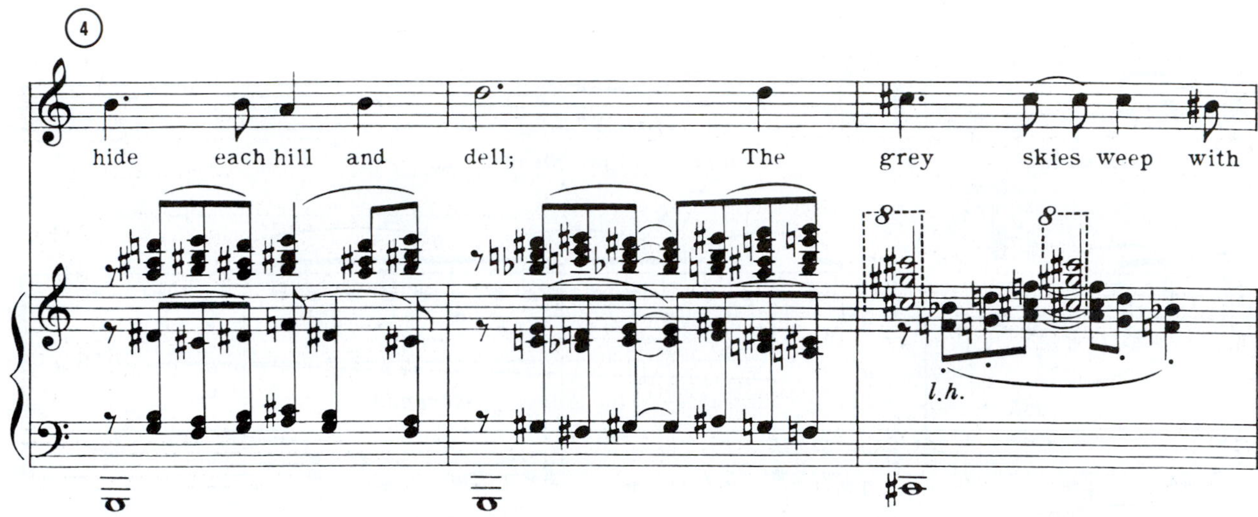

*The group of notes in the r.h. in measures 2, 3, 4, 5 and 16, 17, 18 may be omitted, in which case the l.h. part, with the exception of the low G, may be doubled an octave higher. If the r.h. notes are used they should be scarcely audible.

10
But hap - pier days through mem - ory weaves
più animando
l.h.
r.h.
poco rall. e dim.

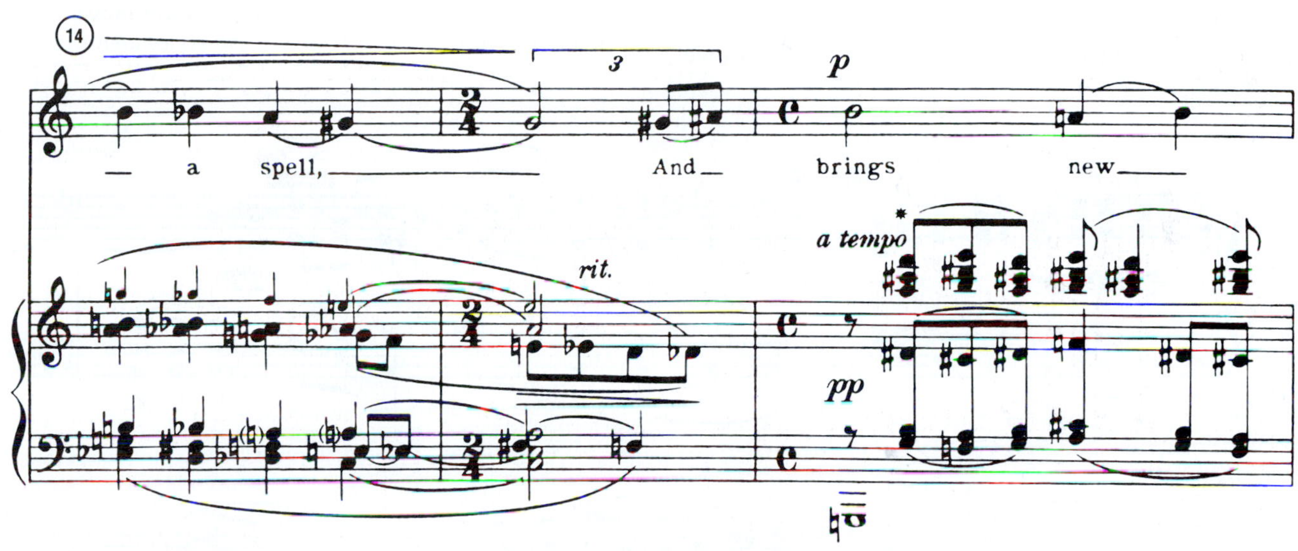
14
a spell, And brings new
rit.
a tempo
p
pp

17
hope to hearts who bid fare - well.
pp
ppp
rall.

Charles Ives

PIANO SONATA NO. 2 ("CONCORD") *Third Movement "The Alcotts"*

The "Concord Sonata" is a four-movement work inspired by four New England literary figures—Ralph Waldo Emerson, Nathaniel Hawthorne, Louisa May Alcott and Henry David Thoreau. Written between 1909 and 1915, it contains some of the most experimental musical techniques of the time. The form, at the broadest level, is dependent on Ives's use of borrowed material and his juxtaposition of different musical styles. Consider in this regard the allusions to a number of well-known musical works—a reflection of the diverse music-making in the Alcotts' house. Note especially the pervasive motive from Beethoven's *Fifth Symphony*. Then consider the more fully developed quotation that occurs later in the movement. How does the use of this pre-existent material serve to create the form? Consider also the tonal centers that are established. Can an overall tonality be said to exist and if so, on what basis? Or is it possible to regard the tonality as progressive—that is, continually moving forward, without returning?

> *Composed 1909–1915*
>
> Related reading: Lawrence Starr, "Charles Ives: The next hundred years—towards a method of analyzing the music," *The Music Review*, Vol. 38, No. 2 (May 1977), p. 101f. An examination of style change in this movement and the form-defining role of the five styles identified.

3
faster
mp
f
ff faster
mf
mf
f
In a gradually
l.h.
excited way.
l.h.
l.h.
ff
ff

faster
accel.
slower
fff
rit.
l.h.
p
f
mf
Moderately again
r.h.
l.h.
faster
rit.
pp
4
Slower and quietly
5
hold back a little
ten.

8
A little faster
mp
poco rit.
13
pp
p
p
hold back a little
17
pp
faster
mp
21
gradually faster
f
25
gradually more animated

f
cresc.
26
accel. - - - cresc.
r.h.
l.h.
27
fast and working up
animando
ff
ff
gradually slower
ff slowly and broadly
3
3
fff
dim. e rit.
ff
f
mp
f
mp
pp
pp
slower

Maurice Ravel

SONATINE *Second Movement: Movement de Menuet*

Maurice Ravel (1835–1937) was a contemporary and friend of Debussy, and he employed many of the same harmonic techniques, but with somewhat greater use of classical forms, a preference for longer melodic lines, and a greater interest in counterpoint. In this sense, his music anticipates the neo-classicism of the 1920s. This movement contains many features that typify Ravel's style. These include planing, modality, lavish use of triadic extensions, and a mixture of functional and non-functional chord successions. Identify the recurring material and determine how it is varied on repetition. Taking the smallest unit that could perhaps be regarded as motivic, examine the ways in which the opening ascending fifth (D-flat–A-flat) governs much of the harmonic and melodic activity of the movement.

26
ppp
en dehors
p
33
Rall.
f
ff
Ped.
Plus lent
39
pp
p en dehors et expressif
Reprenez peu à peu
47
le Mouvt
a Tempo
Sans ralentir
55
Rall.

Béla Bartók

Béla Bartók (1881–1945) successfully united the essence of his native folk music with traditional Western European forms and developmental processes, achieving unity through pervasive motivic relationships. His melodic lines often span a narrow range, feature small intervals, and are based on pentatonic, synthetic or near-Eastern scales and on modes. His harmonies are often the by-products of linear motion. Polytonality, polymodality, clusters, planing and intervallic parallelism are common. Bartók uses the piano and strings percussively and colorfully, calling for such string effects as multiple stops, *glissandi* and snap pizzicato.

Related reading: Mark Nelson, "Folk music and the 'Free and Equal Treatment of the Twelve Tones': Aspects of Béla Bartók's synthetic methods," *College Music Symposium*, Vol. 27 (1987), pp. 59–115. An extended article defining and examining six specific methods by which Bartók arrived at a synthesis of native peasant elements and Western compositional techniques.

MIKROKOSMOS NOS. 59, 91, and 128

Mikrokosmos is a set of 153 piano pieces of graded difficulty, contained in six volumes that were composed between 1926 and 1937. The collection forms not only a sizable source of pedagogical material, but a compendium of Bartók's compositional techniques.

No. 59: "Major and Minor"

No. 91: "Chromatic Invention"

QUESTIONS FOR DISCUSSION

No. 128: "Peasant Dance"

Formal Structure

Into how many principal sections may this work be divided? How are they related?

Melodic/Rhythmic Structure

1. Would you describe the melodic structure as primarily conjunct or disjunct?
2. Study and compare mm. 5–12, mm. 13–20 and mm. 51–57. What features do they share and how are they different?
3. Syncopation—the temporary emphasis on a normally unstressed part of a beat or measure—is produced in several ways in this piece. Can you cite two examples?
4. Locate an example of each of the following:
   a. mirror motion;
   b. cadential extension;
   c. sequence.
5. Identify some large-scale stepwise motions in this piece and explain how they are created.
6. What scale or mode appears to be the basis of the melody between mm. 5 and 28? Remember that, just as in traditional tonal music, certain of the pitches may not be diatonic (i.e., contained within the mode).

Harmonic/Tonal Structure

1. What is the tonal center and how is it established?
2. Describe and compare the harmonic cadences that appear at:
   a. mm. 11–12;
   b. mm. 24–25;
   c. mm. 64–65.

   Do any have modal implications?
3. Describe the harmonic structures that occur in mm. 13–18, mm. 21–23 and mm. 61–66.

Texture/Articulation/Dynamics

1. Describe the role that tempo and dynamics play in creating the form.
2. Can this piece be described as homophonic, polyphonic, or a mixture of the two textures? Explain your answer.

21
pochiss. allarg.
mf
cresc.
f
28 Un poco più mosso, ♩= 120
p
35
mp
42
poco a poco ritard. al
mf
f
sff
sf
dim.
50
Meno mosso, ♩= 92
accel.
p

Béla Bartók

FORTY-FOUR VIOLIN DUETS *Song of the Harvest*

Like the *Mikrokosmos,* this collection of violin duets ranges from simple to complex and contains a variety of compositional techniques. Of particular interest in this work are the pitch and temporal relationships between the two violins. The conflict between the two parts is perhaps symbolized by the discrepancy in key signatures. Is the conflict resolved in the course of the duet? Which of the melodic and harmonic techniques described in the profile on page 465 are employed? On what traditional formal principle is the work based?

6
Più mosso, parlando, ♩ = 88
f
f

11
poco a poco allarg.

16
Tempo I.
poco rit.
p
p

21
Tempo II.
poco a poco allarg.
f
f

28
Tempo I.
rallentando
p
p
pp

(1′27″)

Igor Stravinsky

The output of Igor Stravinsky (1882–1971) was marked by continuous development and dramatic style changes and encompasses practically every genre. Although he displayed an interest in traditional forms and procedures, recombination, superimposition and reorchestration usually take the place of motivic development in his music.

Stravinsky's melodies often have a narrow range, diatonic and repetitive pitch structure, and a modal quality, with frequent meter changes. His harmonic language is at times highly chromatic, pandiatonic or atonal. Stravinsky's textures range from thickly heterophonic to lean and contrapuntal, and ostinatos are common. Sharp timbral contrast is achieved through the use of unusual instrumental combinations and ranges and of solo timbres, especially those of the double reeds.

LE SACRE DU PRINTEMPS

Excerpt One: Introduction and Beginning of Dance of the Adolescents
Excerpt Two: Spring Rounds

Stravinsky composed *The Rite of Spring,* subtitled "Scenes of Pagan Russia," between 1911 and 1913 at the request of Serge Diaghilev for performance by his Ballet Russe. A comparative study can be undertaken between this work and another ground-breaking work from 1912, Schoenberg's *Pierrot Lunaire* (see page 438). Whereas that work is linear-contrapuntal and based on more traditional developmental processes, *Le Sacre du Printemps* is primarily harmonic-rhythmic, and it grows through the succession of undeveloped but associated events. These two works form convenient points of reference for much music that has since been written.

QUESTIONS FOR DISCUSSION

Formal Structure

1. Much of the music of the Introduction can be related to four very general ideas:
   a. a pitch that is either sustained or reiterated;
   b. figures based on major or minor thirds;
   c. diatonic figures containing triadic and pentatonic figures;
   d. a chromatically ascending or descending line.

   Trace the development of each of these ideas.
2. Identify and describe the large, contrasting blocks of sound that are abruptly juxtaposed in the Introduction.

Melodic/Rhythmic Structure

1. Which of the traits summarized in the preceding profile are evident in the opening bassoon melody and the English horn responses? Identify them.
2. How do the horn parts relate to the string parts starting at m. 76 of Excerpt One?
3. How do the bassoon and cello parts beginning at m. 84 relate to each other and to the generative ideas of the composition? What harmonic elements of the texture at mm. 62–65 relate to these parts? Where is the English horn pattern previously heard?
4. Describe the development of the melodic material of Excerpt Two.

Harmonic/Tonal Structure

1. Analyze the reiterated harmony beginning at m. 76 in Excerpt One. Which of its components are heard earlier and which are heard individually later in the excerpt?
2. Locate and describe some examples of planing (melodic/harmonic parallelism) in Excerpt Two.
3. Identify the mode of the passage beginning at m. 15 of Excerpt Two.

Texture/Articulation/Dynamics

1. The climactic moment of the Introduction is an extremely complex texture composed almost entirely of previously heard elements. Locate this point and identify an earlier appearance of each of the textural elements.
2. An innovative string technique is found beginning at m. 62. Identify and explain the technique.

Composed 1911–1913

Related reading: Richard Taruskin, "Russian folk melodies in *The Rite of Spring,*" *Journal of the American Musicological Society,* Vol. 33, No. 3 (1980), pp. 501–543.

Excerpt One: Introduction and Beginning of Dance of the Adolescents

18
Oboe 2.
Cor. ingl.
Clar. picc.
Solo
espress.
Clar. (La)
Clar. basso 2
Fag.
Corni (Fa)
Viol. 2.
V-le
pizz.
dim.
4
23
Fl. gr.
Fl. c-alto in Sol
Oboi 1. 2.
1. Solo
Clar. picc.
Clar. (La)
Clar. basso 1. 2.
Cor. 3. 4. (Fa)
un peu en dehors
Viol. 2.
V-le

27
Fl. gr. 1.2.
3.
Fl. c-alto in Sol
Solo
Oboi 1.2.
Cor. ingl.
Solo (en dehors)
mf
Clar. (La) 1.
2.
Clar. basso 1. 2.
Solo
mf
Fag. 2.
Corni (Fa) 1.
3.4.

32
Fl. gr. 1.2.
2.
Fl. 3 = Fl. picc. 2.
Fl. in Sol
Oboi 1.
2.
mf
Cor. ingl.
Clar. picc.
Solo
legato
mf espress.
Clar. 1.2. (La)
Clar. basso 1. 2.
Corni 1.2.
p
Viol. 1.
Cello Solo
pizz.

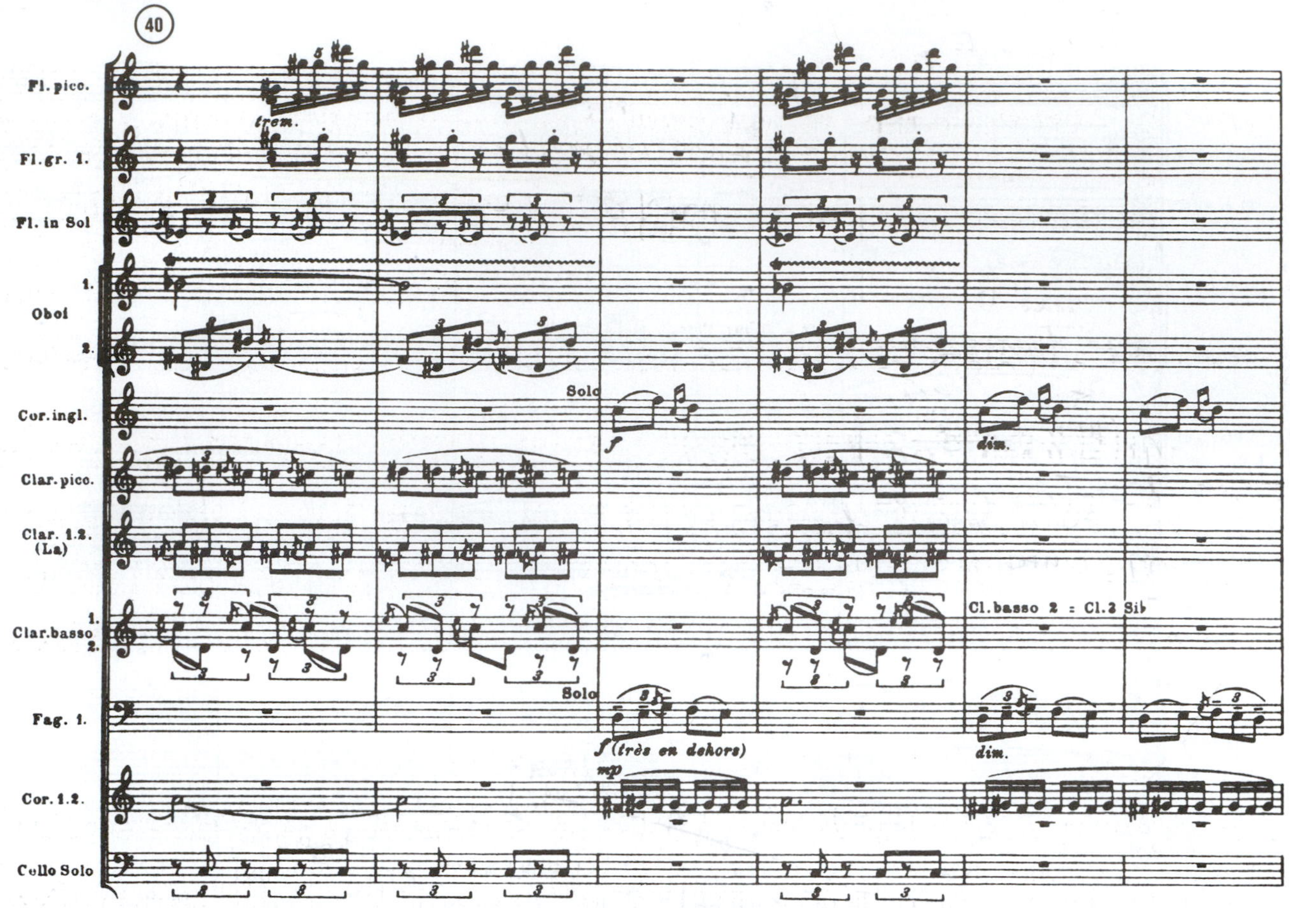

40

Fl. pico.
trem.
Fl. gr. 1.
Fl. in Sol
Oboi 1. 2.
Cor. ingl.
Solo
f
dim.
Clar. pico.
Clar. 1.2. (La)
Clar. basso 1. 2.
Cl. basso 2 = Cl. 3 Sib
Fag. 1.
Solo
f (très en dehors)
dim.
Cor. 1.2.
mp
Cello Solo

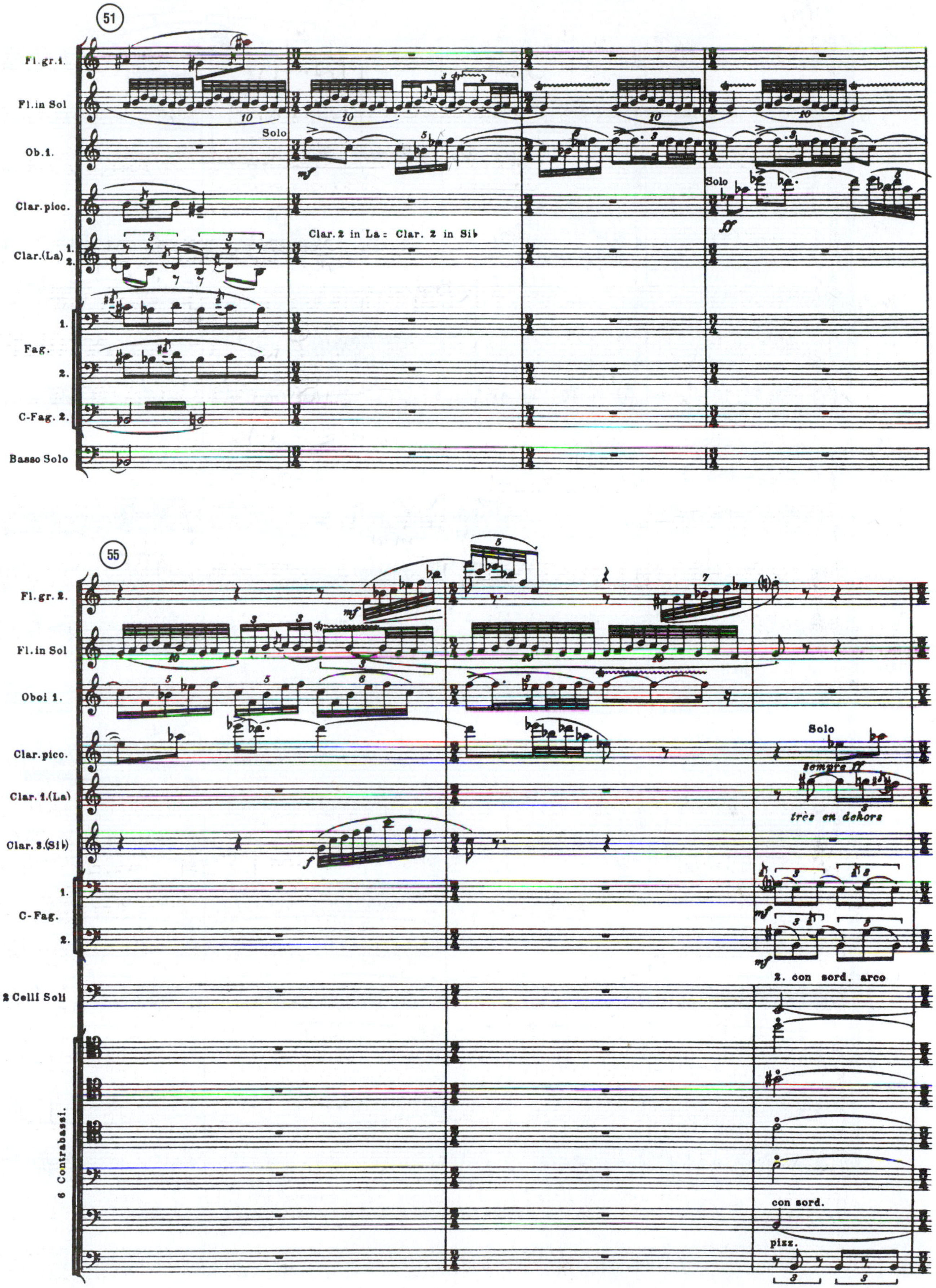

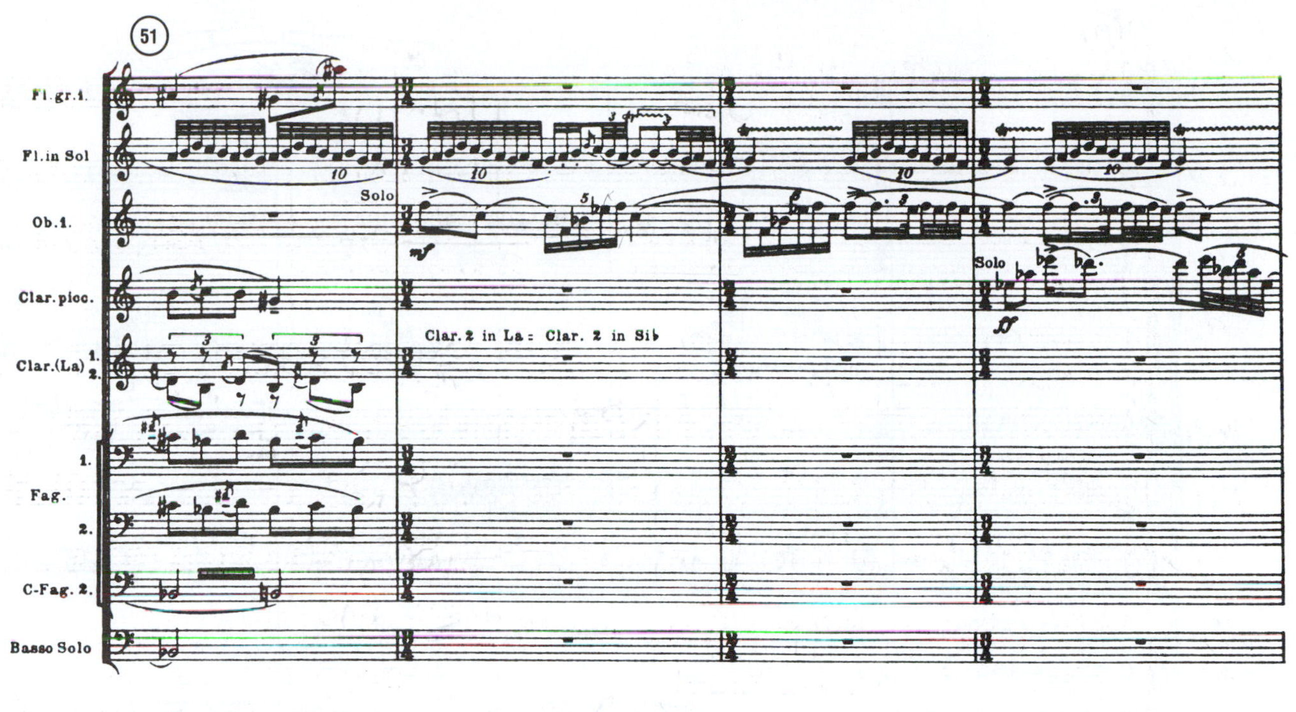

51
Fl. gr. 1.
Fl. in Sol
Ob. 1.
Solo
Clar. picc.
Clar. (La) 1. 2.
Clar. 2 in La = Clar. 2 in Si♭
Fag. 1. 2.
C-Fag. 2.
Basso Solo
55
Fl. gr. 2.
Fl. in Sol
Oboi 1.
Clar. picc.
Solo
sempre ff
Clar. 1. (La)
très en dehors
Clar. 3. (Si♭)
C-Fag. 1. 2.
2 Celli Soli
2. con sord. arco
6 Contrabassi.
con sord.
pizz.

58
Fl. picc.
Flatterzunge
Fl. gr.
Solo (come sopra)
Oboi
Flatterzunge
Solo
Cor. ingl.
Clar. picc.
Clar. 1 (La)
Flatterzunge
Clar. 2 (Si♭)
C-Fag.
con sord.
Tr. picc. in Re
2 Celli Soli
6 Contrabassi

62
Fl. picc.
Fl. gr.
Fl. in Sol
Flatterzunge
Oboi
Cor. ingl.
Clar. picc.
Clar. 1.(La)
Clar.(Sib)
Clar. basso 1.
Fag.
C-Fag.
Cor.
Tr. picc.(Re)
Viol. Solo
sul Sol
V-le
5 Viole
glissando
sul Do
arco
2 Celli
(pizz.)
Soli
6 Contrabassi.

64
Tempo I ♩=50
Fl. picc.
Fl. gr.
Fl. in Sol
Oboi
2. 3.
Cor. ingl.
Clar. picc.
Clar. 1. (La)
Clar. (Sib)
Clar. basso 1.
Solo.
Fag.
(come sopra)
C.-Fag.
to 4th Fag.
Cor.
Tr. picc. (Re)
Viol. Solo.
Viole (div.)
2 Celli Soli.
(senza sord.)
6 Contrabassi.
(senza sord.)
Tempo I ♩=50

67
Clar. picc.
Clar. 1. (La)
Clar. 2.3. (Si♭)
Clar. basso 1.
Fag. 1.
Cor. 1.2.
Viol. 1.
6 Viole Sole
Tutti
pizz.
con sord.
Viole Tutte
Celli Tutti
C-bassi Tutti
Beginning — Dance of Adolescents / Augers of Spring
76
Tempo giusto. 𝅗𝅥 = 50
Cor. ingl.
Fag. 1.2.
Cor.
1.2.3.4.
5.6.7.8.
1&2 senza sord.
sf sempre
Viol. 2.
Viole
Celli
Bassi
arco (non div.)
sempre stacc.
sempre simile
Solo
pizz.
meno f
C7
Tempo giusto. 𝅗𝅥 = 50

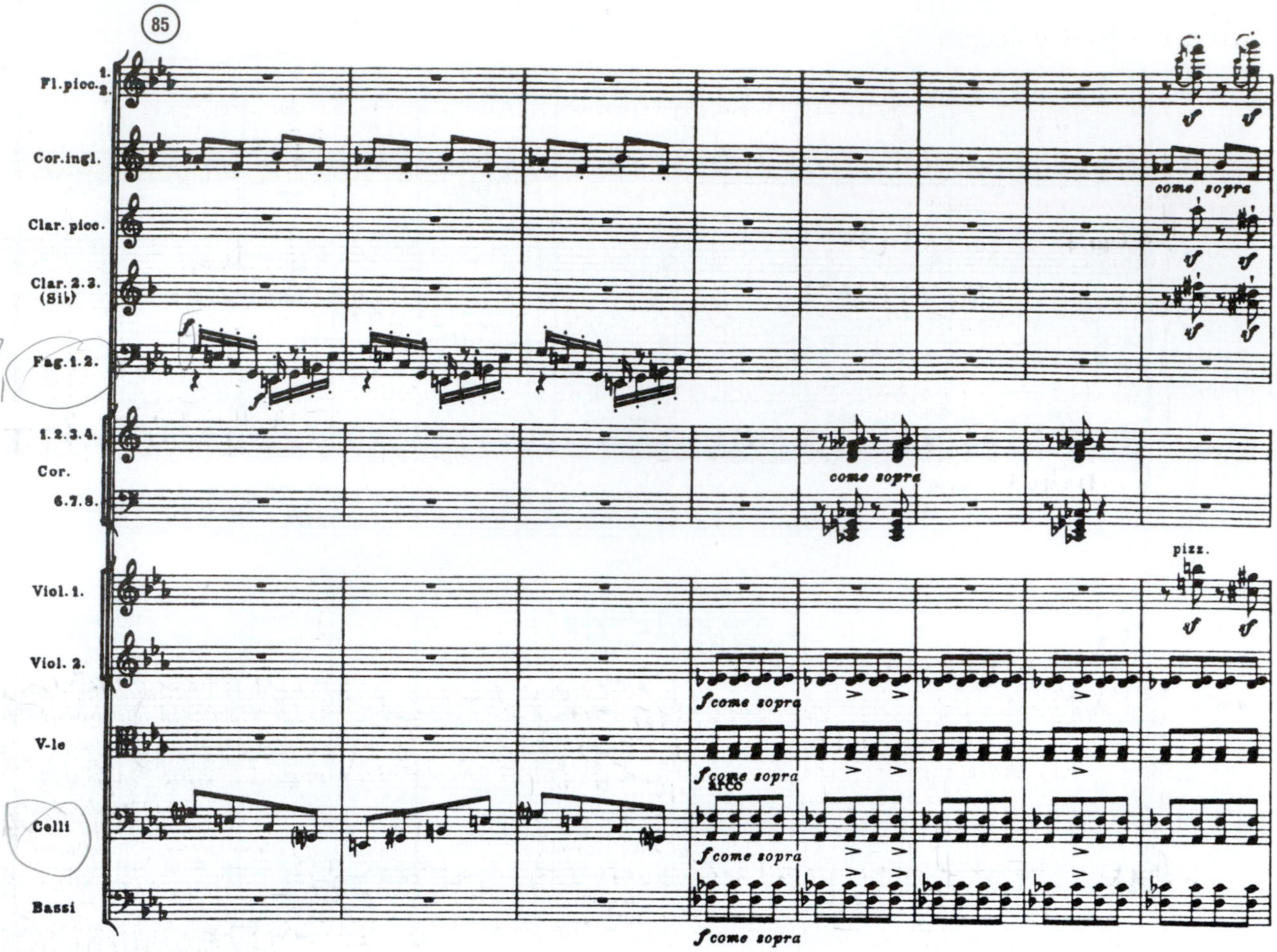

85
Fl. picc. 1. 2.
Cor. ingl.
come sopra
Clar. picc.
Clar. 2. 3. (Sib)
Fag. 1. 2.
1. 2. 3. 4.
Cor.
6. 7. 8.
come sopra
Viol. 1.
pizz.
Viol. 2.
f come sopra
V-le
f come sopra
arco
Celli
f come sopra
Bassi
f come sopra

93
Oboi 1. 2.
Cor. ingl.
Fag. 1. 2.
con sord.
Solo
Tr. 1.
Viol. 1.
pizz.
Viol. 2.
V-le
Celli
Bassi

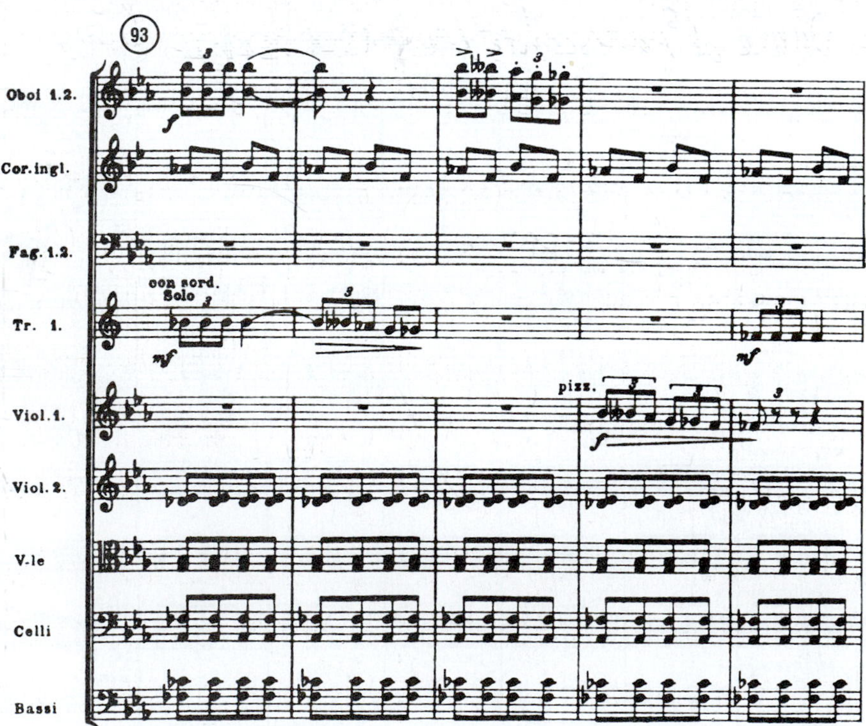

Excerpt Two: Spring Rounds

Tranquillo ♩= 108
1.2.
Fl.gr.
3.
Fl. in Sol
Clar.picc.(Mib)
Clar.basso
p
tr
Tranquillo ♩= 108

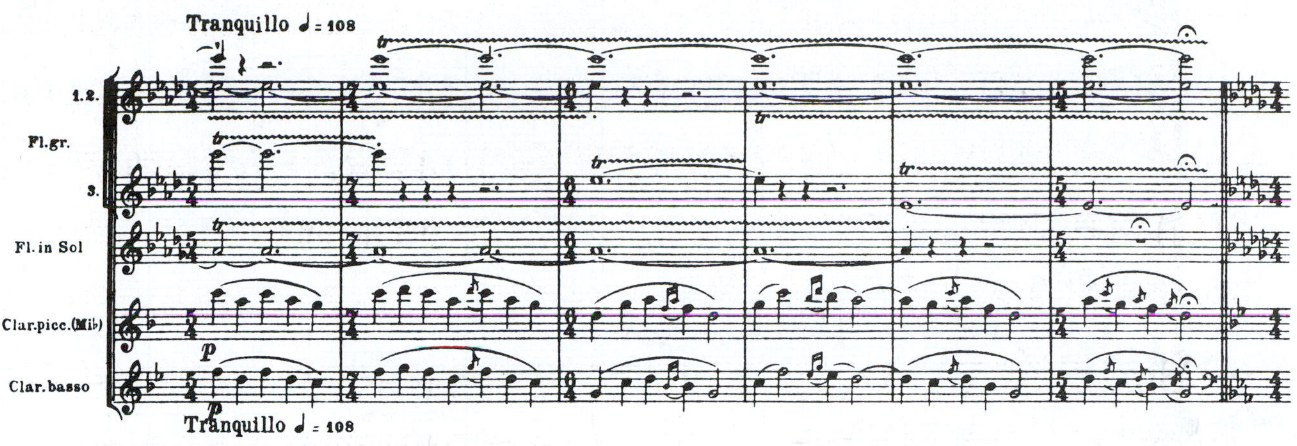

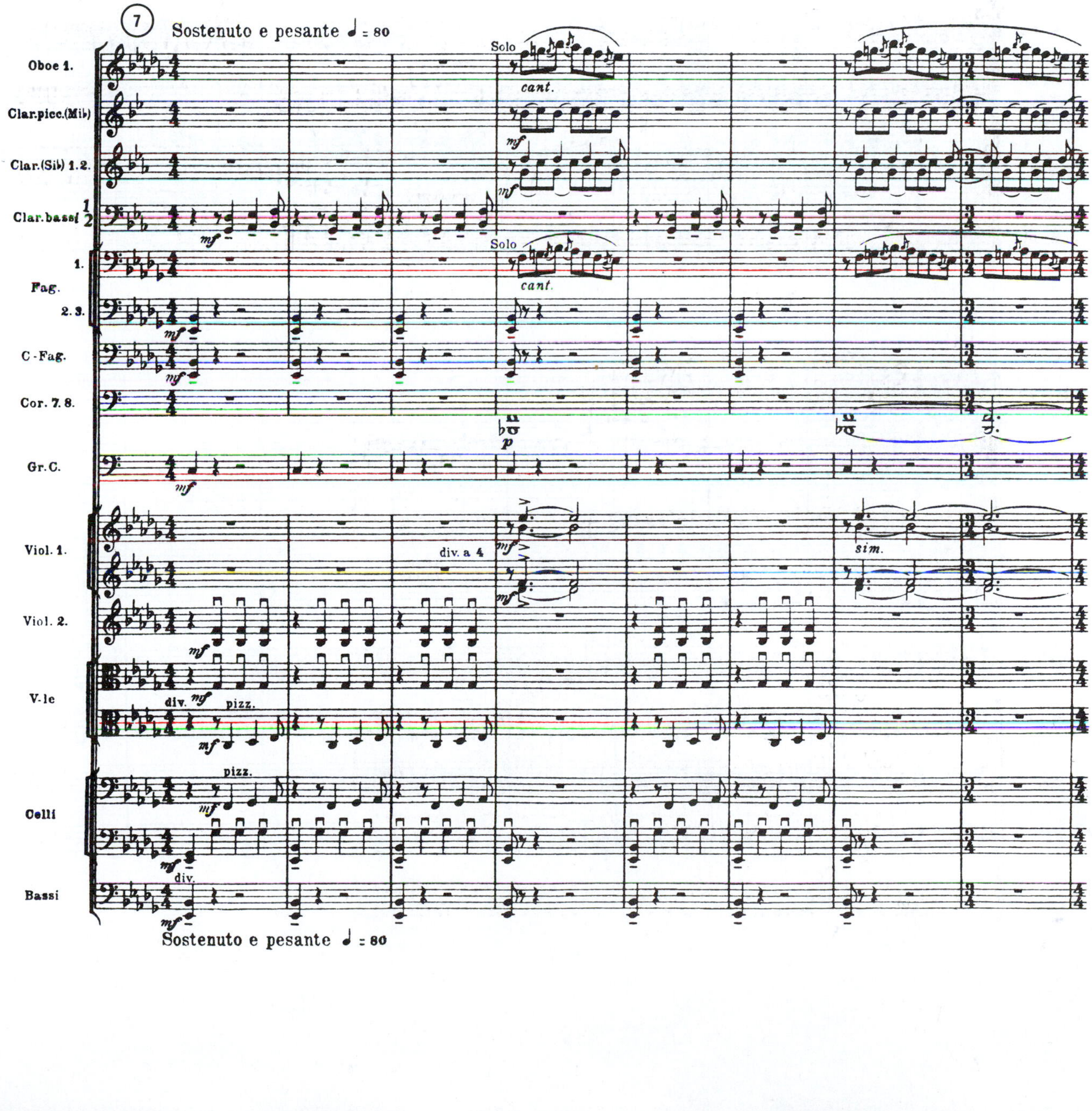

7
Sostenuto e pesante ♩= 80
Oboe 1.
Clar.picc.(Mib)
Clar.(Sib) 1.2.
Clar.bassi 1 2
1.
Fag.
2.3.
C-Fag.
Cor. 7.8.
Gr.C.
Viol. 1.
Viol. 2.
V-le
Celli
Bassi
Solo
cant.
mf
p
div. a 4
sim.
div.
pizz.
Sostenuto e pesante ♩= 80

15
Fl.picc.
Fl.gr.
Fl. in Sol
Oboe 1.
Clar.picc.(Mi♭)
Clar. (Si♭) 1.2.
Clar.bassi 1 2
Fag.
C-Fag.
Cor.
Gr. C.
Viol. 1.
Viol. 2.
4 V-le Sole
Le altre
Celli
Bassi
f e molto cantab.
f e molto cantab.

23
Fl. picc.
1. 2.
Fl. gr.
3.
Fl 3° to Picc 2°
Fl. in Sol.
Oboi
Solo
cant.
Clar. picc. (Mib)
mf
1.
Clar. (Sib)
2.
Clar. bassi 1 2
1.
Fag.
2. 3.
C-Fag.
Cor. 7. 8.
p
Gr. C.
Viol. 1.
Viol. 2.
arco
4 Viole Sole
div.
a 2
(Tutti)
pizz.
Le altre
Celli
Bassi

30
Fl picc
Fl. gr.
Fl. in Sol.
Oboi
Cor. ingl.
Clar. picc. (Mi♭)
Clar. (Si♭)
Clar. bassi
Fag.
C-Fag.
Cor.
Tr. picc. (Re)
Tr. (Do)
Tromb.
Tube
Timp. gr.
Gr. C.
Tamtam.
Viol. 1.
Viol. 2.
V-le
Celli
Bassi
sim.
sempre sim.
ff e molto pesante (sempre)
fassai
molto pesante ma non troppo
gliss.
arco
pizz.
unis.
ff pesante

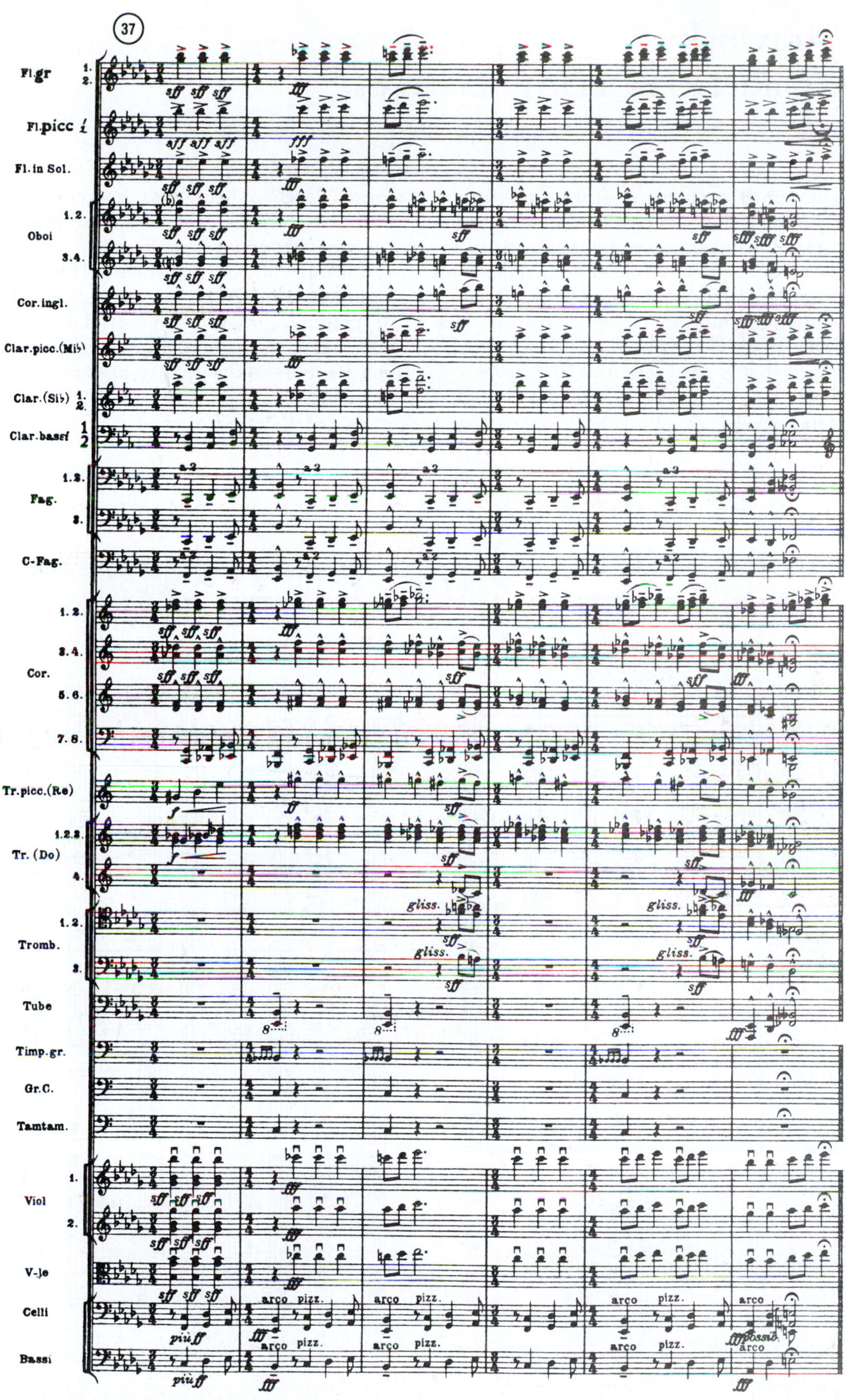
37
Fl.gr 1. 2.
Fl.picc 1
Fl. in Sol.
Oboi 1. 2.
3. 4.
Cor. ingl.
Clar. picc. (Mi♭)
Clar. (Si♭) 1. 2.
Clar. bassi 1 2
Fag. 1. 2.
3.
C-Fag.
Cor. 1. 2.
3. 4.
5. 6.
7. 8.
Tr. picc. (Re)
Tr. (Do) 1. 2. 3.
4.
Tromb. 1. 2.
3.
Tube
Timp. gr.
Gr. C.
Tamtam.
Viol 1.
2.
V-le
Celli
Bassi
a2
gliss.
arco
pizz.
più ff
possib.

Igor Stravinsky

L'HISTOIRE DU SOLDAT *Devil's Dance*

This is the ninth movement from Stravinsky's *L'Histoire du Soldat* ("The Soldier's Tale"), composed in 1917 for a mixed chamber group, narrator and dancer-mimes. The story concerns a soldier who, making his way homeward on leave, is ensnared by the Devil.

Though brief, this movement contains much of the material used in other parts of the work. It also contains much that is representative of Stravinsky's style until his adoption of serial methods in the 1950s. Can you detect an element of repetition at the largest formal level? Where does it occur and how is it different from its original appearance? How many harmonically and texturally static sound blocks can you identify in this movement? How do they differ from each other? Also worth study are the examples of planing, ostinatos, polytonality and implied polymeters. In addition, what possible significance can you attribute to the prominence of the tritone in this movement?

Cl.
Fg.
C.à P.
Tmb.
C.cl.
Vl.
C.B.
poco meno f, ma marc.
sf p sf p etc. simile
ff sub.
très sec sf
2 C.cl.
s.t.
Gr.C.
grande
m.d.
petite
m.g.
bag. en jonc, tête
en capoc
pizz.
poco sf
bag. en jonc, à tête en capoc
au milieu
au bord
mf leggierissimo
sempre p
arco-secco

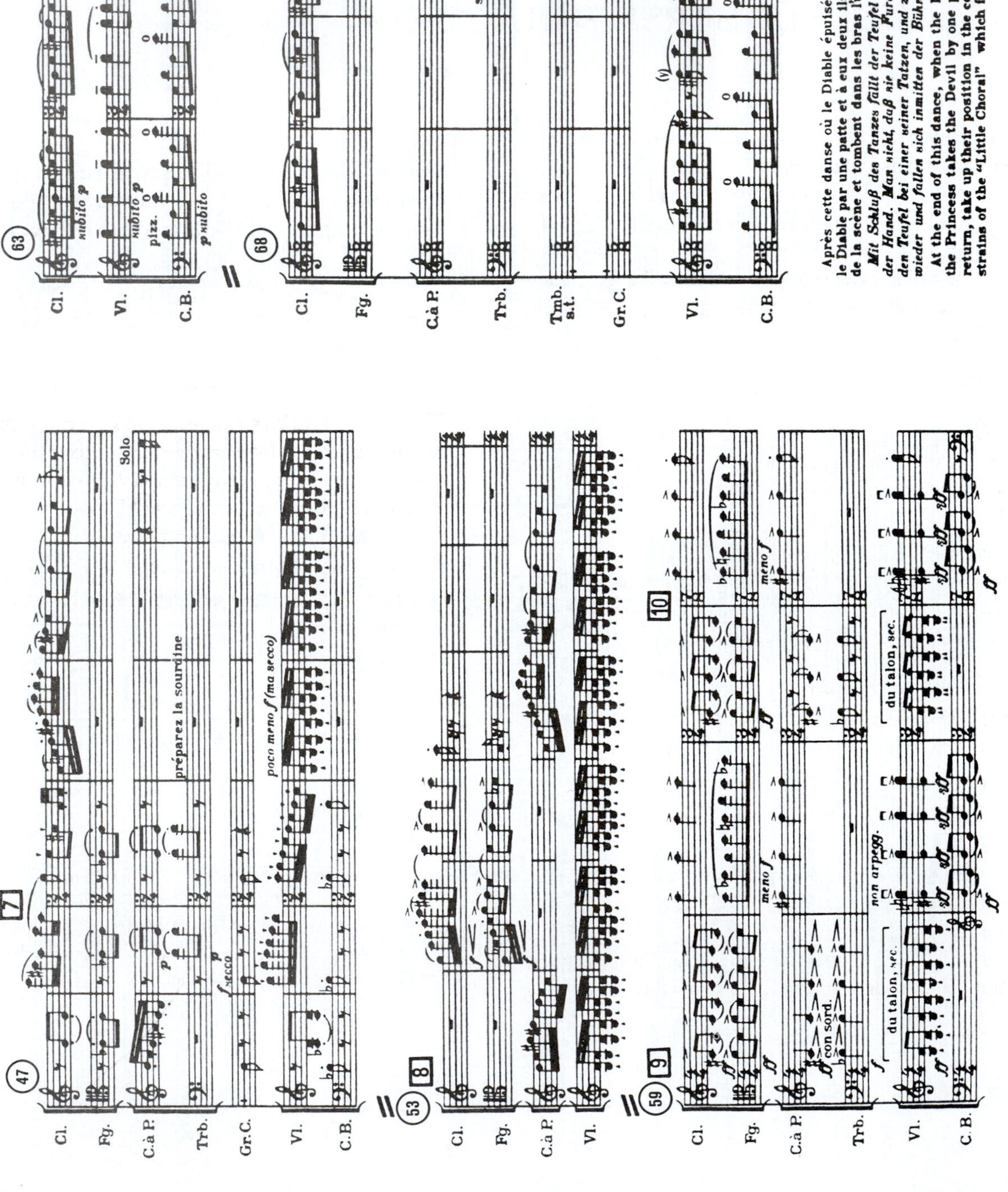

Cl.
Fg.
C. à P.
Trb.
Gr. C.
Vl.
C. B.
Tmb. s.t.
Solo
préparez la sourdine
poco meno f (ma secco)
f secco
con sord.
du talon, sec.
non arpegg.
meno f
subito p
pizz.
p subito
senza sord.
mailloche
trem.
arco
gliss.
molto
Après cette danse où le Diable épuisé tombe à terre sur un signe du Soldat, la Princesse prend le Diable par une patte et à eux deux ils le traînent dans la coulisse. Ils reviennent au milieu de la scène et tombent dans les bras l'un de l'autre sous les sons du „Petit Choral" qui suit.
Mit Schluß des Tanzes fällt der Teufel erschöpft zu Boden. Der Soldat nimmt die Prinzessin bei der Hand. Man sieht, daß sie keine Furcht mehr hat. Dann, auf ein Zeichen des Soldaten, packt sie den Teufel bei einer seiner Tatzen, und zu zweien schleifen sie ihn hinter die Kulisse. Sie kommen wieder und fallen sich inmitten der Bühne in die Arme. Einsatz des kleinen Chorals.
At the end of this dance, when the Devil falls down exhausted, at a sign from the Soldier the Princess takes the Devil by one paw, and between them they drag him off the stage. They return, take up their position in the centre of the stage and fall into each other's arms to the strains of the "Little Choral" which follows.

Anton Webern

Anton Webern (1883–1945) studied with Schoenberg from 1904 until 1908. Like his teacher, he progressed from a late-nineteenth-century tonal idiom, to intensely motivic atonal music, to strictly applied twelve-tone principles. His unusually small output is nearly equally divided between instrumental and vocal works. All are concise. In his music, isolated points of sound acquire the status of musical events. His later works display an interest in canon and mirror forms. Widely disjunct melodies, transparent pointillistic textures, unusual and constantly changing timbres, use of silence, an overall soft dynamic level, and myriad instrumental effects are typical of Webern's style.

FÜNF SÄTZE FÜR STREICHQUARTETT *Third Movement*

Webern completed his "Five Movements" in 1909, contemporaneous with Schoenberg's *Five Pieces for Orchestra* Op. 16, Stravinsky's *The Firebird,* Ives's "Concord Sonata," and Debussy's first book of *Preludes.* In its compact dimensions, sparse textures and intensely motivic construction, Webern's is perhaps the most radical of this diverse and revolutionary group of works.

QUESTIONS FOR DISCUSSION

Formal Structure

1. Where does the principal point of division occur and how is it created? What is the overall form?
2. The movement begins with very short, isolated motives and ends with a comparatively long line. Identify the intermediate steps in this melodic evolution.
3. How would you describe the dramatic shape?

Melodic/Rhythmic Structure

1. Trace the genesis of the figure heard in the first violin at m. 4 and locate all subsequent appearances.
2. Locate an example of:
   a. a melodic figure and its inversion, stated simultaneously;
   b. a three-note figure that contains an identical interval configuration, both melodically and harmonically;
   c. a succession of measures implying a meter other than that indicated by the signature.

Harmonic/Tonal Structure

1. Identify the cell or cells that form the primary harmonic material of the movement. Point out some examples of harmonic structures built upon these cells.
2. Is any single pitch given greater priority in this movement than the others? Can this be said to create a tonal center?

Texture/Articulation/Dynamics

1. This short work contains a variety of color combinations. List a few and describe how they differ from each other. Are certain dynamic levels associated with certain effects? What is the overall dynamic range of the movement?
2. Making use of the terms monophonic, homophonic, lightly polyphonic or highly polyphonic, describe the texture at:
   a. mm. 1–3;
   b. mm. 12–14;
   c. mm. 18–21;
   d. mm. 22–23.

Composed 1909

Related reading: John Rahn, *Basic Atonal Theory* (New York: Schirmer Books, 1980). Detailed, step-by-step instruction in the application of set theory principles to the analysis of atonal music, along with analysis of selected movements by Schoenberg and Webern.

Sehr bewegt (𝅗𝅥 = 84)
ohne Dämpfer
am Steg
pizz.
arco
am Steg
ppp
ff
pp
p
pp
ohne Dämpfer
am Steg
pizz.
arco
pizz.
ohne Dämpfer
am Steg
pizz.
arco
pizz.
ohne Dämpfer
pizz.
sempre ppp
6
pizz.
arco stacc.
col legno
f
ff
col legno
pizz.
col legno
pizz.
arco
pizz.
ppp
11
molto rit.
𝅘𝅥 = 42
pizz.
arco
mf
mp
sehr zart

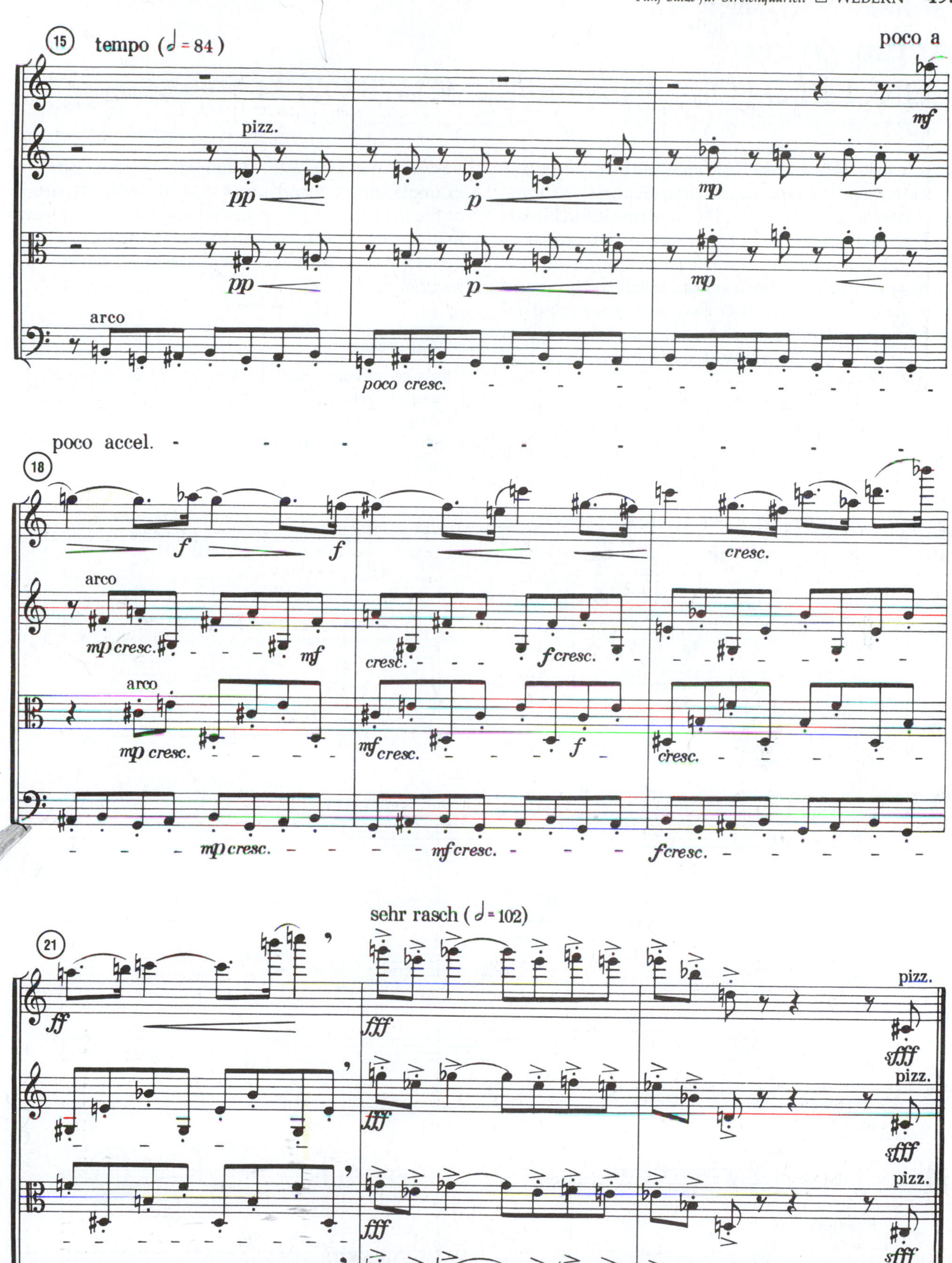
15
tempo (𝅗𝅥 = 84)
poco a
pizz.
pp
p
mf
mp
arco
poco cresc.
poco accel.
18
f
arco
mp cresc.
mf
cresc.
f cresc.
mp cresc.
mf cresc.
f
cresc.
f cresc.
21
sehr rasch (𝅗𝅥 = 102)
ff
fff
pizz.
sfff

Anton Webern

CONCERTO FOR NINE INSTRUMENTS OP. 24 *First Movement*

This work displays the extreme motivic unity and strict twelve-tone methods that characterize Webern's later music. Central is the tone row itself. Notate its first appearance and observe its internal relationships. Now locate the second statement. What row form and transposition level are used? What special relationship between the two row forms exists? Because segments of the various row forms appear identical or nearly so, a row analysis of this movement can be difficult.

Webern appeared to be striving toward a more abstract approach to rhythmic and timbral organization which led to the serial control of these elements by composers such as Babbitt (see his *Semi-Simple Variations* on page 526). Compare rhythmically, for example, mm. 1–3 and mm. 4–5. The rhythmic pattern of the first phrase reappears several times (not always in its "prime" form) and can be seen to relate in a more general way to the rhythmic character of the entire A section.

Composed 1934

Related reading: Joel Lester, *Analytical Approaches to Twentieth-Century Music* (New York: W. W. Norton & Company, 1989), p. 221f. Discussion of the use of a derived series in this movement and in other Webern works.

*Klingen wie notiert (Sound as written)

6
tempo
rit. - - - - tempo
rit. - - tempo
Fl.
Ob.
Kl.
Trp.
pizz.
Dmpf. auf
Gge
pizz.
Dmpf. auf
Br.
Klav.
11
rit. - - - sehr mäßig ♩ = ca 50
Ob.
Kl.
Hr.
Trp.
mit Dmpf.
arco
Gge
mit Dmpf.
arco
Br.
Klav.

17
Fl
Ob.
Hr.
Trp.
Pos.
Gge
Br
Klav.
Flatterzunge
immer mit Dmpf.
ohne Dmpf.
ohne Dmpf.
22
molto rit. - - - sehr gemächlich rit. - -
tempo
Fl.
Ob.
Kl
Trp.
Gge
Br.
Klav.
pizz.
pizz.
arco

tempo
rit. - - - - tempo
rit. - - tempo
28
Kl.
Gge
Klav.
p
f
pp
rit. - - - - tempo
rit. - - - tempo
rit. - - - tempo
33
Fl.
Ob.
Kl.
Trp.
Pos.
Gge
Br.
Klav.
p espr.
ff
arco
pizz.

38
rit. - - tempo
rit. - - tem- po
Fl.
Ob.
Kl.
Trp.
Gge
arco
Br.
Klav.
44
wieder etwas lebhaft
♩ = ca 80
rit. - - - - - - - - - - tempo
ged.
Hr.
Pos.

48
rit. - - - - tempo
rit. - - - - - - wieder sehr mäßig ♩ = ca 50
Ob.
Kl.
Hr.
offen
Gge
mit Dmpf.
mit Dmpf.
Br.
Klav.
53
poco string. - - -
Ob.
Kl.
Hr.
ged.
Trp.
Pos.
Br.
Klav.

58
Flatterzunge
Fl.
Ob.
Kl.
ohne Dmpf.
Gge
ohne Dmpf.
Br.
Klav.
wieder etwas
lebhaft(♩ = ca 80)
63
string.
pesante(♩ = ca.50)
Fl.
Ob.
Kl.
ged.
Hr.
Trp.
Pos.
pizz.
Gge
pizz.
Br.
Klav.

Alban Berg

FOUR SONGS OP. 2 *No. 3 "Warm die Lüfte"*

Alban Berg (1885–1935) studied composition with Schoenberg from 1904 until 1910. Like the music of Schoenberg and Webern, his music evolved from a highly chromatic tonality, to a period of atonal motivic organization, and finally to a personal adaptation of the twelve-tone method. The *Four Songs,* Op. 2 were written in 1908–09, and document his abandonment of functional tonal principles.

Although not as intensely motivic as some of Webern's and Schoenberg's works, this song does contain some important motives, such as the undulating right-hand figure of mm. 1–2 and the tritone interval of mm. 7–8. Trace these two motives. Can you locate a particularly pronounced return of the first four pitches heard in the voice? Parallel motion is one of the song's more prominent techniques. Identify all examples. The widely varied harmonic pallette seems to reflect the composer's search for a new means of tonal organization. Nevertheless, the song is tightly unified and cohesive. What contributes to this effect? Identify the principal points of musical punctuation. How do they relate to the text? What form is created? What features of the text may have induced Berg to use this form? Describe the dramatic high point of the song. Can you point to some clear examples of text painting?

Composed 1908–1909

Related reading: Glen Watkins, *Soundings* (New York: Schirmer Books, 1988), pp. 48–52. A discussion of Berg's connection with Ravel and an enlightening comparison of mm. 18–25 of this work with passages from *Gaspard de la nuit.* (See p. 119 in this regard as well.)

7
frei
langsameres Tempo
Ich will sin - - gen:
Dro-ben hoch im dü - stern Bergforst, es
r.H.
mp
p
meno p
schwach betont.
Ped.
11
poco rit. - - - Noch langsameres Tempo
schmilzt und glit - zert kal - ter Schnee, ein
Mäd - chen in grau - em Klei - de lehnt an feuch - tem
sehr ausdrucksvoll
spitz
mf spitz
Zeit lassen
p
13
accel.
rit.
Eich - stamm, krank sind ih - re zar - ten
Wan - gen, die grau - en Au - gen fie - bern durch
15
accel.
rit.
ff
Dü - ster - rie - sen - stäm - me.
„Er kommt noch nicht.
gliss.
Rit.
Accel.
molto
sffz
molto
gliss.

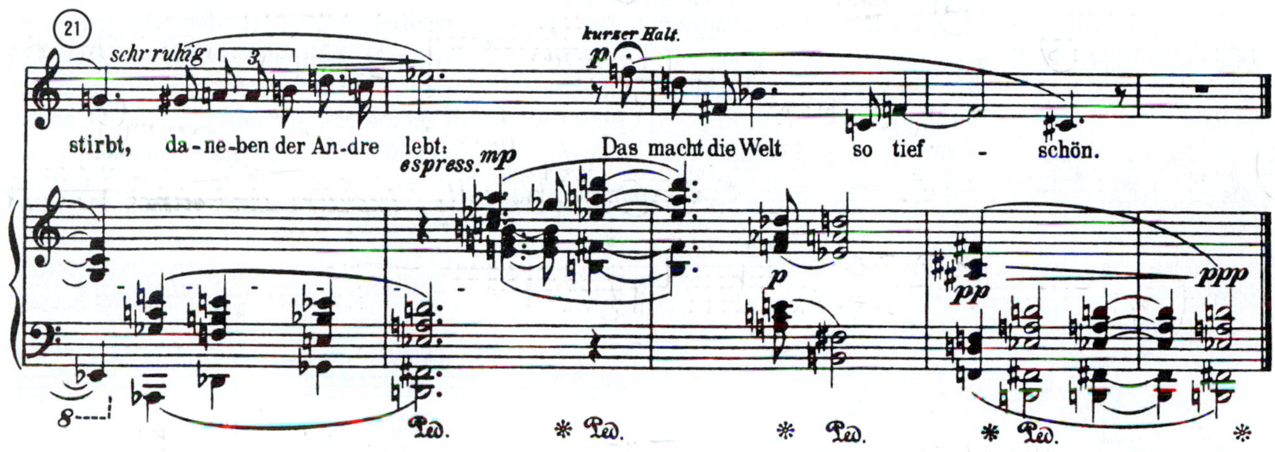

Warm are the breezes, grass sprouts in the sunny meadows,
Listen! Listen, the nightingale is singing.
I will sing:
High above in the dark mountain forest
The cold snows melt and glisten,
A maiden in grey dress is leaning against the trunk of a damp oak tree,
Sickly are her soft cheeks,
Her grey eyes shine feverishly through the dark giant tree trunks.
"He is not coming. He keeps me waiting."
Die! One dies, close by another lives:
This makes the world so deeply beautiful.

Paul Hindemith

LUDUS TONALIS *Fugue No. 5 in E and Interlude*

The *Ludus Tonalis* ("Game of Tones") of Paul Hindemith (1895–1963), published in 1943, is a cycle of twelve fugues, preceded by a Prelude, followed by a Postlude, and connected by Interludes. Each fugue is in a different "key," but tonality is not established through functional harmony in these works. Fugue No. 5 is said to be in E. At what points can E be said to act as a tonic and why? Hindemith's melodies and harmonies favor the intervals of the major second and perfect fourth (and their inversions). Can you point out some notable examples? Can you locate some clear examples of quartal harmonies (which also contain these intervals)?

Examine the structure of the fugue and compare it to any of those by J. S. Bach that you may have studied. Be sure to identify all entrances of the subject, any episodes, and contrapuntal devices (inversion, stretto, invertible counterpoint and so forth).

The Interlude that follows the fugue is a link between it and Fugue No. 6, which is in E-flat. Explain how it acts as a transition between the two tonalities. The sections of this Interlude are clearly indicated. Explain how they relate to each other. Hindemith used the term "step progression" to describe the scalar connection of important pitches in a melodic line. This large-scale stepwise motion (which can occur in any voice) gives his melodies logic and direction. Can you locate any step progressions in this Interlude?

12
18
24
cresc.
f
30
36
stacc.
p

42
stacc.
47
f
stacc.
53
59
mf
cresc.
65
f
stacc.

71
76
Coda
Moderato (♩ ca 80)
Interludium
p
4
cresc.
mf
p
8
pp
cresc.
mf

12
mp
cresc.
15
mf
p
18
più p
cresc.
21
mp
dim.
rit.

Henry Cowell
THE BANSHEE

One of the most innovative American composers of the twentieth century was Henry Cowell (1897–1965). Of his enormous output, perhaps the most prophetic works are the short piano pieces he composed between 1912 and 1935. These works, which made a considerable impact on Cowell's pupil, John Cage, and which were displayed on various tours of Europe, exhibited a new approach to the piano. Among the expanded techniques were the use of fists, forearms and wooden boards to produce thick tone clusters and the use of the hands to brush, pluck or strum the piano strings.

The Banshee (1925), one of the earliest works requiring the pianist to play *inside* the instrument instead of on the keyboard, evokes the image of a figure from Irish folklore who, according to legend, wails over the house of one who is shortly to die. Although the actual sound of the music bears little resemblance to the score, the pitch structure, which helps to define the overall form, is audible. Tonally and technically, the work appears to comprise two components. Can you identify these? How is a final synthesis of the two components achieved? Describe the overall form and note other factors that help to clarify it.

Explanation of Symbols

"The Banshee" is played on the open strings of the piano, the player standing at the crook. Another person must sit at the keyboard and hold down the damper pedal throughout the composition. The whole work should be played an octave lower than written.

R. H. stands for "right hand." L. H. stands for "left hand." Different ways of playing the strings are indicated by a letter over each tone, as follows:

Ⓐ indicates a sweep with the flesh of the finger from the lowest string up to the note given.

Ⓑ sweep lengthwise along the string of the note given with flesh of finger.

Ⓒ sweep up and back from lowest A to highest B-flat given in this composition.

Ⓓ pluck string with flesh of finger, where written, instead of octave lower.

Ⓔ sweep along three notes together, in the same manner as Ⓑ.

Ⓕ sweep in the manner of Ⓑ but with back of finger-nail instead of flesh.

Ⓖ when the finger is half way along the string in the manner of Ⓕ, start a sweep along the same string with the flesh of the other finger, thus partly dampening the sound.

Ⓗ sweep back and forth in the manner of Ⓒ, but start at the same time from both above and below, crossing the sweep in the middle.

Ⓘ sweep along five notes, in the manner of Ⓑ.

Ⓙ same as Ⓘ but with back of finger-nails instead of flesh of finger.

Ⓚ sweep along in manner of Ⓙ with nails of both hands together, taking in all notes between the two outer limits given.

Ⓛ sweep in manner of Ⓒ with flat of hand instead of single finger.

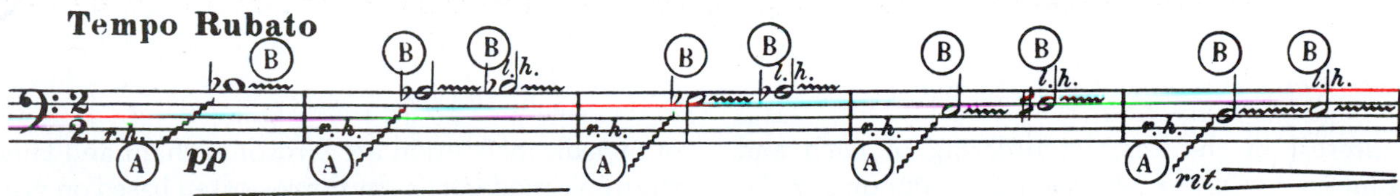

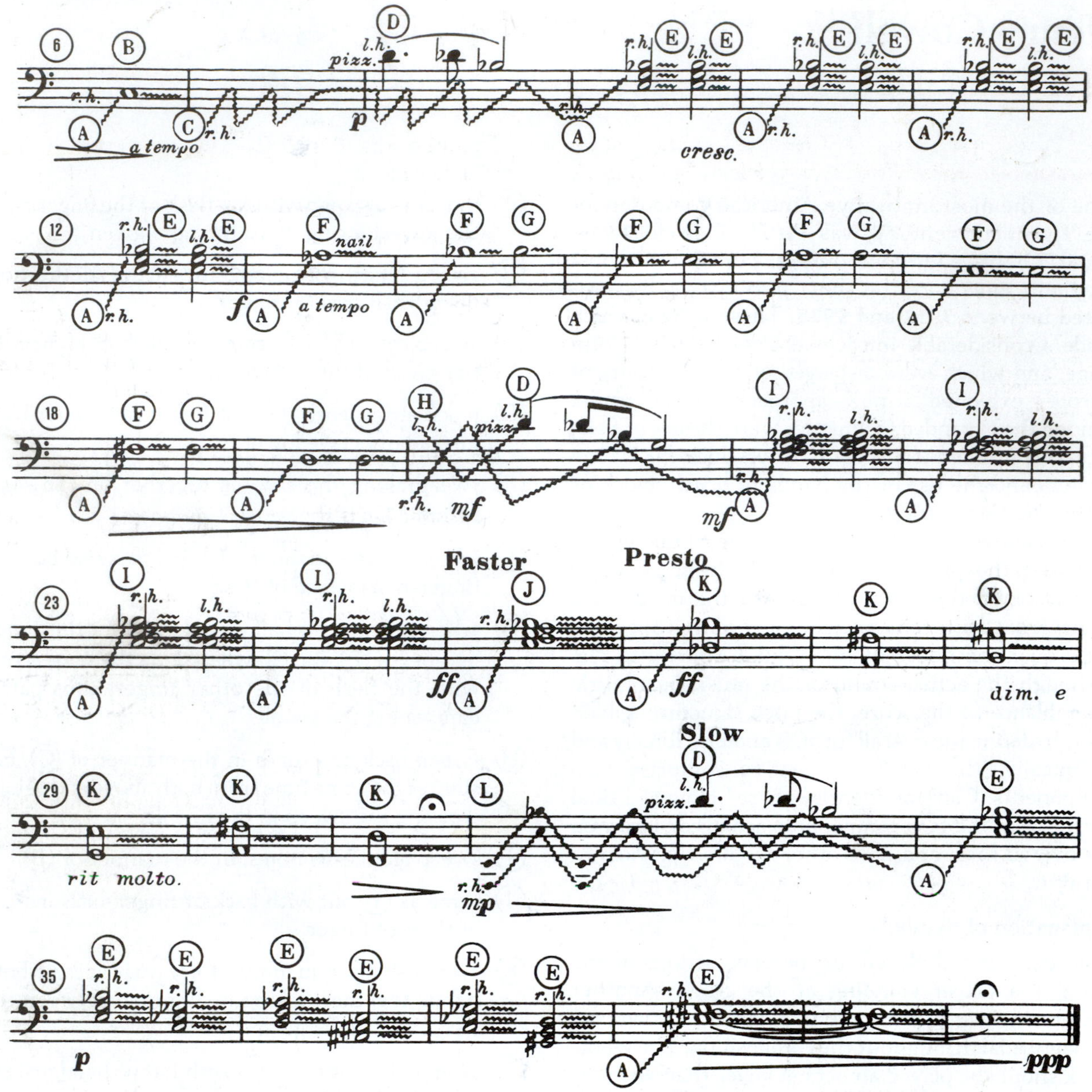

Olivier Messiaen

An interest in the abstract ordering of pitch and rhythm made Olivier Messiaen (b. 1908) one of the most influential figures in the years following World War II, particularly through his pupils, Karlheinz Stockhausen and Pierre Boulez. His works usually contain many movements, in which true development is replaced by the recombination of unchanging elements and large-scale repetition. Among his sources of melodic inspiration are birdsong, chant and Hindu rhythmic modes. His rhythms—often based on prime numbers—are subject to various kinds of augmentation or diminution. His "modes of limited transposition," including the whole-tone and octatonic scales, form both a harmonic and a melodic basis for much of his music. His textures tend to be full and somewhat opaque, containing ostinatos and pedal points.

QUATUOR POUR LA FIN DU TEMPS *Liturgie de cristal*

The *Quartet for the End of Time* was written while Messiaen was a prisoner of war in Silesia. It was completed in January of 1941 and premiered the same month by the composer and three fellow prisoners. The title was inspired by the following passage from Revelations:

> And the angel which I saw stand upon the sea and upon the earth lifted up his hand to heaven, and sware by him that liveth forever and ever, who created heaven, and the things that therein are, and the earth, and the things that therein are, and the sea, and the things which are therein, that *there should be time no longer.*

QUESTIONS FOR DISCUSSION

Formal Structure

1. Do well-defined cadences divide this movement into clearly contrasting sections? Is the music characterized by growth, variation, stasis (lack of change), or intensification?
2. The piano part is isorhythmic. Discover the meaning of this term (the Machaut motet in Unit One is isorhythmic also) and describe its operation in this movement.

Melodic/Rhythmic Structure

1. The clarinet has the principal melody. Though not isorhythmic, much of it relates to a few basic figures, varied and recombined in different ways. Describe the first fifteen measures from this standpoint.
2. Analyze the clarinet passage of mm. 36–38 in terms of scalar content and previously heard material.
3. Analyze the melodic and rhythmic patterns on which the cello part is based.
4. Identify the ideas that form the basis of the violin part and their repetition. What similarities exist between the violin and clarinet parts?

Harmonic/Tonal Structure

1. Does the piano part appear to have its basis in a synthetic scale, a twelve-tone row, or other abstraction? Does the conception appear to be linear or vertical? Do any principles appear to govern the harmonic succession?

Texture/Articulation/Dynamics

1. Describe the overall texture. Does it change or does it remain essentially the same? How are the various textural elements rendered distinct one from another?
2. What is the overall pitch and dynamic range of the movement? Do any of the instrumental parts contain greater dynamic and articulative variety than others? Why might this be so?

(*) *Glissando bref; id. aux passages similaires.*

13
Von
Clar.
Velle
gliss.
C
16
glissando
gliss.
18
gliss.
D

21
Von
Clar.
Velle
gliss.
gliss.
23
Von
Clar.
Velle
gliss.
25
Von
Clar.
Velle
pp
pp
p
gliss.
E

28
Von
Clar.
Velle
gliss.
gliss.
30
8
cresc.
F
32
8
f
dim.
glissando

34
Von
Clar.
Velle
pp
p
gliss.

36
Von
Clar.
Velle
3
G

38
Von
Clar.
Velle
8
glissando
gliss.
p
pp

John Cage

SONATAS AND INTERLUDES *Nos. 1 and 5*

John Cage (b. 1912) has exerted a profound influence on Western music since World War II. Though not extensive, his formal musical training included study in non-Western and folk music with Henry Cowell and counterpoint with Arnold Schoenberg. Since the late 1940s, Cage's interest in Eastern philosophy has resulted in the use of chance elements in his compositions.

Sonatas and Interludes represents a line of Cage's development that began in 1938. In this work, he endows the piano with the timbral variety of a percussion ensemble through the placement of various objects on and between the strings. Because these mutes change both the timbre and the pitch in many cases, the resulting sounds differ greatly from those apparent in the notation. For this reason, it is essential to listen to a recording of this work. On the other hand, the score clearly indicates Cage's formal and rhythmic intentions, the clarity and simplicity of which are perhaps a reaction to the complexity of contemporaneous European developments.

TABLE OF PREPARATIONS

[MUTES OF VARIOUS MATERIALS ARE PLACED BETWEEN THE STRINGS OF THE KEYS USED, THUS EFFECTING TRANSFORMATIONS OF THE PIANO SOUNDS WITH RESPECT TO ALL OF THEIR CHARACTERISTICS.]

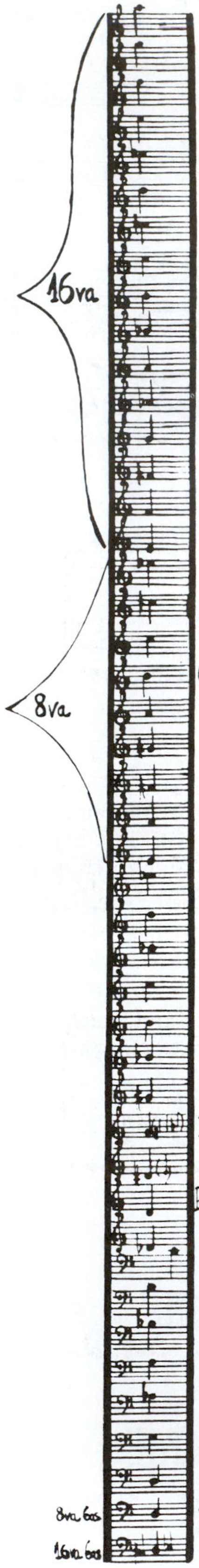

TONE	MATERIAL	STRINGS LEFT TO RIGHT	DISTANCE FROM DAMPER (INCHES)	MATERIAL	STRINGS LEFT TO RIGHT	DISTANCE FROM DAMPER (INCHES)	MATERIAL	STRINGS LEFT TO RIGHT	DISTANCE FROM DAMPER (INCHES)	TONE
				SCREW	2-3	1 1/4*				A
				MED. BOLT	2-3	1 3/8*				G
				SCREW	2-3	1 5/8*				F
				SCREW	2-3	1 13/16*				E
				SCREW	2-3	1 3/4*				E♭
				SM. BOLT	2-3	2*				D
				SCREW	2-3	1 9/16*				C♯
				FURNITURE BOLT	2-3	2 3/16*				C
16va				SCREW	2-3	2 1/2*				B
				SCREW	2-3	1 7/8*				B♭
				MED. BOLT	2-3	2 7/8*				A
				SCREW	2-3	2 1/4*				A♭
				SCREW	2-3	3 3/4*				G
				SCREW	2-3	2 15/16*				F♯
	SCREW	1-2	3/4*	FURN. BOLT + 2 NUTS	2-3	2 1/8*	SCREW + 2 NUTS	2-3	3 1/4*	F
				SCREW	2-3	1 13/16*				E
				FURNITURE BOLT	2-3	1 7/8				E♭
				SCREW	2-3	1 15/16				C♯
				SCREW	2-3	1 1/16				C
	(DAMPER TO BRIDGE = 4 7/16"; ADJUST ACCORDINGLY)			MED. BOLT	2-3	3 3/4				B
8va				SCREW	2-3	4 7/16				A
	RUBBER	1-2-3	4 1/2	FURNITURE BOLT	2-3	1 1/4				G♯
				SCREW	2-3	1 3/4				F♯
				SCREW	2-3	2 5/16				F
	RUBBER	1-2-3	5 3/4							E
	RUBBER	1-2-3	6 1/2	FURN. BOLT + NUT	2-3	6 7/8				E♭
				FURNITURE BOLT	2-3	2 9/16				D
	RUBBER	1-2-3	3 5/8							D♭
				BOLT	2-3	7 1/8				C
				BOLT	2-3	2				B
	SCREW	1-2	10	SCREW	2-3	1	RUBBER	1-2-3	8 1/4	B♭
	(PLASTIC (see G))	1-2-3	2 5/16				RUBBER	1-2-3	4 1/2	G♯
	PLASTIC (OVER 1 UNDER 2-3)	1-2-3	2 7/8				RUBBER	1-2-3	10 1/8	G
	(PLASTIC (see D))	1-2-3	4 1/4				RUBBER	1-2-3	5 7/16	D♯
	PLASTIC (OVER 1 - UNDER 2-3)	1-2-3	4 1/8				RUBBER	1-2-3	9 3/4	D
	BOLT	1-2	15 1/2	BOLT	2-3	14/16	RUBBER	1-2-3	14 1/8	D♭
	BOLT	1-2	14 1/2	BOLT	2-3	7/8	RUBBER	1-2-3	6 1/2	C
	BOLT	1-2	14 3/4	BOLT	2-3	9/16	RUBBER	1-2-3	14	B
	RUBBER	1-2-3	9 1/2	MED. BOLT	2-3	10 1/8				B♭
	SCREW	1-2	5 7/8	LG. BOLT	2-3	5 3/8	SCREW + NUTS	1-2	1	A
	BOLT	1-2	7 1/8	MED. BOLT	2-3	2 1/4	RUBBER	1-2-3	4 1/8	A♭
	LONG BOLT	1-2	8 3/4	LG BOLT	2-3	3 1/4				G
				BOLT	2-3	14/16				D
8va bas	SCREW + RUBBER	1-2	4 7/16							D
16va bas	ERASER (OVER D UNDER C♯ + E♭) AM. PENCIL CO. #346	1	6 3/4							D

*MEASURE FROM BRIDGE.

No. 1

—— = PEDAL

---- = UNA CORDA

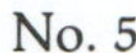

No. 5

Benjamin Britten

SERENADE OP. 31 *"Prologue" and "Dirge"*

This work, written in 1943, consists of six short movements on texts by various English poets. The short Prologue, for solo horn, precedes the six movements and reappears at the end as an Epilogue. It is to be played on natural harmonics (i.e., without valves). It is possible to do this because all the pitches fall within the overtone series of the horn's fundamental tone. However, not all these notes may sound "in tune" with our system of temperament. Can you identify the tones that do not? What mode is suggested? Also examine the melody from the standpoint of phrasing, repetition, variation and the creation of a tonal center.

The Dirge, which is the fourth movement, combines elements of two traditional procedures—the ground and the fugue. Regarding the former, if you have studied Purcell's *Dido and Aeneas* in this anthology, explain how Britten's use of the procedure differs. Regarding the latter, a comparison with Fugue No. 5 from Hindemith's *Ludus Tonalis* will be worthwhile.

PROLOGUE

* *The Prologue to be played on natural harmonics.*

DIRGE
(Anonymous, 15th Century)
Alla marcia grave (𝅗𝅥 = 60)
come un lamento
Voice
Horn in F
Violins I
Violins II
Violas
'Cellos
Basses
This ae nighte, this ae nighte, E-ver-y nighte and alle, Fire and fleet and candle-lighte, And Christe re-ceive
6
thy saule.......... When thou from hence a-way art past, Every nighte and alle, To
ppp marc.
cresc.
fpp
10
Whinny - muir thou com'st at last;......... And Christe re - ceive thy saule..... If
pp marc.
cresc.
13
e - ver thou gav'st hos'n and shoon, E-ver-y nighte and alle,
p marc.
fp

16
Voice
Hn. in F
Vln. I
Vln. II
Vla.
'Cello
Bass
Sit thee down and put them on;.......... And Christe re - ceive thy saule...... If
cresc.
fp cresc.
fp
19
hos'n and shoon thou ne'er gav'st nane, E-very nighte and alle, The
mf marc.
cresc.
22
whinnes sall prick thee to the bare bane;........ And Christe re - ceive thy saule........ From
fp
fp cresc.
f pesante
25
Whin - ny - muir when thou may'st pass, E-ver-y nighte and alle, To
sfp
f stacc. e pesante sempre

28
Voice
Hn. in F
Vln. I
Vln. II
Vla.
'Cello
Bass
Brig o' Dread thou com'st at last; .... And Christe re - ceive thy saule.... From
cresc.
stacc. e pesante
pizz.
arco
31
Brig o' Dread when thou may'st pass, E-ver-y nighte and alle, To
molto largamente
(veloce)
pizz.
arco
f marc.
34
Pur-ga-to-ry fire thou com'st at last; .... And Christe re - ceive thy saule........ If
cresc.
f marc.
37
e - ver thou gav'st meat or drink, E-ver-y nighte and alle, The
dim.
sempre più p
mf

40
Voice
Hn. in F
Vln. I
Vln. II
Vla.
'Cello
Bass
fire sall ne-ver make thee shrink;.. And Christe re - ceive thy saule.............. If
pizz.
43
meat or drink thou ne'er gav'st nane, E-ver-y nighte and alle, The
arco
46
fire will burn thee to the bare bane;.... And Christe re - ceive thy saule................. This ae nighte,
div.
pp dim.
p distinto
50
this ae nighte, E-ver-y nighte and alle, Fire and fleet and candle-lighte, And Christe re-ceive thy saule....
senza ritardando
unis.
pizz.
meno f ma sempre distinto
dim.

Milton Babbitt

SEMI-SIMPLE VARIATIONS

Milton Babbitt (b. 1916) extended the serial process of Schoenberg and Webern, not only subjecting the melodic and harmonic dimensions of his music to rigorous ordering principles, but applying these principles to duration, dynamics and color as well. His use of twelve-tone rows whose first and second hexachords (six-note groups) are constructed from all-combinatorial source sets permits the use of different row forms simultaneously without creating pitch duplication.

Babbitt's forms are often created through the serial process. His often disjunct melodies combine in pointillistic textures. His apparent preference for all-interval rows is the opposite of Webern's preference for limited intervallic content.

Semi-Simple Variations (1957) embodies the variation principle in ways both similar to and different from Schoenberg. You may wish to compare the techniques with those of Schoenberg's *Variations for Orchestra* on page 443.

QUESTIONS FOR DISCUSSION

Formal Structure

1. While it is *possible* to find all twelve notes in the first three measures, the actual row takes two complete variations to unfold. Can you discover it? How are the *other* notes of the texture accounted for? (Hint: Consider the piece to be a *four-voice* texture.)
2. Fill in the blanks:
   a. The first hexachord of P_0 can combine with the first hexachord of P ___, R ___, I ___ or RI ___ (indicate appropriate index numbers) to form all twelve chromatic pitches. Of these forms, the ___ (R, I, RI) form of *any* row will always be combinatorial in this way with its corresponding P statement.
   b. This row is symmetrical in that P_0 is identical with ___ (row form).
   c. How many of the possible intervals of the octave (considering an interval and its inversion to be identical) are present in this row?
3. Which variation is longest and why?
4. *Rotation* refers to a reordering of the notes of a row in some systematic way. How is rotation used to achieve new row forms in Variation 3? Describe the properties of the new rows.

Melodic/Rhythmic Structure

1. Examine Variation 1 for rhythmic repetition, and comment. Then compare Variation 2 to Variation 1. What is the relationship? How is Variation 3 related to Variations 1 and 2?
2. What other rhythmic relationships between variations can you discover?

Harmonic/Tonal Structure

1. Two of the variations provide more vertical combinations of tones than the others. Identify them.
2. Having identified the two "harmonic" variations above, consider the types of sonorities that occur. Do the two variations differ in this respect? Explain how the row forms used affect the types of harmonic structures in the earlier of these two variations.

Texture/Articulation/Dynamics

1. Describe the differences in texture and articulation among Variations 1, 2 and 3. Then explain how Variation 3 differs from Variation 4 in this regard.
2. Describe generally the dynamic character of each of the variations.
3. Explain how register is used as a form-defining element in the first three variations.

Composed 1957

Related reading: Joel Lester, *Analytical Approaches to Twentieth-Century Music* (New York: W. W. Norton & Company, 1989), p. 299f. A discussion and description of combinatorial hexachords, providing a method for determining if a series is combinatorial.

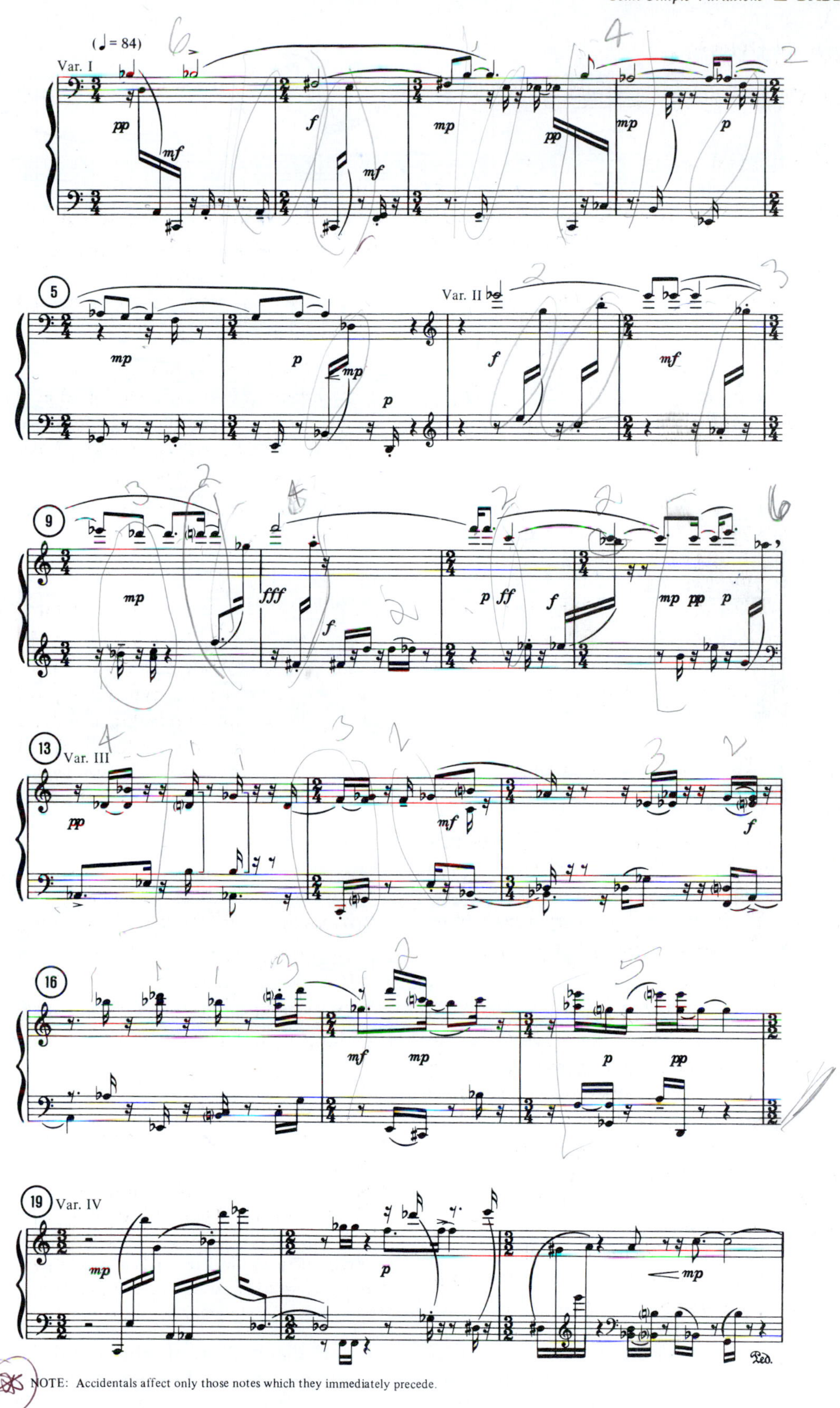

*NOTE: Accidentals affect only those notes which they immediately precede.

Earle Brown

AVAILABLE FORMS I *excerpt*

During the 1950s and 1960s, Earle Brown (b. 1926) experimented with mobile-form works. In these compositions, the individual components were carefully constructed while *their position with respect to each other* was left to chance elements. *Available Forms I* (1961) comprises six score pages, each containing four or five events that can be ordered, repeated or omitted at the discretion of the conductor, who also determines the total time span for each event. This excerpt is the fourth page. Study and describe each event, and explain how the events contrast with each other in terms of timbre and texture. In each event, which elements are very precisely determined and which are indeterminate?

Available Forms I by Earle Brown. © 1962 by Associated Music Publishers, Inc. International Copyright Secured. Used by permission.

George Crumb

MADRIGALS, BOOK I *"Los muertos llevan alas de musgo"*

George Crumb (b. 1929) has a highly personal style that is, in most respects, the antithesis of the abstract, impersonal, serialized music of the 1950s. His "neo-Romanticism" is evident in the programmatic titles and conception of his music and in his intense preoccupation with color.

His four books of *Madrigals,* settings of texts by the Spanish poet Federico Garcia Lorca (1898–1936), were composed between 1965 and 1969. Note the motivic unity in the following selection as well as the unusual instrumental and vocal effects and the meticulous attention to expressive detail. How much of the piece can be related to the opening measure? What sharing of common material occurs among the performers? Every vocal gesture has its origin earlier in the instrumental parts. Locate these origins. In what ways is the text ("The dead wear wings of moss") reflected in the music? If you have studied any of the Debussy works in this unit, identify some obvious influences.

Composed 1965–1969

Related reading: Thomas R. de Dobay, "The Evolution of harmonic style in the Lorca works of Crumb," *Journal of Music Theory,* Vol. 27, No. 2 (Spring 1984), p. 89f.

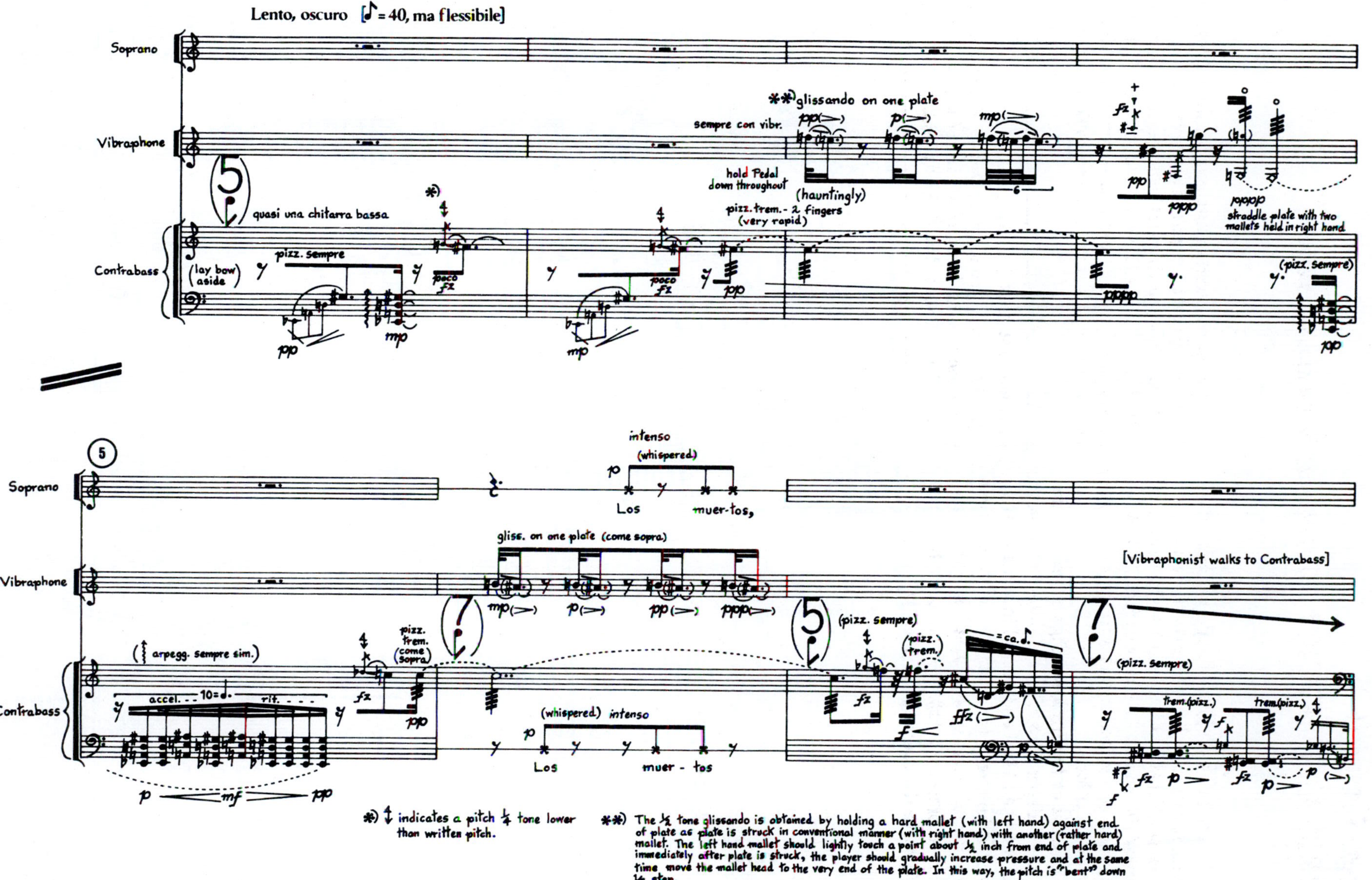
Lento, oscuro [♪ = 40, ma flessibile]
Soprano
Vibraphone
Contrabass
quasi una chitarra bassa
(lay bow aside)
pizz. sempre
poco fz
sempre con vibr.
**) glissando on one plate
hold Pedal down throughout
(hauntingly)
pizz. trem. - 2 fingers (very rapid)
straddle plate with two mallets held in right hand
(pizz. sempre)
Soprano
Vibraphone
Contrabass
intenso
(whispered)
Los muer-tos,
gliss. on one plate (come sopra)
[Vibraphonist walks to Contrabass]
(arpegg. sempre sim.)
accel.
rit.
pizz. trem. (come sopra)
(whispered) intenso
Los muer - tos
(pizz. sempre)
(pizz. trem.)
trem.(pizz.)
*) ‡ indicates a pitch ¼ tone lower than written pitch.
**) The ¼ tone glissando is obtained by holding a hard mallet (with left hand) against end of plate as plate is struck in conventional manner (with right hand) with another (rather hard) mallet. The left hand mallet should lightly touch a point about ½ inch from end of plate and immediately after plate is struck, the player should gradually increase pressure and at the same time move the mallet head to the very end of the plate. In this way, the pitch is "bent" down ¼ step.

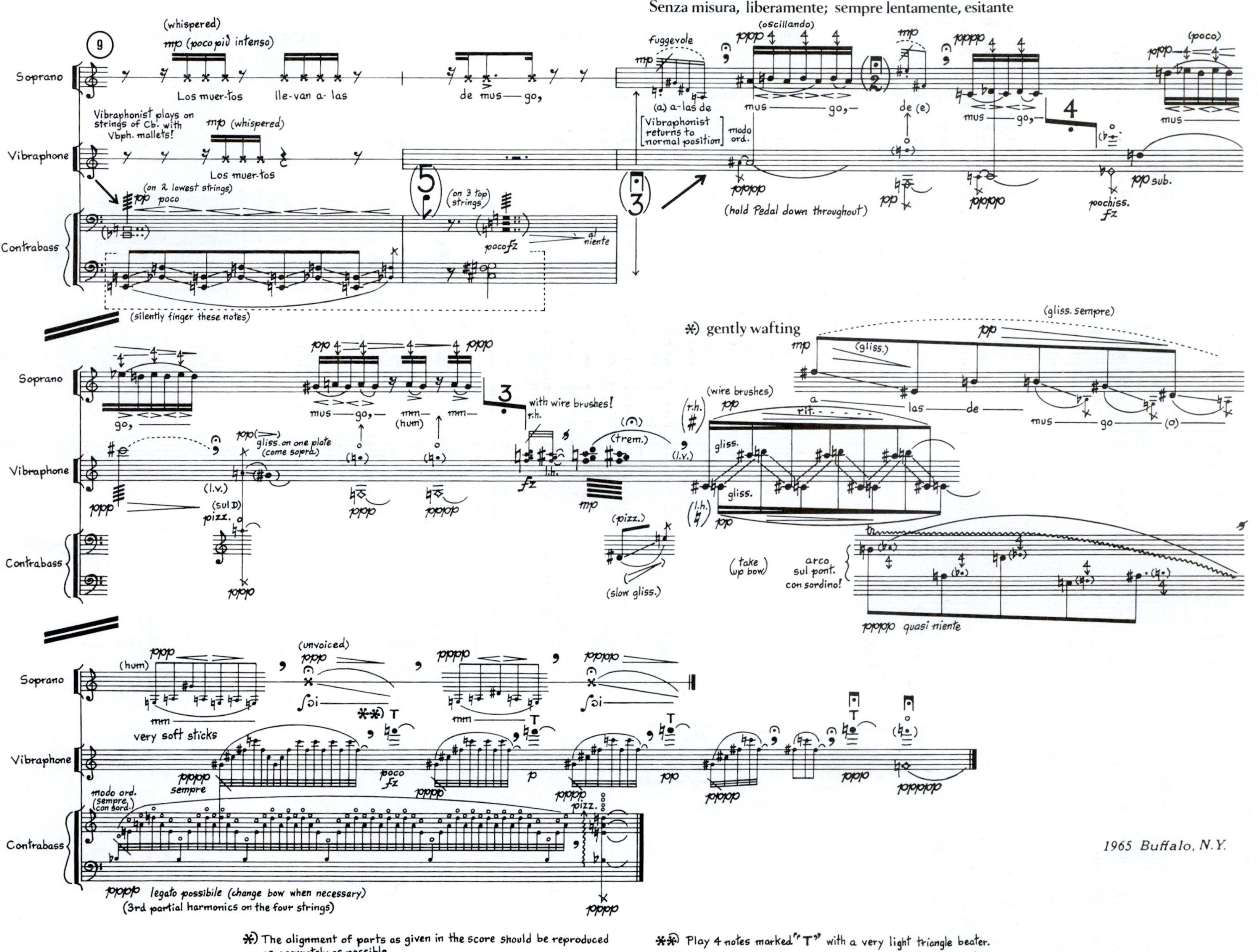

*) The alignment of parts as given in the score should be reproduced as accurately as possible.

**) Play 4 notes marked "T" with a very light triangle beater.

Krzysztof Penderecki
THRENODY FOR THE VICTIMS OF HIROSHIMA *excerpt*

Best known among the younger generation of Polish composers is Krzysztof Penderecki (b. 1933). In this eight-and-one-half minute piece for fifty-two string instruments, musical interest is focused primarily on timbre, texture and dynamics, while discrete pitch plays a relatively minor role. Its three sections (of which only the first is given here) are clearly defined, both cadentially and by the striking contrast between continuous and discontinuous sounds. The continuous sounds consist largely of sustained clusters, which expand or contract and sound against one another in a manner similar to contrapuntal lines. One might, in fact, refer to this sort of technique as "textural counterpoint."

A fascinating aspect of the piece is its notation. Although it probably could have been notated in a traditional manner, Penderecki chose a method that more clearly and directly conveys his musical intent. Study the score carefully, and consider how the various effects would have to be notated traditionally.

Abkürzungen und Symbole
Abbreviations and symbols

Erhöhung um einen Viertelton sharpen a quarter-tone	
Erhöhung um einen Dreiviertelton sharpen three quarter-tones	
Erniedrigung um einen Viertelton flatten a quarter-tone	
Erniedrigung um einen Dreiviertelton flatten three quarter-tones	
höchster Ton des Instrumentes (unbestimmte Tonhöhe) highest note of the instrument (no definite pitch)	
zwischen Steg und Saitenhalter spielen play between bridge and tailpiece	
Arpeggio zwischen Steg und Saitenhalter (4 Saiten) arpeggio on 4 strings behind the bridge	
auf dem Saitenhalter spielen (arco), Bogenstrich über den Saitenhalter (in einem Winkel von 90° zu dessen Längsachse) play on the tailpiece (arco) by bowing the tailpiece at an angle of 90° to its longer axis	
auf dem Steg spielen (arco), Bogenstrich über das Holz des Steges senkrecht zu dessen rechter Schmalseite play on the bridge by bowing the wood of the bridge at a right angle at its right side	
Schlagzeugeffekt: mit dem Frosch oder mit der Fingerspitze auf die Decke klopfen Percussion effect: strike the upper sounding board of the violin with the nut or the finger-tips	
mehrere unregelmäßige Bogenwechsel several irregular changes of bow	⊓V
molto vibrato	
sehr langsames Vibrato mit 1/4 Ton-Frequenzdifferenz durch Fingerverschiebung very slow vibrato with a 1/4 tone frequency difference produced by sliding the finger	
sehr schnelles, nicht rhythmisiertes Tremolo very rapid non rhythmisized tremolo	
ordinario	ord.
sul ponticello	s. p.
sul tasto	s. t.
col legno	c. l.
legno battuto	l. batt.

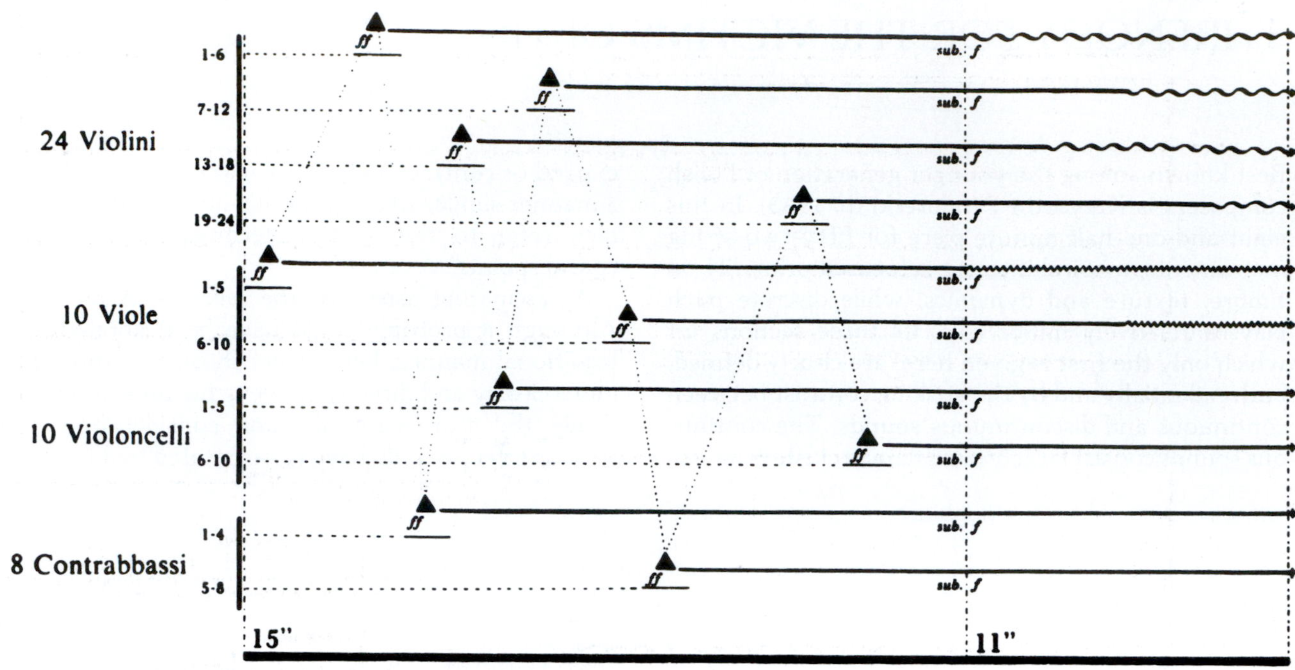
24 Violini
1-6
7-12
13-18
19-24
10 Viole
1-5
6-10
10 Violoncelli
1-5
6-10
8 Contrabbassi
1-4
5-8
ff
sub. f
15"
11"

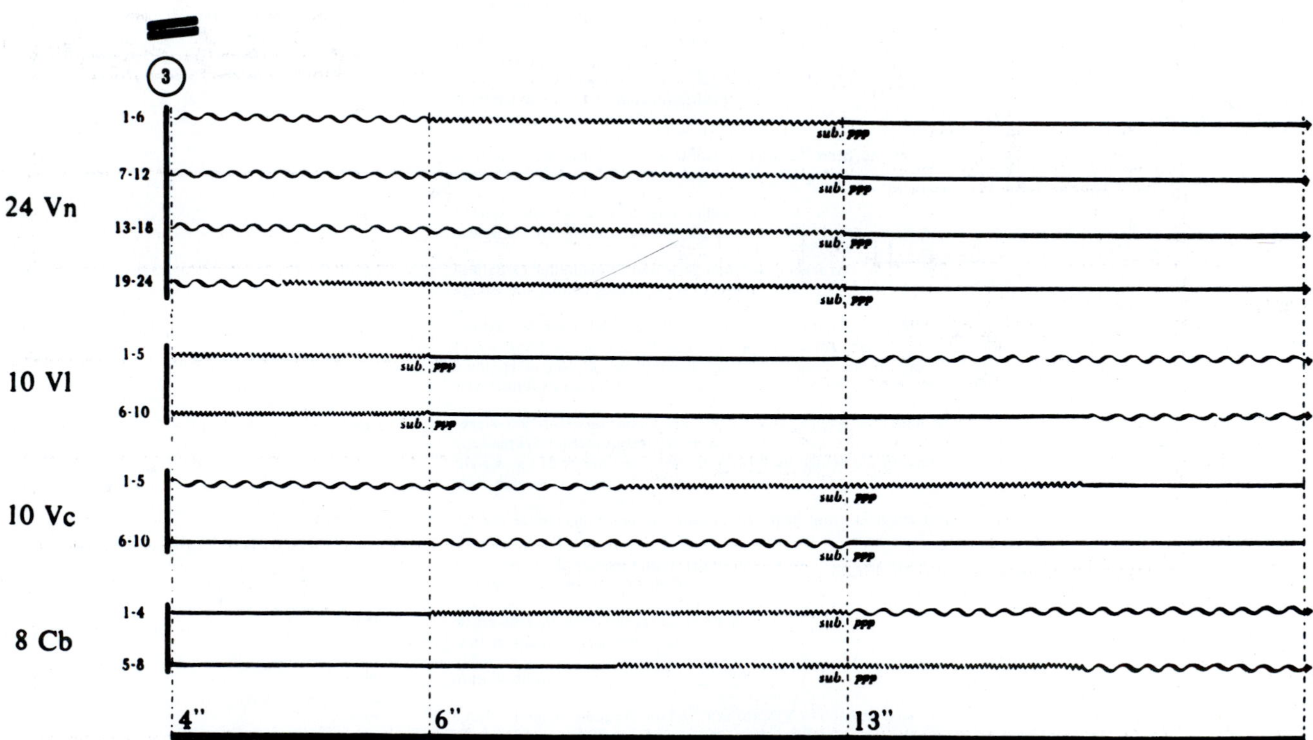
3
24 Vn
1-6
7-12
13-18
19-24
10 Vl
1-5
6-10
10 Vc
1-5
6-10
8 Cb
1-4
5-8
sub. ppp
4"
6"
13"

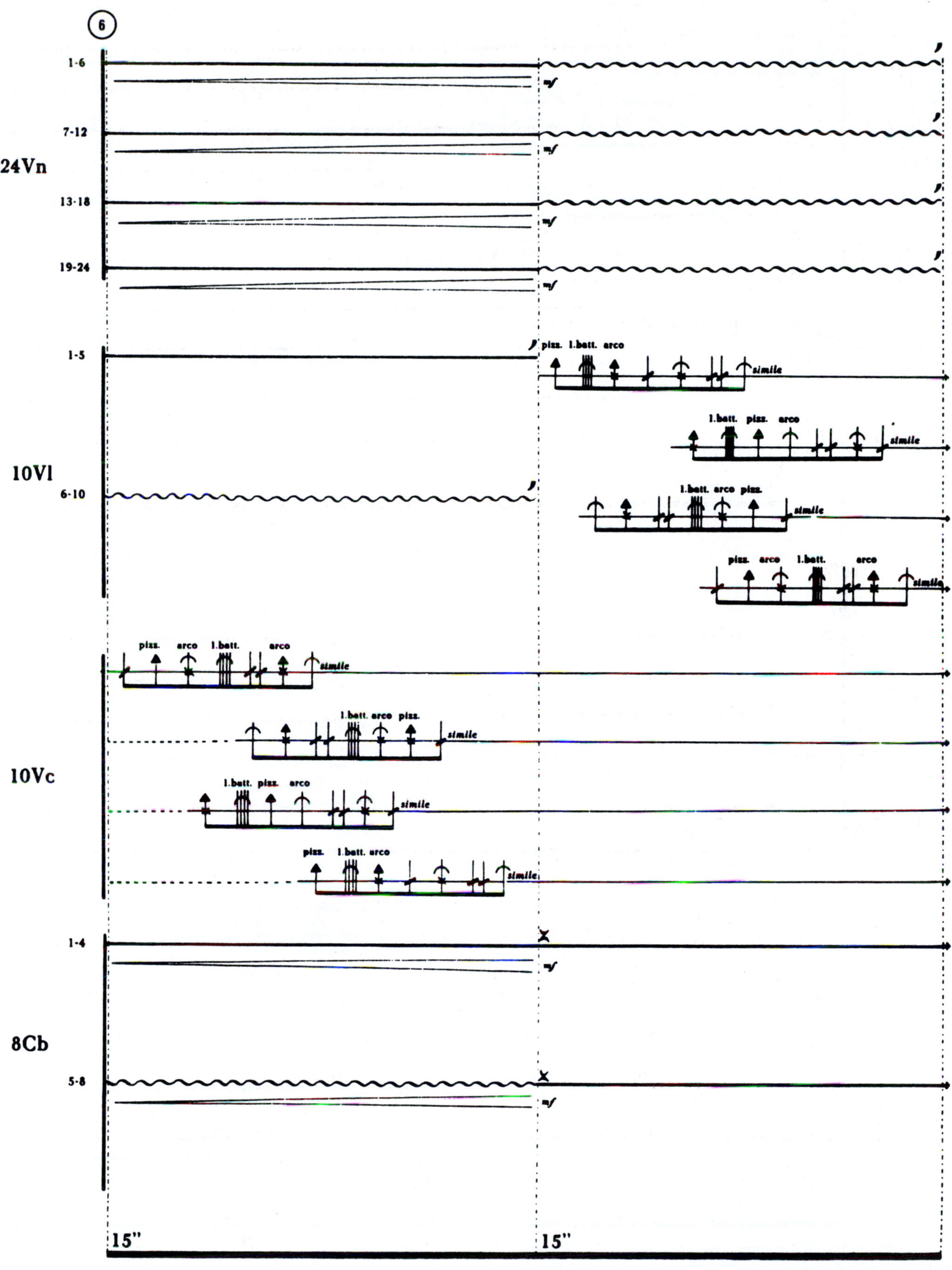
6
24Vn
1-6
7-12
13-18
19-24
mf
10Vl
1-5
6-10
pizz. l.batt. arco
simile
10Vc
8Cb
1-4
5-8
15"
15"

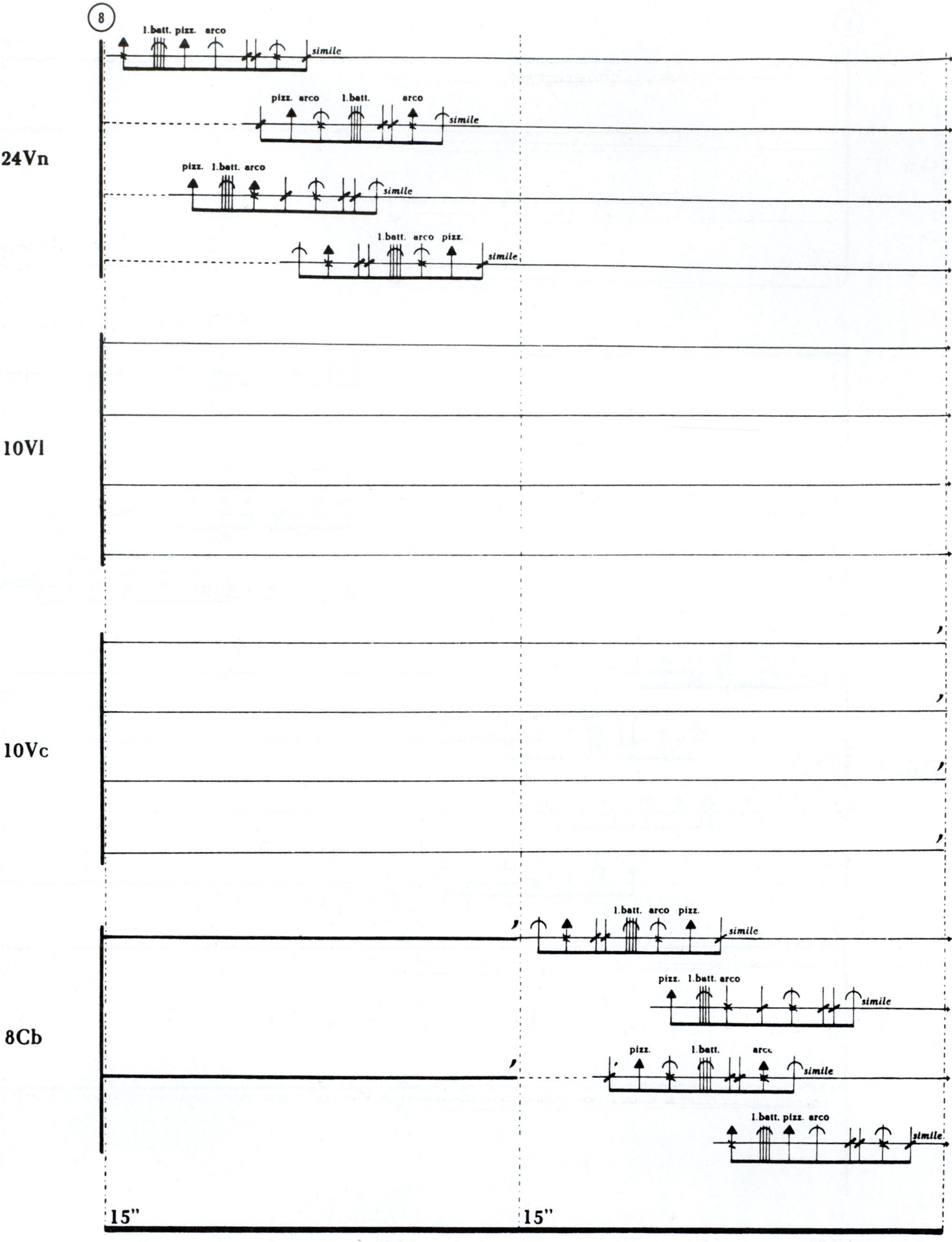
8
1.batt. pizz. arco
simile
pizz. arco 1.batt. arco
simile
24Vn
pizz. 1.batt. arco
simile
1.batt. arco pizz.
simile
10Vl
10Vc
1.batt. arco pizz.
simile
pizz. 1.batt. arco
simile
8Cb
pizz. 1.batt. arco
simile
1.batt. pizz. arco
simile
15"
15"

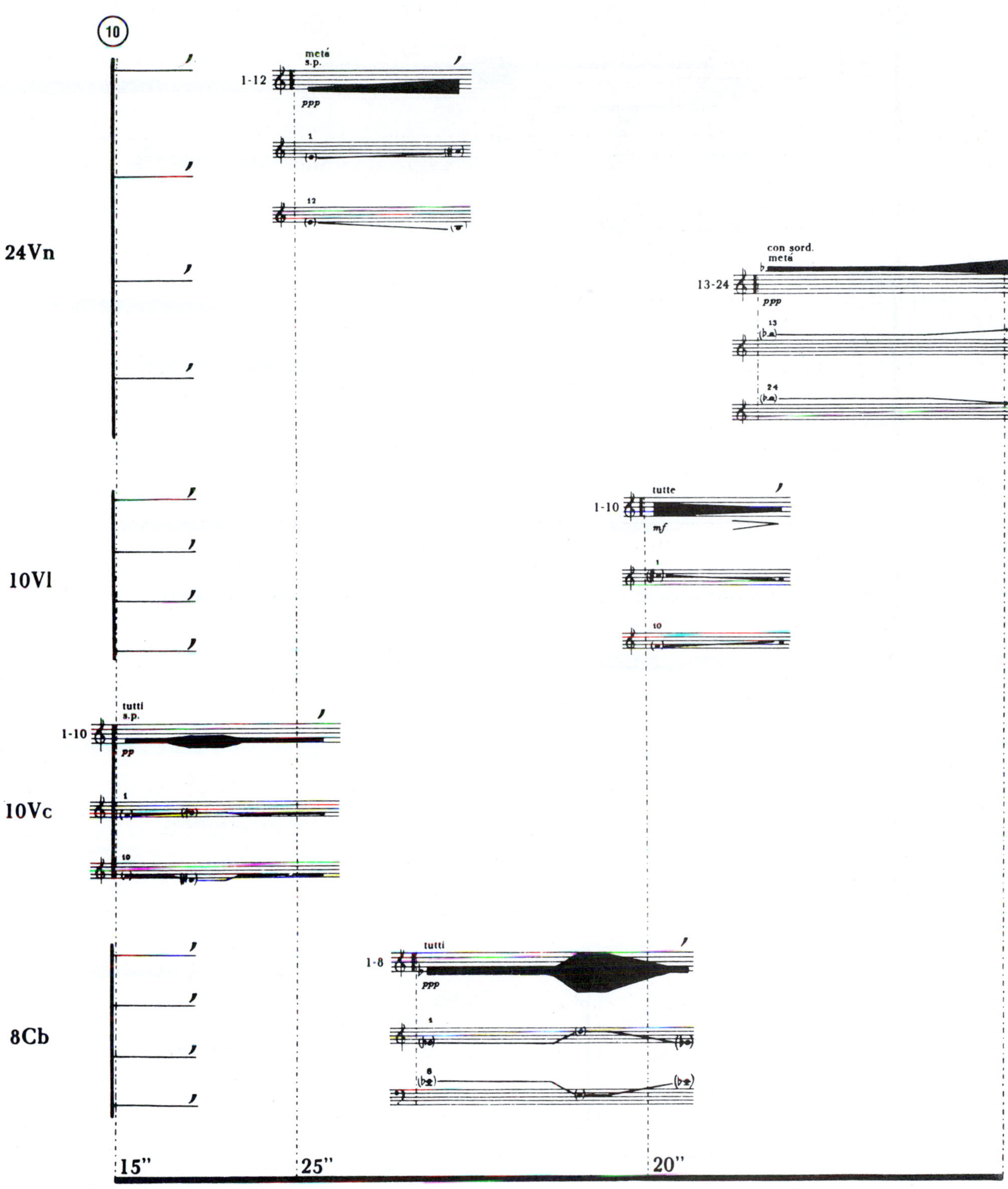
10
metá
s.p.
1-12
ppp
1
12
24Vn
con sord.
metá
13-24
ppp
13
24
tutte
1-10
mf
1
10
10Vl
tutti
s.p.
1-10
pp
1
10
10Vc
tutti
1-8
ppp
1
8
8Cb
15"
25"
20"

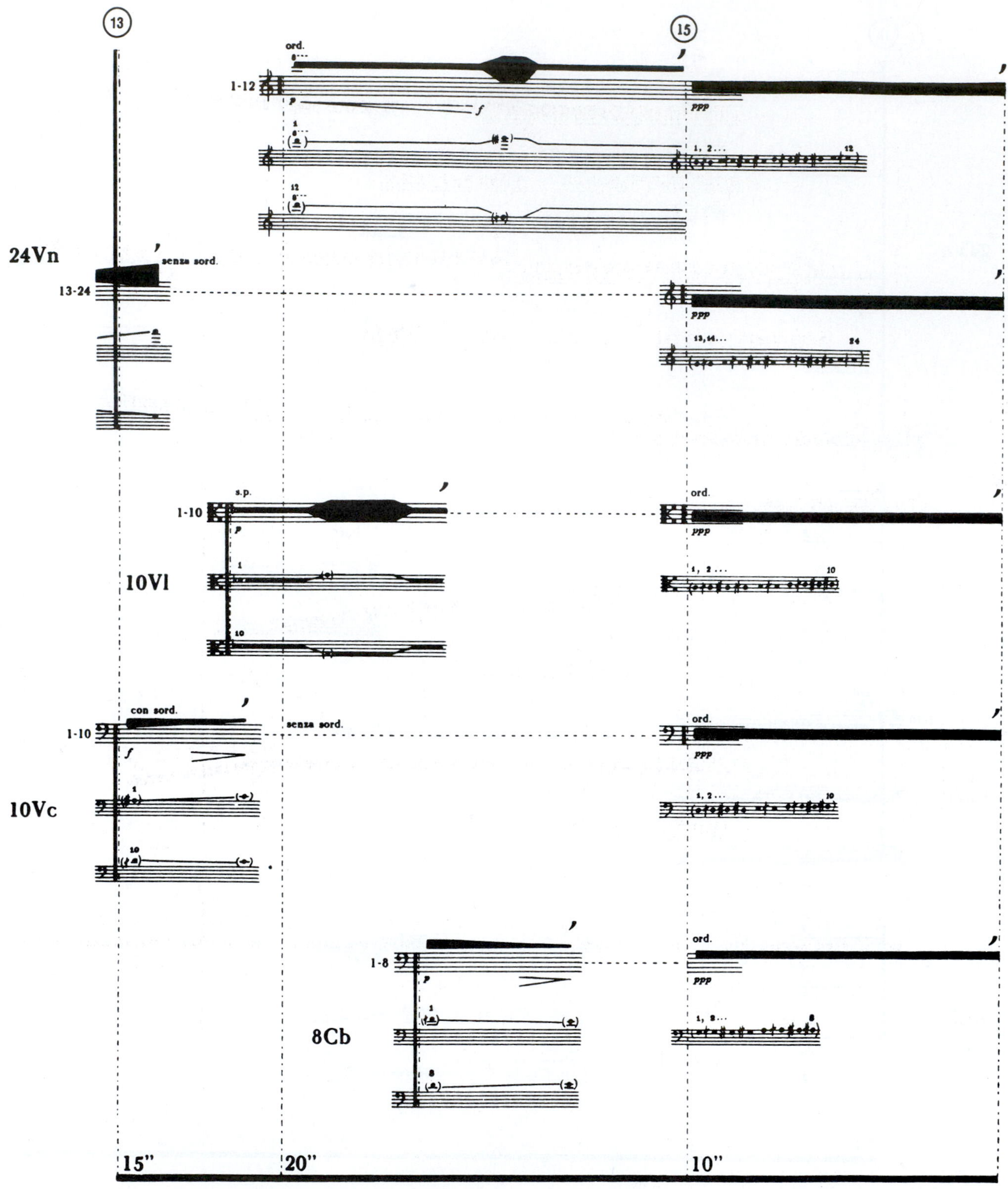

13
15
ord.
1-12
p
f
ppp
24Vn
senza sord.
13-24
s.p.
1-10
10Vl
ord.
con sord.
senza sord.
10Vc
1-8
8Cb
15"
20"
10"

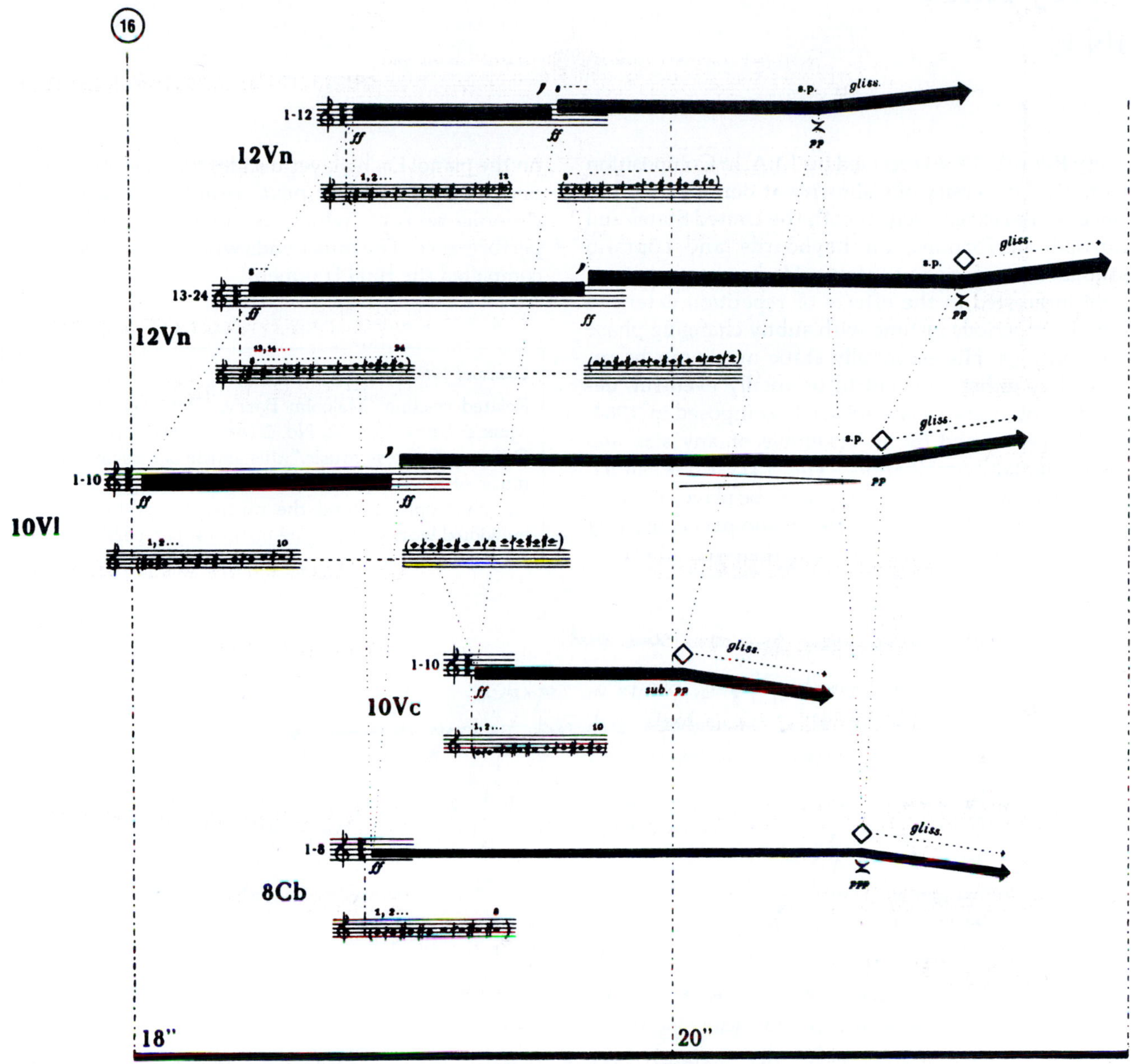
16
1-12
ff
ff
s.p.
gliss.
pp
12Vn
1, 2...
12
13-24
ff
ff
s.p.
gliss.
pp
12Vn
13, 14...
24
1-10
ff
ff
s.p.
gliss.
pp
10Vl
1, 2...
10
1-10
ff
gliss.
sub. pp
10Vc
1, 2...
10
1-8
ff
gliss.
ppp
8Cb
1, 2...
8
18"
20"

Terry Riley

IN C

Terry Riley (b. 1935) received his M.A. in Composition from the University of California at Berkeley and has since toured extensively in both the United States and Europe, performing on keyboards and soprano saxophone in various contexts. He has been particularly interested in the effects of repetition extended over long periods of time with subtly changing phase relationships. His essentially static music can be regarded as either uneventful or totally eventful, depending on one's viewpoint. *In C*, composed in 1964, can be performed by an ensemble of any size and instrumental combination. The fifty-three short, repeatable melodic fragments are to be played in order and in tempo with an unwritten piano part consisting of continuous eighth-notes, using the two highest C's on the piano. Each player decides when to move from one fragment to the next, resulting in a complex canonic texture which is different with every performance. The music ends when the last player has completed the final fragment.

Composed 1964

Related reading: Malcolm Barry, "Reviews of Music," *Music & Letters*, Vol. 62, No. 2 (April 1981), pp. 242–244. Defining "process music," this article is a review of the music of the composer Steve Reich. It is a discussion of the philosophy behind the music, observations about individual works, and some historical perspective.

All performers play from the same part.

there are 53 repeating figures, played in sequence.

They are to be taken consecutively with each performer determining the number of times he repeats each figure before going on to the next.

The pulse is traditionally played by a beautiful girl on the top two octaves of a grand piano. she must play loudly and keep strict tempo for the entire ensemble to follow.

the tempo should be determined by how fast the ensemble can execute the smallest units (16th notes)

All performers must strictly adhere to the tempo of the pulse.

After the pulse has begun to sound each performer determines for himself when to enter on the first figure.

As a general rule the performers should remain within a compass of 4 or 5 figures of each other occassionally trying to merge together in a unison. This means that although each performer is essentially free to repeat a figure as many times as he wishes, he must ultimately abide by the pace taken on by the majority in the ensemble.

The ensemble should sit as close together as is comfortably possible, All performers radiating outward from the pulse who should be in the center.

It is o.k. to amplify instruments that can't naturally play so loud such as strings flutes, harpsichords etc.

All parts should be played at the written pitch. It is generally o.k to transpose up an octave. Transposing down an octave should be discouraged unless several performers are doing so and even then they should be extremely careful in choosing alignments and try to absorb the tendency to stick out.

Since performances often go over an hour each figure can easily be repeated for a minute or longer. (performances could last days, months, a year – a figure for each week with the closing one to start the new year)
Dont be in a hurry to move from figure to figure. Stay on your part and keep repeating it, listening for how it is relating to what the rest of the ensemble is playing. If it sounds like everyone is playing in the same alignment of a figure, you may shift yours to create an opposing alignment.

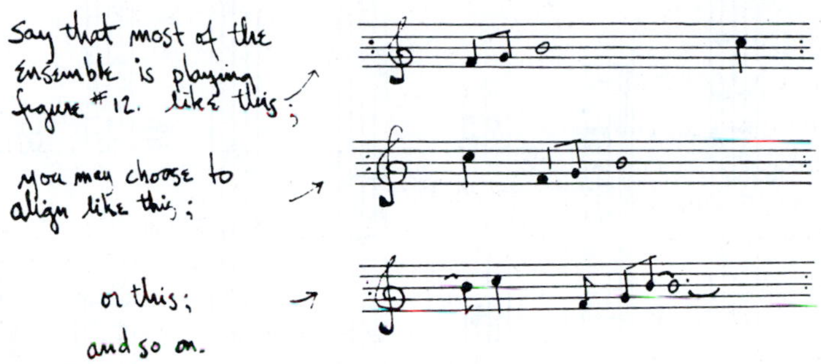

In this way you have not 53 figures but literally thousands and it is part of the creative task of the ensemble to explore the different combinations.

Play at a good loud volume but avoid letting your part get isolated from the others. Make all exits and entrys as unconspicuous as possible.

In order to play continuously without fatigue a figure can be repeated in groups of 4 or 5 with a rest included to form an overall pattern consisting of x number of repetitions plus a rest. The duration of the rest may be equal to the duration of the figure being repeated as illustrated below.

#11.

This makes the part more stable and symetrical and allows it to groove better with the rest of the ensemble, especially if everyone else is stabilized in a pattern formation. However any number of repetitions and any duration of rest is permitted.

Changes should not be dramatic. The sequence should very gradually unfold.
When each performer reaches figure #53 he should stay on that figure until the entire ensemble has arrived and a unison is achieved. The players can then gradually drop out, the pulse continuing a few moments after the rest of the ensemble has finished.

If a performer comes to a figure he cannot play he may omit it.

The ensemble should learn all figures in unison before attempting any combinations. It is essential that everyone play the figures correctly.

Any number of instuments can play. In general the more players, the better it goes. Several keyboard instruments should be used as well as percussion instuments that are tuned such as marimbas, vibraphones and xylophones.

Diane Thome

"THE YEW TREE" *excerpt*

Diane Thome (b. 1942) is Professor of Theory and Composition at the University of Washington. She received degrees in music from Princeton University, the University of Pennsylvania and the Eastman School of Music. A former student of Roy Harris, Darius Milhaud and Milton Babbitt, she has written for a wide variety of mediums—instrumental, vocal and choral, and electronic—and her music has been performed throughout the United States and abroad.

The title of the following selection is a reference to the central image of Robert Strassburg's poem, "Love's Springtime." The music is in two large sections, only the first of which is given. Pitch relationships are tightly controlled. For example, you should be able to identify several motives in the opening violin-viola dialogue that recur when the other instruments enter after m. 12. Observe also how this dialogue grows melodically. What relationship do the many prominent chordal structures bear to it? How does the opening vocal phrase relate? At m. 24 a motive is introduced that undergoes immediate development and reappears several times thereafter. Discuss this. How are the viola and cello related in this measure? To what earlier material can this motive be traced? Describe the interaction between voice and instruments. Notice how rhythmic fluidity is created by the large number of cross-rhythms, especially by the use of triplets against or followed by quintuplets.

"The Yew Tree" was composed in 1979 and is recorded on Crystal Records, with soprano Montserrat Alavedra.

12
A
Fl.
Ob.
Cl.
Bn.
Vn.
Va.
Harp
mp
pp
C♯F♯G♯

15
Piu Mosso
(♩=76)
Fl.
Vn.
Va.
Vc.
Harp
molto legato
pp
mp
sub. pp
poco mf
C♮F♮G♮
ppp
delicato
C♯F♯G♯

Poco Piu Mosso
(♩=88)
18
Ob.
Harp
Cel.
f sub.
pp
ppp
Ped.

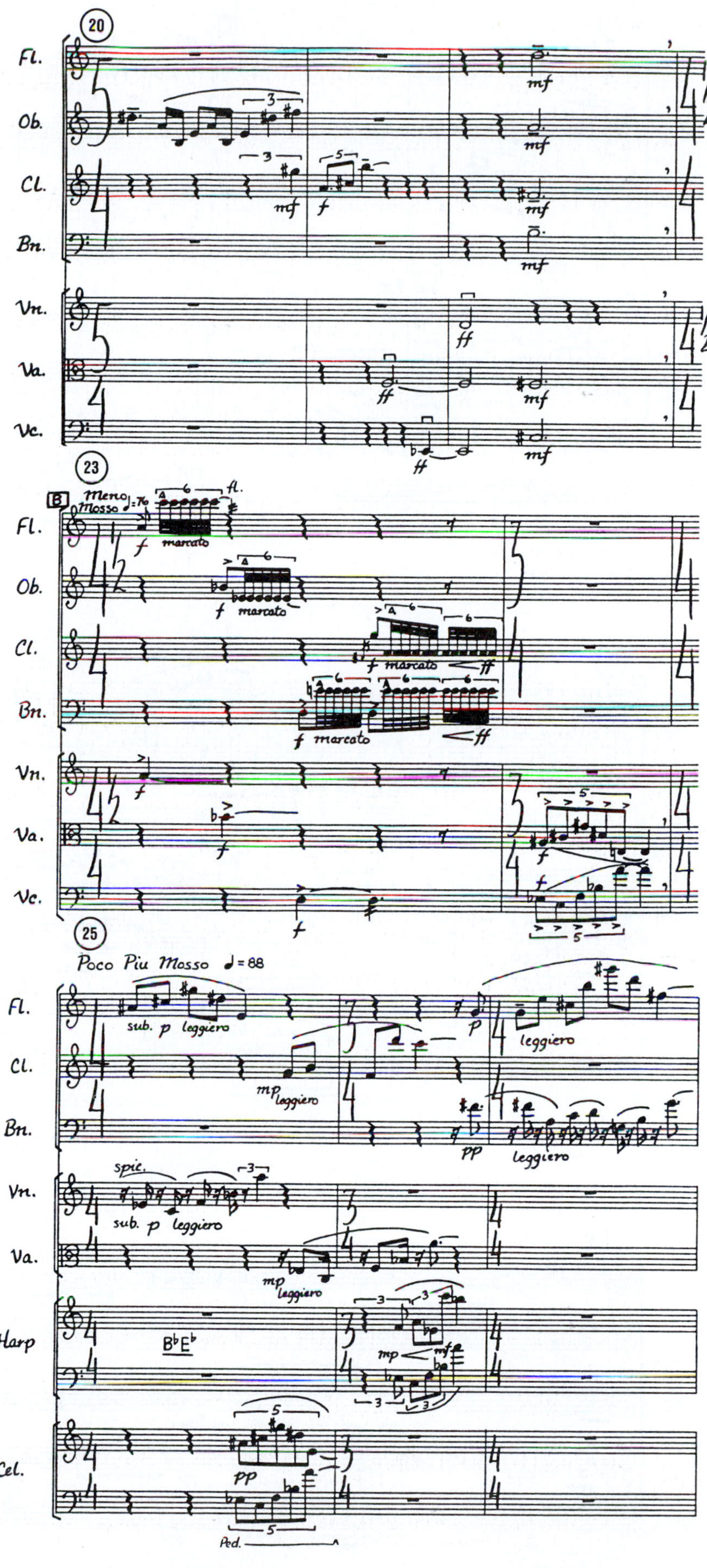
20
Fl.
Ob.
Cl.
Bn.
Vn.
Va.
Vc.
mf
ff
23
B
Meno Mosso ♩=76
fl.
marcato
f
ff
25
Poco Piu Mosso ♩=88
sub. p leggiero
mp leggiero
p
leggiero
pp
spic.
Harp
B♭E♭
mp
mf
Cel.
pp
Ped.

28
C
(♩= 88)
Fl.
Ob.
Cl.
Bn.
Vn.
Va.
Vc.
Sop.
(pizz.)
(arco)
rit. e dim.
(legato)
A mountain echo re

31
Fl.
Ob.
Cl.
Vn.
Sop.
Harp
(joyfully)
fl. tongue
(esp.)
sub. pp
sounds in my heart
This A—pril

34
Fl.
Cl.
Sop.
Vib.
Xylo.
Perc.
morn
the white dove of rhy—thm
Oboist or Soprano plays piece of wood with bell mallet

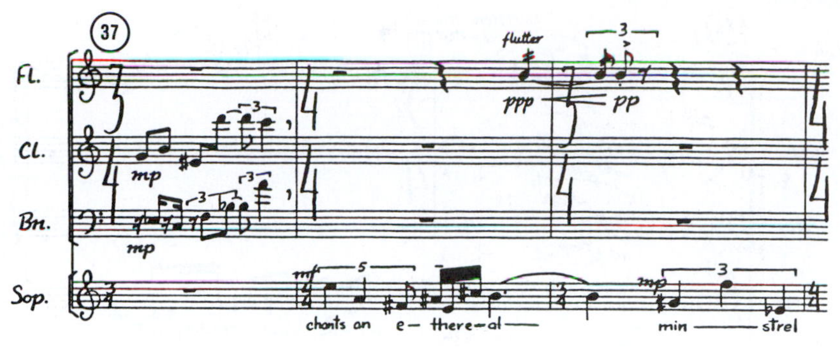
37
Fl.
Cl.
Bn.
Sop.
flutter
ppp
pp
mp
mp
chants an e– there–al
min strel

40
Fl.
Ob.
Cl.
Bn.
Vn.
Va.
Vc.
Sop.
mf leggiero
leggiero
mp
poco mf
pp
pp
pp
pp
poco mp
ff
pizz.
ff
ff
Song

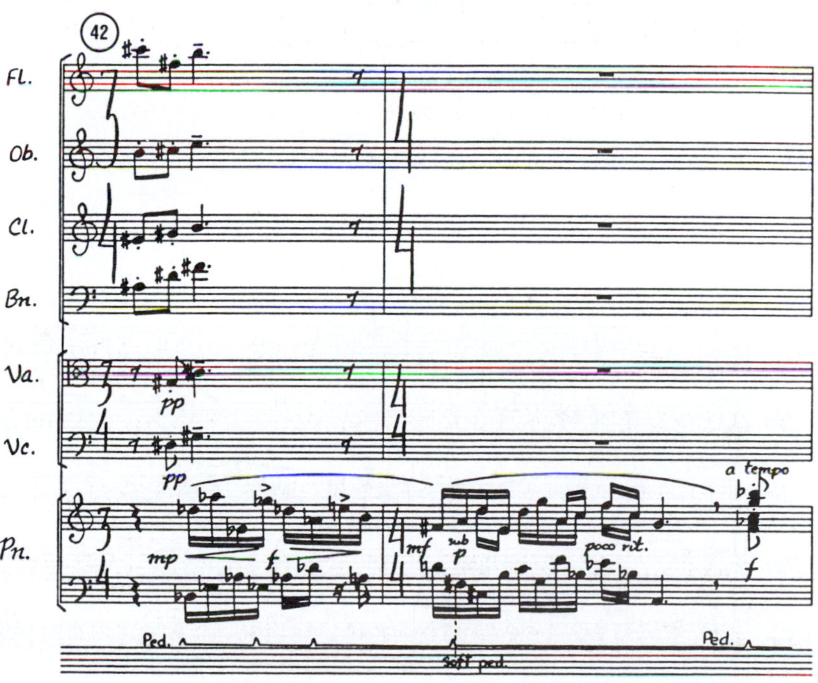
42
Fl.
Ob.
Cl.
Bn.
Va.
Vc.
Pn.
pp
pp
mp
f
mf
sub p
poco rit.
a tempo
f
Ped.
Ped.
soft ped.

44
Meno Mosso
♩=72
D
Vn.
Va.
Vc.
Sop.
Harp
Pn.
esp rit.
esp. rit.
with
gen-tle unpre-tending trills
mp
rit e dim.

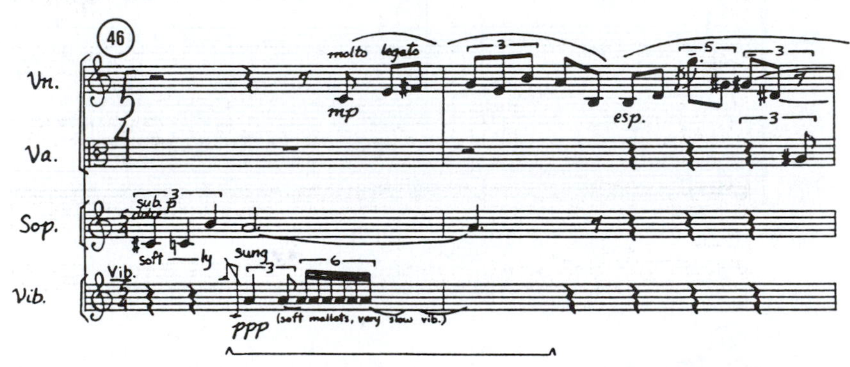
46
molto legato
Vn.
Va.
Sop.
Vib.
mp
esp.
sub. p
soft-ly
sung
(soft mallets, very slow vib.)
ppp

48
Fl.
Vn.
Va.
Vc.
Sop.
pp legato
fl.
ppp
mf
a-mid the thorns and butterflies
the skylark cries
esp.

50
Fl.
Ob.
Cl.
Bn
Vn.
Va.
Vc.
Sop.
flutter
spreading, spreading for — and wide

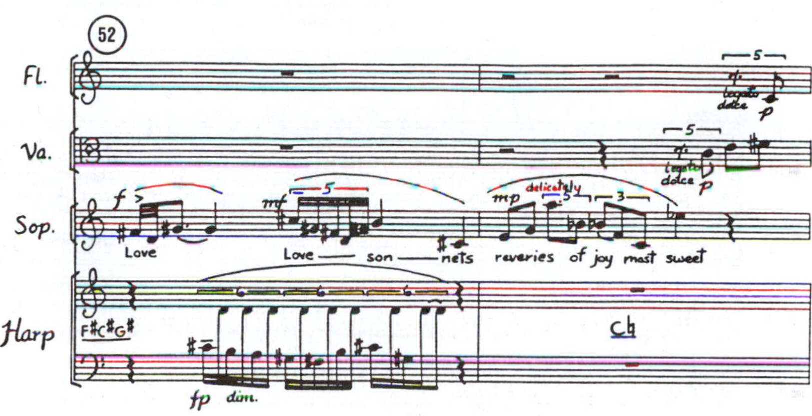
52
Fl.
Va.
Sop.
Harp
legato dolce
Love Love — son — nets reveries of joy most sweet
delicately
F♯C♯G♯
C♮
dim.

54
Fl.
Vn.
Va.
Harp
Pn.
(non Arpeg.)

56
poco rit.
8va
Pn.

57
E
Fl.
Ob.
Cl.
Vn.
Va.
Glock.
Vib.
Cel.
legatis.
legato, esp.
leggierissimo
sul tasto
p dolce
Ped.

GLOSSARY

Additive process A compositional technique frequently employed by Stravinsky and other twentieth-century composers in which a texture is created through the gradual superposition of diverse and unchanging elements. These elements (a melodic figure, a rhythmic ostinato, and so on) typically are heard separately at first. Their subsequent combination and recombination in various registers and instrumental groups may be seen as a form of development.

Aggregate A term meaning "total amount," or "sum." In serial music, it generally refers to the collection of all twelve *pitch classes* formed when two or more voices state different portions of the twelve-tone set.

Alberti bass A type of a broken chord pattern used extensively in Classical keyboard music as a left-hand accompaniment. Developed initially as a means of compensating for the keyboard's lack of sustaining power, the technique was transferred to other instruments, such as the strings, to provide rhythmic animation or momentum.

Aleatoric, Aleatory A term referring to music in which elements of chance are introduced, either in the compositional process or in performance of the work. An associated term is "indeterminacy."

All-combinatoriality A characteristic of certain twelve-tone rows wherein a given form can be used simultaneously with its transposition *and* its transposed inversion without creating pitch duplications. The typical situation is one in which the first hexachords (six notes) of P_0 and P_x (transposition at some level) contain twelve discrete pitches *as do* the first hexachords of P_0 and I_x (inversion at some level). Although normally applied to hexachords, combinatoriality among smaller groups of notes is also possible.

All-interval row A twelve-tone row containing all eleven intervals, assuming an interval and its inversion to be identical — hence, a row containing at least one each of the following: minor second, major second, minor third, major third, perfect fourth and augmented fourth.

Ametric Literally, without meter. The term refers to music in which no prevailing meter, or regularly recurring grouping of beats, can be discerned.

Am Steg A German bowing direction meaning "at the bridge." This instruction for string instruments means to draw the bow across the strings very close to the bridge, producing a hard, "glassy" sound which is rich in overtones.

Anacrusis Upbeat.

Answer, Fugal The imitation of a fugal subject, usually at the level of the dominant.

Arch form A musical structure organized in such a way that the order of the sections appears in reverse beyond a midpoint, such as: A B C B A. The form is found notably in the music of Bartók.

Arco A bowing direction for string instruments meaning "with the bow" — the normal manner of playing.

Antiphonal, Antiphony A texture characterized by the alternation of two or more instrumental or vocal groups. A practically synonymous term is "polychoral."

Atonal, Atonality Meaning the absence of tonality, the term is generally applied to any music which lacks an identifiable tonal center. It is specifically applied to the music written by Schoenberg and his followers between 1909 and 1923 (the year of the formulation of the twelve-tone method of composition).

Augmentation A contrapuntal device in which a melodic phrase or motive appears in note values longer than those of its original appearance.

BACH motive A melodic figure consisting of those pitches which spell the name Bach:

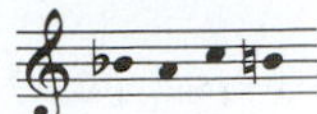

The German B signifies B-flat whereas the German H signifies B-natural. This is due to a misunderstanding which took place in the later Middle Ages in which the sign for B-natural—♮—was mistaken for the letter H. The figure, first used by J. S. Bach himself, has since been employed by many composers.

Basso continuo See Continuo.

Bimodality The use of two modes simultaneously in a composition or a portion thereof. Typically, one voice or group of voices is written in one mode while another voice or group of voices is written in a different mode.

Binary (1) A rhythm characterized by two-part division, resulting in a strong-weak pattern of accentuation. This type of rhythm was considered inferior to triple rhythm in the Middle Ages and only gradually achieved equal standing. (2) Any musical form which divides into two basic parts. While the means of division may vary from piece to piece, the designation usually remains the same: A B. This form was especially common during the Baroque era, being used almost exclusively in the instrumental suites of that period. A common modification involved the "rounding off" of the form with a brief reference to the initial material. See also Rounded binary.

Bitonality The use of two or more tonal centers simultaneously in a musical composition or a portion thereof. The technique was especially common in the music of certain French composers in the early part of the twentieth century and can be found as well in the music of Stravinsky, Copland and Ives.

Breve The longest note value currently used in our proportional system of notation, equivalent to two whole notes. It was the *shortest* value in use during the thirteenth century, being equal to one-half or one-third the value of the longa, a note no longer in use.

Cadential elision The avoidance of a cadence either by joining the end of one phrase to the beginning of the next or by making the end of a phrase in one voice overlap with the beginning of another phrase in a different voice (also termed *cadential overlap*).

Cadential extension Extension of a phrase through repetition or lengthening of its final portion.

Cadential overlap In music of more than one part, the beginning of a phrase in one voice prior to the end of a phrase in another voice.

Cadenza A solo passage, either improvised or composed in an improvisatory style, typically occurring near the end of a composition. It developed from a short interruption of the final cadence in the early Baroque era to a vehicle for extended display of virtuosity in the Classical and Romantic periods. In the Classical concerto, it typically follows a tonic six-four chord and ends with a trill on the dominant which ushers in the final tonic prolongation of the movement.

Caesura A momentary pause in musical activity. The term usually refers to the strongly articulated cadence which precedes the secondary theme in many Classical sonata-form movements.

Canon A composition in which one voice, called the *dux* ("leader"), is imitated throughout by another voice, called the *comes* ("follower").

Canonic imitation The strict imitation of one voice by another for a relatively extended period (usually more than a few measures). If the imitation persists throughout a work or an entire section of a work, the passage is called a canon. If the passage is shorter, the term *canonic imitation* is used instead.

Cantus firmus Literally *fixed song,* a melody (usually preexistent) which serves as the basis for a musical composition. The term is most often used in conjunction with certain music of the Middle Ages and Renaissance, in which a plainsong (chant) melody was given to one part, usually the tenor, in notes of relatively long duration. This melody then served as the foundation around which other, more active, voices were added.

Cellular construction An intensely motivic means of organization employed in the atonal music of Schoenberg and his followers, in which a short motive (often only three or four notes) served as the basis of all or much of the melodic and harmonic content within the composition.

Chaconne A type of continuous variation common in the Baroque era but not limited to it, in which the "theme" or subject of variation is a short harmonic pattern.

Chance elements See Aleatoric.

Change of mode (1) The movement from a major key to its parallel minor or vice versa. (2) The change from a major form of a triad to its minor form or vice versa.

Character variation A type of sectional variation found mostly in the Romantic period in which the theme assumes a highly distinctive character—such as a march or a scherzo—in each of the variations.

Chordal style A highly homophonic texture in which all parts of a multi-voiced composition move together with the same rhythm, creating the effect of a series of chords rather than of individual melodic lines.

Chord mutation A gradual and subtle means of chord change, in which one member of the harmony changes at a time, thereby generating unusual harmonic successions.

Chords of addition Harmonies, usually triadic, which contain one or more added tones, most often a second or sixth above the root. Such chords commonly appear in the music of Debussy.

Chords of omission Harmonies, usually triadic, in which one or more tones is omitted. The third of the chord is most commonly deleted, leaving an open-fifth sound. Such chords are frequently found in the music of Debussy.

Chromatic third relationship Triads with roots a third apart in which at least one of the common tones is chromatically altered (and is thus no longer a common tone), as in: C–E–G and A–C-sharp–E.

Church modes See Modal, Modality, Modes.

Circle of fifths A harmonic motion, especially common in the Baroque and Classical periods, in which chord roots proceed by the interval of a fifth, either upward or downward. Downward movement (e.g., iii-vi-ii-V-I) is the more common and forms the basis for many Baroque sequences.

Closure, Closed cadence A cadence on the tonic or the temporary tonic (if a new key has been established), which imparts a sense of finality to a phrase or section.

Cluster chords Harmonic structures composed of seconds rather than thirds and thus sometimes referred to as *secundal harmonies.*

Coda Originally an expanded final cadence, a coda is an extended ending to a composition or movement that helps to create a convincing close by prolonging and affirming the tonic chord.

Codetta (1) A closing passage to an inner section of a work which performs a function analogous to the coda—to impart a degree of finality by prolonging the final tonic chord of the section. (2) A short coda. (3) In a fugue, a transitional passage which connects two subject entries.

Col legno Literally, "with the wood," a special string instrument effect in which the player either draws the back of the bow across the strings (*col legno tratto*) or taps the strings with the wood of the bow (*col legno battutta*).

Color In isorhythmic compositions, the repeated pitch pattern. The rhythmic pattern is called the *talea.* (See also Isorhythm.)

Coloratura In Classical and Romantic operatic arias, a rapid, virtuosic vocal passage similar to an instrumental cadenza. The term is also applied to sopranos who specialize in singing such parts.

Combinatoriality A characteristic of certain twelve-tone rows wherein a given form can be used simultaneously with its transposition *or* its transposed inversion without creating pitch duplications. If, for example, the first hexachords (six notes) of P_0 and P_x (transposition at some level) *or* I_x (inversion at some level) contain all twelve pitches, the row is said to be combinatorial—specifically, *semi-combinatorial.* If P_0 - P_x *and* P_0 - I_x are combinatorial in this manner, the row is said to be *all-combinatorial.*

Composite rhythm The rhythm that results from the simultaneous combined rhythmic patterns of all voices in a multivoiced composition.

Concertato style The use of contrasting sound sources in certain early seventeenth-century music, which led ultimately to the development of the concerto late in the Baroque era.

Concertino The group of solo instruments (as opposed to the full orchestra—the *tutti*) in the Baroque concerto grosso.

Conjunct Moving by whole-step or half-step.

Con sordino With a mute.

Constructivism The carefully considered application of abstract principles or mathematical models to the composition of music. Found primarily in the fourteenth and twentieth centuries.

Continuo In Baroque music, the figured bass line, which was normally played by a tenor or bass melodic instrument such as the viola da gamba or bassoon and a keyboard instrument.

Continuo homophony The combination of a homophonic texture with rapid harmonic rhythm and a figured bass line that emerged in the concerto of the late Baroque era and ultimately led to the homophonic style of the early Classical period.

Continuous A term referring to forms characterized by uninterrupted musical flow as opposed to clear division into sections. This continuity is generally achieved through the avoidance of strong cadences.

Cross-relation The effect produced by the occurrence of a pitch in one voice followed by its chromatic alteration in another voice (for example, G in the soprano followed immediately by G-sharp in the alto).

Cross-rhythm The simultaneous occurrence of conflicting rhythms, such as an eighth note duplet and triplet.

Countersubject In fugal passages, the musical material that is used more or less consistently to accompany the answer or later statements of the subject.

Declamation, Declamatory A type of musical delivery developed in the early Baroque era in which the singer approximates the rhythms and inflections of natural speech. Music written in such a style is characterized by extensive pitch repetition, lack of wide leaps, syllabic text setting and moderate-to-rapid rhythmic patterns.

Denouement In literature and music, the resolution of conflict that usually follows a dramatic high point.

Development, Developmental That portion of a musical work which involves the manipulation of material set forth in the initial portion of the piece. The term is used specifically in connection with sonata form. Here it refers to the middle section of a movement, characterized by frequent modulations, in which themes heard in the exposition are fragmented, altered and recombined in various ways to produce a feeling of restlessness, instability and conflict.

Diatonic Employing only the pitches of a given scale or mode.

Diminution The restatement of a melodic/rhythmic figure in shortened note values.

Disjunct Melodic lines moving largely by leaps.

Divisi An indication that a passage is to be played by a divided instrumental section.

Dominant caesura See Caesura.

Double stops See Multiple stops.

Double exposition A term used to describe the initial orchestral and solo thematic presentations in the first movement of the Classical concerto. In such movements, the orchestral introduction takes the form of an exposition in its own right, ending, however, in the tonic at the point of the soloist's entry. From this point on, the movement has the general character of a sonata form.

Double fugue A fugue with two subjects, normally containing three sections—a fugue on the first subject, a fugue on the second subject, and a fugue combining both subjects.

Dramatic shape The form of a musical work as created by its psychological or emotional effect. It is normally defined in terms of its areas of peak intensity and the approaches to and resolutions of those moments.

Episode In fugue, an interlude separating entrances of the subject. It may use motives from the subject or entirely new material, but a complete statement of the subject does not occur. A typical fugue consists of a number of episodes and entrances of the subject—singly or in groups—in alternation.

Equal temperament The system of dividing the octave into twelve equal half steps, which has been the basis of keyboard tuning since the nineteenth century. In this system, no interval besides the octave is pure. However, the deviation for each interval is so small as to be hardly noticeable, except by instrumentalists when performing with a keyboard accompaniment. In such cases, the instrumentalist must make constant adjustments in order to play "in tune" with the keyboard.

Event-compression A developmental technique frequently employed by Beethoven and other composers in which a musical figure is repeated a number of times with a gradual shortening or rhythmic *diminution*. Also termed *rhythmic acceleration*, this technique usually results in increased musical intensity and is often used to precede a dramatic high point.

Exposition (1) The first section of a fugue, in which all voices enter in turn with the subject or answer. Subsequent multiple entrances of the subject are sometimes referred to as expositions as well. (2) The first principal section of a sonata-form movement, characterized by the initial presentation of thematic material, the eventual departure from the tonic key area, and the establishment of a secondary key area.

Extrametrical division of a beat A division of the basic pulse which is different from that implied by the prevailing meter (for example, eighth-note triplets in 4/4 meter). The term *borrowed division* is sometimes used as well.

Fauxbourdon A technique found in fifteenth-century music in which a melody is accompanied in parallel motion by two lower voices, forming a series of first-inversion triads.

Figuration A technique found primarily in the Baroque and Classical periods in which stereotyped figures, usually forms of arpeggiation, are used either as embellishment or accompaniment to a melodic line or as a means of variation.

Figured bass A Baroque notational practice in which the keyboard part is written as a bass line with numerals below to indicate the harmonies to be added above. The keyboard player is expected to improvise an accompaniment based upon this line.

Finalis The final, or central note of a church mode, analogous to the tonic in major or minor keys.

Formes fixes Literally *fixed forms*, the three chief forms of thirteenth-, fourteenth- and fifteenth-century French secular music—ballade, virelai and rondeau.

Free tonality Music in which a tonal center is established through means other than functional harmonic relationships.

Free-voiced Compositions in which the number of voices is not fixed but variable.

Fugato A fugal section appearing in a composition which is primarily nonfugal.

Functional harmony, Functional relationship A term referring to the harmonic relationships within the major-minor tonal system. Within a given key, the individual harmonies stand in a hierarchy of importance based on their proximity to the tonic via the circle of fifths and "function" in a certain way as a result. The strongest functional root movement is downward by fifth.

Galante The light, elegant musical style of the transitional period between the Baroque and Classical eras, in which the emphasis was on simple melodies and harmonies and homophonic textures.

Glissando A rapid slide upward or downward between two fixed pitches which produces, on instruments of continuously variable pitch such as the trombone or violin, all intermediate frequencies—hence a continuous, unbroken sound.

Ground, Ground bass A repeated melodic pattern, usually four to eight measures, in the lowest voice of a texture, which serves as the basis for a set of continuous variations. See also Passacaglia.

Half cadence A harmonic cadence in which any chord (often the tonic, subdominant, or supertonic) moves to the dominant, conveying a sense of incompletion and a need for an ultimate resolution.

Hauptstimme Literally "chief voice," a designation employed notably by Schoenberg to indicate that element of the texture which was to be most prominent. See also Nebenstimme.

Hemiola Any rhythmic relationship characterized by a 3:2 ratio, as in three quarter notes in the time of two, or in the accentual differences between 6/4 and 3/2 meters.

Heterophonic A type of texture characterized by the simultaneous occurrence of a melody and its ornamented version. The result, while not sounding homophonic, cannot be considered polyphonic since the lines are not truly independent.

Hexachord Any set of six different pitch classes.

Hocket A medieval polyphonic device in which a melody is broken into single notes sung alternately by two or more voices. Performed rapidly, the result resembles a musical "hiccough"—hence the origin of the term.

Imitation, Imitative The repetition in close succession of a melodic figure by different voices of a polyphonic texture.

Index number In twelve-tone music, a subscript used with prime and inverted forms of the row to designate their levels of transposition. The first note of the original row form is assigned the index number "o" and the initial pitches of subsequent P and I forms are measured in half steps above this pitch and indexed accordingly.

Interlude In the broadest sense, any kind of musical insertion. In song, it usually refers to the instrumental passages which separate or connect the verses.

Internal extension See Interpolation.

Interpolation A means of extending a phrase upon repetition by inserting new material in its mid-portion, also referred to as *internal extension.*

Inversion (1) Turning a melodic figure or a twelve-tone row "upside down" so that its contour is a mirror of the original form, with its upward steps and leaps becoming downward steps and leaps by the same interval and vice versa. In tonal music, melodic inversion is more often diatonic than exact—that is, the interval *quality* may change to accommodate the key signature. (2) A term referring to the disposition of the members of a chord in such a way that the chord root is not in the lowest position.

Invertible counterpoint Polyphony constructed in such a way that the lower part may become the higher part or vice-versa through transposition, most often at the octave but sometimes by other intervals such as the tenth or twelfth.

Involution The application of the principle of melodic inversion to harmonic structures. Thus the involution of a given chord is a mirror of its intervallic structure (for example, the involution of a major triad is a *minor* triad).

Isorhythm Literally *same rhythm*, a fourteenth-century compositional procedure in which an extended rhythmic pattern called a *talea* is repeated a certain number of times throughout the composition. This pattern may or may not correspond in length to the melodic pattern (called the *color*) which is also repeated throughout the composition.

Klangfarben, Klangfarbenmelodie A "melody" composed of changing timbres rather than changing pitches. The idea was first proposed by Arnold Schoenberg as a means of establishing timbre as a parameter equal in importance to pitch and rhythm.

Linear cadence A point of musical repose created by the convergence or divergence of melodic lines rather than by strong harmonic movement.

Major-minor tonality The tonal system which formed the basis of musical composition from the seventeenth through the nineteenth centuries. This system involves two basic modes—major and minor—each containing a tonal center established through an elaborate system of chordal relationships, referred to as functional harmony.

Matrix In twelve-tone composition, a convenient way of representing the forty-eight forms of a row made possible through the transposition of each P, I, R and RI form to all twelve pitch levels. The chart is so constructed that each row form, read from left to right starting at the top, is a P form beginning on successive members of the original inversion (I_0). Thus, P forms are read from left to right, R forms from right to left, I forms from top to bottom, and RI forms from bottom to top.

Meantone tuning The direct predecessor of equal temperament and the only other tuning system to gain widespread acceptance in Western music. It involves the spiraling of slightly diminished fifths (two cents smaller than the 3:2 Pythagorean fifth) both upward and downward from C so as to arrive at a pure (5:4) third above and below this central tone (that is, C-G-D-A-E and C-F-B-flat-E-flat-A-flat). The remaining pitches are then calculated as pure thirds to the already obtained pitches. The result is a system which permits the use of keys up to three flats and sharps but is too dissonant beyond this point for practical use.

Melismata, Melismatic A type of text setting in which a single syllable is sustained over several pitches. (See also Syllabic and Neumatic.)

Metric modulation A rhythmic technique that makes it possible to move smoothly and imperceptibly from one tempo or set of basic durations to another in a mathematically precise and controlled way through the use of common note values. This technique, explored by Elliot Carter, has its harmonic counterpart in common chord modulation.

Metric shift A type of syncopation involving the temporary but extended displacement of the primary accent of a measure.

Mirror imitation The inverted repetition of a melodic figure by a different voice in a polyphonic texture.

Mirror writing The *simultaneous* appearance of a melodic figure and its inversion in different voices.

Modal, Modality, Modes Terms referring to the system of church modes that formed the melodic and harmonic basis of Western music prior to the establishment, in the seventeenth century, of the major-minor tonal system.

Modal cadences Any harmonic cadences, authentic or plagal, which involve harmonies inherent in one of the church modes. For example, a v-I (*minor* dominant to major tonic) is characteristic of the Mixolydian mode and is distinct from either the major or minor authentic cadence.

Modes of Limited Transposition A group of scales so-named by Messiaen because of their limited transpositional possibilities. The *most* limited is the whole tone scale, which can be transposed only once before it duplicates itself. The most frequently used is the so-called octatonic scale, which can be transposed three times before repeating its pitch content. (See also Octatonic scale.)

Monodic Sometimes applied to a monophonic (single line) texture, this term more properly refers to the recitative-like melodies with continuo accompaniment composed in the early part of the seventeenth century in reaction to the intense polyphony of the preceding era.

Monomotivic A term used to describe compositions which are based entirely upon a single motive or its variations.

Monothematic A term used to describe a certain type of sonata-form movement, composed frequently by Haydn and C.P.E. Bach, in which both tonic and dominant key areas of the exposition employ the same theme.

Motor rhythms Strong, driving, repeated rhythms, so called because of their repetitious regularity.

Motto A short, unifying motive, usually announced at the beginning of a work and recalled at various points, often at the beginning of succeeding sections or movements.

Multiple stops A string instrument technique involving the simultaneous sounding of pitches on separate strings. If two pitches are sounded, the term *double stop* is used. If three pitches are sounded, the appropriate term is *triple stop*. Although double stops are the more frequent, triple stops are often playable, especially if one of the pitches involves an open string.

Musica ficta In music of the Middle Ages and Renaissance, the chromatic alteration of certain pitches by performers. In modern editions, such "unwritten accidentals" are indicated by sharps or flats placed *above* the notes to which they apply. Musica ficta was applied most commonly to create a semitone movement *up* to the finalis ("tonic") or *down* to the dominant and to avoid tritone relationships.

Musical rhyme A term normally used in connection with chant and polyphonic music of the fourteenth century, referring to sections within a composition which have identical musical endings.

Nebenstimme A designation employed by Schoenberg to distinguish the main subordinate or auxiliary elements of a musical texture from the most important element (*Hauptstimme*).

Neumatic A manner of text setting in which a single syllable of text is sustained over a small number of pitches, usually two to six. (See Syllabic and Melismatic.)

Node Points of zero amplitude in a vibrating body. Such points occur at the ends of a string or a tube and also at fixed intermediate points, since a body tends to vibrate not only as a whole but also in segments which are 1/2, 1/3, 1/4. . . 1/n of its length.

Non-event A term proposed to describe those portions of a composition whose function is to connect, separate or act as a foil to more important material (which might be termed *events*). For example, the term is frequently appropriate for certain transitional sections in sonata-form movements.

Nonretrogradable rhythm A term used by Messiaen to describe rhythms that sound the same whether played forward or backward.

Octatonic scale Literally, a scale of eight tones. The name has been given specifically to Messiaen's second Mode of Limited Transposition, which features alternating whole and half steps.

Open cadence In tonal music, ending a phrase or section on a chord other than the tonic, resulting in a lack of finality and the expectation of continuation.

Pandiatonic, Pandiatonicism A twentieth-century technique involving the predominant use of the diatonic (as opposed to chromatic) notes within a given key or mode, but without the usual *functional* relationships or traditional treatment of dissonance.

Parallelism Also called "planing," the parallel movement of harmonic structures or of individual melodic lines. An early use of the technique is in the *fauxbourdon* of the fifteenth century. It was established as an important technique in the early twentieth century by Debussy, Satie and others.

Paraphrase technique In the Renaissance, the free elaboration of a chant melody and its use as a basis for Mass composition.

Parody technique A fifteenth- and sixteenth-century technique of Mass composition in which entire portions of a pre-existent polyphonic work are incorporated or used as the basis for a Mass.

Passacaglia A type of continuous variation form common in the Baroque era, in which the theme is a recurring melodic pattern, typically in the bass.

Pentatonic scale Technically, any scale containing only five pitches to the octave. The most common of such scales—prominent in Oriental and African melodies—is composed of major seconds and minor thirds exclusively, as represented by the black keys of the piano.

Period, Periodic A term describing a phrase structure which is characterized by antecedent-consequent relationships and which is clearly and regularly punctuated by cadences.

Permutation In twelve-tone music, any systematic reordering of the notes of a row.

Phrase A basic unit of melodic construction which, having expressed a more or less complete musical thought, comes to a point of relative repose.

Phrase extension The lengthening of a phrase by one of several means. (See also Cadential extension and Interpolation.)

Phrase group A series of phrases which, due to their harmonic independence, do *not* combine to form the larger musical unit known as a *period.*

Phrase member A short (typically two to four measures) melodic unit which constitutes a portion of a phrase.

Phrase overlap See Cadential overlap.

Phrygian cadence A type of half cadence occurring only in the minor mode and designated by the symbols: iv_6 - V. The name derives from the downward movement by semitone of the bass.

Picardy third The conventional Baroque practice of ending a minor key composition or section of a composition on the *major* tonic.

Pictorialism The musical depiction of nonmusical subjects.

Pitch class In twelve-tone music and theory, a note plus all of its octave duplications, including enharmonic equivalents.

Pivot tone A pitch which serves a dual harmonic purpose, acting as a member of two different chords to which it is common. Haydn, Beethoven, Brahms and others frequently used the pivot tone to modulate quickly but logically to a third-related key.

Pizzicato A very common string instrument technique in which the strings are plucked with the finger, producing a dry, staccato sound.

Plainsong A term used to refer to Gregorian chant or other liturgical monophony.

Planing See Parallelism.

Pointillism A twentieth-century compositional technique in which long melodic lines are replaced by fragmented figures in different instruments and registers, producing a kaleidoscopic array of disjointed sounds.

Polychord A harmonic structure consisting of two different chords (usually triads), so spaced or orchestrated that the identity of each chord is retained even though they are sounded simultaneously.

Polymodality The simultaneous use of two or more modes.

Polytonality The simultaneous use of two or more tonalities.

Postlude (1) An organ composition usually played at the end of a church service as the congregation departs. (2) In song, the instrumental conclusion following the last vocal phrase.

Prelude (1) A movement serving as an introduction to a liturgical ceremony or another piece of music. (2) In song, a short instrumental introduction that precedes the vocal entry and serves to set the mood or to establish an accompanimental pattern. (3) The title given to short character pieces written for piano in the nineteenth and twentieth centuries, by composers such as Chopin and Debussy.

Prime The original form of a twelve-tone row or any of its transpositions.

Pythagorean tuning A system of tuning based upon the spiraling of twelve perfect fifths (each with a frequency ratio of 3:2). The twelfth pitch obtained in such a manner, with C as a starting pitch, is a B-sharp which is 23.5 cents (approximately an eighth of a tone) higher than the beginning pitch (transposed to the same octave). Equal temperament, the system now in use, distributes this pitch discrepancy, called a "comma," evenly throughout the octave.

Quartal, Quintal Harmonic structures built upon the intervals of a fourth and fifth instead of a third.

Real (1) In sequence, an exact, interval-for-interval transposition of a melodic figure. Such repetitions almost always entail the use of accidentals and are thus termed *chromatic,* as opposed to diatonic. See also Sequence. (2) In fugue, a term designating an answer which is an exact transposition of the subject to the dominant.

Recapitulation The third principal division of a sonata-form movement, in which the material heard initially in the exposition is repeated, usually remaining in the tonic key with no further modulations such as occur in the exposition.

Recitative A speech-like vocal style used primarily in the fast-paced portions of an opera where the action is rapidly advanced and a large amount of text is involved. It is generally characterized by limited range, pitch repetition, speech-like rhythms and sparse instrumental accompaniment.

Reduction A graph or chart illustrating the most essential elements of a musical passage—the structural pitches and chords which define the basic melodic and harmonic direction and to which the other pitches and harmonies function as embellishments.

Refrain A musical-textural passage which returns several times in the course of a vocal composition, usually at the end of each stanza of a strophic song.

Responsorial One of several ways of performing chant in medieval liturgical services, in which a soloist and chorus sing alternate portions of the chant. It is the most common present-day method of performing chant.

Retrograde The statement of a melodic figure, a twelve-tone row or a rhythmic idea in reverse order—that is, played backward. One of the four basic aspects of a twelve-tone row, the others being Prime, Inversion and Retrograde Inversion.

Retrograde Inversion In twelve-tone composition, the statement of the inversion of a row in reverse order, designated RI.

Rhythmic acceleration A term sometimes used to describe the gradual shortening, or compression, of an event on successive repetitions through diminution or omission of notes. See also Event-compression.

Ritornello (1) A short instrumental passage which returns periodically to punctuate the vocal strophes in an operatic aria. (2) A term used in connection with the Baroque concerto to designate the material of the *tutti* sections—that is, the full ensemble passages, which usually involve the same material and which alternate with passages for the soloists (the *concertino*).

Rondeau (1) One of the three *formes fixes* of medieval music and poetry, which involves a musical and textual repeat structure as follows:

Music: a b a a a b a b
Text: 1 2 3 1 4 5 1 2

(2) A popular Baroque form involving the alternation of a repeated theme (refrain) with new music (*couplets*). This form was especially common in the keyboard suites of French clavecinists such as François Couperin.

Rondo A form frequently used in the Classical period to conclude a multimovement composition such as sonata or symphony and characterized by the alternation of new material with a repeated section. The most common schemes are ABACABA and ABACA.

Rotation In twelve-tone composition, a systematic reordering of the row, usually by moving the first pitch or interval to the last position and advancing all others accordingly. The resulting row is frequently transposed to begin on the same pitch as the original.

Rounded binary A two-part form in which the second part is "rounded off" by a restatement of initial material: A/BA. No clear cadential separation exists in the second part, nor is the final return of the opening material usually of sufficient length to give the effect of a three-part form.

Row forms In twelve-tone composition, the four basic aspects of a twelve-tone row—Prime, Retrograde, Inversion and Retrograde Inversion.

Sectional A term referring to forms which are characterized by a clear division into sections through strong cadential articulation or sharp contrast. See also Continuous.

Segmentation A twelve-tone technique developed mainly by Webern, in which the row, instead of appearing consistently intact, is divided into fragments which are treated in motivic fashion. Frequently in Webern's rows the intervallic content of the various segments is similar or identical.

Semi-combinatoriality See Combinatoriality.

Serial A term applied to music in which at least one parameter is subjected to ordering principles.

Sequence, Sequential A melodic or harmonic pattern repeated in close succession at a pitch level other than the original.

Sesquialtera, Sesquitertia The prefix "sesqui" denotes a fraction whose numerator is larger by one than the denominator. The suffix indicates the quantity of the denominator. Thus, sesquialtera signifies 3:2, sesquitertia signifies 4:3, sesquiquarta signifies 5:4 and so on.

Set A collection of pitches, durations, timbres and so on. The term most often refers to a collection of pitches and is more general than the term "row," since it does not imply a particular ordering.

Set type A means of describing the intervallic content of a collection of pitches, linear or vertical. The group of pitches is placed in the closest possible position, the lowest pitch is assigned the number zero, and the other pitches are measured and indicated in semitones above.

Sonata form, Sonata principle The most important musical form of the Classical period, consisting of three principal divisions—exposition, development and recapitulation—and characterized by the establishment of conflicting key areas in the first part, harmonic exploration and thematic manipulation in the second part and solidification of the tonic in the third part.

Sonata-rondo form A hybrid musical form combining elements of the rondo with elements of sonata form. In this structure, the second episode assumes the character of a development and the last part functions as a recapitulation. A coda may or may not be present.

Sonatina A term commonly used to designate a sonata which is shorter or less difficult than usual. The term *sonatina form* describes a modification of sonata form in which a development section is absent. (This is often referred to as "abridged sonata form.")

Sound blocks Harmonically static masses of sound which typically lack distinguishing melodic and rhythmic features and are thus defined primarily by their texture, register and timbre. Also referred to as *sound masses.*

Source set An unordered collection of pitches or intervals from which rows may be obtained by ordering the members in various ways.

Sprechstimme A type of vocal recitation used most notably by Schoenberg in which specifically notated pitches are merely approximated in performance, with no attempt to maintain the pitch once it has been sounded. The result is halfway between speech and song.

Stasis, Static A term used to describe any musical element which remains essentially unchanged for a period of time. It is frequently used in connection with sound blocks (sound masses) found in the music of Stravinsky and Varèse.

Step-progression The stepwise relationships frequently existing between important pitches in a melodic line that impart a sense of overall direction and logic. Such stepwise connections may be adjacent or separated by several measures.

Stretto In fugue, the imitation of the subject at a short time interval, typically beginning before the subject is completed. Because of the intensity created by this compression, the technique is frequently reserved for later points in the fugal composition.

Strophic A formal structure in which all verses of a song are sung to the same music.

Structural melody (line, chord, pitch) The elements of a melodic or harmonic passage that define its goals or overall direction and thus serve as focal points around which the other elements function as embellishments.

Sul ponticello A direction for a string instrumentalist to bow over or close to the bridge, producing a bright, glassy sound rich in overtones.

Syllabic A manner of text-setting in which each syllable is given a separate pitch. (Compare with Melismatic.)

Symmetrical phrasing Antecedent and consequent phrases of approximately equal length. The norm in music of the Classical period.

Syncopation The placing of emphasis upon normally unaccented portions of a beat or measure.

Synthetic scale Any scale other than the major or minor scales and the church modes that is invented for use in a particular musical composition.

Talea The frequently long, repeated rhythmic pattern of isorhythmic motets, normally independent of the melodic pattern (*color*), which is often of a different length.

Terraced dynamics Instantaneous, abrupt dynamic changes, without crescendo or diminuendo, commonly found in Baroque music. This usage resulted perhaps from the transfer of the harpsichord and organ styles (which involved abrupt changes of stops) to compositions for other instruments.

Ternary (1) A rhythm characterized by three-part division, resulting in a strong-weak-weak or long-short accentual pattern. This type of rhythm was considered superior to binary rhythm until the fourteenth century. (2) Any musical form dividing into three basic parts. The form may be continuous or sectional.

Tetrachord A group of four pitches, normally in stepwise relationship, as in the lower and upper tetrachords of the major scale.

Text painting The practice of reflecting the extramusical ideas projected in the text of a vocal work through the shape of the melodic line, the harmonic structure or the rhythm of the music.

Through-composed A musical form characterized by the lack of sectional repetition, the music being newly composed throughout.

Tonal (1) A term referring to music based upon the major-minor tonal system, as opposed to music based upon the church modes. (2) A sequence in which the repetition is modified so that all pitches remain diatonic (within the key). This type contrasts with the *real* sequence, which involves an exact, interval-for-interval transposition. (3) A fugal answer which is modified in certain ways according to the harmonic characteristics of the subject.

Tonal shift An abrupt move to a new tonal center without the benefit of the more gradual modulatory process.

Tonicization, Tonicize A process whereby a non-tonic chord is caused to sound temporarily like a tonic by preceding and supporting it with its own dominant, leading tone and/or hierarchy of chordal relationships.

Transformation A gradual change in the features of a theme during the course of a musical composition. Unlike the technique of development, it normally does not involve fragmentation. Rather, the theme as a whole acquires a different character as the music progresses.

Trichord Any group of three different pitch classes.

Tremolando, Tremolo A rapid pitch reiteration produced on string instruments by the small, rapid up-and-down (back-and-forth) motion of the bow.

Truncation The shortening of a phrase, usually by omission of some latter portion.

Tutti A designation directing that the entire ensemble play. It is often used to refer to the *ripieno*, or full ensemble, as opposed to the *concertino*, or soloists, in the Baroque concerto grosso.

Voice exchange One of the earliest variation techniques, in which two voices simply exchange parts on repetition, creating a timbral variation with respect to the original. In early music, the technique is called *Stimmtausch*. It remains a basic orchestrational technique to the present day.

Well-temperament A close approximation and the direct forerunner of equal temperament, in which all keys are usable although the more remote tonalities are somewhat more dissonant than the tonalities closer to C (the "home tonality").

Whole tone scale A six-note scale made up of pitches a whole tone apart.

Word painting See *Text painting*.

READY REFERENCE

Selected Harmonic Topics in Music Theory

Students' understanding of particular chord types, cadences and other harmonic resources of music is greatly enhanced by study of specific examples from the musical literature. Instructors of music theory, too, often need ready access to examples of particular types of chords or progressions. The following listing is designed to simplify the search for such resources within the compositions included in this anthology. Their ordering corresponds to the sequence in which they are most commonly presented in freshman and sophomore theory courses. I have sought to select examples that are as clear and straightforward as possible, and that are uncomplicated by complex textures, non-chord tones and the like. Whenever possible, I have also sought to include examples from different style periods.

Mostly diatonic triads (with dominant seventh chords) in root position and inversion

Mozart, *Piano Sonata* K. 332, II: mm. 1–4 **219**
Schubert, *Originaltänze* Op. 9, No. 3: mm. 1–8 **309**
Schumann, "Soldier's March" **334**
Chopin, *Valse* Op. 69, No. 2: mm. 1–32 **336**

Triads in second inversion

Cadential six-four chord
Mozart, *Piano Sonata* K. 332, I: m. 95 **216**
Beethoven, *Piano Sonata* Op. 26, III: m. 15 **266**
Schubert, *Impromptu* Op. 142, No. 2: m. 45 **319**
Pedal (embellishing) six-four chord
Haydn, *String Quartet* Op. 76, No. 3, II: mm. 8–9 **195**
Beethoven, *Piano Sonata* Op. 53, I: mm. 23–29 **270–271**
Schubert, *Originaltänze* Op. 9, No. 3: m. 6 **309**

Seventh chords

Dominant seventh chord
In root position
Haydn, *String Quartet* Op. 20, No. 5, I: mm. 17–18 **178**
Schubert, *Originaltänze* Op. 9, No. 23: m. 7 **309**
Schubert, "Pause": m. 8 **314**
Beethoven, *Piano Sonata* Op. 13, II: mm. 43, 71 **264–265**
In first inversion
Bach, *Prelude* No. 1 in C major from *WTC I:* m. 3 **116**
Haydn, *String Quartet* Op. 20, No. 5, I: m. 2 **178**
Schumann, "Soldier's March": m. 20 **334**
In second inversion
Beethoven, *Piano Sonata* Op. 13, II: m. 19 **263**
Beethoven, *Piano Sonata* Op. 10, No. 1, III: m. 18 **260**
Schubert, *Impromptu* Op. 142, No. 2: m. 2 **318**
In third inversion
Beethoven, *Piano Sonata* Op. 13, II: m. 1 **263**
Beethoven, *Piano Sonata* Op. 26, III: mm. 2, 10 **266**
Schumann, "Valse noble": m. 3 **322**
Schumann, "Nordic Song": m. 2 **335**
Diminished seventh chord
In root position
Couperin, "Passacaille": mm. 1, 2 **75**
Haydn, *Piano Sonata* H. XVI:37, I: m. 56 **189**
Beethoven, *Piano Sonata* Op. 26, III: m. 17 **266**
In first inversion
Mozart, *Piano Sonata* K. 332, I: m. 25 **215**
Beethoven, *Piano Sonata* Op. 7, III: m. 35 **256**
Beethoven, *Piano Sonata* Op. 13, II: m. 48 **265**
Fauré, "Chanson d'Amour" Op. 27, No. 1: m. 19 **396**
In second inversion
Bach, *Prelude* No. 1 in C major from *WTC I:* m. 14 **117**
Haydn, *Piano Sonata* H. XVI:37, I: m. 53 **189**
Chopin, *Valse* Op. 69, No. 2: m. 22 **336**
In third inversion
Schumann, "Valse noble": m. 1 **322**
Brahms, *Sonata No. 1 for Clarinet and Piano* Op. 120, II: m. 43 **383**
Wolf, "Gebet": m. 14 **390**

Half-diminished seventh chord
In root position
Bach, *French Suite* No. 6, Sarabande: m. 18 **132**
Haydn, *String Quartet* Op. 76, No. 3, II: m. 3 **195**
Schumann, "Ich will meine Seele tauchen": m. 1 **329**
In first inversion
Schubert, "Die Liebe hat gelogen": m. 4 **310**
Chopin, *Valse* Op. 69, No. 2: m. 14 **336**
Wolf, "Gebet": m. 21 **391**
In second inversion
Beethoven, *Piano Sonata* Op. 13, II: m. 50 **265**
Schubert, "Ungeduld": m. 17 **313**
In third inversion
Couperin, "Passacaille": m. 26 **75**
Chopin, *Valse* Op. 69, No. 2: m. 7 **336**
Non-dominant seventh chords
Satie, *Trois Gymnopedies*, No. 1: mm. 1–12 **433**
Non-dominant seventh chords in succession
Mozart, *Piano Sonata* K. 332, I: mm. 61–65 **215**
Brahms, "O Tod, wie bitter bist Du": mm. 18–22 **387**
Ravel, *Sonatine*, II: mm. 9–11 **463**

II. Cadences

Authentic
Mozart, *Eine kleine Nachtmusik*, I: m. 14 **223**
Schubert, "Pause": m. 8 **314**
Schumann, "Soldier's March": mm. 31–32 **335**
Schumann, "Nordic Song": m. 20 **335**

Plagal
Schumann, "Ich will meine Seele tauchen": mm. 21–22 **330**
Wolf, "Gebet": mm. 30–32 **391**

Half
Bach, *Cantata No. 78*, Chorale (No. 7): m. 4 **158**
Mozart, *Piano Sonata* K. 332, II: m. 4 **219**
Beethoven, *Piano Sonata* Op. 26, III: mm. 11–12 **266**

Deceptive
Haydn, *Piano Sonata* H. XVI:37, III: mm. 21–22 (minor), mm. 25–26 (major) **192**
Beethoven, *Piano Sonata* Op. 7, III: mm. 53–54 **256**
Beethoven, *Piano Sonata* Op. 53, I: mm. 248–249 **280**

Phrygian
Josquin, "Agnus Dei" from *Missa Mater Patris:* mm. 28–29 **23**
Couperin, "Passacaille": mm. 11–12, 133–134 **75, 79**
Schumann, "Wenn ich in deine Augen seh": mm. 8–9 **328**
Schumann, "Nordic Song": m. 4 **335**

III. Chromatic Chords

Secondary functions
V and V_7
of ii
Mozart, *Eine kleine Nachtmusik*, I: m. 28 **223**
Beethoven, *Piano Sonata* Op. 13, II: m. 6 **263**
Schumann, "Nordic Song": m. 19 **335**

- German
    - Haydn, *String Quartet* Op. 20, No. 5, I: m. 9 **178**
    - Mozart, *Piano Sonata* K. 332, I: m. 35–36 **215**
    - Schubert, *Impromptu* Op. 142, No. 2: m. 28 **319**
    - Schubert, "Pause": m. 66 **317**
- Enharmonic German
    - Schubert, "Die Liebe hat gelogen": m. 16 **311**
- Doubly augmented four-three chord
    - Wolf, "Gebet": m. 6 **390**

Borrowed harmonies (from minor mode)

- ii° and $\text{ii}^{ø7}$
    - Schubert, *Impromptu* Op. 142, No. 2: m. 45 **319**
    - Schumann, "Ich will meine Seele tauchen": m. 5 **329**
    - Wolf, "Gebet": m. 3 **390**
    - Wolf, "Wer sich der Einsamkeit ergiebt": m. 19 **393**
- iv
    - Schumann, "Valse noble": m. 37 **322**
    - Chopin, *Nocturne* Op. 9, No. 2: mm. 10, 29 **341–342**
    - Brahms, "O Tod, wie bitter bist Du": m. 26 **388**

Altered dominants

- Schubert, "Pause": m. 40 **316**
- Wolf, "Gebet": mm. 1, 4 **390**
- Fauré, "Chanson d'Amour" Op. 27, No. 1: m. 21 **396**

Ninth chords

- Haydn, *Piano Sonata,* H. XVI: 37, II: m. 3 in d; m. 7 in F **191–192**
- Schumann, "Das ist ein Flöten und Geigen": m. 1 in d **331**
- Chopin, *Valse* Op. 69, No. 2: mm. 66, 92 **338**
- Wolf, "Gebet": m. 13 **390**

IV. Modulation

by common chord to relative major

- *Der Prinzentanz* (anonymous lute dance): m. 1 **54**
- Bach, *Invention* No. 13 in A minor: m. 3 **105**
- Handel, *Suite* No. 4 in D minor, Gigue: m. 2 **162**
- Chopin, *Valse* Op. 69, No. 2: mm. 32–33 **337–338**

by common chord to relative minor

- Mozart, *Die Entführung aus dem Serail,* Act I, No. 5: mm. 40–41 **229**

by common chord to dominant

- Bach, *Prelude* No. 1 in C major from *WTC I:* m. 5 **116**
- Mozart, *Die Entführung aus dem Serail,* Act II, No. 8: mm. 18–19 **234**
- Mozart, *Piano Sonata* K. 332, II: mm. 6–7 **219**
- Beethoven, *Piano Sonata* Op. 7, III: m. 12 **255**

by common chord to other keys

- to VI
    - Mozart, *Die Entführung aus dem Serail,* Act I, No. 5: mm. 49–50 **230**
    - Beethoven, *Piano Sonata* Op. 7, III: m. 54 **256**
    - Chopin, *Mazurka* Op. 17, No. 2: mm. 24–25 **344**
- to VII
    - Beethoven, *Piano Sonata* Op. 7, III: mm. 38–39 **256**

Chromatic

- Mozart, *Die Entführung aus dem Serail,* Act I, No. 5: mm. 58–61 **230**
- Beethoven, *Piano Sonata* Op. 7, III: m. 112 **257**

INDEXES

Note: Numbers in **bold** type refer to pages (usually, only the number of the first page is given); numbers in parenthesis ( ) refer to measures.

Index I
Musical Devices and Techniques

Index II
Harmonic Index

Note: The chorale harmonizations of Johann Sebastian Bach and others are not included among the sources cited in this index.